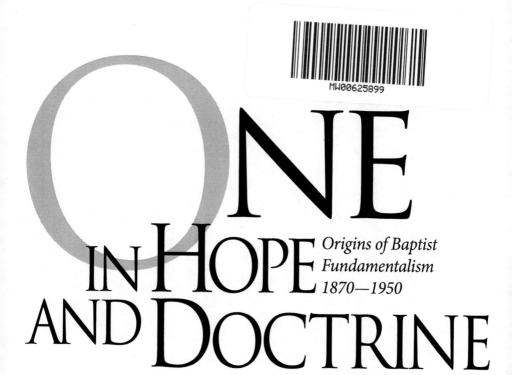

ONE
IN HOPE
Origins of Baptist
Fundamentalism
1870—1950
AND DOCTRINE

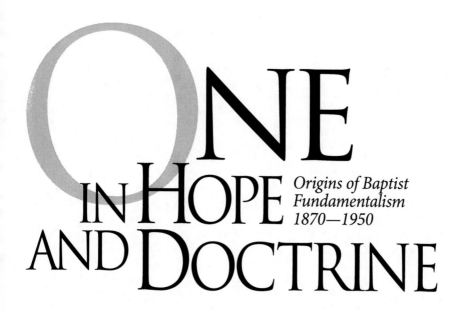

ONE IN HOPE AND DOCTRINE

Origins of Baptist
Fundamentalism
1870—1950

KEVIN BAUDER & ROBERT DELNAY

Regular Baptist Books
Arlington Heights, Illinois

One in Hope and Doctrine
© 2014 Regular Baptist Press • Arlington Heights, Illinois.
www.RegularBaptistPress.org • 1-800-727-4440
RBP5128 • ISBN: 978-1-60776-660-5

Second printing—2016

Contents

The Development of
BAPTIST FUNDAMENTALISM
in North America

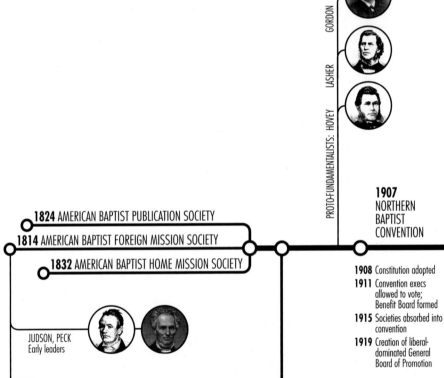

PROTO-FUNDAMENTALISTS: HOVEY   LASHER   GORDON

1824 AMERICAN BAPTIST PUBLICATION SOCIETY

1814 AMERICAN BAPTIST FOREIGN MISSION SOCIETY

1832 AMERICAN BAPTIST HOME MISSION SOCIETY

JUDSON, PECK
Early leaders

1814
FIRST TRIENNIAL CONVENTION
Period of North/South Unity

1907
NORTHERN
BAPTIST
CONVENTION

1908 Constitution adopted
1911 Convention execs
allowed to vote;
Benefit Board formed
1915 Societies absorbed into
convention
1919 Creation of liberal-
dominated General
Board of Promotion

1845
SOUTHERN
BAPTIST
CONVENTION

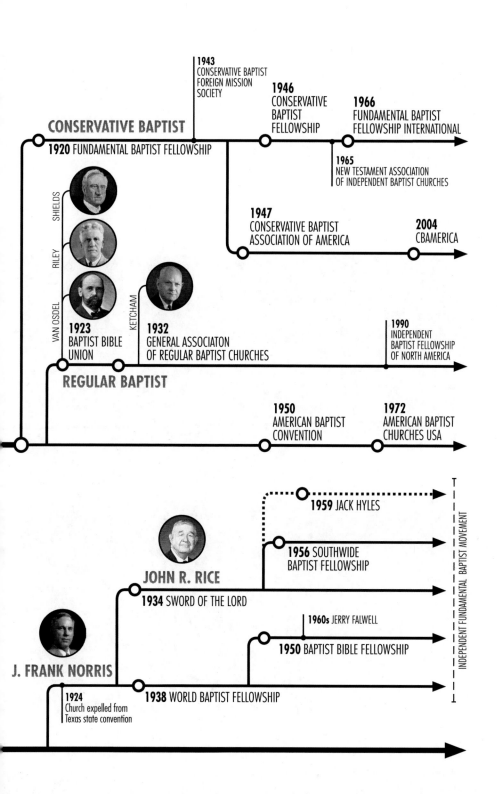

1943
CONSERVATIVE BAPTIST
FOREIGN MISSION
SOCIETY

1946
CONSERVATIVE
BAPTIST
FELLOWSHIP

1966
FUNDAMENTAL BAPTIST
FELLOWSHIP INTERNATIONAL

CONSERVATIVE BAPTIST

1920 FUNDAMENTAL BAPTIST FELLOWSHIP

1965
NEW TESTAMENT ASSOCIATION
OF INDEPENDENT BAPTIST CHURCHES

SHIELDS

RILEY

VAN OSDEL

KETCHAM

1947
CONSERVATIVE BAPTIST
ASSOCIATION OF AMERICA

2004
CBAMERICA

1923
BAPTIST BIBLE
UNION

1932
GENERAL ASSOCIATON
OF REGULAR BAPTIST CHURCHES

1990
INDEPENDENT
BAPTIST FELLOWSHIP
OF NORTH AMERICA

REGULAR BAPTIST

1950
AMERICAN BAPTIST
CONVENTION

1972
AMERICAN BAPTIST
CHURCHES USA

1959 JACK HYLES

1956 SOUTHWIDE
BAPTIST FELLOWSHIP

JOHN R. RICE

1934 SWORD OF THE LORD

1960s JERRY FALWELL

1950 BAPTIST BIBLE FELLOWSHIP

INDEPENDENT FUNDAMENTAL BAPTIST MOVEMENT

J. FRANK NORRIS

1924
Church expelled from
Texas state convention

1938 WORLD BAPTIST FELLOWSHIP

Belden Avenue Baptist Church youth group, 1945.

Preface

J. R. R. TOLKIEN opened *The Lord of the Rings* with the statement, "This tale grew in the telling." That has also been our experience. To understand the story, one must know the story of how it was written. It began when one of us, Robert Delnay, approached Regular Baptist Press with a brief history of the Conservative Baptist movement. The editor was interested, but he thought that the narrative was too focused to attract much attention. He suggested expanding the tale to include the history of the Regular Baptist movement. At that point, the other one of us, Kevin Bauder, was brought into the picture.

Delnay spent decades gathering sources for his Conservative Baptist history. He also did significant research on the Regular Baptist movement, writing his dissertation on the Baptist Bible Union. Bauder wrote a master's thesis on Oliver W. Van Osdel, arguably the founder of the General Association of Regular Baptist Churches. He also wrote a short history of the founding of the GARBC, a copy of which is in the offices of the GARBC and Regular Baptist Press. The result was that we were tasked to work together with the goal of producing a history of Northern Baptist fundamentalism.

We both welcomed the collaboration. We have known each other since the early 1980s, when Delnay was a professor and Bauder a student at Denver Baptist Theological Seminary. We have become friends, kept in touch, and sought each other out whenever possible. For us, the opportunity to share this labor came as a Providential gift.

Naturally, each of us carries his experience into the story. Our experience includes being reared in Baptist fundamentalism, though in different generations. Delnay grew up attending Wealthy Street Baptist Church in Grand Rapids, Michigan. He can still recall the pulpit manners of Oliver W. Van Osdel and Amy Lee Stockton. He was baptized by David Otis Fuller. He graduated from Northern Baptist Theological Seminary and interviewed for ordination in the American (Northern) Baptist Convention. He was later

ordained in a Conservative Baptist congregation. He was an active partici-
pant in the battles within the Conservative Baptist movement, a professor in
more than one Conservative Baptist school, and has taught in several Regular
Baptist institutions. He was the founding dean of Faith Baptist Theological
Seminary in Ankeny, Iowa.

A generation younger, Bauder was baptized by a church planter working
under the Fellowship of Baptists for Home Missions. He grew up in Regular
Baptist churches and attended a Regular Baptist college (Faith Baptist Bible
College) and seminary (Denver Baptist Theological Seminary). He was ordained in a Regular Baptist church and later held membership in a church
that identified with the Sword movement. He served as president of Central
Baptist Theological Seminary of Minneapolis, whose roots were firmly in the
Conservative Baptist Hard Core. He still serves on the board of the old Min-
nesota Baptist Convention, now renamed the Minnesota Baptist Association.

Both of us have been seminary professors. Among other courses, we have
each taught Baptist history and fundamentalist history. We each bring to this
story, not only research and documentation, but a lifetime of the people we
have known, the concerns they have shared, and the stories they have told.
Mostly we have written about what we can document, but here and there we
have told the story as we know it to be, even if we cannot quite prove it.

When we began, we thought we were writing a rather brief and quite popular history. No comprehensive narrative of the development of Baptist fundamentalism has ever been written. The consequence is that much of the history
has been forgotten. Most present-day Baptist fundamentalists (of whatever
sort) do not really know how their movement began or how it has developed.
Our goal was to fill this void, focusing particularly upon Northern Baptist
fundamentalism.

We never intended to produce a scholarly history. We wanted to write a
book that would be accessible, not only to pastors and students, but to ordinary church members. We wanted to help them understand where they were
and how they got there. We wanted to help them discover where they stood
in the story of their ecclesiastical and theological tradition.

As we set about the task of organizing, researching, and writing, however, we found that the story needed to be longer and more detailed than we
had originally envisioned. As we attempted to tell the story chronologically,
geographical concerns became less important. We found that the story of
Northern Baptist fundamentalism was incomplete without a large part of the
story of Southern Baptist fundamentalism. Eventually enough of the Southern story came into the narrative that we could no longer designate the work
simply as a history of Northern fundamentalism—though, as will be evident,
that is still where the emphasis lies.

As the story lengthened and gained detail, we had to divide it into two volumes. The natural division was at the end of the 1940s and beginning of the 1950s. The Conservative Baptist movement had just taken shape, rejecting attempts at merger by the Regular Baptists. John R. Rice was producing his polemics against Lewis Sperry Chafer, coloring a whole branch of Baptist fundamentalism. J. Frank Norris's movement was on the verge of splintering, after which Norris himself would die. The mid-1950s would bring new concerns and new battles, providing the ideal opening for the second volume.

In the process of writing, our commitment to document the story also rose. In a few places we have retained some of our original unsupported observations; in those places the tale will read more like a memoir. We have also used secondary sources to a greater degree than is usual in a strictly scholarly publication. Nevertheless, the greatest part of the story can now be substantiated by interested readers, and researchers will find more than enough to launch them into new discoveries. We have carefully transcribed the primary sources cited in this history. The reader will notice that some quotations use unconventional spellings and variant grammar, which we have reproduced exactly from the original document. But if a source gives an incorrect fact that could cause significant confusion, we have judiciously added *sic* to alert the reader.

The goal of a purely popular history was abandoned long ago, but we have still tried to avoid writing an academic tome. While we have sought to avoid both informality and sentimentality, we have attempted to tell a story that is as readable as it is worth reading. Those who wish for either a casual yarn or a rigorously scholarly narrative are likely to be equally disappointed. Our hope is that they will be in the minority.

A word should be said about the perspective from which this tale is told. The earlier part of the story is viewed primarily through the eyes of Oliver W. Van Osdel. The latter part is examined mostly through the thick lenses of Robert T. Ketcham. The continuity between these two figures as the primary leaders of the Regular Baptist movement will become evident in the narrative. We thought it particularly important to emphasize Van Osdel. While not as public as some other fundamentalists, his influence would be difficult to overstate. He was undoubtedly the single most important figure in the Regular Baptist movement until 1934, when the leadership went to Ketcham. Furthermore, his story has not been told in any published history of fundamentalism. This is unfortunate, because good documentation is (or was) available.

Which brings us to sources. Sixty years ago, Delnay was permitted to examine T. T. Shields's papers in the vault at Jarvis Street Baptist Church in Toronto. Forty years ago he had access to Chester Tulga's papers in the offices of the Fundamental Baptist Fellowship (sadly, these papers were ransacked repeatedly during the ensuing years). Notes and copies made during this period form part of the documentation for our story.

Thirty years ago, Van Osdel's papers filled a couple of boxes on the second floor of the administrative wing in the old Wealthy Street Baptist Church building. Bauder was allowed free access and permission to photocopy whatever he liked. Those copies are still in his possession. The church has subsequently moved (it is now Wealthy Park Baptist Church in Grand Rapids), and the church's archives have been donated to the University of Michigan.

Wealthy Street had a few back issues of Van Osdel's paper, the *Baptist Temple News*. More of these were found in the archives of Grand Rapids Baptist Seminary. While a complete run probably does not exist, photocopies of both collections are kept by Bauder, who hopes to edit and publish Van Osdel's writings for the use of historical researchers.

Walnut Street Baptist Church in Waterloo, Iowa, has moved and changed its name to Walnut Ridge Baptist Church. The church graciously permitted Bauder to spend a couple of days going through its old files, including books of the minutes of both church and deacons. This reading closed some of the gaps in the story. Pastor Joel Dunlap was especially helpful in locating materials. He also took Bauder to visit the grave of the Rev. P. B. Chenault.

The General Association of Regular Baptist Churches has also granted full access to its archives, including files of correspondence and minutes of both associational and council meetings. The association has also been digitizing early copies of the *Baptist Bulletin* and posting them for the use of researchers. One interesting custom of early GARBC leaders was to mimeograph important correspondence for circulation. These mimeo copies were produced with such a high degree of accuracy that we have felt comfortable citing the circulation copies instead of original drafts in some cases.

The Brimson Grow Library at Northern Baptist Theological Seminary gave gracious access to materials pertaining to Amy Lee Stockton and John Marvin Dean. Theirs are two stories that need to be told at length. Both will be fascinating to read when they are written.

The Norris papers have been microfilmed by the Historical Commission of the Southern Baptist Convention. Copies of the microfilm can be found at the Billy Graham Center at Wheaton College and in the Earl K. Oldham Library at Arlington Baptist College. Arlington is the continuation of the school that Norris founded, but the originals of his papers do not appear to be on campus. Thanks are due to professor Greg Adams and librarian Vickie Bryant for providing access to the microfilms.

Not surprisingly, the library of the Central Baptist Theological Seminary of Minneapolis has been a trove for information on the Conservative Baptist movement. In addition to the papers of Richard V. Clearwaters, it includes much else related to fundamentalist history and to Minnesota Baptist history in particular. Furthermore, much of the documentation that we have accumulated in preparing this volume will be archived there for the use of future researchers.

Certain other acknowledgements are in order. Debra Bauder not only offered inspiration at important moments, but proofread the entire text. Chris Ames rendered valuable assistance in preparing the text and bringing the notes into conformity with the latest edition of the *Chicago Manual of Style*. Kevin Mungons offered counsel and encouragement from the offices of Regular Baptist Press, exhibiting astonishing patience as the task developed and changed. Jonita Barram offered her editorial expertise and kept us out of trouble more than once.

The story of how liberalism took over the Northern Baptist institutions (the first chapter of this book) could not have been told without the assistance of our colleague Jeff Straub. His doctoral dissertation at Southern Baptist Theological Seminary dealt with exactly this area.[1] He was selfless with his research and helpful with his advice. We hope that by the time this book appears, his dissertation will be well along the road to publication.

The administration of Central Baptist Theological Seminary has gone out of its way to liberate Bauder to work on this project, and certain donors have gone out of their way to support his writing efforts. In a small seminary, every professor wears multiple hats. President Sam Horn and vice presidents Jonathan Pratt and Brent Belford have from the beginning committed themselves to relieving Bauder of as much extraneous responsibility as possible.

Several individuals have read all or parts of the text and have offered helpful criticism. Jeff Straub was one of the most important. So were Ralph Warren and Fred Moritz. Through the years both George Houghton and Myron Houghton have shaped this book, though neither was necessarily aware of it. Needless to say, no one mentioned here bears any responsibility for the errors that remain in the book.

One more word. The authors are committed to the notion that the only person who cannot become disillusioned is the one who holds no illusions to begin with. For that reason, we have not attempted to whitewash or sugarcoat any aspect of the history of Baptist fundamentalism. We affirm the doctrine of total depravity, and we recognize that even the redeemed will be sinners until they see Jesus. We are old enough to know that depravity works its way out even in Christian service. Fundamentalists are not exempt from this dynamic, and their history features fools, predators, toadies, hypocrites,

---

1. Jeffrey P. Straub, "The Making of a Battle Royal: The Rise of Religious Liberalism in Northern Baptist Life, 1870–1920" (PhD diss., Southern Baptist Theological Seminary, 2004).

power grabbers, and character assassins as well as humble servants, insightful leaders, and heroic warriors. We fundamentalists struggle with *akrasia* and *hamartia*, just as other Christians.

Our goal in this book is to tell the truth, in the proportions as well as in the details. Doubtless we have sometimes failed to do so, perhaps not by getting the facts wrong, but by presenting them in some disproportionate manner. Nevertheless, we do not feel called upon to cover up the mistakes and sins of fundamentalism past. Those, too, are part of the story—indeed, they were sometimes the main forces in shaping it.

We believe that fundamentalism is a good idea. It is a great idea. It is, in fact, a biblical idea. The idea, however, has been implemented by flawed and sinful people. One can find plenty in the fundamentalist movement of which to disapprove, but we are convinced that the liabilities of the movement can be attributed to sources other than the idea. Even with its liabilities the fundamentalist movement was better than any alternative during the period of which we are writing.

This tale has grown in the telling, but it is still a tale. More than anything, we wanted to tell a story that has never before been heard. It is at some points an astonishing story, but it is a true one. We hope that it is one you will enjoy reading.

Northern Baptist Leaders, 1922.

1 Liberalism and the Northern Baptist Convention

BRACING HIMSELF against the February cold, a tall, graying gentleman stepped from the train and into the winter of Grand Rapids, Michigan. He wore spectacles and a broad-brimmed hat. Puffs of his breath condensed on his moustache in the chilly air. The year was 1909, the man was Oliver W. Van Osdel, and he was returning to Grand Rapids to shepherd the Wealthy Street Baptist Church.

Van Osdel had briefly pastored the small congregation nearly fifteen years before. He had discovered that the church could not grow without a new building, but the church refused to build and Van Osdel left for another ministry. Now the old facility had been condemned and construction was imperative. The church called Van Osdel to return, and he agreed.

Only days after Van Osdel's arrival, two men appeared at his front door. They introduced themselves as a minister and a deacon from Calvary Baptist Church. They asked to visit with the new pastor. Van Osdel welcomed them into his home, and they began to unfold their story.

As in many cities, the Baptist churches of Grand Rapids had organized an association to assist their work together. For many years the association had provided a venue for church planting and other projects. Recently, however, controversy had erupted. The disagreement centered on Fountain Street Baptist Church. Fountain Street had been organized in 1846 as the First Baptist Church of Grand Rapids, settling on its current name in 1877. It had once been known for gospel preaching and for planting new churches. In fact, Wealthy Street Baptist Church had been started by Fountain Street.

Fountain Street occupied the most impressive church building in Grand Rapids, and it had the largest membership. Nevertheless, rumors were flying about the theology in its pulpit. As early as the 1890s it had begun to back away from strong preaching about an authoritative Bible or a substitutionary atonement. Its pastor at that time, J. Herman Randall, expressed sympathy

17

for the popular new theology of liberalism. The arrival of Pastor Alfred W. Wishart, however, was what precipitated the controversy.

Wishart was smallish, perhaps five-and-a-half feet tall, and just over 120 pounds, but his theological stature was gargantuan. Before Fountain Street Church called him in 1906, he had already established a reputation for controversy. In Trenton, New Jersey, he had both pastored the Central Baptist Church and edited the *Trenton Times*. He used these two roles to break up the city's gambling ring, close its red-light district, and expose political corruption.[1]

The year before he came to Grand Rapids, Wishart published his theory of Christianity. He saw religion as the experience of God, common to all humanity, arising from the fact that God puts His own life in the life or soul of humanity. Wishart posited that God "manifests himself to man, immediately in man's soul, and indirectly through nature and history." This universal experience of God is what constitutes religion. At different times and in different places, people have described or expressed their experience in different ways, but their expressions are secondary while their experiences are primary.[2]

According to Wishart, some of these expressions are better than others. He believed that a few remarkable individuals have achieved such clear perception of God, and exhibited so transparently their experience of Him, that they have left a deep and enduring influence upon the religious life of humanity. The best among these extraordinary individuals is Christ. On the divine side, Christ expressed the life of God so fully that God could be said to speak to humanity through Him. On the human side, Christ fully exemplified the religious spirit of a man seeking after God. He was both the "most beautiful expression of the life of God in the soul of man," and the "noblest example of what a truly religious man ought to be."[3]

Christ's mission was to give humans "a true consciousness of themselves and of the God whose life dwells in them." If people wanted to "find rest for our souls in the sweet fellowship with the Eternal Life of the universe," then they needed to emulate Christ. Wishart was clear at this point: "This emulation is our salvation." The imitation of Christ would lead to transformation for the individual and, eventually, for society, because those who were transformed by following Christ would give themselves to serve their fellow humans.[4]

1. A description of Wishart's pastorate can be found in James D. Bratt and Christopher H. Meehan, *Gathered at the River: Grand Rapids, Michigan, and Its People of Faith* (Grand Rapids: Grand Rapids Area Council for the Humanities and William B. Eerdmans Publishing Company, 1993), 89–105.
2. Alfred W. Wishart, *Primary Facts in Religious Thought* (Chicago: University of Chicago Press, 1905), 4.
3. Ibid., 90.
4. Ibid., 92, 96–98.

What about the Bible? For Wishart it was not an infallible revelation, but rather a book of religious experience. Its great value lay in "arousing the soul to a sense of its needs and of pointing the way to life." The Bible contained conflicting views and perspectives, and the modern reader had to discriminate "between the true and the false, the good and the bad, in the Bible."[5]

Wishart's system was exactly that version of theology that became known as *liberalism*, or, sometimes, *modernism*. Because it originated in Germany, it was sometimes called *German theology* (usually by its opponents, especially after World War I). Given Wishart's views and his aggressive demeanor, a collision among Grand Rapids Baptists was unavoidable. It came just two years after his arrival, during the 1908 annual meeting of the Grand Rapids Baptist Association. The highlight of the meeting was a sermon, delivered by a venerable minister named Rose, defending the deity of Jesus Christ. Probably with Wishart in mind, someone moved that the sermon should be printed and distributed to all the churches. Immediately Wishart stood and stated that the sermon would offend the Fountain Street church. This blunt denial of the deity of Christ created an uproar that went far beyond the adjournment of the associational meeting.

Now, two representatives of the Grand Rapids Association sat in Van Osdel's home. They claimed that the churches found the situation intolerable. They had determined to act. Since Van Osdel was the new pastor in town, they wanted to know where he stood.

What happened next could be viewed as the beginning of Baptist fundamentalism. Before that story can be told, however, two older stories first need to be repeated. The first is the development of organization among Baptists in America, and especially in the North. The second is the rise of the liberal theology that found expression in Alfred Wishart.

Northern Baptist Organization

Baptists prize the autonomy of the local church. They have always rejected every attempt to subject individual churches to the outside authority of bishops and synods. Nevertheless, this commitment to autonomy should not be understood as a preference for utter independence. Baptist churches have tried to work together for several reasons. First, some tasks have proven too large for most individual churches to accomplish alone. Second, persecution has sometimes forced Baptists to find greater safety in their united numbers. Third, common concerns and issues have often led Baptists to try to speak with a united voice.

5. Ibid., 118–19.

From their earliest days as an identifiable movement, Baptists have organized church fellowship around associations. One of the earliest and most
prominent Baptist associations in America was the Philadelphia Association.
Originally organized in 1707 by churches in Pennsylvania, New Jersey, and
Delaware, the Philadelphia Association eventually added churches in New
York, Connecticut, Maryland, Virginia, and the Carolinas. Other Baptist associations included the Charleston Association (1751), the Sandy Creek Association (1758), and the Kehukee Association (probably 1769). As groups of
churches began to form their own local associations, the Philadelphia Association gradually shrank to serve churches in and around Philadelphia.[6]

By the early nineteenth century, Baptist churches were scattered through-
out the United States. Many fellowshipped with some local association, but
Baptists had no organization at the national level. That changed when Luther
Rice returned from India in 1814.

Rice was a Congregationalist who sailed for India as a missionary in 1812.
He and Adoniram Judson, who sailed in a separate ship, intended to labor
together for the salvation of souls in south Asia. Arriving in Calcutta, however,
Rice discovered that Judson had been studying his Greek New Testament
during the voyage and had converted to Baptist principles. Shortly thereafter,
Rice himself accepted Baptist views. Both missionaries were immersed, as
were their wives. Accompanied by recommendations from William Carey
(the famous British missionary to India), Rice was sent back to America to
seek missionary support among Baptists.

Rice was received warmly by churches in New York, Boston, Baltimore,
and Washington. People responded to his plea to support Judson, but Rice
was frustrated by the lack of a national organization to coordinate the effort.
He began to meet with Baptist leaders throughout the country, encouraging
them to form an agency to promote and coordinate the work of missions.

Baptists held their first national meeting, called the General Missionary
Convention of the Baptist Denomination in the United States of America, for
Foreign Missions, in Philadelphia in 1814. Subsequently, the gathering was
held every three years, and it soon became known simply as the Triennial
Convention. One of its first acts was to form a permanent missionary society,
the American Baptist Missionary Union. The new convention appointed Rice
as its missionary and commissioned him to travel through the United States
to promote the work of missions.

6. Any standard Baptist history should trace the development of Baptist organization in
America. Three of the more important histories are Henry C. Vedder, *A Short History of the
Baptists* (Philadelphia: American Baptist Publication Society, 1907); Robert G. Torbet, *A His-
tory of the Baptists*, 3rd ed. (Valley Forge: Judson Press, 1963); H. Leon McBeth, *The Baptist
Heritage: Four Centuries of Baptist Witness* (Nashville: Broadman Press, 1987).

Almost immediately a difference arose over the form of organization. Luther Rice, followed by Baptists in the South, wanted to organize Baptist work according to the associational principle. Associations were under the control of messengers appointed by churches. If the missionary work was organized associationally, then it would be accountable to the churches. Baptists in the North, however, were concerned that the chain of accountability could work in the opposite direction. Associations had sometimes displayed a tendency to intrude into the affairs of their fellowshipping churches. Northern Baptists, led by Francis Wayland, perceived a danger that the associational principle could give agencies such as missionary organizations a way to manipulate the churches. Consequently, they wanted the missionary work to be controlled by a society or service organization comprised of individual members. Each society member would also be a member in good standing of a Baptist church, but the service organization itself would be operated independently.

At least initially, those who favored the service-organization model prevailed. The American Baptist Missionary Union was an autonomous agency with individual membership. The Triennial Convention was, at first, simply the gathering of the membership of the society. Soon, however, Baptists began to organize other agencies, and with each new agency the tension between North and South increased. The Northerners were happiest with service organizations. The Southerners wanted associational accountability. The ABMU was a service organization, but its public representative, Luther Rice, favored the associational principle.

Before long, Rice was pushing the ABMU to include home missions in its work. He witnessed the need for Baptist church planting firsthand as he crisscrossed the country on horseback or surrey carriage. In 1815 he met John Mason Peck who, under Rice's influence, committed himself to the task of planting churches in the western United States. Peck was initially sent out by the ABMU, but in 1820 that organization decided to focus more pointedly on foreign missions. Peck resigned from the American Baptist Missionary Union and continued his work under the auspices of a local society in Massachusetts. Eventually (1832), Peck helped to found the American Baptist Home Mission Society.

Another service organization was added in 1824. Impressed with the need for Christian literature, Baptists organized the Baptist General Tract Society, renaming it the American Baptist Publication Society two years later. Then, seeing the need for an educated ministry, the Triennial Convention also authorized Rice to establish an educational institution. The result was Columbian College in Washington, D.C. (later given up by Baptists and renamed George Washington University).

As Baptist work began to grow, so did tensions over the form of organization.

Northerners favored service organizations, while Rice and many Southerners were committed to the associational principle. During the 1820s several factors combined to exacerbate this tension. Part of the problem was centered in education: Rice's promotion of Columbian College was interfering with Francis Wayland's promotion of Brown University, an older and nominally Baptist institution. Wayland presented himself as a champion of service organizations in opposition to Rice's promotion of the associational principle. The tension was further aggravated by Rice's rather loose form of management: though he controlled funds for both missions and education, money that was given to one sometimes found its way into the other.

By 1826 a whispering campaign against Rice was in full operation. Rumor had it that he had misappropriated the funds of the ABMU. At the Triennial Convention, Rice angrily denied the charges and demanded an investigation. He got the investigation and it eventually cleared him, but not before the board dismissed him as its missionary. From that point onward, the Triennial Convention was firmly under the hand of those who took Wayland's view.

The organizational question, however, continued to fester just under the surface. With each meeting of the Triennial Convention, Baptists from the South felt increasingly marginalized. Unfortunately, this was the very time when slavery was also becoming an issue. These two problems together led Southern Baptists to withdraw from the Triennial Convention in 1845 and to organize their own Southern Baptist Convention. From the beginning, the SBC followed the associational principle. The exodus of the Southerners left the Triennial Convention more firmly committed than ever to doing its work through independent service organizations.

After the War Between the States, the Triennial Convention began to meet annually, typically during the week of Pentecost. These meetings became known as the Anniversaries, or sometimes as the May Meetings. The big three societies were the American Baptist Missionary Union (later renamed the American Baptist Foreign Mission Society), the American Baptist Home Mission Society, and the American Baptist Publication Society. These were joined by smaller organizations: the American Baptist Education Society, the Women's Home Society East, the Women's Home Society West, the Foreign Bible Society, and the Young People's Union. All of the organizations met the same week in the same hall, but each maintained its own identity.

Before the turn of the century, Baptists also organized several seminaries throughout the country. The most important of these were Newton, Hamilton (later renamed Colgate), Rochester, Crozer, and the Baptist Union Theological Seminary near Chicago. The last school was part of the old University of Chicago, but it broke away and moved to Morgan Park. In 1892 John D. Rockefeller provided funding for a new University of Chicago under the leadership of William Rainey Harper, and the Morgan Park seminary was brought on campus as the divinity school of the new university.

In his *Short History of the Baptists*, Henry Clay Vedder closed his presentation of the nineteenth century with some telling observations. After recounting how the Baptists had increased in numbers, wealth, and influence, he went on to note trends that he saw as dangerous to the future of their testimony. One of these was the weakening conviction of the centrality of the Bible in all they tried to do; in other words, he saw the corrosive influence of German theology. Another was a decline of discipline in the churches. Third, he pointed to a change in the character of preaching, resulting in fewer adult conversions and more members coming in through the Sunday School and the young people's societies. Finally, he noticed the enlargement of the denominational societies, leading to a desire to unite the work under a single great convention.[7]

The Rise of Liberal Theology

Probably the leading doctrinal development of the nineteenth century was liberalism or modernism, also known as German higher criticism. A fusion of rationalism, materialism, and pietism (of the kind that placed experience above Scripture), it fed on higher criticism and evolutionism. By 1860 probably all the German universities had accepted it, although Tübingen was considered the citadel. This new theology was rooted in an optimism based on confidence in fundamental human goodness. The modernists employed a Christian vocabulary while radically redefining the supernatural aspects of the Christian faith. Near the end of the century, a few American seminary graduates had the money and resources to finish their education in Germany. They came home convinced of what they had heard. As they entered ministry, they settled in professorships and influential pulpits, giving them the best opportunity to spread their new theology. In 1900, few North American Baptists had any real awareness of the enormity of the defection. By 1920 hardly a denominational college still held to the faith of its founders.[8]

What was liberalism or modernism? The answer to this question is complicated by the fact that it came in different varieties. Later students of the period have even debated how to use the names. Some scholars see *liberalism* and *modernism* as interchangeable terms. Others use the name *liberalism* to denote only some of the variations, while reserving the term *modernism* for others. Nevertheless, all varieties were influenced by the same ideas. The

---

7. Vedder, *History*, 379–83.
8. An exception was Augustus Hopkins Strong, president of Rochester Divinity School. See his *Systematic Theology: A Compendium* (Valley Forge: Judson Press, 1907), ix.

differences arose only from the proportions in which these influences were combined.[9]

All versions of liberalism emphasized the beneficence of God. From the liberal point of view, the primary feature of the divine nature was goodness or kindness. Accordingly, liberals liked to speak of God as the Father, not only of saved people or professing Christians, but of all humanity. The corollary to this universal "fatherhood of God" was (as it was expressed at the time) a universal "brotherhood of man." God was understood to stand in a paternal relationship of intimacy, generosity, tenderness, and compassion toward all people, with the implication that they ought to adopt a similar attitude toward one another.

Liberals differed in the degree to which they saw God as a personal being. Virtually all of them emphasized divine immanence, or nearness, more than they emphasized God's transcendence, or otherness. For many (and this number grew as time went by), God was not really distinguishable from the world process itself. This view stood in marked contrast to traditional Christianity, in which God was thought to be a sovereign ruler who stood outside of and above His creation. Liberalism began to erode the distinction between creature and Creator. As William R. Hutchison notes, for liberals, God was "immanent in human cultural development and revealed through it."[10]

Given this understanding of God, liberals naturally adopted an optimistic view of human nature. If God is universally the father of humans, then humans must universally bear the marks of divinity. They might possess a rough exterior, but they have enough goodness in them to transform the world. Liberalism emphasized this essential uprightness and was naïvely confident in human progress.

The liberal belief in human goodness and progress was reinforced by the then-new theory of Darwinian evolution. Most (not all) conservative Christians were reluctant to accept any theory of evolution, but liberals found that it gave them an explanatory framework for human growth and advancement. The uniqueness of the human race consisted not in its special creation by God, but in the degree to which humans had progressed toward the divine ideal. At any rate, liberals would never have entertained the possibility of contradicting what they saw as the best of modern science.

---

9. Some of the variations were explored by Kenneth Cauthen, *The Impact of American Religious Liberalism* (New York: Harper and Row, 1972), while the commonalities are developed by William R. Hutchison, *The Modernist Impulse in American Protestantism* (Durham, NC: Duke University Press, 1992). An early, hostile summary and critique of liberal theology was J. Gresham Machen, *Christianity and Liberalism* (Grand Rapids: Eerdmans, 1923). Machen insisted that liberalism and Christianity were distinct religions. While many differed with this assessment, few questioned the fairness of his summary.

10. Hutchison, *Modernist Impulse*, 2.

Having accepted evolution as a biological theory, liberals were quick to apply it to social and religious development. Religion became a reflection of human mental development. Consequently, the history of Hebrew religion was rewritten to allow for progress from an early polytheism through henotheism to monotheism, with a corresponding development in moral values. The Bible—especially the Old Testament—had to be rearranged in order to accommodate this revised understanding of Israelite theology. The theory of evolution fed directly into liberal criticism of the biblical text.

The liberals' strong emphasis upon human goodness inevitably altered their understanding of sin. Liberals acknowledged that people were still imperfect, but the doctrine of progress told them that these imperfections could be overcome. The unfolding marvels of medicine, technology, and industry seemed to substantiate this hypothesis, as did the recent abolition of slavery in the United States. From the liberal point of view, sin (such as it was) certainly did not call for divine wrath. Humans were too good to be sent to Hell—and on any account God was too good to send them there.

With virtually one voice, liberals denied that a wrathful God could have required propitiation. Consequently, the historic Christian understanding of the atonement had to be revised. From a liberal point of view, Christ certainly did not suffer as the sinner's substitute or receive the condemnation that the sinner deserved. Instead, the atonement was an example and an influence. By dying sacrificially on the cross, Jesus displayed the magnificent love that God bears toward human beings. For the liberal, this display of sacrificial love provided a pattern or example that people should follow in their pursuit of God. More than that, it awakened within them an answering love toward God and toward their fellow humans. Few doctrines were more offensive to liberals than the teaching that Christ had to endure God's wrath on behalf of sinners.

Of course, liberals could not and did not deny that people sometimes behaved in destructive and selfish ways. What they denied was that these destructive and selfish acts constituted an inexcusable offense to God or brought condemnation upon those who committed them. Liberals denied that guilt was the problem, that justice demanded retribution, and that Christ suffered to satisfy God's justice. Even the worst of people had a divine spark within, and this spark could be fanned into a flame. When ministering to people the focus should not be upon their personal guilt or the evil that they had done, but upon the good that was in them and upon which they might build.

To a very large extent, liberals relocated sin from individuals into social structures. While they certainly believed that individuals could and did do wrong things, they were more concerned about the social structures that placed people in impossible situations. Individual acts such as theft, drunkenness, or prostitution were seen more as symptoms, while the causes lay in social and economic inequality, oppressive industrialism, and predatory enterprises such as the liquor trade. While one might help the individual drunkard or prostitute, the important thing was to challenge the structures that fostered their practices.

In other words, liberals wanted a gospel that was not merely (or even mainly) personal, but social. The older gospel brought an announcement that Christ had acted in space and time to secure the forgiveness of sins. Liberals, however, began to reimagine the gospel as an endeavor to transform society. In the name of the gospel they began to challenge social ills such as poverty, crime, ignorance, child labor, drunkenness, gambling, tenement living, unsanitary conditions, poor hygiene, and the exploitation of labor. Their efforts were bolstered by their commitment to the doctrine of progress and their strong belief in the essential goodness of human nature.

A key component in the social gospel was the liberal understanding of the kingdom of God. Modernists adopted a postmillennial view of the future in which a golden age was the goal of human activity on earth. This golden age would mean the elimination of social ills and the elevation of human dignity, and it is what liberals thought of as the kingdom of God. The joy, peace, and fruitfulness of the kingdom would constitute the full manifestation of God's presence on earth—though without anything like the bodily presence of Jesus. Liberals committed themselves to bringing in such a kingdom.

Who, then, was Jesus? As liberals understood Him, Jesus was the first Christian. He was an example of faith. He served as a model to show how people ought to live for God. Like all humans, Jesus was divine—but He was not uniquely God incarnate. He did reveal God through His teachings, but He also revealed the tremendous potential for good that lies within human nature. He was a sort of prototype of what God wanted all people to become.

Liberals generally downplayed the role of the miraculous in Jesus' life. They often understood the resurrection to mean that the influence of Jesus lives on in His followers. Since Jesus was not uniquely God, they saw no need for a virgin birth. Since they understood the kingdom of God to be an ethical development within the flow of history, they saw no useful purpose in Jesus' miracles. Indeed, they believed that miracles were an offense to the modern mind. The important thing about Jesus was His ethical teaching. Liberals saw in the message of Jesus the supreme elevation of morality and altruistic service. The goal of the Christian was to live the same kind of ethical life that Jesus lived. Jesus was a guide and pattern for the religious person.

In fact, liberals often insisted upon distinguishing the Jesus of history from the Christ of faith. The Jesus of history was the teacher who had actually lived in Judea and Galilee during the first century. The Christ of faith was the supernatural person whom the church had invented by adding generations worth of legend to the stories of Jesus. From the modernist perspective, the miraculous Christ contributed little to modern Christianity. Rather, liberals were interested in the Jesus of history, and particularly in His ethical teachings. They launched upon a so-called quest for the historical Jesus to discover those teachings by reading between the lines of the Gospels.

The distinction between the Jesus of history and the Christ of faith reveals something about how the liberals were using the Bible. They saw the Scripture as neither inerrant nor infallible. They ridiculed the notion of verbal inspiration. Rather than accepting the complete Bible as a revelation of God, they viewed it as a record of religious experience. They believed that the Bible exhibits different religious experiences, some of which are better and some worse. Parts of the Bible (particularly the ethical teachings of Jesus) could still speak to moderns and help to spur human progress. Other parts had to be rejected as expressions of primitive religious perspectives and experiences that had now been superseded.

Liberals fully accepted and employed a higher critical approach to the text of Scripture. Higher criticism is a discipline that asks questions about how texts were composed. It is concerned with issues like authorship, date, and place of composition. Influenced as they were by the theory of social and religious evolution, liberals often used higher critical techniques to challenge traditional understandings of the Bible.

For example, liberals accepted the Documentary Hypothesis, which asserts that the Pentateuch could not have been written by Moses. Rather, original documents were prepared by a Jahwist and an Elohist, supplemented by a Deuteronomist, and combined by a priestly redactor (sometimes this theory was referred to as the JEDP theory). Likewise, liberals believed that the book of Isaiah was the product of at least two authors, the original Isaiah (who wrote chapters 1–39) and a later pseudonymous poet whom they called Deutero-Isaiah (who wrote chapters 40–66). The Synoptic Gospels were not written by Matthew, Mark, and Luke, but were the product of generations of storytelling in which the repeated tellings added Jesus' miracles and supernatural claims to the stories.

In short, religious liberalism or modernism completely transformed Christian theology. Liberalism held new and different views of God, humanity, sin, judgment, atonement, salvation, the kingdom of God, Christ, and Scripture. Virtually no part of historic Christianity was left unchanged by the liberal approach to religion.

In view of the radical nature of religious liberalism, two further questions must be asked. The first is why the liberals made these changes. Why did they commit themselves to a radical revision of Christianity? The second is how a religion that was so different from historic Christianity could manage to capture virtually all of the mainline Protestant denominations, and particularly how it could capture Northern Baptists.

The *why* question is easier to answer. As William R. Hutchison notes, modernism was "first and most visibly . . . the conscious, intended adaptation of religious ideas to modern culture."[11] Liberals were not trying to destroy Christianity. In fact, they were trying to save it. They believed that the old supernatural religion of the Bible could not stand up to the challenges of modern science—and the spirit of the age told them that the scientific method was the surest way to certain knowledge. Consequently, Christianity had to be adapted so as to eliminate any conflict with modern science. It had to make room for evolution. It had to make room for the "assured results" of biblical criticism. It had to make room for the optimistic view of human nature that had been proliferated during the Enlightenment. The liberal response was to relocate authority from the written text of Scripture to the inner experience of God. Jesus became the best exemplar of this experience, and Christianity became the process of following Jesus as He served God. Effectively, liberals removed the core of Christianity from the sphere of knowledge and transferred it into the sphere of sentiment.

During the half century from 1870 to 1920, liberalism gained de facto control of nearly all of the mainline Protestant denominations. In particular, by 1920 it held such a tight grip on Northern Baptists that it could not be shaken loose, even by concentrated efforts. How could liberals gain so much power? What factors explain their success? That is a story that needs to be told.

Liberalism among Northern Baptists

American denominations of all sorts experienced controversy during the years leading up to the Civil War. They endured arguments over Calvinism, missions, Freemasonry, Bible translation, organizational structure, and, most of all, slavery. These controversies had produced deep divisions in many denominations, including Baptists.

As they emerged from the war, it seemed as if Baptists and other Christians had adopted Lincoln's spirit of malice toward none and charity toward all. For some decades controversy dropped to a minimum while a new attitude of forbearance and catholicity swept across American Christianity. This new atmosphere of tolerance provided exactly the right environment for the new theology of liberalism to flourish. At the end of the war, hardly a liberal could be found among Baptists anywhere. Half-a-century later, however, a leading Baptist would write, "At the present all the older theological seminaries of the

11. Hutchison, *Modern Impulse*, 2.

North have on their faculties scholars of the modern type who are outspoken in their acceptance of modernistic views of the Bible and of the evolutionistic philosophy, and no one of them, so far as the writer is aware, has among its professors a stalwart and aggressive advocate of the older conservatism."[12]

The progress of liberalism began in the schools. It was first detected in classrooms, publications, and addresses at denominational gatherings like the Baptist Autumnal Conferences and (later) the Baptist Congresses. Eventually it spread to the denominational structure and pulpits of Northern Baptists. Almost invariably the first evidence of liberal theology was its view of the Bible. The abandonment of inerrancy or infallibility (these were not always neatly distinguished) was itself a departure from historic Christianity, and it usually foreshadowed other departures that would soon follow.[13]

One of the first identifiable liberals among Northern Baptists was Thomas Fenner Curtis. An educator, Curtis had for years devoted himself to preparing Baptist ministers at the University of Lewisburg in Pennsylvania. During the mid- to late 1860s his theology began to change. He resigned from the university and moved into the shadow of Harvard. There he wrote *The Human Element in the Inspiration of the Scriptures*. While Curtis professed to believe in the inspiration of the Bible, he insisted that inspiration did not require infallibility. The biblical writers could be mistaken in matters of science, history, and even in their doctrinal teachings.[14] While Curtis's work provoked some controversy, its influence was limited for the moment. What it did accomplish was to open the door for subsequent scholars to teach and publish liberal views.

Before long, Southern Baptists were facing a more serious situation—and it was one that ended up affecting Baptists in the North as well. Crawford Howell Toy was installed as professor of Old Testament at Southern Baptist Seminary in 1869. During his installation address he noted that the conclusions of secular science should be used to interpret the Bible. Within a few years he was beginning to accept critical views on issues like creation and the date of certain biblical books. The president of Southern Baptist Seminary, James P. Boyce, pressured Toy to keep these views to himself, but the professor continued to teach them. In 1878 he began to put his views in print, which

12. Albert Henry Newman, *A History of the Baptist Churches in the United States*, 6th ed. (Philadelphia: American Baptist Publication Society, 1915), 518.

13. The most comprehensive discussion of the liberal takeover among Northern Baptists is found in Jeffrey Paul Straub, "The Making of a Battle Royal: The Rise of Religious Liberalism in Northern Baptist Life, 1870–1920" (PhD diss., Southern Baptist Theological Seminary, 2004). See also Norman H. Maring, "Baptists and Changing Views of the Bible, 1865–1918 (Part I)," *Foundations* 1 (July 1958): 52–75; Maring, "Baptists and Changing Views of the Bible, 1865–1918 (Part II)," *Foundations* 1 (October 1958): 30–61.

14. Thomas Fenner Curtis, *The Human Element in the Inspiration of the Scriptures* (New York: D. Appleton, 1867), 314–32.

brought accusations of heresy. After a year of public controversy, Toy resigned his professorship. He later accepted a teaching post at Harvard, where he drifted into Unitarianism.

Toy's views were spread among Northern Baptists by his students. One of these, David Gordon Lyon, went on to take his PhD from the University of Leipzig. Toy was instrumental in bringing Lyon to Harvard in 1882. Whereas Toy had disassociated himself from Baptists, Lyon went on to propagate a liberal theory of Scripture in his addresses at the Baptist Autumnal Conferences.

These conferences, which later developed into the Baptist Congress, began with an 1882 meeting in Brooklyn, New York. The purpose of the Baptist Autumnal Conferences and the Baptist Congress was to provide a platform for Baptist leaders to address current issues. From the beginning the conference aimed for theological breadth, allowing participants to present papers without fear of recrimination. Organizers such as George Dana Boardman and Norman Fox were at least somewhat sympathetic to liberal views. As the Baptist Congress grew, it became an important venue for the open discussion of liberal theology. It gave liberals a platform to present their views with near impunity.

Within a couple years after Toy's departure from Southern Baptist Seminary, Baptists in the North were facing a comparable situation. Ezra Palmer Gould had graduated from the Newton Theological Institution in 1868. He had been asked to remain as a teacher by President Alvah Hovey, and then was elevated to full professor in 1870. Over the years Gould's teaching became increasingly liberal, resulting in complaints to the board in 1881. As tensions rose, the board appointed a committee of five to investigate the situation and return with a recommendation. In a split decision, the committee recommended that Gould be removed from teaching. In 1882 the trustees acted to dismiss Gould, also in a split decision.

Gould's firing sparked considerable controversy among Baptists. Some voices called for toleration, liberty, and diversity—an appeal that would become a liberal staple during the ensuing years. Then a second controversy erupted over a commentary that Gould was supposed to publish with the American Baptist Publication Society. The editor wanted him to take a more orthodox position in certain comments. Gould refused. Eventually he accepted a teaching position in an Episcopalian seminary, later receiving Episcopal ordination.

Although Gould was no longer teaching in a Baptist institution, his influence among Baptists continued through those whose lives he had touched. For example, W. H. P. Faunce (who became president of Brown University) and Albion Small (later president of Colby College and founder of the department of sociology at the new University of Chicago) were among his students, and both became notorious liberals. He had also started a friendship with a young pastor named William Newton Clarke, and his influence contributed greatly to Clarke's drift into liberalism.

When Clarke came as pastor to Newton Center, Massachusetts (home of Newton Theological Institution), he was already beginning to incline toward liberal theology. Even as a young man he had experienced difficulty accepting some biblical perspectives. As he matured in pastoral ministry, he rejected the verbal inspiration and inerrancy of Scripture. He also began to accept the new evolutionary theories of Charles Darwin, and these forced him to revisit several aspects of his Christian faith. His first published work, a commentary on Mark, aroused significant controversy among Baptists because of its incipient liberalism. Friendship with Ezra Gould was just the catalyst that Clarke needed to propel him into a fully liberal theology.[15]

Clarke was actually a member of the board at Newton when Gould was fired. Shortly after the firing he left Massachusetts for a teaching position at Toronto Baptist College (later McMaster University), where he was assured that his liberal ideas would be tolerated. After five years in Canada he accepted a pastoral position in Hamilton, New York, the home of Hamilton Theological Institution.

Hamilton (later renamed Colgate Theological Seminary) was one of four old Baptist seminaries in the Northeast. The others were Newton (in Newton Center, Massachusetts), Rochester (in Rochester, New York), and Crozer (in Upland, Pennsylvania). A fifth seminary was located in the Midwest under the umbrella of the old University of Chicago. It was the Baptist Union Theological Seminary, which eventually relocated to Morgan Park, Illinois.

The Hamilton seminary was affiliated with Madison University, and both were presided over by Ebenezer Dodge. Dodge also taught theology in the seminary. Theologically, he was a transitional figure. On the one hand, he insisted upon a hearing for newer theological perspectives. On the other hand, he remained committed to the older Baptist orthodoxy. When Dodge suddenly died in early 1890, the school needed to find a replacement quickly for his teaching duties. Since Clarke was already pastoring in Hamilton, and since he already had experience as a professor, he was asked to take over Dodge's classroom responsibilities.

Clarke's influence as a professor at Hamilton (Colgate) was far-reaching.

---

15. The commentary appeared in unusual form. The cover read *Commentary on Mark and Luke*, the title page showed the title as *An American Commentary on the New Testament*, ed. Alvah Hovey, but the volume contained only William Newton Clarke's commentary on the Gospel of Mark (Philadelphia: American Baptist Publication Society, 1881). Clarke later recalled the story of his changing views in William Newton Clarke, *Sixty Years with the Bible: A Record of Experience* (New York: Charles Scribner's Sons, 1909). The work is a kind of theological autobiography.

To his teaching he brought a warm, pious, irenic spirit that students found nearly irresistible. He gave himself to teaching and writing, and for two decades became a prominent influence toward liberal theology among younger Baptists. His *Outline of Christian Theology* (first published in 1894) became the first great systematization of religious liberalism by an American theologian. His *Use of the Scriptures in Theology* spelled out in detail the liberal approach to the Bible. Clarke became the first liberal to remain permanently in a Baptist seminary.[16]

While Clarke managed to establish himself pretty firmly at Hamilton, a younger liberal, Nathaniel Schmidt, was less successful. Schmidt was from Sweden, but he had received his master's degree from Madison University in Hamilton, New York. For a short time he pastored a Swedish Baptist church in Manhattan, where he befriended Walter Rauschenbusch and Leighton Williams. In 1888 he returned to Hamilton to teach Greek and Semitic languages. He spent time at the University of Berlin in 1890, after which he was given a full professorship at Hamilton.

Even before Schmidt traveled to Berlin, he was being pressured to keep quiet about some of his more liberal views. After he resumed his duties, word spread quickly that he had adopted a critical approach that was unfriendly to Scripture. While Schmidt had an undoubted reputation for brilliance, even some of his peers were uncomfortable with his conclusions. Sylvester Burnham, dean at Hamilton, had started out as one of Schmidt's defenders, but by 1896 Burnham had grown so uncomfortable with Schmidt's views that he threatened to resign.

In the middle of 1896, the American Baptist Education Society recommended that Schmidt be dismissed from Hamilton. The board of the school asked for Schmidt's resignation with only one dissenting vote. This prompted a letter of protest from Walter Rauschenbusch. At Cornell University, President Jacob Gould Shurman created a teaching position specifically for Schmidt.

Schmidt's forced resignation prompted sufficient controversy that even the secular papers took notice. The public consensus was that Schmidt had been treated shabbily. The trustees, who were not prepared for such negative publicity, quickly adopted a broadened policy on academic freedom. The lesson was not lost on other Baptists who were involved in higher education. Boards and administrations quickly became more tolerant of liberalism. Schmidt was probably the last modernist to be dismissed from one of the old Northern Baptist seminaries for theological reasons.

One liberal who benefitted from this increased latitude was Walter

---

16. William Newton Clarke, *An Outline of Christian Theology*, 20th ed. (New York: Charles Scribner's Sons, 1912); Clarke, *The Use of the Scriptures in Theology* (New York: Charles Scribner's Sons, 1906).

Rauschenbusch. Years before, fresh out of Rochester Theological Seminary, Rauschenbusch had taken the pastorate of the Second German Baptist Church in Manhattan. This little congregation was located in the heart of New York's infamous Hell's Kitchen, near the equally notorious Tenderloin District. Rauschenbusch found himself ministering to a community that was dominated not only by poverty and inhumane living conditions, but also by drunkenness, gambling, prostitution, and other vices. He became convinced that the mission of Christianity was to address the human suffering that now confronted him every day. In spite of a weak constitution and growing deafness, he threw himself into the task. In addition to his pastoral ministry, he began to edit a worker's paper called *For the Right*.

Pastoring in Hell's Kitchen brought Rauschenbusch into contact with other ministers who shared his burden. That is how he met Nathaniel Schmidt, who at the time was pastor of a Swedish Baptist church. Another important contact was Leighton Williams of Amity Baptist Church on West 54th Avenue. Both geographical proximity and a common interest brought these three together. Their great goal was to decide how Christianity could address the social concerns that were common to all of them.

They had not yet answered this question when Schmidt left to teach at Hamilton in 1888, and then Rauschenbusch was granted a sabbatical to travel to England and Germany in 1891. Before the friends went their separate ways, however, they made the acquaintance of a Pennsylvania pastor, Samuel Batten. He suggested that the answer to their question could be found in a new understanding of the kingdom of God, which, he noted, was the center of Jesus' teaching.

Rauschenbusch pondered this suggestion as he toured Europe, working out the implications of the kingdom of God for the church's mission of social betterment. The construct that he developed was called the "social gospel," and it sought to apply Christian ethics to social problems. Economic inequality, racial tension, child labor, prostitution, drunkenness and comparable evils were to be challenged, not by individual conversions to Christianity, but through measures like education, labor unions, and legislation. Vigorously pursued, these progressive measures could usher in a social golden age, a kind of secularized millennium.

After Rauschenbusch returned from Europe, he and his friends committed themselves to labor for the kingdom through social betterment and to promote a social understanding of the gospel. In 1892 they decided to form a small society to encourage one another in the advancement of the social gospel. They called their fellowship The Brotherhood of the Kingdom, and it held its first meeting the next year.

Each summer the Brotherhood of the Kingdom would meet near

Marlborough-on-the-Hudson, at a country home owned by Williams's family. With the social gospel as their focus, pastors and scholars would gather to argue with each other, encourage each other, and present papers to one another. The meetings of the Brotherhood provided an opportunity for interchange between liberals of different denominations. Over time it became a center for liberal strategy. Its main focus, however, was always the implementation of the kingdom of God on earth.

In 1897 Augustus H. Strong invited Rauschenbusch to join the faculty at Rochester Theological Seminary. Strong was personally committed to Baptist orthodoxy as he understood it, but his understanding of orthodoxy was rather more open than that of some others. For instance, he allowed for the evolution of the human race, and he was willing to entertain the possibility that belief in inerrancy was not essential to biblical authority. Later in life he would speak out against religious liberalism, especially when it was found on the mission field. Nevertheless, Strong's invitation to Rauschenbusch was one of the key events in the advance of liberal influence.

Strong knew that Rauschenbusch was a liberal when he hired him. In fact, he counseled Rauschenbusch to be cautious in expressing his views, and especially in voicing denials of traditionally held doctrines. Rauschenbusch hardly ever followed this counsel. Nevertheless, Strong not only employed Rauschenbusch, but promoted him and kept him on the faculty at Rochester. Rauschenbusch's most important influence came, not while he was a pastor in Hell's Kitchen, but while he was a teacher for A. H. Strong.

His professorship at Rochester gave Rauschenbusch the leisure to write. His first major work, published in 1907, was *Christianity and the Social Crisis*. This work was a kind of personal manifesto on the social gospel. A best seller for its day, this book made Rauschenbusch famous and galvanized the social gospel movement. Two years later (the same year that Van Osdel moved to Grand Rapids), Rauschenbusch published a second volume, *Prayers of the Social Awakening*. His blueprint for change, *Christianizing the Social Order*, appeared in 1912, followed shortly by *Dare We Be Christians?* Rauschenbusch's influence began to wane during the Great War, but he kept publishing. *The Social Principles of Jesus* was meant to popularize the social gospel through group study by young adults. *A Theology of the Social Gospel* still caused a sensation when it appeared after the armistice.[17]

Alfred Wishart, pastor at Fountain Street Church when Van Osdel arrived

---

17. Walter Rauschenbusch, *Christianity and the Social Crisis* (London: Macmillan, 1907); Rauschenbusch, *Prayers of the Social Awakening* (Boston: Pilgrim Press, 1910); this volume was also published under the title *For God and the People*; Rauschenbusch, *Christianizing the Social Order* (New York: Macmillan, 1913); Rauschenbusch, *Dare We Be Christians?* (Boston: Pilgrim Press, 1914); Rauschenbusch, *The Social Principles of Jesus* (New York: Woman's Press, 1917); Rauschenbusch, *A Theology for the Social Gospel* (New York: Macmillan, 1918).

in Grand Rapids, had been strongly influenced by Rauschenbusch's theory of the social gospel. Rauschenbusch's ministry in Hell's Kitchen had become Wishart's model in Trenton. Wishart then became a direct pipeline for the social gospel into Grand Rapids. Rauschenbusch was not the only influence upon the young liberal, however, nor was he necessarily the most important. Wishart had also been shaped—profoundly so—by his education at the University of Chicago.

The old University of Chicago had occupied a ten-acre site donated by Stephen Douglas (of the Lincoln-Douglas debates) just off Lake Michigan near Cottage Grove and 35th Avenue. Affiliated with the university were a law school (now the Northwestern University School of Law) and the Baptist Union Theological Seminary. The old university faced financial difficulties almost from its founding in 1857. An offer of free land attracted the seminary, and in 1877 it relocated to Morgan Park (now part of Chicago's Far South Side). When the university failed in 1886, the seminary had already been operating independently for some time.

Oliver Van Osdel attended the Baptist Union Theological Seminary while it was still connected with the old University of Chicago. He left seminary early for several years of pastoral ministry, then returned to complete his training in Morgan Park. The president of the seminary was George W. Northrup, who doubled as professor of systematic theology. Most significantly, the young William Rainey Harper became professor of Hebrew and cognate languages in 1879.

Van Osdel and Harper quickly formed a friendship. Van Osdel was older, a Civil War veteran, and a family man. He had already pastored three churches and faced his first ecclesiastical battles. Harper, while younger, was an undisputed genius. When Harper's dying brother came to live in his home, the Van Osdels shouldered the responsibility for his care. Harper reciprocated with warmth toward Van Osdel's young son, Edgar. Their games took a different twist from those usually played between adults and children—Van Osdel was surprised one day to hear his son recite the entire first chapter of Genesis in Hebrew.

After Van Osdel was graduated, the two friends drifted apart, though they did not quite lose touch. Van Osdel went on to pastor churches in Kansas and Texas. In 1888, two years after the closure of the old University of Chicago, Harper left Morgan Park for Yale. Chicago Baptists were already attempting to gather financing for a new university. Van Osdel accepted the pastorate of First Baptist Church in Galesburg, Illinois, in 1889 just as anticipation was mounting. Within a year, John D. Rockefeller of Standard Oil agreed to donate $600,000 to open the new university, provided other donors could raise another $400,000. He wanted Harper to become the president of the university, but Harper insisted upon another million dollars for the divinity school. Rockefeller agreed, and the new University of Chicago opened for classes in the fall of 1892.

The Harper who built the new university, however, held rather different convictions from the professor who had taught Van Osdel his Hebrew in Morgan Park. Sometime during the '80s, Harper had passed through an intellectual crisis. During his studies he found himself drawing conclusions that required him to deny the Davidic authorship of one of the psalms that, according to the Gospels, Jesus Himself attributed to David. Hour after hour Harper paced in his study, trying to decide whether to terminate his line of study. In the end, he pressed forward, embracing a critical approach to Scripture.[18]

Once Harper had accepted liberal theology—especially a higher critical approach to the Bible—he became an evangelist for that view. In 1888 he began an interchange on "The Pentateuchal Question" with a Presbyterian scholar, W. H. Green of Princeton Seminary. Green attacked and Harper defended the critical approach to the Pentateuch (Green eventually put his articles into book form).[19] Harper's interest was broader than scholarly debate, however. He wanted to introduce ordinary church members to the liberal view of Scripture. To accomplish this goal he organized summer schools and edited popular publications such as *The Old Testament Student*. When he became the president of the new University of Chicago, he began to use the power of his institution to spread liberalism.

The Morgan Park seminary became the divinity school of the new university. The older professors were not identifiably liberal, but they were at the upper end of their teaching careers. Harper quickly added his own choices to the faculty, then used the retirements of the older professors to add even more. In the long run, the faculty of the divinity school boasted some of the best-known names in American liberalism: Ernest DeWitt Burton, Shailer Mathews, Shirley Jackson Case, George Burman Foster, and Gerald Birney Smith. Under the leadership of these individuals, the divinity school of the new University of Chicago became the single most important force for advancing liberalism among Northern Baptists.

Of the so-called Chicago School, Foster was the most openly radical. So extreme were his pronouncements that he was formally excluded from the Chicago Baptist ministers' conference. Eventually Foster asked to be

18. Shailer Mathews, *New Faith for Old: An Autobiography* (New York: Macmillan, 1936), 63.

19. The episode is mentioned by Edward J. Young, *An Introduction to the Old Testament* (Grand Rapids: William B. Eerdmans, 1964), 139. See W. H. Green, *The Unity of the Book of Genesis* (New York: Charles Scribner's Sons, 1895); Green, *The Higher Criticism of the Pentateuch* (New York: Charles Scribner's Sons, 1895).

transferred from the divinity school to the philosophy department of the university. Harper may have felt relieved, but Foster's influence continued.

Shailer Mathews probably held views that were as radical as Foster's, but he made a point of articulating them more carefully. Originally hired to teach New Testament, Mathews rose to become dean of the divinity school. He was a skilled administrator and a consummate ecclesiastical politician. Mathews also represented the interests of the Chicago school and of liberalism in general during the formation of the Northern Baptist Convention.

The Northern Baptist Convention

By the turn of the century, Northern Baptists had organized a number of important institutions. They operated a foreign mission society, a home mission society, a publication society, an education society, various women's organizations, a young people's union, and an assortment of educational institutions. The larger societies still held their annual meetings together during the week of Pentecost.

Numbers of influential Baptists were growing restless with the Anniversaries and wanted a more powerful, efficient organization for the churches. Some of these were wealthy men who had been giving massive amounts to the two main mission agencies, both of which were running significant deficits. In 1895 the combined shortfall of the foreign and home societies was about $460,000—a princely sum in those days. The general secretaries would try to ease financial emergencies by approaching the rich to make up the deficit. The most notable giver was John D. Rockefeller, but his patience was wearing thin. He would typically offer a matching gift that the secretaries could use to motivate other givers, but by early in the new century he was pressuring Baptists to adopt a more businesslike organization.

Aware of the need for a more central organization, Shailer Mathews saw the possibility of using it as a platform to advance liberalism. Accordingly, at the fall 1906 meeting of the Chicago Baptist Association he had a resolution introduced. It appealed to the secretaries of the big three societies (foreign missions, home missions, and publication) to call a meeting with a view to organizing a Northern Baptist Convention. The resolution also stated that if the three did not act by December, then the secretary of the Chicago Baptist Association would be authorized to call such a meeting.[20]

20. For a well-researched account of the founding, see Robert E. McClernon, "The Formation of the Northern Baptist Convention" (BD thesis, University of Chicago, 1956). See also Mathews, *New Faith for Old*, 63. Additional perspective on the founding and operation of the convention can be found in Paul M. Harrison, *Authority and Power in the Free Church Tradition: A Social Case Study of the American Baptist Convention* (Carbondale, IL: Southern Illinois University Press, 1959).

The three secretaries conceded, and on December 11, 1906, called for the meeting. At the 1907 Anniversaries in Washington, D.C., Mathews was appointed chairman of the steering committee. He had a draft constitution ready to offer. By the end of the week he had led the organizing of the Northern Baptist Convention. Perhaps not surprisingly, the desk jobs went to modernists, although the elected officers were often conservatives. The first president was New York Governor Charles Evans Hughes. The vice president under him was Harry Pratt Judson of the University of Chicago. The general secretary was William C. Bitting.

Many have said that the convention was once fundamental, but that the liberals later got control of it. The documents say it differently: modernists put the convention together from the very beginning and they never lost control.[21] The general secretaries and the executives were modernists all through the history of the establishment. Within a few years of the founding, that influence would make itself felt.

In 1908 the convention met in Oklahoma City and adopted the constitution. A key question was how the existing societies would be related to the new NBC. At the Portland, Oregon, meeting in 1909 the convention adopted a resolution affirming that each society was independent of any union with the Northern Baptist Convention. Until 1915 that resolve seemed to hold: the societies' reports in the Annual had their own page numbering. From that year on, the Annuals were paginated consecutively. For another ten years the societies conducted their own business meetings. In the Seattle meetings of 1925, at the discussion of the Hinson resolution, the chair for the first time failed to yield the gavel to the society president.[22]

In 1911 the convention altered the bylaws so as to give the salaried executives the right to vote. This turned out to be a powerful liberal device to control any floor vote. Also in 1911 the convention created the Ministers and Missionaries Benefit Board. Instigated by Rockefeller and initially backed by his money, the M&M Board (as it was known) was a retirement program for the convention's ministers and missionaries. Those who participated in the program would contribute a small percentage of their salaries, which would be matched by contributions from their churches. The board would then manage those funds to secure the best rate of return. In principle, the M&M Board could provide a comfortable retirement for Christian servants who might otherwise be destitute. In practice, this program became a very effective tool

---

21. Mathews, *New Faith for Old*, 113.
22. Robert Leonard Carlberg, "The Development of Centralizing Tendencies in the Northern Baptist Convention 1907–1946" (ThM thesis, Eastern Baptist Theological Seminary, Philadelphia, 1947), 72.

to prevent pastors from leaving (or worse yet, pulling their churches out of) the convention.

A third decision in 1911 would also have a significant influence upon the future of the Northern Baptist Convention. In that year the convention voted to merge with the majority of the Northern or Randall Line of Free Will Baptists. Free Will Baptists had always been more open on matters related to church membership, sometimes allowing unimmersed individuals to join their churches. This policy, sometimes called "Open Membership," was typically rejected by more mainstream Baptists. The merger of these two groups brought a number of Open Membership churches into the Northern Baptist Convention, as well as a larger number of churches that did not see Open Membership as an issue. This merger would prove to be a deciding factor in some of the controversies of the 1920s.

That development, however, still lay in the future. When Oliver Van Osdel moved to Grand Rapids in 1909, the Northern Baptist Convention was in its infancy. Conservatives supported the convention because of its organizational and financial advantages. Liberals supported it because it gave them a tool that they could use, first to secure their own position, and then to spread their control into places they would never otherwise have been able to reach. Within a decade many conservatives would begin to realize the magnitude of the blunder that they had made, but they would never be able to recover the lost ground.

Keys to Liberal Success

At the end of the Civil War, liberal theology could hardly have been detected among Baptists of the North. By 1909 a liberal like Wishart could block an entire association from publishing an orthodox defense of the virgin birth of Christ. Furthermore, liberals had formed the Northern Baptist Convention to gain an iron grip upon Baptist organizations—a grasp that would eventually extend to the churches themselves. Another decade would pass before Baptist conservatives would organize to thwart the liberal juggernaut. They would have no way of knowing that they were already beaten.

How could the theological current turn so swiftly against Baptist orthodoxy? What carried liberalism to such swift acceptance? Several considerations help to answer this question.

First and most obviously, the intellectual climate of Western civilization was changing rapidly during the late nineteenth and early twentieth centuries. The philosophical theories of Kant and Hegel were being imported into America, as were the comparable theological systems of Schleiermacher and Ritschl. Darwin's new theory of evolution had carried the day among the intelligentsia.

The acceptance of biblical criticism paralleled the growth of historical and literary criticism in other disciplines. During this transition, religious liberalism appeared to be dressed in the latest intellectual fashions.

Second, the liberals themselves were bright and even brilliant young men. They had studied in the most prestigious universities (usually German), and they flourished in the new academic climate. They were a generation upon whom respectable schools could be built, and the administrations of those schools viewed them with something akin to awe. Men like Walter Rauschenbusch and William Rainey Harper became religious celebrities. They gained influence rapidly and could not easily be challenged.

Third, once liberals became symbols of academic respectability, the public (including the religious public) was willing to protect them. Academic freedom became more important than orthodoxy. The board at Hamilton learned this lesson the hard way when they fired Nathanial Schmidt. They never forgot the beating that they took in the press—nor did the boards of the other seminaries. From the firing of Schmidt onward, liberals were safe in the schools.

Fourth, educational leaders often failed to realize how radical liberalism really was. One factor that contributed to this failure was the theological imprecision of the generation that came immediately prior to liberalism. While Presbyterians had the Princeton theologians to articulate a careful case for orthodoxy, Baptists had few educational leaders who meticulously engaged theological issues. For example, during the early debate over Thomas Fenner Curtis's book on biblical inspiration. Henry G. Weston wrote to Alvah Hovey of Newton Theological Institution saying, "I am all at sea, except so far as a dogged belief in inspiration goes, without being able to define what 'Inspiration' is, or what its metes and bounds are. . . . I want you to give me what ideas you can conveniently put on two pages of note-paper. I'll fight for them to the death, for I shall heartily believe just what you say."[23] Not long after writing this letter, Weston found himself in the presidency of Crozer Seminary. Such vagueness provided an environment that was conducive to theological innovation.

From their side, the liberals learned to keep a low profile, at least until they had gained public support and captured positions of influence. Compared to the old orthodoxy, even the moderate liberals held radical ideas. Nevertheless, they wrapped their ideas in the language of orthodoxy, especially during their public presentations. As they employed the older terms, however, they gave them new definitions. Liberals in 1909 could still speak of the inspiration

---

23. Henry G. Weston to Alvah Hovey, 6 December 1867, in *Life and Letters of Alvah Hovey*, ed. George Rice Hovey (Philadelphia: Judson Press, 1928), 161.

of Scripture, but their theory of inspiration was miles away from the beliefs (however inchoate) of Baptists before the Civil War.

Liberals also manifested the appearance of godliness and Christian devotion. Men like William Newton Clarke earned reputations as pious, warmhearted teachers. They were irenic and zealous for the kingdom of God. Many Baptists found it difficult to believe that men with whom they had knelt in earnest prayer could actually be undermining or even betraying the faith.

Because they did not appreciate the radical nature of liberalism, older administrators tended to remain unconcerned about the younger professors on their faculties who were adopting more modernistic views. They seem to have viewed liberalism as a phase or a passing theological fad, assuming that their young professors would eventually grow out of it. They believed that these bright young thinkers could eventually be influenced toward orthodoxy. In the meanwhile, the young liberals could be kept under control. Consequently, A. H. Strong hired and kept Walter Rauschenbusch on his faculty at Rochester, even though he could also express great concern over the progress of liberalism.

> Under the influence of Ritschl and his Kantian relativism, many of our teachers and preachers have swung off into a practical denial of Christ's deity and of his atonement. We seem upon the verge of a second Unitarian defection, that will break up churches and compel secessions, in a worse manner than did that of Channing and Ware a century ago. American Christianity recovered from that disaster only by vigorously asserting the authority of Christ and the inspiration of the Scriptures. . . . Without a revival of this faith our churches will become secularized, mission enterprise will die out, and the candlestick will be removed out of its place . . . as it has been with the apostate churches of New England.[24]

Hard words, those, and timely. How ironic that the man who wrote them was at that very moment employing one of the best-known and most influential liberal theologians of his generation. Whatever concerns Strong may have felt about the growth of modernism, he did not allow them to affect decisions about hiring at his own seminary.

In fact, Strong typifies the imprecision of the age. On the one hand, he objected to liberalism. On the other hand, he wished to distance himself from anything like real conservatism. At the end of his life, he was still hoping to stake out a mediating position between liberalism and fundamentalism. In his last book, he wrote,

24. Strong, *Systematic Theology*, ix.

I desire to recognize whatever of truth there is in the theory of evolution and in the conclusions of the higher criticism. . . . I hold, therefore, middle ground between the higher critics and the so-called fundamentalists, and believe it possible for them both to reconcile their differences by a larger view of the deity and omnipresence of Christ. He is "our Peace," and he holds in his girdle the key to all our problems. It is with hope of doing something to bring about such a reconciliation, that I print this new statement of doctrine.[25]

A fifth way that liberals gained influence was through denominational churchmanship. Northern Baptists had many local associations and state conventions, not to mention service organizations at every level. The multiplication of institutions required a great many employees and volunteers to administer their work. These included not only institutional presidents and convention secretaries, but a variety of middle-level managers, fundraisers, editors, publicists, field directors, and other coordinators. The complexities of Baptist organization had created many wheels to be turned, and the people who turned them performed a valuable task. Liberals willingly accepted these positions, integrating and ingratiating themselves within the denominational structure. Through their hours of denominational service they quietly made themselves indispensible.

Shailer Mathews typified the liberal commitment to churchmanship. As professor and later dean at the Divinity School of the new University of Chicago, he devoted much of his time and attention to Baptist organization. He pushed Baptists to form the Northern Baptist Convention when they were already feeling the need for a unified organization. By inserting himself into leadership, he was able to structure the new convention in ways that were favorable to liberal acceptance and, ultimately, liberal control. He had already served as president of the convention (1915) before the fundamentalist controversy erupted.

Finally, liberalism flourished among Northern Baptists because the liberals built strong networks for mutual support and protection. Among Baptists, liberals were among the most influential planners and participants at the Baptist Autumnal Conferences and the later Baptist Congresses. Liberals also worked across denominational lines through organizations like the Brotherhood of the Kingdom and the Liberal Congress of Religion (also known as the American Congress of Liberal Religious Societies, or simply the Congress of Religion).

The Liberal Congress of Religion grew out of the World's Columbian Exhibition of 1893. Also known as the Chicago World's Fair, the exhibition featured

---

25. Augustus Hopkins Strong, *What Shall I Believe: A Primer of Christian Theology* (New York: Fleming H. Revell, 1922), 8–9.

a two-week Parliament of the World's Religions (Sept. 11–27), which brought together representatives from both Eastern and Western faiths. Capitalizing on the momentum created by the Parliament, the first of the Liberal Congresses met in Chicago the following May. Meeting over the next decades, the congress provided a forum for religious liberals of different backgrounds to exchange ideas.

All of these venues, as well as others that operated on the state or local level, gave liberals an opportunity to develop and test their theology, to offer mutual encouragement, and to provide mutual assistance when one of them came under ecclesiastical fire. Through the relationships that they developed at these forums, liberals were able to engage, defend, and promote one another. This was a key element in their strategy to influence the denominations, including the Northern Baptists.

Conclusion

Less than a decade into the new century, proponents of modernist theology were firmly entrenched among Northern Baptists. They held key positions in education and publication. Their influence was spreading in the mission agencies. They had begun to occupy important pulpits. Perhaps most importantly, they had been able to engineer the formation of the Northern Baptist Convention in a way that would allow them to influence the churches directly.

When Oliver Van Osdel found himself facing the liberalism of Alfred Wishart, he was confronting a theology that had been given a forty-year head start among Northern Baptists. Organized opposition at the national level was still more than a decade away. In Van Osdel, however, liberalism encountered an intractable foe. While he did not know Wishart, he did know how to respond to error. The story of Baptist fundamentalism really begins with his reply to the two men sitting in his home during the winter of 1909.

Adoniram Judson

Alvah Hovey

George Lasher

2 Early Opposition to Liberalism

THE VISITORS IN VAN OSDEL'S HOME were H. H. Ford and James Whitney, pastor and deacon from Calvary Baptist Church of Grand Rapids. They spoke for the conservatives in the Grand Rapids Baptist Association. As Van Osdel later recalled, they stated that, "owing to the unbearable arrogance of the liberals, action had been decided upon." Then they demanded that Van Osdel tell them where he stood.[1]

The answer to this question led to something unprecedented, but the question itself was not new. Liberalism had been growing in Northern Baptist circles for at least four decades. Some Baptists had become alarmed by its progress, and some had tried to oppose it. Van Osdel and other Grand Rapids Baptists reacted in the light of these past responses to liberalism.

Opposition in Baptist Institutions

Early objections to liberalism arose from multiple sources, though only rarely within the seminaries. The denominational papers were sometimes filled with the controversy. On rare occasions, conservative voices warned against liberalism in public meetings such as the Baptist Congresses. On the whole, however, opposition to liberalism remained at the level of a relatively mild protest.

Opponents of liberalism began to raise questions in print during the early 1880s. For example, in 1882 O. S. Stearns of Newton reviewed a book that took a critical approach to the Old Testament. He warned that it was "a damaging and a dangerous book," comparing it to the "voice of the sirens." Nevertheless, he warned, "Let us not conquer the sirens by copying Ulysses, closing our ears to their song with uncritical wax."[2]

1. *Baptist Temple News,* January 29, 1921, 2.
2. O. S. Stearns, "The Old Testament in the Jewish Church," *Baptist Quarterly Review* 4 (1882): 251–52.

Hesitation about liberalism was also expressed by Alvah Hovey at the Baptist Autumnal Conference of 1883. Hovey was president at Newton and one of the most important Baptist theologians of his generation. In his keynote address he questioned whether the new theology was simply a change of expression or whether it represented a change in the principles that were expressed.[3]

Hovey partly answered his own question. He stated that the critical treatment of the Pentateuch was of a "disturbing character; for in this field the new criticism cannot prevail without destroying root and branch our confidence in the writings of that volume as a revelation of the Lord's will." While recognizing the destructive nature of the new approach, however, Hovey insisted that "the investigation, the controversy, must and should go on."[4] This puzzling ambivalence became typical of many who opposed the new theology. On the one hand, they recognized its dangers, but on the other hand, they did not wish to seem closed-minded. Consequently, they did little to expunge liberal influences from their fellowship.

Also in 1883 Howard Osgood of Rochester Seminary published an article that contrasted modern critics' conclusions with Jesus' teaching about the Old Testament. He noted that the "newer school" stamped as "fiction and fraud" much that Jesus declared to be the Word of God. Osgood insisted that this difference amounted to a "direct and colossal contradiction" concerning which no compromise was possible.[5]

Osgood's assessment was repeated but then blunted in an address that he delivered at the Baptist Autumnal Conference later that year. He first applauded the use of impartial, scientific principles in the study of Scripture, insinuating that liberals lacked impartiality. He charged, "What lean and beggarly specimens the works of many modern critics would be if all pure dogmatism were eliminated from them." He assaulted the supposedly "undeniable criteria" of liberal critics, stating that such criteria were worthless when applied to modern writings. Then he suddenly reversed himself: "For all that modern criticism brings us as the tested product of sound investigation, every intelligent lover of the Bible will be grateful. All ill-founded or unfounded theories about the Bible are only passing clouds."[6] A century and a half after Osgood offered this naïve counsel, destructive biblical criticism is more influential than ever.

3. Alvah Hovey, "Opening Address," *Proceedings of the Second Annual Baptist Autumnal Conference* (Boston: Baptist Missionary Rooms, Tremont Temple, 1883), 5.

4. Ibid.

5. Howard Osgood, "Jesus Christ and 'The Newer School of Criticism,'" *Baptist Quarterly Review* 5 (1883): 117.

6. Howard Osgood, "Modern Biblical Criticism: Its History and Method," *Proceedings of the Second Annual Baptist Autumnal Conference* (Boston: Baptist Missionary Rooms, Tremont Temple, 1883), 59–60.

Other writers also expressed concerns about the destructive criticism of the Bible. One was P. S. Evans, who acknowledged copyists' errors in the biblical manuscripts, but refused to question the Mosaic authorship of Deuteronomy or to assent that Daniel's prophecies were written after the fact. "You cannot disintegrate and lacerate the Word of God," he said, "tearing out here a leaf and there a leaf, and still hold the Church to its allegiance. Do this and you destroy the very substance of our faith."[7]

One steadfast opponent of the new theology was George William Lasher, editor of the popular *Journal and Messenger*. Lasher first involved himself in the controversy over Crawford Toy at Southern Baptist Seminary. Within a few years he took the orthodox side in opposing Ezra Palmer Gould, who was then teaching at Newton. When Nathaniel Schmidt was forced out of Hamilton, Lasher was among the few who expressed approval. After the founding of the new University of Chicago, Lasher directed his fire at both William Rainey Harper and George Burman Foster. Even William Newton Clarke came under scrutiny in the *Journal and Messenger*. While Lasher developed a personal friendship with Walter Rauschenbusch, he remained a critic of the social gospel. Lasher further devoted the pages of his paper to the ongoing defense of orthodox Baptist teaching. He kept up his opposition to liberalism until his death in 1920, only months before the beginning of the fundamentalist controversy.[8]

In 1895 the liberal author Norman Fox touched off a controversy in the *Baptist Quarterly Review*. Fox argued that the apostles' writings were no more inspired than their acts or their oral utterances. Subscribers to the *Review* reacted strongly. Caught by surprise, the editors reminded their readers that they permitted "considerable freedom of discussion." They chided that a quarterly review "is not intended for babes, but for thinking men." Matters that might be inappropriate in a popular paper or in the pulpit were perfectly admissible for its intended readers. The truth did not need to be protected, they said: it only needs "a fair field and no favor."[9]

That issue of the *Review* also featured a symposium on "The Inspiration of the Apostles." The symposium consisted of a series of more-or-less critical responses to Fox's article. Two are worth mentioning in particular.

Heman Lincoln of Newton opened his response by noting that if Fox's principles were sound, then "a reconstruction of Baptist theology is inevitable. [I]f there be no infallible inspiration in the Bible; if its writers were liable to

---

7. P. S. Evans, "Liberty and Toleration," *Baptist Quarterly Review* 5 (1883): 175–76.

8. Jeffrey P. Straub, "George William Lasher—Baptist Proto-Fundamentalist," *Detroit Baptist Seminary Journal* 11 (2006): 135–50.

9. Norman Fox, "The Inspiration of the Apostles in Speaking and Writing," *Baptist Quarterly Review* 7 (1885): 469–82; Fox, "The Future of the Review," *Baptist Quarterly Review* 8 (1886): 94–95.

error in the apprehension of the statement of truths; if its teachings are to be corrected by conscience and common sense, the old foundations have given way, and the final standard of appeal is lost." He insisted that without an infallible Bible, human reason would become the ultimate authority.[10]

George D. B. Pepper of Colby University offered a similar assessment. He posed the question, "What authority belongs to the apostolic teaching contained in our New Testament writings?" In answer he wrote, "We cannot rank our New Testament below our Old Testament, and so we hold of the former, as Christ and the apostles did of the latter, that in quoting, we may name indifferently either God or the writer, and that when we can say 'Thus it is written,' we have struck bottom and can stand fast."[11]

By the early 1890s liberals had learned to use meetings such as the Baptist Autumnal Conferences to their advantage. A noteworthy episode occurred in 1892, when the conference set aside special time for presentations on biblical inspiration. A Philadelphia pastor, T. A. T. Hanna, spoke strongly in favor of biblical inerrancy, insisting that Jesus' handling of the Scripture left no room for critical denials. In rebuttal, D. G. Lyon argued that whether or not the Bible contained errors, its strength lay in its great moral teachings, which were of eternal value. Lyon was followed by J. B. G. Pidge, who maintained that present errors in the manuscripts might well indicate the presence of errors in the autographs. He further opined that Hanna had not offered a scintilla of proof for his assertions. Against Lyon and Pidge, Howard Osgood and J. W. Wilmarth both insisted upon biblical inerrancy, but then Nathaniel Schmidt (who had recently returned from studies in Germany) stated that he thanked God for errors in the Bible. These, said Schmidt, included not only matters of history and science, but also matters of morals and religion. Ezekiel Robinson, president at Brown University, took the platform and, responding by name to Hanna and Osgood, argued that the Bible certainly does exhibit the marks of human infirmity.

As the day progressed, these presentations and discussions became increasingly tense. Different parties in the crowd interrupted speakers on both sides with applause. By the time Robinson had finished his refutation of Hanna and Osgood, the atmosphere was brittle. Since Robinson and Pidge had both directed their remarks toward him personally, Hanna was given the opportunity to respond. Extemporizing, he stated that the division among Baptists was deeper than he had supposed. To Pidge's slight that he had offered no proof, Hanna retorted that he had offered the Word of God as proof. He then added,

10. Heman Lincoln, "The Inspiration of the Apostles," *Baptist Quarterly Review* 8 (1886): 65.

11. George D. B. Pepper, "The Inspiration of the Apostles," *Baptist Quarterly Review* 8 (1886): 74, 77–78.

"In some cooler moment, when [Pidge] goes before his God, let him take that to him." The audience responded to this jab with hisses.[12]

This exchange shows that the debate between liberals and conservatives was heating up. Between the two was a moderate party, devoted mainly to organizational concerns. Osgood and other conservatives continued to denounce the new theology, but the moderates viewed both positions as factions within a broader Baptist brotherhood. From the moderates came calls for the two sides to live in harmony with one another.

An example of the moderate position is an article published by Eri Hulbert in the *Standard* of Chicago, one of the most important Baptist papers. Hulbert had been on the faculty of the Baptist Union Theological Seminary when it moved from Morgan Park to become the divinity school of the new University of Chicago. He served as dean of the divinity school during its first fifteen years.

Hulbert called the two parties *progressives* and *conservatives*. While he believed that the two groups held much in common, he acknowledged that progressives (liberals) had reached a different understanding of God, Christ, human nature, and Scripture. Wondering aloud whether the two parties would fight, Hulbert offered the following observations.

> If the old and the new are to fight it will be a fight all along the line, among pastors, between schools, in churches, associations, conventions, national societies. It will extend to our young people, seminaries, mission fields, religious press, to all our organized denominational activities.... If both parties are to invite and keep up a satanic spirit Satan will deservedly get them both in the end, and, perforce, the denomination will go to the devil.[13]

The bulk of the article consisted of an extended appeal for the two sides to tolerate each other. Hulbert believed that by working together, progressives and conservatives could give Baptists a better Bible, a better theology, a better education, a better ecclesiasticism, a better missionary endeavor, a better sociological activity, and a better young people's influence. Particularly interesting are his remarks on a better theology.

> Thirty, twenty, fifteen years ago our seminaries served out a theology which some of the conservative pupils are disposed to retain, but which to their progressive teachers has become obsolescent. The theology of the future may not be the "new theology" of today, but it will

12. The story is retold by Norman H. Maring, "Baptists and Changing Views of the Bible, 1865–1918 (Part II)," *Foundations* 1 (October 1958): 34–36. Maring's research lies behind much of this section.

13. The article was republished as Eri B. Hulbert, "The Baptist Outlook," in *The English Reformation and Puritanism With Other Lectures and Addresses* (Chicago: University of Chicago Press, 1908), 441.

be a vast improvement on the old theology of yesterday. It will not revolve around metaphysical abstractions nor deal largely in proofless and profitless fictions.[14]

These words and much else in Hulbert's article reveal that he was not a disinterested mediator. He was dean of a divinity school led by one of the greatest liberal minds of the day. His faculty included outspoken defenders of liberalism. His plea for toleration exemplifies a tactic that liberals learned to deploy with great skill.

The plea for toleration was always a plea that affected only the conservatives. The liberals were not trying to oppose conservatives within the denomination. In fact, they needed the conservatives' money to survive: they could not trust Rockefeller to finance the whole thing for them. Nothing would have been more disastrous for the liberals than if the conservatives had simply left them with the denominational machinery. They could not have supported the structure for a year.

Liberals did not want the conservatives to go away, for the simple reason that conservatives constituted a vast majority of Northern Baptists. The real danger—the thing liberals feared—was that conservatives would unite with a single resolve to move against them. If at this early stage those who held orthodox theology had acted in concert, using their votes, their money, and their influence, they could have ended liberalism within their denomination almost immediately.

One reason that they did not is because they listened to the plea for toleration. Liberals were happy to allow conservatives to voice orthodox theology, just as long as the conservatives did not begin to grow confrontational. What they dreaded was some event that would turn the conservatives into militant challengers. Consequently, they used collegiality as a solvent to dilute conservative opposition and prevent it from crystallizing. Whenever conservatives began to put on a confrontational face, liberals would wax eloquent about unity, toleration, and the importance of denominational goals. They were able to sway many with these pious-sounding words.

Opposition from the Bible Conference Movement

Not everyone was oblivious to the trend. In 1875 some six men met in Chicago, probably in E. P. Goodwin's church, to share in Bible study. Their two great concerns were liberal theology and the literal interpretation of prophecy. Their meeting later came to be known as "the Believers' Meeting." Out of it came a resolve to meet the following year. Eventually these meetings

14. Ibid., 444–45.

produced the prophetic conference movement (New York in 1878, Chicago in 1886, and so on), the Bible conference movement (Niagara, Seacliff, and 150 to 200 more), and even the Bible school and faith missions movements. Fundamentalism itself nearly half a century later can be considered a direct product of the movement begun in Chicago, 1875.[15]

Though he was not present in Chicago, A. J. Gordon, pastor of Clarendon Street Baptist Church in Boston, soon became one of the principal leaders of the Believers' Meeting for Bible Study. In October 1878 Gordon began publishing a periodical called the *Watchword*. While the publication was interdenominational in flavor, Gordon himself was deeply involved in Baptist life. He was a graduate of Brown and Newton. Not only did he pastor a prominent Baptist church, but he also served as a member of the board at Newton. His words carried weight in Baptist circles.[16]

Gordon was as alert to liberalism as any leader of his generation. The first page of the first issue of the *Watchword* took aim at those who wanted to appeal to Christ's personal authority while "depreciating the plenary inspiration of Scripture." The second issue offered criticism of liberals who "disparage the use of the Old Testament, as a book belonging to a past age and to an outgrown religion."[17] Clearly Gordon intended to use his magazine to oppose liberalism.

As modernism grew more popular, Gordon was unimpressed. He argued that liberalism was the "religion of human nature" because it made no "stern claims." He believed that liberalism provided an easy path for those who were careless and easygoing in their convictions. He quipped,

> You never find men backsliding into Orthodoxy. You never find men drifting into high Calvinism. And you never will till you find water running up hill and iron floating upward in air. On the contrary, one has to climb to get into this kind of faith, trampling on pride and self-esteem, and holding himself rigidly up to that conviction which is hardest to receive, that human nature is naturally depraved and needing regeneration, and that God is righteously holy and must punish sin.[18]

---

15. Norman C. Kraus, *Dispensationalism in America* (Richmond: John Knox Press, 1958), 72ff. Kraus puts the date at 1876. George W. Dollar put the date as 1875, which seems to follow more of the sources. *A History of Fundamentalism in America* (Greenville, SC: Bob Jones University Press, 1973), 72.

16. On A. J. Gordon see George G. Houghton, "The Contributions of Adoniram Judson Gordon to American Christianity" (ThD diss., Dallas Theological Seminary, 1970); Ernest B. Gordon, *Adoniram J. Gordon: A Biography* (New York: Fleming H. Revell, 1896); S. M. Gibson, "Adoniram Judson Gordon, D.D. (1836–1895) Pastor, Premillennialist, Moderate Calvinist, and Missionary Statesman" (PhD diss., University of Oxford, 1997).

17. *Watchword*, October 1878, 1; *Watchword*, November 1878, 17.

18. *Watchword*, May 1880, 141.

The next year Gordon was handed an opportunity to act on his convictions. That was the year that protests were raised over the liberalism of Ezra Palmer Gould at Newton. Gordon was a member of the board at Newton and served on the committee of five who investigated the professor. Gould was dismissed from Newton by vote of the board in 1882—the only successful firing of a liberal professor from a Northern Baptist seminary.

Much of Gordon's influence went into building the Bible conference movement. He was an important leader of the Believers' Meeting for Bible Study (sometimes known as the Niagara Bible Conference). He spoke regularly at D. L. Moody's Northfield Conference. He was also heavily involved in promoting the international prophecy conferences of 1878 (New York) and 1886 (Chicago). These conferences brought him into contact with conservative leaders from other denominations. They gave him a position of leadership among younger Northern Baptists such as I. M. Haldeman, A. C. Dixon, and the very young W. B. Riley. The Bible conferences also provided an opportunity to take the case against liberalism directly to ordinary church members.

The planners of these conferences believed that premillennialism erected a bulwark against modern theology. They viewed the literal interpretation of prophecy as a breakwater to halt the tide of "jelly-fish theories evolved out of man's erratic consciousness, pride, and self-will." They saw the anticipation of Christ's return as an antidote for the "feverishness of the age" and the race after theological novelties.[19]

Gordon attempted to import the spiritual intensity of the prophetic conferences directly into Baptist life. On May 27, 1890, a group of Baptist pastors met in Chicago to organize a great convention for Bible study. The meeting was held in Brooklyn that fall under the name "Baptist Pastors' Conference for Bible Study." To no one's surprise, the conference elected Gordon as president. Ira Sankey led the singing. Besides Gordon, speakers at the conference included I. M. Haldeman, A. C. Dixon, Edward T. Hiscox, Clarence Larkin, and George C. Needham. Several of the addresses were later published in book form.[20]

Like the nondenominational Niagara Conference, the Baptist Pastors' Conference on Bible Study focused upon biblical prophecy understood from a premillennial perspective. Also like Niagara, a key concern of the attendees was liberal theology. Samuel M'Bride set the tone of the conference in his welcoming address.

19. George C. Needham, "Reasons for Holding the Bible and Prophetic Conference," in *Prophetic Studies of the International Prophetic Conference* (Chicago: Fleming H. Revell, 1886), 216.

20. While it was intended as a conference for Baptist ministers, the meeting allowed at least one Presbyterian to add his name to the membership role, largely at the behest of Gordon. "Wouldn't Open Baptist Doors to a Premillennial Presbyterian," *Brooklyn Daily Eagle*, November 20, 1890, 4:00 edition, 6.

Perilous times have come. The Old Book is being assaulted as never before. The batteries of hell have opened upon it. The forces of evil are confederated for its destruction. From every quarter within the Church, as well as without, men are assailing it with a virulence and a violence hitherto unheard of. Instructors and infidels, doctors of divinity and defamers of divinity, professors of religion and protestors against religion, higher critics and critics for hire, are seeking to undermine the Word of God and blow up the rock on which we stand. . . . We have no sort of sympathy with what is called the higher criticism, or any other work of darkness. We take no stock in Elohistic or Javistic documents. We have no need of Redactors. We believe that all Scripture is God-breathed; that men spake from God, being moved by the Holy Spirit; that every chapter, verse, line, jot, and tittle of the original parchments was inspired.[21]

The planners of the conference saw the doctrine of Scripture as a special concern. Typically, liberalism first evidenced itself by attacking the inspiration of the Bible, while orthodox Christianity built upon the Bible as the Word of God. Consequently, the first major address of the conference, delivered by F. E. Tower of Bristol, Connecticut, was an extended defense of the inspiration and authority of the Bible. Speaking extemporaneously, Tower took a full hour to examine higher critical assumptions, attacking the liberal theory of partial inspiration and defending the plenary inspiration of Scripture.[22]

By the end of the conference, the crowd had packed Centennial Baptist Church and overflowed into a nearby Presbyterian church building. The excitement was palpable, creating the impression that Gordon was building a movement not only to advance premillennialism, but also to oppose modernism. No wonder. For these leaders, liberal theology was a matter of spiritual life and death. They sincerely believed that liberalism gave bad answers to the most urgent problems of the human condition.

According to Gordon, keeping a moral person moral was no great challenge, but changing the immoral outcast into someone sober and respectable took a supernatural Spirit working through a supernatural gospel.[23] He wrote, "Go into the liberal churches where they boast so loudly of their ethical preaching, and their high morality, and their strict integrity; and ask them how many drunkards they picked from the gutter last year, changing them into sober men who can pray and sing praises to God. They cannot show you one, and they are condemned by this test."[24]

Gordon exhibited little patience toward Christians who held orthodox

21. Samuel M'Bride, "Address of Welcome," in George C. Needham, *Primitive Paths in Prophecy* (Chicago: Gospel Publication Company, 1891), 12–13.

22. "The Baptist Conference for Bible Study," *Watchword*, January 1891, 27–28.

23. Adoniram J. Gordon, *Yet Speaking* (New York: Fleming H. Revell, 1897), 71–72.

24. Ibid., 72.

theology but who tried to maintain cordial relations with liberals. He vented this frustration in an article about "Good Men Recommending Bad Books," in which he deplored the tendency of Bible-believing professors to recommend liberal works of biblical criticism. Gordon wrote, "[W]e suggest that he who teaches the evangelical faith, and commends his students to rationalistic books, may do more harm by his citations than good by his expositions."[25]

In spite of Gordon, conservative seminaries tried to make peace with liberalism. This was one of the motivations that led him and others to establish an alternative form of theological training, the Bible institute. They also had another motivation. Since they believed that the second coming of Jesus was near, they wanted to prepare a host of Christian workers to participate in the worldwide spread of the gospel. The Bible institutes were not originally intended to educate Christian leaders, but to prepare workers to help in the task of worldwide evangelism.

While others may have differed, Gordon never intended the Bible institute to replace the theological seminary. In fact, he remained on the board of Newton Theological Institution until his death. As Gordon saw it, seminaries should educate the leaders, but leaders needed help. The Bible institutes would provide a shorter course of study to train workers who could carry out the task of missions under the direction of seminary-trained leaders.

In 1889 Gordon opened the Boston Missionary Training School (now Gordon College) in the basement of Clarendon Street Baptist Church. It was one of several early Bible institutes. Gordon made it clear that the institute would not provide the background that students could get in college and seminary. The point was to "call out the reserves" and produce a "large force of *lay workers*" for the mission field. Graduates would learn the English Bible, they would know how to lead a soul to Christ, and they would be able to instruct converts in the simple principles of Christianity.[26]

The creation of the Boston Missionary Training School was highly controversial. Critics accused it of offering shortcut training for ministry. They worried that a large influx of lay workers would create financial difficulties for mission agencies that were trying to keep an adequate number of missionaries

25. Adoniram J. Gordon, "Good Men Recommending Bad Books," *Watchword*, June 1895, 82.

26. Adoniram J. Gordon, "Short-Cut Methods," *Watchman*, November 7, 1889, 1, cited by Houghton, "Contributions of Adoniram Judson Gordon," 193–94. See also Ernest B. Gordon, *Adoniram Judson Gordon*, 260–61. Some of the other Bible institutes that were founded about this time included the Missionary Training Institute (New York, 1882, now Nyack College), Moody Bible Institute (Chicago, 1886), and later the Practical Bible Training School (Johnson City, New York, 1900, now Davis College), Northwestern Bible and Missionary Training School (Minneapolis, 1902, now Northwestern College), the Bible Institute of Los Angeles (Los Angeles, 1908, now Biola University), and the Philadelphia College of the Bible (Philadelphia, 1913, now Cairn University).

on the field. They were concerned that lay workers would proceed without adequate supervision from ministers. Worst of all, these lay workers would probably want to teach premillennialism to their converts.[27]

Certainly Gordon had sympathizers among Baptists, but he now attracted a new body of denominational opponents. Over the next decades, the gap between those who supported the official Baptist leadership and those who supported the Bible schools continued to widen. The rift worsened when graduates of the Bible institutes began to accept pastorates in American churches. While hostility was rarely expressed openly, an ongoing tension existed between those who were responsible for the denominational machinery and those who occupied themselves with the Bible conferences and Bible schools.

Greeted by skepticism from the denominational boards, leaders of the Bible conference movement also began to organize their own mission agencies. Many of these were interdenominational in character: the Christian and Missionary Alliance (1887), Cape General Mission (1889), Central American Mission (1890), South East Africa General Mission (1891), Sudan Interior Mission (1893), and a host of others. In their structure, these missions reflected what was sometimes called the "faith principle." Cut off from denominational support, both missionaries and sending agency relied directly upon the giving of Christian people and churches for support.

The Bible conferences, the training schools, and the faith missions were all aspects of one larger movement. Not surprisingly, A. J. Gordon was involved with all three. He put forth his philosophy of missions in a series of lectures that was later published as *The Holy Spirit in Missions*. This volume provides a glimpse into the thinking of these institutions.

For Gordon, the purpose of missions was not to win the world, but to witness to the world. The elect, called by the Holy Spirit, would respond to the message, but Christians should not anticipate a worldwide turning to Christ. Because the Spirit was the one who chose the elect, the task of witnessing had to be carried out with an awareness of His presence and power. Consequently, missionaries should be called to their task by the Holy Spirit, and they must surrender to their calling in submission to the Spirit. The Spirit who calls is also the Spirit who enables, so missionaries must pursue their task with a conscious dependence upon Him. For Gordon, the work of missions was a matter of daily faith in the Spirit.[28]

Adoniram Judson Gordon died in 1895. He was not yet sixty years old. After

---

27. The denominational papers were full of the controversy. For an example, see the discussion between E. H. Johnson, H. N. Murdoch, J. F. Elder, and Henry C. Mabie, "Missionary Training Schools—Do Baptists Need Them?"*Baptist Quarterly Review* 12 (1890): 69–100.

28. Adoniram J. Gordon, *The Holy Spirit in Missions* (New York: Fleming J. Revell, 1893), passim.

his death, the Bible conference movement (with the institutes and the faith missions) continued to develop in one direction while Baptist denominationalism developed in another. As the denominational colleges and seminaries slipped into liberal theology, conservatives turned increasingly to the Bible institutes for ministry preparation. Men who were trained in Bible schools eventually became a large contingent among conservative Northern Baptists.

By the turn of the century, however, orthodox opposition to liberalism stalled. Conservatives within the denominational agencies found themselves checked by liberal pleas for tolerance. Gordon's untimely death robbed the Bible conference movement of its most important Baptist leader. Conservatives were going to have to regroup before they would be able to mount any concerted resistance to modernism. That regrouping began in the home of Oliver W. Van Osdel during the winter of 1909.

The Grand River Valley Baptist Association

Conservatives in the Grand Rapids Baptist Association already had a vague plan when they sent Ford and Whitney to meet with Van Osdel. They had decided to disfellowship Alfred Wishart and Fountain Street Church. Their problem was that they had never done that sort of thing, and they really had no idea how to proceed.

Van Osdel was viewed as a gray eminence among Northern Baptists. He had already pastored at least eight churches, built at least three buildings, been honored with a doctorate from Shurtleff College, and was widely recognized as the founder of the Baptist Young People's Union. As a fundraiser first for his own church building projects and then for McMinnville College (now Linfield College), he had developed a working relationship with some of the most important figures in Baptist organization.

Surprisingly, Van Osdel was going through a personal theological transformation when he reached Grand Rapids. This shift had begun several years before, when he had invited W. B. Riley to preach a series of messages at First Baptist in Spokane. Riley was the pastor of First Baptist Church in Minneapolis, and he was emerging as one of the most important leaders in the Baptist contingent of the premillennial Bible conference movement. He was able to combine Baptist convictions with enough breadth to work alongside men of other denominations in conferences, Bible institutes, and faith missions.

While Riley was a committed premillennarian, Van Osdel had never really examined eschatological questions. His own views were vaguely amillennial, but under Riley's enthusiasm he began to see more and more biblical justification for premillennialism. He also began to perceive a natural connection between postmillennial eschatology and the liberal social gospel with its talk of bringing in the kingdom. By the time he arrived in Grand Rapids, he was seriously considering premillennialism, and before many months passed, he had embraced it.

Riley introduced Van Osdel to many of the premillennial Baptists in the Bible conference movement. This meant that the veteran pastor stood with a foot each in two Baptist camps. On the one side, mainstream Baptists recognized him as a leader in denominational life. On the other side, he threw himself into the growing premillennial movement with its conferences, schools, and missions. Van Osdel was ideally situated to bring these two camps together. If the conservatives could win him over to their side, their cause would be immeasurably strengthened.

As it turned out, Van Osdel did not have to be won over. He already bore the scars of significant ecclesiastical controversy, and he had already made up his mind about liberalism. He had watched an old friend, William Rainey Harper, build the new University of Chicago into a bastion of liberal theology. More personally, his own son Edgar had been won to liberalism, probably through Harper's influence.

Most likely Van Osdel did not yet know J. Gresham Machen, and it would be years before Machen began to write explicitly against liberalism. When it came to modernist theology, however, Van Osdel took the same view that J. Gresham Machen would eventually put into print: liberalism was not Christianity. It was a different religion entirely. It did not even belong to the same class of religions as Christianity.[29]

From the moment that he heard about Wishart's pronouncements, Van Osdel determined to break fellowship with Fountain Street Church. He began to meet with Baptist conservatives to find a way to oust the erring congregation from the Grand Rapids Baptist Association. To their surprise, the conservatives discovered that the group's bylaws contained no provision for disciplining a heretical church. It seemed that they had no choice except to embrace fellowship with a modernist assembly.

Van Osdel determined not to let that happen. From his viewpoint, liberals were not Christians and no Christian fellowship was possible with them. If the liberals could not be put out of the Grand Rapids Baptist Association, then the conservatives would have to try something else—and Van Osdel knew what. He proposed that all of the orthodox churches should abandon the association. This separation would place Fountain Street in sole possession of the name and meager resources of the old association, but it would leave the conservatives free to form a new fellowship. The orthodox churches of Grand

---

29. J. Gresham Machen, *Christianity and Liberalism* (Grand Rapids: Eerdmans, 1923), passim.

Rapids would begin their own Baptist association, and it would be free from liberal influence.

It was a radical idea. While it had small disadvantages (the conservatives would be surrendering an organizational structure and a few resources), it would permit orthodox Baptists to rebuild quickly and would free them from fellowship with an apostate theology. The conservatives trusted Van Osdel's experience and insight, and they quickly decided to accept his counsel.

This decision would take time to implement. Baptist churches vote individually to fellowship with associations, and they have to vote individually to withdraw fellowship. The Grand Rapids Baptist Association counted around sixteen churches in its fellowship, including Fountain Street. Of these, fourteen were determined to separate and to form a new fellowship. Before they could do that, the pastors needed to lead their congregations through the process, and then to plan a new structure. Finally, the entire group met on September 21, 1909, just one week before the old Grand Rapids Baptist Association was scheduled to assemble at Fountain Street.

During the intervening months, Van Osdel arranged to have observers from the separating churches continuously in the services at Fountain Street. These witnesses kept careful records of Wishart's theological pronouncements, and Van Osdel began to compile a list of the doctrines that the liberal pastor denied or perverted. These included the final authority of Scripture; the miracles of the Bible; the virgin birth of Christ; the deity of Christ; the vicarious death of Christ; the bodily resurrection of Jesus; the origin, nature, and eternal consequences of sin; the personality of the Devil; the necessity of regeneration; and the biblical demand to be separated from the world.[30]

Armed with this list, the messengers of the churches approved a letter to be sent to the Grand Rapids Baptist Association. In it, they pointed out that they were "completely out of harmony with the views of Fountain St. Church as set forth in published sermons and interviews, and as represented by witnesses." Since the bylaws of the Grand Rapids Baptist Association were "too indefinite and inadequate" to deal with a heretical church, fourteen churches were now announcing their withdrawal from its fellowship in order to form the Grand River Valley Baptist Association. The letter continued,

> Dear Brethren, the name Baptist has been rendered inestimably precious by the blood of the martyrs who have sacrificed all for these truths that we might become heirs with them of the Grace of God. The skepticism which denies to the Christ the glory that is His due cannot be covered by smooth speech, and specious reasoning. Labels of "new,"

---

30. Grand River Valley Baptist Association, letter of separation to the Grand Rapids Baptist Association (22 September 1909).

"modern," and "scholarly" cannot hide the enmity which attempts to rob Christ of His right to Deity and the throne of the universe.

Where such positions are taken we can see nothing ahead "but a certain fearful expectation of judgment and fierceness of fire which shall devour the adversaries."[31]

Evidently, only one church remained with Fountain Street in the old group. Even so, the remnants of the old Grand Rapids Baptist Association did not simply fade away. When the old association met the following week at Fountain Street Church, the floor was packed with denominational dignitaries. The editor of the *Standard* came over from Chicago. Prominent pastors attended from Detroit, Lansing, and Kalamazoo. Meeting with the secular press, these luminaries announced that while certain churches might have withdrawn from the Grand Rapids Baptist Association, the denomination had not. When the state convention met the next month in Alpena, Alfred Wishart was asked to lead a discussion of methods in social service. Then he was elected a director of the convention.[32]

During the next decade, the Michigan convention made it clear that it was backing the Fountain Street Church and the old association. As the older group rebuilt, one of its leaders, E. L. Killam, was chosen by the state convention as a district superintendent and then as convention secretary. The Grand River Valley Baptist Association was virtually ostracized, but more and more men from the liberal group appeared on the state convention platform every year.

The new association elected Van Osdel as its first moderator, but he did not remain in official leadership for long. He was the sort of man who moved others into responsible positions as quickly as possible. As one biographer wrote,

His leadership was not the type which with clarion call rallied people around an outstanding personality. It was rather that of giving sage advice, constantly analyzing issues for people to realize, accept, and then rally to a principle. Generally, the principle also pointed the way the movement should take. His leadership was peculiar in that he worked with and through people, bringing them to the place of acting, rather than acting for them.[33]

In one important way, however, Van Osdel's leadership was felt keenly. In 1912 he began publishing a little paper called the *Baptist Temple News.*

31. Ibid. The biblical citation is from Hebrews 10:27. In view of the later involvement of Wealthy Street Baptist Church in the King James Only movement, it is interesting that the letter quotes from the American Standard Version of 1901.

32. Oliver W. Van Osdel, "A Little History," *Baptist Temple News*, October 18, 1919, 3–4; "Michigan Baptist Convention," *Standard*, October 30, 1909, 24.

33. John H. Wilson, "The Life of Dr. Oliver W. Van Osdel and the Influence of His Ministry at the Wealthy St. Baptist Church, Grand Rapids, Mich." (University of Michigan: unpublished paper for Lewis G. Vander Velde, January 18, 1958), 12.

Originally it was hardly more than a church bulletin: a half-sheet of paper folded in half. Eventually it grew larger (though rarely more than four pages) and began to include Bible studies, devotionals, denominational news, and editorials. Within a few years it became the unofficial voice of the Grand River Valley Baptist Association. Though he held no office, Van Osdel was widely recognized as the association's de facto leader.

His leadership was further enhanced by the obvious prosperity of the ministry at Wealthy Street. Before a decade lapsed, the church erected a magnificent new building and added nearly 900 to the membership roles. It organized a Bible institute in 1912. In addition to maintaining older acquaintances such as I. M. Haldeman (pastor of the First Baptist Church of New York City), Van Osdel took initiative to introduce both the church and the association to a new generation of spiritual leadership. He formed close relationships with W. B. Riley (pastor of First Baptist Church in Minneapolis), James M. Gray (president of Moody Bible Institute), R. E. Neighbour (evangelist and pastor), and William L. Pettingill (one of the founders of Philadelphia School of the Bible). In 1916 Methodist evangelist Bob Jones held six weeks of meetings at Wealthy Street, then in 1918 presided over the dedication of the church's new building.[34] Under Van Osdel's ministry, Wealthy Street blossomed into one of the leading churches in its city.

Increasingly, Van Osdel turned the pages of the *Baptist Temple News* against liberals and liberalism. In March 1919 he publicly rebuked one of the district superintendents of the Baptist Mission Board of the State of Michigan. The superintendent, Joshua Roberts, had written glowingly of a missionary pastor who spent most of his ministry in social activity. Van Osdel responded, "We are told Joshua used to preach the Gospel once—now he seems to be otherwise engaged." He continued,

> Is this the way our missionary work is being advanced in the state? Is this the way the missionary money of the Baptist churches of Michigan is to be invested? Well, we are out of it. We have no disposition to invest missionary money to aid in the distribution of "Clark's Sixty Years With the Bible," nor for the dissemination of the modern liberalistic propaganda, nor for keeping the cows out of the city streets. Our business is to preach the ever-blessed Gospel of Christ's saving grace.[35]

Later that year, the *Baptist Temple News* censured the American Baptist Publication Society, which had produced a paper that pleaded for tolerance

---

34. *Baptist Temple News*, August 4, 1912, 4; *Baptist Temple News*, November 23, 1918, passim. Van Osdel wrote of the young Jones, "Every time we heard him speak we approved of his message. Every time we met him we loved him more. During the months since his departure he has had our deep affection and our prayers."

35. Oliver W. Van Osdel, "A Wonderful Preacher," *Baptist Temple News*, March 22, 1919, 1, 3.

while advocating a liberal view of Scripture. Van Osdel was contemptuous. He accused the society of prostituting its resources and called its authors "weak and skeptical men who are destitute of a Christian experience and without knowledge of the Scriptures." These words would hardly endear him to denominational officials, but they provided a compass for a growing number of Baptists even beyond the Grand River Valley Baptist Association.[36]

Michigan convention officials tried to hit back by attacking Van Osdel's allies. One of these was A. L. Ritts, pastor of the Baptist church in Mount Pleasant. Unhappy with Ritts's support of Van Osdel, officials from the state convention engineered a meeting of the Saginaw Valley Association to call a council for a review of Ritts's ministry. The council, packed by handpicked denominational sympathizers, dutifully issued a denunciation of the pastor. Convention officials then carried this condemnation to the *Standard*.

Unabashed, Ritts was soon called to a pastorate in Sturgis. Convention officials followed him there and again managed to stir up opposition among the inactive members of the church. In frustration, Ritts and the interested members simply began a new church. Putting their twist on the story, the convention officials denounced him in the *Standard* as a divider of churches. Van Osdel, incensed, defended Ritts and claimed that convention officials had tried the same tactic at Wealthy Street.[37]

Ritts had been preceded in Mount Pleasant by E. L. Killam, who then went on to become the secretary of the Michigan convention. Subsequently, Killam became editor of the *Standard* in Chicago, a position that he still held. From across the lake, he used his paper to fire verbal salvos into Michigan. In 1919 Isaac Van Westenbrugge, association moderator and pastor of Second Baptist Church in Grand Rapids, delivered the doctrinal sermon at the Grand River Valley Baptist Association. Van Westenbrugge used the address to raise concerns about several Northern Baptist agencies. The *Standard* denounced his sermon as "an attack as dirty as it is vicious," then continued, "this is where those of us who still believe in a Judgment Day have a bit of an advantage over those who don't, but we confess that sometimes it is difficult to wait." Van Osdel spoke in defense of Van Westenbrugge: "All honor to him. The *Standard*'s talk of judgment is harmless as far as he is concerned."[38]

Whatever the opposition, Van Osdel never relented in his assault upon Michigan Baptist liberalism. In an article titled "Where Shall We Educate Our Sons and Daughters?" he examined notes from the classes of professor

---

36. Oliver W. Van Osdel, "American Baptist Publication Society," *Baptist Temple News*, September 20, 1919, 1–4.

37. Oliver W. Van Osdel, "Rev. A. L. Ritts," *Baptist Temple News*, October 18, 1919, 1, 3; Oliver W. Van Osdel, "Outrages," *Baptist Temple News*, August 7, 1920, 3.

38. Oliver W. Van Osdel, "A Little History," *Baptist Temple News*, October 18, 1919, 4.

Hermon Severn at nearby Kalamazoo College, a Baptist institution. He concluded, "If his whole Bible course is fairly illustrated by what we have before us, we should not expect the students to have much faith when done with it."[39]

Someone from the University of Chicago made the mistake of sending Van Osdel a review copy of Shirley Jackson Case's book, *The Revelation of John.* Van Osdel devoted nearly an entire issue of the *Baptist Temple News* to his critique. After summarizing the contents of the book, Van Osdel questioned whether Case subscribed to any of the fundamental doctrines. He answered himself: "As we have read the book we have received the impression, from what he says, that he does not believe any of these things." Of people like Case, Van Osdel wrote, "They masquerade as friends, when they are the most deadly foes. Are these men honorable?"[40]

Early in 1920 Van Osdel resumed this theme. He noted that the denominational colleges had been built by the sacrifices of "those who loved the Lord Jesus Christ better than life." These people intended their gifts to support godly teachers who loved the Bible. In spite of their intentions, however, many denominational schools were now teaching "the religion of Cain and of Satan," denying the necessity of regeneration, the efficacy of Christ's blood, and other fundamental doctrines. According to Van Osdel, these teachers were parasites, not men of honor. He added, "Benedict Arnold was a paragon of nobility when compared with them." He concluded, "These gentlemen have no vital Christian experience. They do not know the Word of God and their pretensions about facts, science and history are but the noise they make to divert attention from their ignorance. Surely the present age is an age of dishonor so far as many schools can make it so."[41]

One of the charges that Van Osdel's opponents brought against the Grand River Valley Baptist Association was that they had left the Baptist denomination. Van Osdel retorted that in the fifty years of his ministry he had never discovered a Baptist denomination to quit. He continued,

> One of the perils facing real Baptist churches today, is the Satanic endeavor to bring Baptist churches under convention control. There are no such persons as "officials" among Baptists, and the men who are endeavoring to create such by the processes of the Northern Baptist (?) Convention . . . to control things are leading away toward the Pope. . . . We stoutly refuse to be coerced. . . . We are Baptists with all that means of independence. If any of the brethren are alarmed by the noise of the machine, and Samson-like have been shorn of their Baptist locks, and

39. Oliver W. Van Osdel, "Where Shall We Educate Our Sons and Daughters?" *Baptist Temple News*, December 6, 1919, 1–2.

40. Oliver W. Van Osdel, "The Revelation of John," *Baptist Temple News*, December 20, 1919, 3.

41. Oliver W. Van Osdel, "An Age of Dishonor," *Baptist Temple News*, January 10, 1920, 1–2.

have gotten under the sweep of Dagon's mill and like it, and want to stay there, we pity them and pray for them. We are not there and do not intend to be placed there.[42]

Led by Van Osdel, the Grand River Valley Baptist Association went beyond local separation and effectively placed an embargo upon giving to the state convention in Michigan. Van Osdel stated bluntly: "We will not invest missionary money in missionaries or teachers who are destructive [critics] of the Bible and liberals in belief." Instead, Van Osdel urged the Grand River Valley Baptist Association to support weak churches that the state convention board had cast off. Instead of supporting the American Baptist mission board, he recommended that Bible-believing churches support the faith missions such as China Inland Mission and Africa Inland Mission.[43]

At the same time, Van Osdel was growing more concerned about the ministers who were being ordained in Michigan. Under his influence, the churches of the Grand River Valley Baptist Association began to ordain ministers separately from the Michigan convention. He noted that he had attended several recent ordination councils in which the candidates held liberal views. These men, he said, were being ordained and even sent out under the foreign mission society, where they were "not refused appointment on account of false doctrine." He asked, "Will Baptists continue to stand for this sort of thing?"[44]

By 1920 Van Osdel had come to see the Michigan convention and its institutions as an ecclesiastical machine. He believed that it was being used by unscrupulous men to advance an anti-biblical agenda, and he had become convinced that these men were willing to use the convention machinery to destroy their opponents. More than that, he felt increasingly that the power of this machine was being directed personally against him.

He saw evidence of this conspiracy at a prophetic Bible conference that Wealthy Street hosted in February 1920. This conference grew out of W. B. Riley's World's Christian Fundamentals Association, which had been founded in 1919. The WCFA represented a coalition based in the old Bible conference movement. Van Osdel had participated in founding the WCFA, then he had brought W. B. Riley, James M. Gray, and J. C. Massee to Grand Rapids for a regional meeting in June 1919.

Now, in February 1920, he hoped to rally those Michigan Baptist pastors who had roots in the Bible conference movement. This meeting would be

42. Oliver W. Van Osdel, "Quitting the Denomination," *Baptist Temple News*, January 17, 1920, 1–2.

43. Oliver W. Van Osdel, "Ordination at Hastings," *Baptist Temple News*, January 24, 1920, 1; Van Osdel, "What Do We Advise?" *Baptist Temple News*, February 14, 1920, 1–3.

44. Oliver W. Van Osdel, "What About It?" *Baptist Temple News*, February 14, 1920, 4.

explicitly Baptist. It was an elaborate affair, involving the cooperation of about twenty pastors from across lower Michigan. Part of the announced purpose of the conference was to "warn against present-day apostasy."[45]

From Van Osdel's point of view, the conference was a huge success. Though not usually given to hyperbole, he stated that "there probably never has been a meeting in Michigan so momentous for real Baptists as this Conference." He praised the prayer meetings, the addresses, the fellowship, and the "deep spiritual power" of the gathering. He recommended that the conference be duplicated every quarter at a different location in Michigan.[46]

The only blight on the conference was the attendance of uninvited and unwelcome convention officials. Reporting on their presence, Van Osdel adopted a mocking tone, priding himself that the conference attracted the censure of the "machine."

> Several of the Master Mechanics of the Machine were present the first day, ostensibly because it was a Michigan Baptist affair. . . . Well, they came and at the first opportunity attempted to test the sentiment of the conference for the machine, by starting to crank it, but the ignition system failed to work—there was no explosion, just silence, things did not start as was anticipated, and the mechanics left in disgust—disgust so deep that it is said they reported to their fellows who were eagerly awaiting their verdict that "The Conference was the wickedest and most damnable thing that had ever come to Michigan."[47]

By this time, the *Baptist Temple News* was reaching beyond the state of Michigan. Increasingly, Van Osdel began to write about events within the Northern Baptist Convention. His main opposition, however, came from the Michigan convention. This antagonism only served to heighten Van Osdel's scorn of liberalism. Responding to a liberal declaration that had been adopted in Lansing, he wrote, "Many so-called Baptists, Baptist leaders and Baptist churches are liberals and Unitarians, just cheap one horse infidels, and any one who exalts them exalts the devil."[48]

In spite of his censure of liberalism and conventionism, however, Van Osdel was mainly a pastor. He poured his life into his congregation, and people responded to his ministry. By April 1920 the church had gained more than a thousand new members during his tenure. During 1918 and 1919 Wealthy Street baptized more new converts than any other Baptist church in Michigan.

45. "Call for a Michigan Baptist Prophetic Bible Conference," *Baptist Temple News*, January 31, 1920, 1–2.

46. Oliver W. Van Osdel, "The Recent Conference," *Baptist Temple News*, March 6, 1920, 1–2.

47. Ibid.

48. Oliver W. Van Osdel, "That Lansing Declaration of Faith," *Baptist Temple News*, March 13, 1920, 4.

It had sent twenty missionaries, pastors, and other Christian workers out of its membership. It had another ten in training.[49]

The visible success of Wealthy Street was a constant irritation to the Michigan officials. In the face of Van Osdel's jabbing, they felt that they had to do something. The convention board met in Traverse City during May 1920 to strategize. H. C. Gleiss of the Detroit Baptist Union and P. A. Waite of Owosso had prepared resolutions denouncing Van Osdel as a "radical dispensationalist" and vowing to fight him to the last ditch. The board adopted the resolutions, and Gleiss told the press that the convention intended to halt Van Osdel, "even if it require actual confiscation of his church buildings, which belong to Michigan Baptists of orthodox belief."[50]

Van Osdel got his first news of the Traverse City meeting when he read about it on the front page of the *Grand Rapids Herald*. Astonished, he first insisted that the report must be mistaken. As he became convinced of its veracity, however, he responded by observing that "if these men meeting in Traverse City have made these threats, they are not Baptists at all." He insisted that each Baptist church was free to choose its own belief and practice according to the decision of the majority of the congregation. The threats of the convention board were, "ridiculous, revolutionary, injurious, unscriptural, and unbaptistic."[51]

A week later Van Osdel published an open letter to the state board. He still found it difficult to believe that the reports could be entirely accurate. Yet the board of managers had neither denied nor clarified the story. Still incredulous, Van Osdel wrote,

> We beg to say to you, that you have exceeded your powers. You are the creatures of the churches, just plain servants and not officials, elected for the care of the missionary interests of the denomination in the State. You were not elected to pass resolutions condemning the churches and defaming the pastors that made your Board possible . . . but simply to attend to the duties incumbent upon you as servants of the churches.
>
> If you are correctly reported as laying plans to begin a program of confiscation and persecution, you are not Baptists at all. You are traitors to every Baptist interest. We humbly suggest that you go to school and learn something about Baptist history, Baptist principles and Baptist usage. It is unfortunate that you have been swept off your

---

49. Oliver W. Van Osdel, "By Their Fruits Ye Shall Know Them," *Baptist Temple News*, April 17, 1920, 4.

50. "State Baptist Board of Managers Calls Dr. Van Osdel 'Radical Dispensationalist,'" *Grand Rapids Herald*, May 19, 1920, 1. Seventeen years later, Van Osdel's successor, David Otis Fuller, reprinted excerpts of the article in the *Baptist Temple News*, July 4, 1937, 1–3.

51. Oliver W. Van Osdel, "That Board Meeting," *Baptist Temple News*, May 22, 1920, 1–2.

feet by your prejudices and your lust for power. Your action must work injury to our great cause.[52]

Over the next weeks Van Osdel returned to this matter over and over again. Nearly every issue of the *Baptist Temple News* contained some reference to it, coupled with some reproof of the convention officials. In particular, Van Osdel singled out Gleiss for repeated spankings. In late June, he accused Gleiss and others of conspiring to "wrest the property from the Sand Creek and South Lansing" churches. When W. T. Roberts, secretary of the Michigan convention, tried to justify that action in the *Michigan Baptist*, Van Osdel accused him of "cheap pettifoggery." Roberts had also suggested that his embattled colleague Gleiss was "a prince." Van Osdel retorted that Gleiss might be the "prince of persecutors." Furthermore, Roberts tried to excuse the Traverse City meeting by blaming the *Herald* article for its report. By now, however, Van Osdel was beyond conciliation. He wrote, "We are not surprised Mr. Roberts that it looked a little ugly to you when you saw it in cold print."[53]

By now the *Baptist Temple News* had become a major irritant to the Michigan Baptist Convention. Unable to answer Van Osdel factually, convention officials resorted to the accusation that he employed undue severity and that the paper did "nothing but sting." Van Osdel replied that they only felt stung because he had opposed their pet projects. "If the brethren keep out of the way," he said, "they shall not get stung." He insisted that he would not consider "weakening our testimony," that is, softening his language. Instead, he said, "We hope to make it more intense."[54]

Van Osdel was true to his word. During the following weeks he published articles exposing liberalism and conventionism in the seminaries, in the Michigan convention, in the Northern Baptist Convention, and in other agencies. More than that, he began to talk explicitly about separation. Noting the biblical commands of 2 Corinthians 6:14 and 17, he stated, "When men therefore who profess to be Baptists, extend the hand of fellowship to, and join in labor under the same yoke with men who deny or ignore the most vital and sacred teachings of the Word of God, they are indeed anti-Scriptural and anti-Baptistic."[55]

An episode in early August 1920 revealed how the state convention board had been working behind the scenes. Van Osdel had been called as a witness in a lawsuit concerning the Baptist church in Sand Creek, Michigan. A faction within the congregation, advised by the state convention board, was trying

52. Oliver W. Van Osdel, "An Open Letter to the State Board," *Baptist Temple News,* May 29, 1920, 2.
53. Oliver W. Van Osdel, "Persecution Begins," *Baptist Temple News,* June 22, 1920, 1. Van Osdel, "An Attempted Explanation," *Baptist Temple News,* July 10, 1920, 1.
54. Oliver W. Van Osdel, "The Temple News Sting," *Baptist Temple News,* July 17, 1920, 2–3.
55. Oliver W. Van Osdel, "The Board's Complaint," *Baptist Temple News,* July 31, 1920, 2.

to win the church's name and property from the majority. The interests of the Michigan convention were represented by W. T. Roberts, who also appeared on the witness stand. During the course of the testimony, it came out that the state convention had been appealing to the United States Post Office to deny second-class mailing privileges to the *Baptist Temple News*. Van Osdel later commented, "We knew that the liberals had tried to get the little paper thrown out of the mails, but we did not know the exact source of opposition. Now we know."[56]

Convention officials, looking for some weapon to use against Van Osdel, tried to invoke the millennial question to divide the Grand River Valley Baptist Association. Several churches in that association held premillennial views, but the group had never taken any official position on the timing of the Lord's return. When the association was formed, Van Osdel himself was still amillennial, and several postmillennial congregations fellowshipped with the group. According to Van Osdel, millennialism had never been an issue within the association "until the apostasy came on and the liberals began to masquerade as Baptists." He argued that the only issue for the Grand River Valley Baptist Association was loyalty to the Bible, and that the convention officials were pushing the millennial issue so as to divide conservatives who were otherwise united and who formed a majority of the churches.[57]

Van Osdel was also incensed at the repeated assertion that the Grand River Valley Baptist Association had left the denomination. In the Sand Creek trial, W. T. Roberts had testified that the Grand River Valley group was a rival organization running opposition to the Michigan Baptist Convention. At least one official wrote that the association had separated from the state convention and was like a different denomination, quipping that a church might as well join the Methodists as to join the Grand River Valley Association. Van Osdel responded bluntly, "All of these sentiments and many others of the same sort are utterly false."[58]

In mid-August the courts ruled against the convention-supported minority in the Sand Creek case. Van Osdel led the Grand River Valley churches in raising money for the legal expenses of the beleaguered church. Roberts, who still hoped to discredit Van Osdel, found the rule in the Grand River Valley bylaws that allowed the association to disfellowship an errant church or pastor. Roberts published the rule in the *Michigan Baptist* and called it medieval. Van Osdel responded with an article in which he accused liberals of what he called "Medievalitis," or the fear of becoming medieval. He accused Roberts of violating the rules of the Michigan convention by his involvement in the

---

56. Oliver W. Van Osdel, "The Sand Creek Case," *Baptist Temple News*, August 7, 1920, 1.
57. Oliver W. Van Osdel, "Dextrous Lying," *Baptist Temple News*, August 7, 1920, 2–3.
58. Ibid., 2.

Sand Creek case, and he publicly challenged Roberts to write and publish a rule "that is more Scriptural and Baptistic than the rule of the Grand River Valley Association."[59]

Within weeks the Sand Creek situation exploded again. The court decision had strictly enjoined the minority from interfering with the pastor or the majority, but on September 1 the minority attempted to take physical possession of the building. The majority retreated to the church basement and held a prayer meeting while the minority took votes to fire the pastor, adopt new rules of order, appoint a pulpit committee, and invite W. T. Roberts to appear in the pulpit. These actions were brought to the attention of the judge, who held the minority in contempt of court and enjoined them from using the property at all. Roberts had accepted the invitation to preach, but did not hear about the citation for contempt or the injunction against the minority. When he walked into the building on September 4 and found himself facing the wrong congregation, he beat a hasty retreat and took the next train home. When Van Osdel heard about the episode, he poked fun at the convention secretary, but he also noted that Roberts's expenses were paid by state missionary funds. He noted, "Mr. Roberts is the Secretary of the Convention, and the Convention Board has the power any day to command him to stay away from Sand Creek and let the Sand Creek church alone."[60]

Roberts and other officials were paid by the convention, and conventions were supported out of the missionary budgets of the churches. For Van Osdel, this meant that missionary money was going directly to support liberalism and conventionism. Consequently, he encouraged conservative churches to look for other ways of channeling their missionary monies. He pointed to the faith missions, many of which practiced believer immersion. He stated that Wealthy Street had sent fifteen of its young people to Nyack and Moody to prepare for missionary service under these agencies. He also recommended Riley's Northwestern Bible Institute, the Bible Institute of Los Angeles, and the Philadelphia Institute of the Bible. He predicted that the Grand River Valley Baptist Association would form a permanent council to work with William Haas and his Mid-Africa mission.[61]

Clearly, Van Osdel was turning to the missions and schools of the old Bible conference network as a replacement for denominational missions and schools. As more churches joined him in this turn, the denominational agencies felt the financial pinch. Van Osdel was costing them money, and that was something they had to deal with.

---

59. Oliver W. Van Osdel, "Apropos," *Baptist Temple News*, August 14, 1920, 2–3.

60. Oliver W. Van Osdel, "Mr. Roberts and the Sand Creek Decision," *Baptist Temple News*, September 11, 1920, 2.

61. Oliver W. Van Osdel, "The Faith Missions," *Baptist Temple News*, September 18, 1920, 2.

In late September the judge suddenly reversed himself in the Sand Creek case. The minority in the church was led by the legal trustees of the corporation, and the judge decided that the decision of the trustees carried more weight than the decision of the congregation (as it would in some non-Baptist churches). This action put the control of the whole organization in the hands of the minority. Particularly outrageous to Van Osdel was the fact that the trustees included unbaptized persons, and that W. T. Roberts had testified under oath that a person could be a member in good standing of a Baptist church without being baptized. Van Osdel asked, "Brethren, conservative brethren, is it not about time for a protest? Whose turn will come next to appear in court?"[62]

For his part, Van Osdel did protest, and vigorously. Just as importantly, the Grand River Valley Baptist Association met that week. It passed a resolution warning churches to take action to safeguard their property. It passed another resolution decrying the "unscriptural and unbaptistic persecution of our fellow brethren and churches." A third resolution insisted upon a full and clear statement of faith from the Michigan convention's Kalamazoo College, stipulating that the statement should be signed by every member of the faculty and board.

In another important move, the Grand River Valley Baptist Association voted to change its name. For several years it had been attracting attention from churches outside of the actual Grand River drainage, so a broader name seemed appropriate. Also, the churches wanted a name that would distinguish them from the growing number of liberals in Michigan institutions. Against Van Osdel's advice, the fellowship finally decided to call itself the Michigan Orthodox Baptist Association. While Van Osdel disliked the name, he supported it once it had been chosen: "We have taken the word ORTHODOX to show to any interested that we are standing by the precious, God-given truths revealed in the Bible."

The greater concern was that the Michigan convention was already trying to treat the Grand River Valley group (now named the Michigan Orthodox Baptist Association) as a rival convention. Van Osdel had already confronted W. T. Roberts over this point, and "told him plainly that he had not told the truth." In a letter to Grant M. Hudson, general director of the Michigan convention, the officers of the newly renamed Michigan Orthodox Baptist Association bluntly stated that "we have no thought of giving up our rights in the Convention."[63]

62. Oliver W. Van Osdel, "The Sand Creek Church Out and Injured," *Baptist Temple News*, September 25, 1920, 1–2.
63. Oliver W. Van Osdel, "Michigan Orthodox Baptist Association," *Baptist Temple News*, October 9, 1920, 1–4.

Relations between the Michigan Baptist Convention and the Michigan Orthodox Baptist Association had already been strained to the breaking point. In August, convention officials had met with Van Osdel and a group from the Grand River Valley Association at the Gull Lake conference ground, hoping to find some middle ground. Rather than compromising, Van Osdel had heightened his opposition to liberalism. Subsequently, the convention had appointed a committee to "consider the relations of the Association with the State Convention." One of the committee was Frank E. Leonard, a leading member of the Fountain Street church, whose involvement was a portent of the direction that the committee would take. The committee demanded that the Grand River Valley Baptist Association send a delegation to meet with them in Battle Creek. The association refused for two reasons. First, the date that the committee selected was in the middle of the Grand River Valley Association's annual meeting. Second, the leadership of the association believed that no conciliation was possible until the convention was willing to sever fellowship with liberal churches. [64]

This attitude had finally become intolerable to the Michigan convention. The committee returned a report recommending that the Michigan Orthodox Baptist Association be disfellowshipped by the Michigan Baptist Convention. The committee seized the change in name as evidence that the Grand River Valley group intended to form a rival convention. Consequently, when the recommendation came to the floor, not a single dissenting vote was cast. The Michigan Orthodox Baptist Association found itself suddenly thrown out by the convention.[65]

These decisions, made late in 1920, moved Van Osdel and the Michigan Orthodox Baptist Association into an entirely new stage of organization. On the one hand, they now had to develop their own mechanisms for ordination, recognition, pastoral searches, missions, and even education. Because the churches of the association were accustomed to acting for themselves, these matters were readily addressed. The number of fellowshipping churches nearly doubled over the next ten years.

On the other hand, finally liberated from the tensions within the Michigan Baptist Convention, Van Osdel was able to turn his attention to national affairs. Here he was not alone. In Michigan he had been a pioneer of separation from liberalism. On the national stage, however, he was joined by other, more prominent figures. While he was accorded the dignity of an elder statesman, he was only one voice among many who decried liberalism within the

64. Sheldon Quincer, "A History of the Grand Rapids Association of Regular Baptist Churches" (mimeographed paper for the 50th Annual Meeting, Sept. 23–25, 1958), 11; *Baptist Temple News*, October 9, 1920, 3–4.

65. *Baptist Temple News*, November 13, 1920, 3.

Northern Baptist Convention. That is the story that will be explored in the next chapter.

Before turning attention to that story, however, two other early efforts to resist liberalism should be mentioned. The first is the founding of Northern Baptist Seminary in Chicago. The second is the publication of *The Fundamentals*.

Northern Baptist Seminary

Even without the issue of liberalism, Illinois Baptists experienced definite tensions during the latter half of the nineteenth century. These tensions tended to mirror the social divisions of the state, in which the interests of greater Chicago were often pitted against the interests of everyone else. Socially, Baptists around Chicago often appropriated influences from the East and even from Europe, while Baptists in southern Illinois were more influenced by the culture and mores of the American South.

Illinois Baptists were already divided, even before the conflict over liberalism began. During the last decade of the nineteenth century, however, liberalism became a major issue. The new University of Chicago, founded by William Rainey Harper in 1892, quickly emerged as the most visible and outspoken center for the advancement of liberalism among Baptists. Having begun with a substantially liberal faculty, the divinity school became more modernistic by the year.

Baptists in Illinois had organized a state convention during the 1840s. The associations within the state convention reflected the differences between the Chicago Baptists and Illinois Baptists from further south. Specifically, Baptists in southern Illinois were among the first to register their concern over the liberalism of the new University of Chicago. In 1896, however, they agreed to give the new university a ten-year trial and to judge the university by its product.

The new university had Rockefeller money behind it. Probably no opposition could have halted its growth as a proselytizing center for liberal theology. Nevertheless, Illinois Baptists were keenly aware that the divinity school was growing more radical. Those in southern Illinois were particularly alarmed by the trend.[66]

The final blow came in 1906 with the publication of George Burman

66. Parts of this story can be found in Charles Harvey Arnold, *Near the Edge of the Battle: A Short History of the Divinity School and the "Chicago School of Theology" 1866–1966* (Chicago: The Divinity School Association, The University of Chicago, 1966); Arnold, "The Death of God—06," *Foundations* 10 (1967): 331–53; Charles Chaney, "Diversity: A Study in Illinois Baptist History to 1907," *Foundations* 7 (1964): 41–54; Perry Stackhouse, *Chicago and the Baptists: A Century of Progress* (Chicago: University of Chicago Press, 1933); Warren Cameron Young, *Commit What You Have Heard: A History of Northern Baptist Theological Seminary 1913–1988* (Wheaton, IL: Harold Shaw Publishers, 1988).

Foster's *The Finality of the Christian Religion*. Foster had long been among the most outspoken of the Chicago liberals. He was already so controversial that in 1905 he was moved from the faculty of the divinity school to the university's department of philosophy. His book, however, broke new ground.

In the past, liberals had often couched their expressions in terms that were calculated to allay the fears of ordinary Christians. Foster always despised this tactic, and he deliberately avoided it in *The Finality of the Christian Religion*. "If the author should sometimes hold back the truth for prudential reasons, he does not see how his fellow-pilgrims could know when he was telling what he believed to be the truth, and when he was holding the truth back for reasons of policy." Foster was sharply critical of those churches in which the "theological Christ" still supplanted the "real Jesus of history, whose spirit alone is the life of our spirit." He understood Christianity to be not a religion of facts, but of timeless values, a "religion of spirit and personality." His purpose in the book was to destroy "authority-religion" in order to "define Christianity as religion of the spirit, with a view to determining whether the highest spirit of the modern world can and will in the long run call itself Christian." The effect of Foster's work was not only to reject orthodoxy, but actually to go beyond liberalism and to anticipate some of the more radical theologies that would develop during a later generation. Echoing the German Philosopher Friedrich Nietzsche, Foster declared that "a God outside the cosmos is dead." [67]

In his destruction of what he called "authority-religion," Foster's contempt was unsparing. He stated that the inspiration of the Bible was "untrue historically and impossible psychologically." He noted that even in antiquity some friends of Christianity had expressed scruples about the creation account as well as the "revolting narratives" of Lot, Judah, and others. The truth of Scripture and Christianity could not be vindicated by any appeal to the miraculous, for "an intelligent man who now affirms his faith in such stories as actual facts can hardly know what *intellectual* honesty means." The rejection of the miraculous even applied to the bodily resurrection of Jesus, the theological importance of which was "far out of proportion to the evidence."[68]

These statements could not be ignored. Perhaps to his own surprise, Foster's book became an instant phenomenon. Almost at the same time, William Rainey Harper died, depriving Foster of his principal protector. Controversy erupted within the Chicago Baptist Association. John Roach Straton, pastor of the Second Baptist Church, publicly excoriated the book. Then Austen K. DeBlois of First Baptist Church offered a resolution to the Ministers' Council of the Chicago Baptist Association declaring that "the views set forth in this

67. George Burman Foster, *The Finality of the Christian Religion* (Chicago: University of Chicago Press, 1906), xii–xiii, 9, 177.
68. Ibid., 87, 88, 132, 135.

book are contrary to the scriptures, and that its teaching and tendency are subversive of the vital and essential truths of the Christian faith." This resolution was approved by a vote of 48 to 22.[69]

While the censure passed by a substantial majority, the fact remained that twenty-two Chicago ministers had voted against it. Some of these arranged the publication of a protest against the resolution. Among the signatories of the protest were university figures such as Shailer Mathews, Thomas W. Goodspeed, Gerald Birney Smith, Theodore G. Soares, and Ernest DeWitt Burton. Foster's pastor at Hyde Park Baptist Church, John L. Jackson, also signed the protest.[70]

Already on their guard, Baptists in southern Illinois reacted viscerally. They immediately met to plan the formation of a new state convention. In 1907 they organized the Illinois Baptist State Association, which they quickly aligned with the Southern Baptist Convention. Initially, about a quarter of the state's 1,200 churches went with the new association, and by 1920 around half of the local associations in Illinois had identified with it.[71]

The furor had not died down when in 1908 Foster was invited to lecture for the Philosophic Union of the State University of California. He used the occasion to popularize the themes that he had expressed in *The Finality of the Christian Religion*. The next year he published these lectures as a volume of nearly three hundred pages, *The Function of Religion in Man's Struggle for Existence*. In his introduction, Foster stated that he was aiming the book at young men and women who were seeking after truth. In other words, *The Function of Religion* was Foster's attempt to bypass controversy with the older conservatives and to propagandize the next generation directly.[72]

Foster had pushed the Chicago Baptists as far as they were willing to go. He was summoned by the Ministers' Council to defend his understanding of the deity of Christ, but he refused to appear. Led by its president, Johnston Myers, the Ministers' Council then voted to remove Foster from its fellowship and called upon him to resign his Baptist ordination. The Ministers' Council also requested that Hyde Park Baptist Church remove Foster from its fellowship. Hyde Park, home church for many of the university liberals, ignored the request. Retaining both his membership in Hyde Park and his Baptist ordination, Foster then went on to serve a couple of Unitarian churches.[73]

69. Jeffrey Paul Straub, "The Making of a Battle Royal," 236–39.

70. Ibid., 240.

71. Some information is available online at the website of the Illinois Baptist State Association (http://www.ibsa.org/history, accessed May 13, 2013); see also Young, *Commit What You Have Heard*, 12.

72. George Burman Foster, *The Function of Religion in Man's Struggle for Existence* (Chicago: University of Chicago Press, 1909), viii–xi.

73. Straub, "The Making of a Battle Royal," 240–45; Young, *Commit What You Have Heard*, 12–14.

As the modernism of the University of Chicago became increasingly obvious, many Baptists throughout the Midwest began to wish for a more orthodox seminary to serve their region. Many of their hopes focused upon Second Baptist Church in Chicago, which had led the charge against Foster. The church shared the vision for a new training institution, but John Roach Straton left its pastorate in 1908. The church went without a pastor for two years while the hope of a new seminary languished.

Henry Mabie, secretary of the American Baptist Home Mission Society, was one of the few denominational executives to oppose liberalism openly. He shared the desire of Second Baptist Church and of Midwestern Baptists in general to open a conservative seminary. He provided the key by recommending John Marvin Dean to the pulpit of Second Baptist Church. He also urged Dean to accept the church's call.

Dean became the pastor of Second Baptist Church in the middle of 1912. He was one of the most energetic and colorful Baptists of his era. Self-educated, his only degree was an honorary ThD conferred by Northern Baptist Theological Seminary in 1917. He had entered ministry during the mid-1890s, then served as a YMCA chaplain for American troops in the Philippines during the Spanish-American War. After the war, Dean pastored in Seattle, Washington, and then San Jose, California. He left pastoral ministry in 1912 to work with the "Men and Religion Forward Movement," an interdenominational endeavor whose goal was to involve men and boys in Christian work. This was the point at which Mabie convinced Dean to take the pastorate at Second Baptist. Dean remained at Second Baptist only five years, then moved on to the pastorate of First Baptist Church in Pasedena, California. During the late 1920s he ministered at Hinson Memorial Baptist Church in Portland, Oregon, where he helped to establish Western Baptist Theological Seminary. Dean also held pastorates in Honolulu, Hawaii, and Roanoke, Virginia, besides serving as a chaplain in the Civilian Conservation Corps.

A born organizer and promoter, Dean was exactly the man to establish a seminary for Second Baptist Church. He recruited his first student, Amy Lee Stockton, before the seminary had been publicly announced. During the summer of 1913, Stockton (who went on to become a well-known fundamentalist evangelist) was on the program at the Pacific Coast Young People's Conference in Seattle. After hearing her speak, Dean told her that he was opening a seminary that fall and offered to enroll her as its first student. Delighted with the proposal, she became one of seven students in the first class.

Northern Baptist Theological Seminary formally opened on September 10, 1913. The enrollment increased from seven in 1913 to thirty-five the second year, then fifty-six in 1915. In 1916 the seminary held its first commencement with two graduates, one of whom was Stockton. Within a few years, Northern established its own campus and placed its governance under a self-perpetuating board. During the 1920s it developed a core faculty consisting of William Fouts (Old Testament), Julius R. Mantey (New Testament), Faris D. Whitesell (practical theology), and Peder Stiansen (church history and dean of the seminary). These four were the backbone of the seminary for three decades. Into the 1950s Northern remained the most important institution for Baptist conservatives who wanted graduate-level training for ministry.

Northern was founded to resist liberalism, but its early leaders insisted upon linking it to the Northern Baptist Convention. Some of their reasons may have been sentimental, but others were frankly financial. In 1919 the Northern Baptist Convention voted to participate in the New World Movement, a branch of the Interchurch World Movement. Essentially a capital campaign (the NBC agreed to raise $100 million), the New World Movement was biased toward liberalism from the beginning. In fact, the convention's participation in the New World Movement was one of the main factors that led to the rise of fundamentalism in 1920. The leadership of Northern Baptist Theological Seminary, however, saw an opportunity to gain needed funding for the school.

In June 1919, the board of Northern Seminary applied to the Education Board of the Northern Baptist Convention for official recognition. The secretary of the board was Frank W. Padelford and its president was Ernest D. Burton. Both men were friendly toward the University of Chicago—in fact, Burton taught in the divinity school. Both men were expected to oppose Northern's application. Consequently, the application assured the Education Board that Northern Baptist Theological Seminary was committed to full harmony with the aims of the denomination.[74]

In spite of this assurance, the Education Board remained skeptical. Its initial response required Northern to dismantle its graduate programs and to function as a Bible institute. Animated correspondence flowed in both directions as Northern repeated its intention to function as a convention school. Finally Northern insisted that if it was denied recognition, it would carry the matter to the floor of the convention in 1920. Faced with this threat, Padelford and Burton reversed themselves and the Education Board granted recognition.

On the very eve of the fundamentalist controversy, Northern Baptist Theological Seminary had invested significant moral and political capital to align itself with the convention. When the controversy broke out, some personnel at Northern sympathized with the fundamentalist position, but the school always supported the convention. Although it was organized as a protest against

74. Young, *Commit What You Have Heard*, 44.

liberalism, Northern could never really be identified as a fundamentalist institution. It did, however, train many pastors and missionaries who would later align with the fundamentalist movement.

The Fundamentals

In October 1906, Amzi Clarence Dixon arrived in Chicago. Though he came to pastor the nondenominational Chicago Avenue Church (soon to be renamed Moody Church), Dixon was a committed Baptist. Before moving to Chicago, he placed his personal church membership in the First Baptist Church of Cambridge, Massachusetts. Still technically a Baptist, Dixon joined the Ministers' Council of the Chicago Baptist Association, where he became an outspoken critic of Foster, of the University of Chicago, and of modernist theology.[75]

Dixon had grown up in North Carolina and attended Southern Baptist Theological Seminary. He had pastored churches near Baltimore, Brooklyn, and Boston, and in 1911 he would take the pastorate of Spurgeon's Tabernacle in London. By the time he moved to Chicago, he had already established a reputation as an apologist for Christian orthodoxy and, indeed, as an opponent of the Chicago theology.

In 1905 Dixon preached a sermon in which he declared that "when Mr. Rockefeller learned that a prominent representative of Chicago University was tearing the Bible to pieces in a course of lectures, he ordered the lecturer to cancel his engagements and go to Europe for the purpose of purchasing a library." The sermon was subsequently published in the *Boston Herald* and brought to the attention of Shailer Mathews in Chicago. Challenged privately by Mathews, Dixon not only refused to retract the charge, but declared that the "lecturer" he had in mind was none other than William Rainey Harper. Controversy between the two erupted in the Baptist press, particularly in the *Examiner* and the *Standard*. Mathews also took the unusual step of attacking Dixon in the secular papers, beginning with *The Outlook* of New York. Before long the story spilled over into other papers such as the *Literary Digest* and even the *New York Times*.[76]

---

75. For Dixon's life see Helen C. A. Dixon, *A. C. Dixon: A Romance of Preaching* (New York: G. P. Putnam's Sons, 1931); Jeffrey Shane Mayfield, "Striving for Souls by the Power of God: The Life of Amzi Clarence Dixon" (PhD diss., Southern Baptist Theological Seminary, 2010); Donald Lewis Martin Jr., "The Thought of Amzi Clarence Dixon" (PhD diss., Baylor University, 1989).

76. The main public exchange appeared in *The Examiner*: "A Statement by Professor Shailer Mathews," *The Examiner*, May 11, 1905, 586; "Dr. Dixon's Reply to Professor Shailer Mathews," *The Examiner*, June 8, 1905, 715; "Professor Mathews Rejoinder," *The Examiner* June 8, 1905, 716. Additional correspondence appeared in *The Standard*, June 10, 1905, 14. For secular accounts see "Ministerial Irresponsibility," *The Outlook*, May 20, 1905, 164–65 [source

This episode was still festering when Dixon took the pastorate of the Chicago Avenue Church the following year. He arrived in the middle of the Foster controversy, and he actively campaigned for Foster's removal from the Ministers' Council. After Foster published *The Function of Religion*, Dixon was asked to respond by the YMCA of Los Angeles. He delivered a sermon that was reprinted in the *Bible Student and Teacher* and published as a pamphlet by the Bible Institute of Los Angeles. Titled, *"Destructive Criticism vs. Christianity"—An Expose of Fosterism*, the address criticized Foster both for his denial of fundamental doctrines and for his advocacy of evolution.[77]

Present during Dixon's YMCA address was one of the Stewart brothers, owners of the Union Oil Company. Lyman and Milton Stewart had made a good bit of money, much of which they donated to Christian enterprises. Now they had a vision for a publishing project, and they wanted Dixon to head it up.[78]

The idea was to produce a series of twelve short books filled with essays defending Christian orthodoxy. Dixon would be given oversight of an editorial that would solicit contributions from noteworthy Christian leaders. The books, collectively titled *The Fundamentals: A Testimony to the Truth*, would be sent free of charge to every minister, missionary, or other Christian worker for whom the committee could find an address.

Dixon accepted the challenge and organized the Testimony Publishing Company to complete the project. The first volume appeared in February 1910. Dixon edited the first five books before taking the pastorate of Metropolitan Tabernacle in London. Louis Meyer was appointed in his place, and when Meyer died, R. A. Torrey completed the project. The last of the twelve volumes, some of which were sent to over three hundred thousand individuals, was released in 1915. Once stocks of the individual books were depleted (around three million altogether), the Bible Institute of Los Angeles printed a four-volume edition.

The publication of *The Fundamentals* was not simply a Baptist enterprise. The sixty-four or so individual writers (some essays were anonymous) included significant diversity. L. W. Munhall was a Methodist evangelist. Princeton theology was represented by B. B. Warfield, and low-church Anglicanism by Dyson Hague and H. G. C. Moule. C. I. Scofield was only one of several

of the quotation above]; "Ministerial Irresponsibility," *Literary Digest*, May 27, 1905, 785; "Raps Chicago University," *New York Times*, May 25, 1905, 2.

77. Amzi Clarence Dixon, *"Destructive Criticism vs. Christianity"—An Expose of Fosterism* (Los Angeles: Bible Institute of Los Angeles, 1909); A. C. Dixon, "Destructive Criticism vs. Christianity: An Expose of Fosterism," Part I, *Bible Student and Teacher* 12 (June 1910): 447–51; Part II, *Bible Student and Teacher* 13 (July 1910): 35–40.

78. The story is told concisely by Gerald L. Priest, "A. C. Dixon, Chicago Liberals, and The Fundamentals," *Detroit Seminary Journal* 1 (1996): 125–28.

who represented the premillennial Bible conference movement. Among others, H. W. Webb-Peploe represented the Keswick movement. Oberlin geologist George Frederick Wright contributed to the work, as did the great Scottish professor James Orr. Other significant names included Arno C. Gaebelein, James M. Gray, A. T. Pierson, Philip Mauro, G. Campbell Morgan, E. Y. Mullins, Sir Robert Anderson, George W. Lasher, J. C. Ryle, Charles Trumbull, and W. H. Griffith Thomas. Regardless of their differences, these names represented some of the best-known defenders of Christian orthodoxy during their generation.

In some cases, the writers contributed essays that they had already published elsewhere. Absent from the series was any discussion of areas in which Christians disagreed, such as the timing of the Lord's return or denominational distinctives. What did the series include? The contents have been nicely summarized by Ernest R. Sandeen.

> The ninety articles published in these volumes divide quite evenly into a group of twenty-nine articles devoted to safeguarding the Bible, another group of thirty-one articles providing an apologetic for doctrines other than the Bible, and a third group of thirty articles devoted to personal testimonies, attacks upon variant forms of belief, discussions of the relationship of science and religion, and appeals for missions and evangelism. The whole series seems to be fabricated like a wheel—its central hub composed of articles related to the Bible, surrounded by general doctrinal articles arranged like spokes leading to the rim where more practical or peripheral concerns were handled. The twenty-nine contributions devoted to the Bible seem to be divided in the same manner. Seven might be classified as panegyrics and two others discussed archeological confirmation of biblical statements. But fifteen authors either directly attacked higher criticism or contested the critics' interpretation of specific passages. Five articles were taken up with discussions of the doctrine of inspiration.[79]

How did *The Fundamentals* influence American Christianity? Answers differ. Both Ernest Sandeen and George Marsden see the work as the highest expression of an unofficial coalition between premillennialists and Princeton theologians. George Dollar said that "Fundamentalist fellowships never used this as a complete statement of their faith, since literalism in prophecy, imminency of the Lord's Coming, and a premillennial stand are not found in them. These booklets should be hailed as the Fundamentals of Orthodoxy," by which Dollar meant primarily the Princeton theology. Robert Lightner, who admits to being influenced by Stewart G. Cole, says, "Fundamentalism as a

---

79. Ernest R. Sandeen, *The Roots of Fundamentalism: British and American Millenarianism, 1800–1930* (Chicago: University of Chicago, 1970; repr. Grand Rapids: Baker Book House, 1978), 203–04.

movement started, therefore, in 1909 with the publication of its manifesto." According to Norman Furniss, "The series expatiated the 'Five Points' that were to become the *sine qua non* of fundamentalism. . . . The conservatives' creed was now reduced to clear essentials."[80]

Several observations are in order. First, although the series was titled *The Fundamentals*, it did not invent the notion of fundamental doctrines. Historically, fundamental doctrines have been understood as the affirmations that are essential to the existence of Christianity. Arguably, the early expressions of the "rule of faith" and the first great doctrinal statements (the Apostles' Creed, the Nicene Creed, the Athanasian Creed, the formula of Chalcedon) were attempts to specify certain fundamental doctrines. The concept of fundamental doctrines became very important to the Reformers and their heirs. More than that, the distinction between fundamental and non-fundamental doctrines had been discussed extensively in nineteenth-century American Christianity, especially by the Old School Presbyterians. In paying attention to these boundary doctrines, the publishers of *The Fundamentals* were attempting nothing new.[81]

Second, *The Fundamentals* was probably not written for the benefit of modernists. Dixon and company hardly hoped to convince liberals of their errors, wishing rather to strengthen orthodox Christians and to answer their questions. The volumes were virtually ignored by liberal scholars. Modernists persisted in the theological and institutional direction that they had already established. The entire series was largely a matter of preaching to the choir.

Third, *The Fundamentals* did not really represent a coalition or movement. The direction for the series was established primarily by Dixon and his editorial committee. After Dixon left for England, the next two editors came from the committee itself. The authors of the individual articles were sought because of their reputations or because the editor thought they could make some particular contribution. While surprisingly diverse, they were not the sort of individuals who regularly collaborated or who saw themselves as more than distant fellow laborers. They were not so much a community as an aggregation, brought together by the choices of the editors.

What good did *The Fundamentals* do? Plenty. It refocused the attention

---

80. Sandeen, *Roots of Fundamentalism*, 188–207; George M. Marsden, *Fundamentalism and American Culture: The Shaping of Twentieth Century Evangelicalism 1870–1925*, 2nd ed. (New York: Oxford, 2006), 118–23; Dollar, *History of Fundamentalism*, 175; Robert P. Lightner, *Neo-Evangelicalism* (Des Plaines, IL: Regular Baptist Press, 1965), 38; Norman F. Furniss, *The Fundamentalist Controversy, 1918–1931* (New Haven: Yale University Press, 1954; repr., Hamden, CT: Archon Books, 1963), 13.

81. For the discussion of fundamental doctrines within Old School Presbyterianism, see Kevin T. Bauder, "Communion of the Saints: Antecedents of J. Gresham Machen's Separatism in the Ecclesiology of Charles Hodge and the Princeton Theologians" (PhD diss., Dallas Theological Seminary, 2001).

of biblical conservatives upon the most important truths of Christianity. From deep within Christian history and the unfathomable wealth of biblical revelation, these truths resonated with the echoes of God's own voice. *The Fundamentals* stirred the hearts of God's people, awakened their souls, and focused their awareness upon the most important teachings of inscripturated revelation.

The time was not yet ripe for an ecclesiastical battle. By the time *The Fundamentals* had completed publication, the First World War had intervened. Torn by the concerns of global conflict, people were distracted from the equally important contest that would have to be made for the faith once delivered to the saints. When the Great War was over, however, Bible believers would be ready to confront their other great enemy, the enemy that was subverting Christian institutions and leading them into apostasy. They would be ready to challenge liberalism.

W. B. Riley at the pulpit of First Baptist Church, Minneapolis.

3 The Fundamentalist Fellowship

THE NORTHERN BAPTIST CONVENTION was under the control of modernists from the moment it began. During the 1910s liberals consolidated their grip on the machinery, not only of the NBC itself, but of the state conventions, the schools, and the publication work. While many of the more conservative Baptists were preoccupied with the Great War, liberals looked for ways to spread their influence. In 1911 employees of the convention and its subsidiaries received the right to vote on convention business. The publication society (now Judson Press) took on an increasingly liberal editorial policy. Growing numbers of modernists were sent to the mission field. By 1920 hardly a Baptist college in the North still taught an inerrant Bible or a literal creation.

Few among the faithful seem to have had any real awareness of the defection that had quietly taken place within their denomination. True, Van Osdel was challenging liberalism in Grand Rapids, and Chicago Baptists organized Northern Baptist Seminary in protest against the modernism of the University of Chicago. Early in 1910 W. B. Riley of Minneapolis traded letters with Johnston Meyers and S. T. Ford of Chicago, discussing the possibility of a preconvention conference that year. Riley in particular seems to have perceived the inroads that modernism had made. Yet no conference was called for another decade.[1]

Some Baptists participated in the publication of *The Fundamentals*, but that series tried to challenge liberalism intellectually rather than organizationally. It refocused the attention of American Christians on the importance of doctrines that liberals rejected, but it did little to show exactly where modernism had gained control. It provided even less guidance for Baptists who needed a strategy to challenge modernism within their own organizations.

---

1. Robert George Delnay, "*A History of the Baptist Bible Union*" (ThD diss., Dallas Theological Seminary, 1963), 19–20.

Even during the war years, conservatives occasionally managed to express their dissatisfaction with the liberal leadership of the convention. Shailer Mathews later recalled a rudimentary protest movement in 1916. "An effort had been made to organize an anti-convention movement which, while it amounted to nothing, was none the less symtomatic of increasing opposition to the very moderate progressive policy of the denomination. In fact, one of its leaders wrote me that this would be the last Northern Baptist Convention ever held."[2]

A key figure in galvanizing the opposition to liberalism was William Bell Riley. Since 1897 Riley had pastored the First Baptist Church of Minneapolis. He also established the Northwestern Bible and Missionary Training School. Still in his forties, Riley's energy made him a force in both Baptist life and the Bible conference movement.

Riley already had a record of opposition to liberalism. For example, in 1909 he responded to Foster's *Finality of the Christian Religion* with a book titled *The Finality of the Higher Criticism*. Though Riley did not contribute to *The Fundamentals*, his concern over liberalism was growing. In 1917 he issued a volume, *The Menace of Modernism*, in which he argued that a confederacy of conservatives was the need of the hour.[3]

In keeping with this sentiment, Riley vigorously promoted a Bible Conference on the Return of our Lord, held in Philadelphia on May 28–30, 1918. The call for the conference was published over thirty-six signatures, including such prominent names as L. W. Munhall, W. H. Griffith Thomas, Cortland Myers, James M. Gray, William L. Pettingill, C. I. Scofield, R. A. Torrey, and Charles G. Trumbull. Several of these leaders were Baptists, with Riley among the most influential of them. He spoke five times during the conference.

While the Philadelphia meeting was billed as a conference on premillennialism, its speakers also sounded the alarm against modernism. The spirit was summed up by Cortland Myers in his address, "War on German Theology." After calling upon his audience to fight liberalism to the finish, he declaimed,

---

2. Shailer Mathews, *New Faith for Old: An Autobiography* (New York: Macmillan, 1936), 114.

3. William B. Riley, *The Finality of the Higher Criticism: Or the Theory of Evolution and False Theology* (n.p., 1909); Riley, *The Menace of Modernism* (New York: Christian Alliance Publishing Company, 1917), 154–81. The standard biography of Riley is William Vance Trollinger Jr., *God's Empire: William Bell Riley and Midwestern Fundamentalism* (Madison: University of Wisconsin Press, 1990). See also C. Allyn Russell, "William Bell Riley: Accusative Fundamentalist," in *Voices of American Fundamentalism* (Philadelphia: Westminster Press, 1976), 79–106; George W. Dollar, *A History of Fundamentalism in America*, 112–22; Trollinger, "One Response to Modernity: Northwestern Bible School and the Fundamentalist Empire of William Bell Riley (Midwest, Minnesota)" (PhD diss., University of Wisconsin–Madison, 1984); Ferenc Morton Szasz, "Three Fundamentalist Leaders: The Roles of William Bell Riley, John Roach Straton, and William Jennings Bryan in the Fundamentalist-Modernist Controversy" (PhD diss., University of Rochester, 1969).

We will have no German rationalism for our authority. We will have only the Christ of the Book for our authority. I hate this traitorous stuff. Yes, I hate it! I have seen too much of it. I see the abominable curse working its way now into the churches and in the hearts of my fellow ministers. I see it damning our theological seminaries. I hate it! I hate it! I hate the new theology as I hate hell, from which it came![4]

The gathering issued a call for a second conference, also to be held in Philadelphia, during the last week of May in 1919. While the earlier conference had supposedly focused upon premillennialism, the 1919 meeting was explicitly a World Conference on Christian Fundamentals. The six thousand attendees met in three of the largest halls in the city.

Riley opened the meeting with an attack upon liberalism. Most of the succeeding messages focused upon fundamental doctrines that liberalism denied: the verbal inspiration and inerrancy of Scripture, the transcendence and personality of God, the full deity and humanity of Christ, the reality of Satan and human sin, and the substitutionary atonement. Some of the sermons emphasized the need for revival. Others focused upon biblical prophecy—this was still a premillennial meeting. Riley closed the conference with a message on the Great Commission.

The attendees voted to form a permanent organization: the World's Christian Fundamentals Association. Riley was chosen as president, and the group adopted a nine-point confession consisting of several fundamental doctrines plus premillennialism. Reports and resolutions indicated that the association planned to become involved in education, publication, Bible conferences, and missions.[5]

The World's Conference on Christian Fundamentals was followed by regional conferences across America. The most prominent preachers—men like A. C. Dixon, W. H. Griffith Thomas, W. B. Riley, J. C. Massee, and Charles Blanchard—immediately left Philadelphia for preaching tours throughout the country, attempting to transfer the momentum into other strategic centers of biblical orthodoxy. Riley wanted not only to found an organization, but to generate a movement.

He succeeded. The World's Christian Fundamentals Association was probably the first organization in the nationwide protest movement that would soon be labeled *fundamentalism*. Alarm over liberal theology had reached a critical point, and many conservatives determined that they had to do something to oppose it. Because the WCFA was interdenominational, it was not in

---

4. Cortland Myers, "War on German Theology," in William L. Pettingill, et al., *Light on Prophecy* (New York: Christian Herald Bible House, 1918), 181–82.
5. The reports and addresses were published in a single volume, *God Hath Spoken* (Philadelphia: Bible Conference Committee, 1919).

a position to counteract liberals within the Northern Baptist Convention. Still, several of the most prominent leaders within the WCFA (including Riley) were Northern Baptists. The 1919 meeting of the Northern Baptist Convention overlapped the Philadelphia meeting by two days. News from the convention gave the WCFA crowd plenty to be concerned about. The same sense of alarm that led them to organize the WCFA would lead these men to erect a parallel movement within the NBC.

The 1919 Denver Convention

The Northern Baptist Convention met in Denver, May 21–27, 1919. This was the first convention after the war. To this point, liberals had kept their program more-or-less in the background. Events at the 1919 convention, however, proved that they were strong enough to push their agenda. Several decisions at Denver revealed the liberal influence to those who had the eyes to see.

Most of these decisions stemmed from a report of the Layman's Committee on Survey. During the previous year, the leadership of the convention had wanted to prepare to confront the post-war order. The committee had been appointed "to make a survey of our present denominational work and report to the Convention what, in its judgment, the denomination should undertake to do."[6] The committee's report, published in a book of 151 double-column pages, covered every aspect of Northern Baptist work. Its sixteen recommendations were listed in the final two pages.

The first was that "as a denomination we record our acceptance of the conception that the mission of the Christian Church is to establish a civilization, Christian in spirit and in passion, throughout the world."[7] The significance of this recommendation appears to have escaped the conservatives until after its adoption. Many of their leaders were attending the Philadelphia conference anyway. Upon consideration, however, they realized that the recommendation was postmillennial at best. More than that, it committed the convention to a program of civilization at the expense of personal evangelism and discipleship. In light of theological developments among Northern Baptists, it could only be taken as an expression of the liberal social gospel that had been promoted by Rauschenbusch, Mathews, and others.

The next five recommendations in the committee's report spoke generally about foreign missions. The next three dealt with home missions. Number ten urged the convention to increase the work in Latin America, "That we

---

6. *Report of the National Committee of Northern Baptist Laymen Section II: Survey of the Fields and Work of the Northern Baptist Convention* (New York: National Committee of Northern Baptist Laymen, 1919), 1.
   7. Ibid., 150.

may help prepare those Republics for the new day in their land." Number eleven proposed to study the social situation in America, so as to "speak with authority and helpfulness in the crisis which now faces the nation."[8] These recommendations further expounded the convention's commitment to a social gospel.

The twelfth recommendation was to increase funding for the Ministers and Missionaries Benefit Board. All Northern Baptist ministers had an interest in funding the M&M Board. Any increase in support by the convention would pay dividends at retirement. The only problem was that a minister who left the Northern Baptist Convention would keep only his personal investment in the board. This problem did not seem significant in 1919, but within a decade convention officials would be able to use the M&M Board to enforce the loyalty of conservative pastors. Pastors who stood to lose most of their retirement would think twice before leaving the convention, however apostate it became.

Recommendation number fifteen was to establish a denominational weekly paper under the control of the Northern Baptist Convention. To this point, Northern Baptists had relied upon independent papers such as the *Standard* of Chicago (a mouthpiece for the liberals) or the *Journal and Messenger* (consistently conservative under the editorship of George William Lasher). The committee recommended, and the convention agreed, that the time had come for an official paper. Launched in January 1920 as the *Baptist*, the new periodical absorbed the two older papers plus the *Pacific Baptist* and *Zion's Advocate*. The only major Northern Baptist paper to continue independent publication was the conservative *Watchman Examiner* under the editorship of Curtis Lee Laws.

To the annoyance of conservatives throughout the Northern Baptist Convention, the *Baptist* immediately followed the trajectory set by the old *Standard*. Robert T. Ketcham later gibed, "The first squawk it ever gave was unbaptistic."[9] Worse still, the convention sent the *Baptist* directly into the homes of church members. This gave liberals a way to circumvent conservative pastors and to influence individual Baptists directly. These pastors could hardly have welcomed the paper.

More was to come. The sixteenth and final recommendation of the Layman's Committee on Survey involved the Northern Baptist Convention in a scheme to raise $54 million for the work of the convention and its agencies. When the recommendation reached the floor of the convention, optimistic delegates raised the number to $100 million.

Where did this enthusiasm come from? Perhaps it arose partly from

8. Ibid., 150–51.
9. Robert T. Ketcham, recorded interview with Robert Delnay, April 7, 1962.

sensibilities that carried over from the recent war. People in a later century have forgotten both the horrors and the idealism that went with trench warfare and mustard gas. Who has any notion of the despair that seeped out from a seemingly interminable conflict? Who still appreciates the awful bloodletting, resulting in somewhere near twenty million combat deaths, none of which gained much advantage or ground? Americans made the sacrifices because they were told that this would be the war to end all wars. When in exhaustion and despair the fighting finally ended, their idealism was not yet gone, and some of it expressed itself in what was called the Interchurch World Movement.

Conceived in a Presbyterian meeting in about December 1918, the Interchurch offered the promise of a great campaign to fulfill the task of Christianizing the world. Each denomination would work in its own section of the vineyard, and each church would set and fulfill its own goal. The total amount to be raised across all denominations was one-and-one-half billion dollars. By early 1919 the New York office was spending about $1 million a month just promoting the movement, and John D. Rockefeller Jr. was a major backer.

When the Laymen's Committee on Survey recommended a campaign for $54 million, it had its eye on the Interchurch World Movement. Baptists adopted their own name for the campaign, the New World Movement. The $100 million that the convention actually voted was an astonishing sum. Then conservatives realized that some percentage of every dollar was destined to finance liberal enterprises. The conservatives were just becoming aware that their giving to the convention was already helping the liberals, and they resented being asked to support liberalism even more.

The Denver convention took one additional action that alarmed conservatives throughout the North. A separate laymen's committee—this one on the relations of the convention's boards and societies—had been asked to develop a plan for more efficient operation. Though it had been founded to eliminate duplication among Northern Baptist agencies, the structure of the NBC was still both complicated and inefficient. The committee recommended creating a new General Board of Promotion that would oversee and coordinate the work of all of the agencies. The board was envisioned as a representative body of about 140 members who would review the work of the convention and its societies, formulate policy, and oversee fundraising for the convention and its subsidiaries. The recommendation was adopted without significant dissent.[10]

Upon consideration, conservatives realized that the General Board of Promotion represented an enormous centralization of power within the NBC.

---

10. *Annual of the Northern Baptist Convention 1919* (Philadelphia: American Baptist Publication Society, 1919), 187–201.

More alarmingly, they realized that the structure of the board required about three-fourths of its 150 members to be convention executives or representatives of convention subsidiaries. More and more, the Northern Baptist Convention was being run like a corporation, and several layers of bureaucracy insulated the convention executives and other employees (the salaried servants, as they were called) from accountability to the voting delegates, let alone to the churches. This structure would make the liberals virtually invulnerable.

By the time the Denver convention was concluding, the World's Conference on Christian Fundamentals (WCFA) was already underway. Many Baptist conservatives attended the latter meeting rather than the convention. Others must have left the convention early—in 1919 the journey from Denver to Philadelphia took some days. Before long, however, conservative pastors throughout the nation began to feel the effects of the Denver decisions. In January their church members received the first issue of the *Baptist*. By that time, churches were being pressured to participate in the New World Movement. April 25 was set aside as the big Sunday when the convention leaders hoped to raise $100 million in cash and pledges.

The New World Movement did not sit well with conservative pastors. Van Osdel wrote in the *Baptist Temple News* that Wealthy Street had no intention of cooperating in the "GREAT DRIVE for one hundred millions." He continued, "If God and His precious Word had been given their rightful place, and if there had been enough of prayer and faith there would have been no call for a drive." Over the next months Van Osdel attacked the New World Movement repeatedly in his paper, and by March or April 1920 these attacks became weekly.[11]

Other pastors came to similar conclusions. One was Robert T. Ketcham, the young shepherd of First Baptist Church in Butler, Pennsylvania. Officials from the state convention had urged him to lead the church into the program. Upon closer inspection, however, he connected the New World Movement with the statement of purpose from the Layman's Committee on Survey, that is, to create a "civilization, Christian in spirit and passion." He decided that the whole agenda was liberal and postmillennial and refused to cooperate. He wrote a small pamphlet to explain his conclusion to his church. Somebody sent a copy of the pamphlet to W. B. Riley, who, with Ketcham's permission, reprinted it and sent hundreds of thousands of copies around the Northern Baptist Convention.[12]

11. Oliver W. Van Osdel, "The Drive," *Baptist Temple News*, November 22, 1919, 2.
12. Robert T. Ketcham, "A Statement of the First Baptist Church, Butler, Pennsylvania, with Reference to The New World Movement and the $100,000,000 Drive" (Butler, PA: First Baptist Church, 1920); Ketcham, recorded interview with Robert Delnay, April 7, 1962. For a comparable response, see Oliver W. Van Osdel, "The Church Adjusting Itself to the Age," *Baptist Temple News*, February 28, 1920, 1.

In April, Riley issued his own denunciation of the $100 million drive. While he expressed several reservations, his principal objection was that the plan called for $31 million to go to Northern Baptist schools. He observed that nine-tenths of the schools were devoted to "Germanized, Rationalistic interpretations of Scripture," and argued that giving the schools "Thirty-one Million additional dollars, is to sell out to Modernism even our sword."[13]

By March, Robert E. Neighbour became convinced that a public protest needed to be made. Originally a Southern Baptist, Neighbour had just been called to First Baptist Church in Elyria, Ohio. He first organized a couple of local conferences to address the issue, but he wanted something larger. He wanted a national meeting to confront the liberalism of the Northern Baptist Convention.

Neighbour began by writing to an old friend, Oliver Van Osdel, who had already been in communication with W. B. Riley. Van Osdel agreed that a national conference was needed, but he was hesitant to launch it immediately. For one thing, he believed that the time was too short to plan a conference before the Northern Baptist Convention met in Buffalo. For another, he had just received word from Jasper C. Massee of New York, who was already working with a committee to organize a protest meeting in Buffalo.

Van Osdel was skeptical about Massee's chances. "At present," he wrote, "the liberals are in possession of the schools and all of our boards, and there is no possibility of removing them as far as I am able to see." When Neighbour suggested that they could plan their conference after the convention, Van Osdel replied that everyone would be in a hurry to get home. He added, "[We] could succeed better by having our own time and issuing our own call."[14]

Van Osdel thought that they should let Massee's protest run its course. He was willing to allow Massee an opportunity to confront liberalism in the convention, but he was convinced that the protest was doomed. To Neighbour he wrote, "Here we feel sure that his scheme will accomplish nothing." [15]

J. C. Massee was pastor of the Baptist Temple in Brooklyn, and would soon go on to become pastor of Tremont Temple, an historic Baptist church in Boston. According to reports, Massee would hire an elocutionist to critique his Sunday sermons. If so, the investment was worthwhile—he became one of the best known preachers of his day. He eventually built the congregation at Tremont Temple into a crowd of around four thousand.[16]

Like Neighbour, Massee believed that the hour had come for a protest.

13. William B. Riley, "Can Baptists Indorse the Hundred Million Dollar Drive?" *Baptist Temple News*, April 24, 1920, 2. Capitalization is *sic*.

14. Oliver W. Van Osdel to Robert E. Neighbour, April 17, 1920; Van Osdel to Robert E. Neighbour, May 17, 1920.

15. Ibid., May 17, 1920.

16. Joseph M. Stowell Jr., interview by Kevin T. Bauder, June 23, 1982. See also C. Allyn Russell, "J. C. Massee: Moderate Fundamentalist," in *Voices of American Fundamentalism*, 107–34.

Early in 1920 he gathered twenty-five Baptist ministers for a private conference in Brooklyn. The group determined to sponsor a conference immediately before the Northern Baptist Convention in Buffalo. The conference would become a focal point to raise an outcry against rationalism, worldliness, materialism, and centralization in the convention. The gathering appointed a committee of seven, including Curtis Lee Laws, John Roach Straton, and J. C. Massee as chairman, to plan the meeting.

The timing was right. Church members were beginning to understand what had happened. They only had to read the *Baptist* to see where their money was going. The convention was asking them to support a pledge campaign to promote a modernist agenda. They were supposed to help Christianize the world. They were to put $31 million into schools that rejected the cross. The facts had become incontrovertible, and conservative frustration had reached a boiling point.

The $100 million drive was already in trouble. On the appointed Sunday in April, churches took up their pledges. That afternoon thousands of Baptists, mainly young people, went door-to-door begging money for the New World Movement. The program fizzled, eventually netting only about three-fifths of the projected funds. The embarrassment of this failure was worsened by the fact that some agencies had already spent the money that they planned on receiving.

This was the atmosphere when Massee, Laws, and their committee published a call for a "Conference on 'The Fundamentals of Our Baptist Faith'" to be held immediately prior to the Northern Baptist Convention. The call drew attention to the widespread influence of liberalism in the convention, insisting that "the vast majority of our Baptist people are as loyal as were our fathers to our Baptist principles." It stated that "there rests upon us as Baptists an immediate and urgent duty to restate, reaffirm, and reemphasize the fundamentals of our New Testament faith."[17]

The call was signed by 156 Baptist leaders, many of whom later became prominent within Baptist fundamentalism. It sparked excitement throughout the convention. For decades conservatives had been chafing under the growing confidence of the modernists. Now it was time to hit back. Buffalo promised to be a convention where Bible believers would finally get the opportunity to squelch liberalism.

Van Osdel was still skeptical. He noted the planned protest in the *Baptist Temple News*, acknowledging that "protests are proper, but possibly somewhat delayed." He also noted that liberals had been leading the convention

---

17. "To All Baptists Within the Bounds of the Northern Baptist Convention," *Watchman Examiner*, May 20, 1920, 652.

from the time that it was organized, and they now controlled the schools, the paper, the publication society, and the boards and committees. "Orthodox brethren, however, have stood by and said, 'we must not become antagonistic or do anything divisive. We must keep together and be patient and love these brethren into line.'"[18]

From Van Osdel's perspective, this tactic had been disastrous. It had allowed the liberals to become so entrenched that they could no longer be dislodged. "And now comes the smiling protest and the declared purpose to begin gradually to weed the liberals out of the convention, little by little, year by year. Can this be done? Not if there is anything to be learned from experience and the Word of God."[19]

The 1920 Buffalo Convention

Although the Brooklyn committee hoped that a couple of hundred people might attend the preconvention conference, somewhere between two and three thousand packed the hall. The conservatives seriously thought that they might regain control of their denomination. Their leader, Massee, was an avowed conservative and a man of recognized stature. In his opening address, he summarized the concerns of the assembly. These included the teaching of radical theology and materialistic evolution, the "gospel of social betterment," the increase of open membership, and the inability of the churches to hold convention agencies accountable.[20]

On the other hand, Massee's address also hinted at an approach that was to prove ruinous for the conservatives. He gave repeated assurances of loyalty to the convention. He bluntly stated that "we would not write nor consent to the writing of a formal creed." He also summarized his personal attitude toward the conflict: "We will not go with swords sharpened to the conflict, but with spirits prayerfully called to unity on the basis of our historic evangelical Baptist faith."[21] Few seem to have discerned from these words the disaster that Massee's leadership was about to become.

Frederick L. Anderson of Newton Theological Institution reflected the same lack of determination. On the one hand, he sounded concerned enough. On the other, Anderson, like Massee, insisted that he would "oppose any creedal statement whatever in the Northern Baptist Convention, or any other

---

18. Oliver W. Van Osdel, "Those Protests," *Baptist Temple News*, May 15, 1920, 1.
19. Ibid., 2.
20. Curtis Lee Laws made reference to the numbers in "Pre-Convention Days at Des Moines," *Watchman Examiner*, June 30, 1921, 811; Jasper C. Massee, "Opening Address," in Curtis Lee Laws, et al., *Baptist Fundamentals* (Philadelphia: Judson Press, 1920), 4–6.
21. Ibid., 7, 11.

formal gathering, because it would be sure to be regarded as an attempt to impose that creed on all Baptists contrary to their liberty in the gospel."[22]

Other voices, however, were more forceful. A. C. Dixon devoted his entire message to a sustained attack upon evolution and biblical criticism. W. W. Bustard confronted the social gospel by arguing, "While it is good to clean up a community, it is better to clean up the people who live in the community, for the reformation of society is made possible only through the regeneration of human nature." John Marvin Dean preached a ringing defense of the deity of Christ, concluding that "a great hour is upon us. Vast victories are within our grasp. Northern Baptists! let us repudiate apostasy. Let us demand a leadership in our denomination that is above suspicion."[23]

A unique and perhaps impromptu address was delivered by J. W. Porter, a visiting Southern Baptist pastor and editor of the *Western Recorder*. Porter exhorted the crowd to "earnestly contend for the faith." In unambiguous terms he stated that the "success of the Interchurch World Movement would mean the recrucifixion of Christ." He gibed that "when some of our brethren become as liberal with their dollars as they are with the doctrines committed to their keeping, they will have as much, or more money, than the Interchurch Movement promised them." Porter went on to say that he would rather misappropriate entrusted funds than the entrusted faith. He concluded by offering to publish the conference addresses in book form, an offer that was politely declined.[24]

These speeches were more in keeping with the mood of the crowd. Best of all was W. B. Riley's address on modernism in the schools. The core of his presentation revolved around three fundamental doctrines: the inspiration and inerrancy of the Bible, the true deity of Christ, and the necessity of the new birth. He insisted that these teachings were essential for Baptists and that Baptists had never been reluctant to express them.

On the subject of creeds, Riley's address was a direct refutation of Massee and Anderson. He pointed to the long history of Baptist confessions, maintaining that Baptists do universally subscribe to a specific set of beliefs about God, Christ, the Bible, and the ordinances. To those who objected that there are no infallible interpreters of the Bible, he replied, "The question is an altogether different one—have we an inspired and an infallible volume to interpret?"[25]

22. Frederick L. Anderson, "Historic Baptist Principles," in Curtis Lee Laws, et al., *Baptist Fundamentals* (Philadelphia: Judson Press, 1920), 19–21.

23. A. C. Dixon, "The Bible at the Center of the Modern University," in Curtis Lee Laws, et al., *Baptist Fundamentals* (Philadelphia: Judson Press, 1920), 119–40; W. W. Bustard, "The Baptist Program of Evangelism," in Laws, et al., *Baptist Fundamentals*, 143; John Marvin Dean, "Northern Baptists and the Deity of Christ," in Laws, et al., *Baptist Fundamentals*, 92.

24. J. W. Porter, "An Unexpected Message," in Laws, et al., *Baptist Fundamentals*, 109–15.

25. W. B. Riley, "Modernism in Baptist Schools," in Laws, et al., *Baptist Fundamentals*, 171.

Shifting to a discussion of the denominational colleges, Riley posited that the only reason to have a Baptist school was to conserve Baptist precepts and principles. That, however, was just what the colleges were failing to do. He noted the widespread teaching of evolution and biblical criticism, accompanied by the denial of biblical authority and inerrancy. He contended that if a single Northern Baptist college taught the fundamentals without contradiction, it would surge to instant popularity with the backing of the conservatives behind it.[26]

Riley went on to indict the seminaries, beginning with the divinity school at the University of Chicago. Members of the Chicago faculty had recently edited and contributed to a volume in which there was "not one article of the Baptist Confession of Faith that is not opposed and practically destroyed by the volume." He buttressed his point with lengthy quotations from the book.[27] He went on to discuss Rochester and Crozer, then implied that the other seminaries except Northern were similarly liberal. This was news to no one, but Riley was making the point as it had rarely been made.

After his assault upon the seminaries, Riley concluded that the entire denomination was in danger. Its distinctive doctrines were being denied, its distinctive mission was being disparaged, and its distinctive influence was being destroyed. Modernism was about to overthrow the whole structure. If that should happen, concluded Riley, "let it not be said to the shame of Baptists that they were engaged as 'pipers of peace' at the very time when their denomination perished."[28]

Of all the addresses, Riley's most fit the mood of the crowd. These people were tired of being pressured to support liberalism. They were ready for a battle, and they decided to fight it on two fronts. First, they would call for an independent commission to investigate the schools. Second, they would press the convention to sell the *Baptist* to the highest bidder. Having committed themselves to these initiatives, they appointed Massee to lead the fight on the convention floor.

On the first afternoon of the convention, Massee presented the resolution for an investigation of the schools. It called for a commission of nine to investigate both the stated position of the schools and the specific beliefs of the teachers. Topics of inquiry were to include the inspiration of Scripture, the deity of Christ, the atonement, the resurrection, the return of the Lord, the spiritual nature of the church, the necessity of regenerated, baptized church membership, the "unchanged nature" of the ordinances, and the responsibility

---

26. Ibid., 172–78.
27. Ibid., 178–81; the book Riley was citing is Gerald Birney Smith, ed., *A Guide to the Study of the Christian Religion* (Chicago: University of Chicago Press), 1916.
28. Riley, "Modernism in Baptist Schools," 185–87.

of carrying out the Great Commission. The resolution further specified that no trustee or teacher in any school could serve on the committee, but named nine of the conservatives to its membership.[29]

When the resolution came up for debate, H. J. White of Connecticut presented a substitute resolution. White's motion affirmed soul competency and rejected the imposition of any doctrinal test "by either political or ecclesiastical authority." Then it called upon ministers and teachers to "maintain and proclaim the gospel of Jesus Christ in all its simplicity, purity, and power." Furthermore, it declared that "we will not seek to have dominion over one another's faith." Finally, it requested the schools to put out a statement "which may give assurance to the denomination of their fidelity to the Saviour." White's resolution did agree to a committee of nine to "inquire into the loyalty" of the schools, investigating the method of appointing trustees in each institution. This substitute resolution, however, was very far from the original in both spirit and function.[30]

Spirited debate followed. John Roach Straton of Calvary Baptist Church in New York City attacked White's substitute resolution point by point amid heckling and protests from the floor. Massee tried to modify his original resolution, which led to further debate. Then, surprisingly, Massee reversed himself and accepted the substitute resolution, which was immediately adopted by the convention. The president of the convention was empowered to appoint the committee of nine and the committee was given money for its investigation.

The conservative initiative had effectively been neutralized, and by accepting the substitute motion, Massee had become complicit in its defeat. At that point W. B. Riley, whose name had been on the list of commission members in the conservatives' original resolution, rose to announce that he would not serve as a member of the new committee. His action probably reflected the disgust of many: this was more of a victory for the liberals than for the conservatives.[31]

The General Board of Promotion then presented a report on the convention's involvement in the Interchurch World Movement. By now nearly everyone knew that participation had been a mistake. It was in danger of becoming an embarrassment. The report recommended that the Northern Baptist Convention would discontinue its involvement in the movement. If this seemed like a victory to the conservatives, their spirits were dampened by the fact that the report also obligated the convention to raise $2.5 million for the expenses of the Interchurch. In spite of some maneuvering by the liberals, this recommendation passed.

29. *Annual of the Northern Baptist Convention 1920* (Philadelphia: American Baptist Publication Society, 1920), 48–49.
30. Ibid., 60–61.
31. Ibid., 60.

Finally Massee moved that "the convention now instruct the Board of Promotion to sell the *Baptist* to the highest bidder."[32] The paper had become a sore spot with conservatives. It was openly modernistic, it did not represent the great majority of Baptists in the North, and it was being heavily subsidized from mission funds. Massee's motion caught the liberals by surprise, and at first they responded with jeers and catcalls. Then a strange thing happened. As one conservative eyewitness recalled,

> We were going! People were just anxious to get a crack at that and vote it. It took the other crowd by surprise, and they had a little hurried conference there on the platform, and then one of them made a substitute motion that it be referred to a committee for further study. Presently Massee said, "Well now look, brethren, we ought to show ourselves to be Christians, and let's not be too radical. Let's give it to the committee and let them study it and wade their way through it, and bring it back next year." Well, by the next year they had their guns in place and we just never had anything after that.[33]

The substitute motion actually required that "the whole question of denominational journals be referred to a special committee, to be appointed by the President, composed of all elements and views held among us, and to report to this annual meeting of the convention." This was not at all the same thing as a motion to sell the offending periodical. The adoption of the substitute motion was a genuine, if rather ad hoc, liberal victory.

With the votes to win behind him, why did Massee accept the substitute motion? On the one hand, he did want liberals removed from control of the convention. On the other hand, he evidently believed that this goal could be accomplished without rancor or harsh words. At any rate, the conservatives' most important initiative came to nothing.[34]

From one perspective, the conservatives accomplished very little at the Buffalo convention. They failed to win a single decisive victory. Their leadership vacillated in the heat of battle. Because of uncertain leadership, they were outmaneuvered by an unprepared minority on the convention floor. This outcome looked much more like defeat than like victory.

From a more strategic perspective, however, conservatives could still reckon the Buffalo conference and convention as a major step forward. They had begun to function more or less cohesively. They had discovered that they could act and that they would not be ignored—in a word, that they had power. They were beginning to develop a consciousness of themselves as a distinctive body.

32. Ibid., 124.
33. Ketcham, interview.
34. Ibid.; J. C. Massee to Robert Delnay, July 27, 1962.

But just who were they? Neither the conference group nor their opponents seemed to be quite sure. After the convention, Curtis Lee Laws gave this question a bit of thought and a couple of paragraphs in the *Watchman Examiner*. He insisted that premillennialism was not the issue: "Standing solidly together in the battle for the reenthronement of the fundamentals of our holy faith were premillennialists, post-millennialists, pro-millennialists and no-millennialists." Then he wrote,

> We here and now move that a new word be adopted to describe the men among us who insist that the landmarks shall not be removed. "Conservatives" is too closely allied with reactionary forces in all walks of life. "Premillennialists" is too closely allied with a single doctrine and not sufficiently inclusive. "Landmarkers" has an historical disadvantage and connotes a particular group of radical conservatives. We suggest that those who still cling to the great fundamentals and who mean to do battle royal for the fundamentals shall be called "Fundamentalists." By that name the editor of *The Watchman-Examiner* is willing to be called.[35]

Though the group was still maturing, it had an identity, an agenda, and now a name. Doctrinally, its core concern was Christian orthodoxy. Ecclesiastically, it combined the traditions of Baptist denominationalism (Massee and Laws) with the emphases of the Bible conference movement (Riley and Dixon). None of this was really new: such combinations had been taking place for at least half a century. What was new was this group's attitude. Faced with a seemingly intractable modernism, they had decided to fight. Furthermore, they had decided to fight, not as individual ecclesiastical warriors, but as a coalition. They intended to stand together and to do what they could to eliminate the influence of liberalism within the Northern Baptist Convention. They not only clung to the great fundamentals, they meant to "do battle royal" for them. What set fundamentalism apart from earlier conservative movements was not orthodoxy, but militancy.

The 1921 Des Moines Convention

During the year of 1920–1921, the *Baptist* continued to publish.[36] The Interchurch World Movement went into receivership with millions in debts. The committee on schools began its investigation, soliciting specific proof of liberalism from the Baptist public.

By now the Great War was well over and the twenties had begun to roar.

---

35. Curtis Lee Laws, "Convention Side Lights," *Watchman Examiner*, July 1, 1920, 834.
36. The *Baptist* continued to publish until the bottom year of the Depression, when in 1933 it was merged with *The Christian Century*. Both had been published in the same building.

In New York City, John R. Straton had been pastor of Calvary Baptist Church for just two years. In his mid-40s, Straton was both outgoing and outspoken. He identified with the fundamentalists from the very beginning, organizing a Fundamentalist League in New York City and rising to prominence as one of the movement's most public figures. During the 1920s he would campaign against liquor, prostitution, gambling, and dancing. He would also defend women's rights, fair wages for workers, and the right of African-Americans to be received as members in white churches (Calvary Baptist led by example). He became famous for his public debates on both moral and theological issues. *New Yorker* magazine referred to him as the "Meshuggah of Manhattan."[37]

In Grand Rapids, Van Osdel was fighting his own battle with the Michigan Baptist Convention. The convention-backed lawsuit against Sand Creek Baptist Church was absorbing his attention, but he still found time to help R. E. Neighbour set up a structure that would skirt the convention apparatus for supporting missionaries. Neighbour was trying to form a kind of clearinghouse that would transmit funds to missionaries without taking any percentage for expenses. Van Osdel endorsed Neighbour's plan, but he also wanted something more enduring.

Initially, Van Osdel wanted the Grand River Valley Baptist Association to set up a permanent council to cooperate with the work of William Haas in mid-Africa. The vision, however, grew beyond western Michigan. In October, representatives from churches in Ohio and Michigan organized the General Council on Cooperating Baptist Missions, popularly known as the Mid-Africa Mission. This organization (now known as Baptist Mid-Missions) would go on to become one of the most important mission agencies within Baptist fundamentalism.[38]

Hoping for support in the Sand Creek lawsuit, Van Osdel appealed to Massee. The reply was less than satisfactory. He complained to Neighbour, "I have a letter from Dr. Massee in which he indicates that 'if' the things that have been published in the Temple News are true, and I do not exactly understand why he puts the 'if' in, but he says, 'if these things are true', he will go before the Northern Baptist Convention with a protest against this sort of litigation."[39]

Van Osdel was even less pleased with Curtis Lee Laws and the *Watchman Examiner*. On his view, Laws spent too much time giving favorable exposure

37. Stanley Walker, "The Meshuggah of Manhattan," *New Yorker*, April 16, 1927, 25. For more on Straton, see George W. Dollar, *A History of Fundamentalism in America*, 135–143; C. Allyn Russell, "John Roach Straton: Accusative Fundamentalist," in *Voices of American Fundamentalism*, 47–78.

38. Oliver W. Van Osdel, "The Faith Missions," *Baptist Temple News*, September 18, 1920, 2; Oliver W. Van Osdel to R. E. Neighbour, October 12, 1920.

39. Oliver W. Van Osdel to R. E. Neighbour, October 12, 1920.

to the enemy. He wrote to James M. Gray (president of Moody Bible Institute), "If only the Watchman-Examiner had backbone enough to stand always in the same place, then its utterances might have force."[40]

His mood did not improve when Laws ran a page featuring Fountain Street Church in Grand Rapids. Van Osdel was incensed, especially since Laws had refused space to feature the dedication of the Wealthy Street building. He wrote to Laws that Christianity in Michigan had "no greater menace than the same Fountain Street Church. Mr. Wishart announces himself as an out and out liberal, refusing to believe the Bible as a whole and turning aside from the fundamentals and practically all of the things which make a man a Baptist at all." Van Osdel went on to wonder whether there was really any difference between Laws's *Watchman Examiner* and the *Baptist*. [41]

By this time the Michigan Orthodox Baptist Association had already been ejected from the Michigan Baptist Convention. Wealthy Street was still nominally part of the Northern Baptist Convention, but Neighbour and Van Osdel continued to talk about a separatist fellowship. They were particularly irked by the lack of communication from Massee and the Brooklyn committee. Everyone understood that another preconvention conference was in order, but no one was getting much information. In early June, Neighbour wrote to Van Osdel wondering what was going on. Van Osdel wrote back that "Dr. Massee has not taken me into his confidence in any way as to what he is intending to do." Far from it—Massee communicated his disapproval of Van Osdel's leadership in Michigan. Van Osdel complained to Neighbour,

> We have been in this contest for the past twelve years and you also have possibly the same length of time. About twelve months ago Dr. Massee awoke to the plan of doing something and he insists that we shall abandon our own convictions and follow him. He appears to be asking for our patronage, but not our cooperation.
>
> My feeling about the convention is that the forces there will be about evenly divided. If the conservatives are in the majority, the liberals will become very noisy and break up the convention. If the liberals are in the majority there will be nothing left for the conservatives but to pack their grips and go home. So that in either case I am not anticipating there will be anything done unless there may be a compromise. And you and I are not just now in the attitude of a compromise.[42]

In 1921 the NBC met in Des Moines, enduring the heat of late June. The preconvention conference opened only the day before the conference began. Seven men spoke during the course of the conference.

40. Oliver W. Van Osdel to James M. Gray, November 15, 1920.
41. Oliver W. Van Osdel to Curtis Lee Laws, January 25, 1921.
42. Oliver W. Van Osdel to R. E. Neighbour, June 7, 1921.

As during the previous year, Massee delivered the opening address. This year he adopted a less concessive tone. He pointed to "wide-spread propaganda" that would prevent the convention from accepting any doctrinal test of fellowship. He admitted that Baptists had always "refused to subscribe to a formal and an authoritative creed." Nevertheless, he insisted that Baptists had persistently set forth their beliefs in confessions, and that these confessions had served as a basis for fellowship between churches. In a surprise move, he began to argue that a common basis of fellowship required a common confession, whether old or new. [43]

With considerable emotion, Massee related how four young people whom he had sent to Baptist schools came back with their faith shaken. The schools were guilty of "moral impatience" and doctrinal laxity. Consequently, many of the younger ministers "now deny almost in toto the great fundamentals of the faith as held by the fathers and as still held by the majority of our churches." Massee warned that the schools were in danger of discrediting all Baptist doctrines.[44]

What was to be done? Massee stated that compromise was unthinkable. The solution lay in some formal action for a basis of fellowship, that is, a confession. Massee proposed that the convention should adopt "a statement of belief to which all teachers in all Baptist educational institutions shall be required to give annual assent in writing, cutting off from denominational support and sponsorship all schools refusing such fellowship and faith."[45]

In keeping with this proposal, the Brooklyn committee presented a brief statement to the conference. Since it built upon the work of Frank Goodchild, pastor of Central Baptist Church in New York, it became known as the "Goodchild Confession." It was far from an exhaustive creed, consisting only of a preamble and seven brief articles. The preamble disavowed any attempt to adopt "a creed to which allegiance is demanded," but expressed the desire to restate the "foundation doctrines of our faith." Surprisingly, the article on the Bible did not address the issue of inerrancy. The third article was perhaps the most significant.

> We believe in Jesus Christ, God's only begotten Son, miraculous in His birth, sinless in His life, making atonement for the sins of the world by His death. We believe in His bodily resurrection, His ascension into heaven, His perpetual intercession for His people, and His personal visible return to the world according to His promise.[46]

---

43. J. C. Massee, "Opening Address," in Curtis Lee Laws, et al., *Baptist Doctrines* (n.p.: Jasper C. Massee, 1921), 9–13.

44. Ibid., 14–17.

45. Ibid., 17–19.

46. "A Confession of Faith," *Watchman Examiner*, June 30, 1921, 805; the confession has

This statement was almost as significant for what it did not say as for what it did. It contained no explicit statement of either the unique deity or true humanity of Jesus Christ. It did not mention a virgin birth, though it did specify a miraculous one. It left the question of the millennium unaddressed. As historian Grant Wacker has noted, "All in all the Confession was a remarkably delicate formulation for a group of men who claimed that they were prepared to do 'battle royal' for the faith delivered unto the fathers."[47] Still, no modernist could honestly assent to it. After some debate, the men in the conference agreed that it sounded acceptable. They voted to offer it in a resolution to become the convention's official doctrinal statement. Massee was again appointed to lead the fight on the floor.

During the convention itself, the report on the schools was delivered on Thursday morning. The investigating committee had included some conservatives, including chairman Frank Goodchild. It had advertized in both the *Baptist* and the *Watchman Examiner* for information "touching the character of the teachers and the teaching in our schools." According to the report, what the committee received was "exceedingly meager," and consisted of "the most general statements, the vaguest accusations, rumors and grievances of doubtful origin, trivial matters of complaint, and small and rather unworthy criticism." The committee had planned to base its investigation upon these accusations, but declined to "seek the proof of charges which others made of which they submitted no proof whatever, nor to trace rumors to their source, nor to include in our report quotations of unsubstantiated assertions or accusations."[48]

Lacking direct accusations that could be investigated, the committee decided to proceed by sending questionnaires to the schools. Most of the schools responded, though President W. H. P. Faunce of Brown University rebuffed the questionnaire. Members of the committee also paid perfunctory visits to several institutions. Meanwhile, Massee had been conducting his own investigation by sending questionnaires to graduates of the schools. The committee incorporated Massee's results into its report.

In its conclusion, the committee found that "here and there" a teacher had "departed from the Baptist faith." While a few of these instances had become notorious, they could be dealt with adequately by the schools themselves. These few instances did not detract from the committee's confidence that the schools were doing a work "of which the denomination may well be proud." In

been reprinted in William L. Lumpkin, *Baptist Confessions of Faith* (Valley Forge, PA: Judson Press, 1969), 382–83.

47. Grant Wacker, *Augustus H. Strong and the Dilemma of Historical Consciousness* (Macon, GA: Mercer University Press, 1985), 144.

48. *Annual of the Northern Baptist Convention 1921* (Philadelphia: American Baptist Publication Society, 1921), 58–59.

short, the committee gave the schools very high marks, acknowledging only a trivial problem with liberalism.[49]

Mild as it was, this slight element of censure was still too strong for some. One committee member, Franklin W. Sweet, issued a minority report that criticized the majority for not affirming clearly enough the teachers' loyalty to Christ. The convention adopted Sweet's report along with the committee's. Then, when Frank Padelford delivered the report of the Board of Education, he took a clear swipe at Massee: "It is the business of the Board of Education to know the conditions that obtain in our schools. We believe we do know them. . . . We have not depended upon questionnaires sent to students." Padelford denounced the charges against the schools as "largely false." He insisted that undermining faith in these institutions was "little less than criminal."[50]

Sweet and Padelford need not have worried. The report stated its concerns so mildly that they were easily overlooked. In fact, the newly elected president of the convention, Helen Barrett Montgomery, would later announce, "Our schools, after investigation, have been given a clean bill of health." That was the official word that was repeated throughout the denomination. Conservatives (including Goodchild) objected, but the damage was done.[51]

This report was just about what the fundamentalists had expected. Undeterred, they prepared for debate when Massee introduced the Goodchild Confession. They were ready to see it through, present in full strength to back the move. As they waited, they heard report after report and motion after motion. Then the closing gavel fell, and Massee had never even put the confession on the floor.

It turned out that this failure was not Massee's alone. Writing in the *Watchman Examiner*, Laws commented,

> The fundamentalists had no desire to plunge the Convention into controversies of this kind, and so they decided not to ask the Convention to adopt the confession which had been so heartily adopted at the Conference on Fundamentals. It seemed to us that this decision was all the more commendable in view of the fact that the Convention was overwhelmingly conservative. . . .[52]

Which fundamentalists did Laws have in mind? The entire fundamentalist conference could hardly have reconvened to discuss the matter, and no record indicates that they did. The decision may have been made by Massee and Laws on their own initiative, or it may have involved the entire Brooklyn committee.

49. Ibid., 93.
50. Ibid., 98, 108–09.
51. Frank M. Goodchild, "A Correction," *Watchman Examiner*, December 15, 1921, 1587.
52. Curtis Lee Laws, "Convention Sidelights," *Watchman Examiner*, July 7, 1921, 834.

Either way, rank and file fundamentalists were denied the opportunity to vote for the confession on the convention floor. That was damaging enough. Even worse was Laws's rationale. By his own admission, he and Massee were willing to forego a near-certain victory in order to avoid a controversy. If the fundamentalists shook their heads in bewilderment, no one can blame them.

For a second year the fundamentalists left the convention having accomplished nothing of substance. Every initiative that they had authorized had been thwarted, either by maneuvering from the opposition or by the vacillation of their own leaders. So far, Van Osdel's prognostications had proven appallingly accurate. The question was whether the fundamentalists would be able to accomplish anything at their third meeting.

The 1922 Indianapolis Convention

Almost immediately after the Des Moines convention, the Brooklyn committee announced plans to call another preconvention conference in 1922 (the convention was originally scheduled to meet in Seattle, but the meeting place was later moved to Indianapolis). Reactions began almost immediately. The West Washington convention made an appeal to suspend all preconvention conferences. The newly elected president of the convention, Helen Barrett Montgomery, suggested that the fundamentalist conference should be canceled and the day devoted to prayer.

Van Osdel noted that fundamentalists had begun to organize committees and fellowships in several states. While he still disapproved of Massee's leadership, he encouraged people to support these smaller organizations. He also encouraged them to write to Massee and to contribute financially to the expenses of the fundamentalist conferences. He himself sent Massee a check for $100 (equivalent to more than $1,100 in 2010 dollars). When Massee asked C. H. Heaton of Lansing to organize a group in Michigan, Van Osdel gave Heaton his public support.[53]

Neighbour wanted to prepare a joint letter, over the signatures of several Baptist pastors, applying a bit of pressure to Massee and the Brooklyn committee. Van Osdel told Neighbour that the Brooklyn committee was too sensitive to respond well to what they would perceive as dictation. Instead, he suggested that each of the proposed signatories write separately to Massee asking for his full plan, and then write again with their suggestions if Massee's proposals were unacceptable.[54]

Following his own advice, Van Osdel wrote to Massee asking for

53. Oliver W. Van Osdel, "A Michigan Association of Baptist Churches," *Baptist Temple News*, November 19, 1921, 1.
54. Oliver W. Van Osdel to R. E. Neighbour, November 18, 1921.

information. He noted that five months had passed since the Des Moines convention, but no clear agenda had been articulated. He assured Massee that support was growing, but cautioned him that some kind of educational campaign would have to precede the convention or the fundamentalists' efforts were likely to stall.[55]

What Massee sent back was disquieting. He had begun writing conservatives all across the country, soliciting funds to bail out the financially troubled missions work of the Northern Baptist Convention. Laws was making the same appeal in the pages of the *Watchman Examiner*, and it was being repeated by Joshua Gravett, fundamentalist leader in Colorado. Laws had gone so far as to say that "they who refuse to participate in the burdens of the denomination lose right to voice in the conduct of its affairs."[56]

This move left Van Osdel perplexed. He argued that the convention was in trouble only because the liberals were in power. Churches (including Wealthy Street) had sought or created other venues to support missions. They had made commitments from which they could not easily detach themselves. For Van Osdel, there was only one thing that the denominational boards should do: "Come out immediately with a bold statement declaring that all liberals, new theology men and modernists shall be removed from the Boards and the Mission Fields at the earliest date possible." Why should the conservatives feel justified in taking up the work of the bankrupt boards?[57]

Massee, however, persisted in trying to prove his loyalty to the denomination. The Board of General Promotion had suggested that conservatives could designate their funds, and Massee verged on endorsing the suggestion. He also began to conduct joint conferences between conservatives and liberals. He further proposed that the conservatives raise $2 million to start their own school under the auspices of the convention, effectively surrendering the other institutions to the liberals. Alarmed, Van Osdel wrote that he did not want any liberal money. "I am a Baptist and I want only what belongs to Baptists and I utterly refuse to join hands with Unitarians and men who are untrue to our work." He expressed his wish to gather support and money for Massee's movement, but indicated that Massee's approach would prevent him from doing either.[58]

To these concerns, Van Osdel received no answer. A month later he wrote again, stating his fears more directly: "[T]he fact that you and Dr. Laws are so extensively engaged in an endeavor to aid in the New World Movement leads some of us to believe that it is not likely that very much will be planned

55. Oliver W. Van Osdel to J. C. Massee, November 18, 1921.
56. "How Colorado Baptists See It," *Watchman Examiner*, March 2, 1922, 278.
57. Oliver W. Van Osdel to J. C. Massee, December 2, 1921.
58. Oliver W. Van Osdel to J. C. Massee, January 9, 1922.

in connection with the next Convention, except to try, to pay the debts." He pointed out that many conservatives felt that they had no voice in convention affairs, and that they wanted an organization that would make their concerns heard. Van Osdel then stated that he and others were thinking about forming a Baptist Bible Union to meet that purpose. He elaborated,

> My advice has been for delay in the formation of such a Union until after the next Convention. But now that your Committee seem to be engaged in an endeavor to make up the indebtedness incurred by the Board of Promotion, some of us are feeling anxious to be doing something.
>
> Our thought is not to leave the denomination, not to create division, but to put ourselves in a position where we can help the brethren who are wavering, to line up on the right side.
>
> I am writing this letter because I want to know your mind. I wish you to write me fully. You certainly will not blame us for becoming anxious that something decided should be done very soon.[59]

In fact, Neighbour and Van Osdel had already begun to plan the organization of the Baptist Bible Union. Massee, however, agreed to devote himself to the fundamentalist cause rather than to balancing the convention's budget, and the Baptist Bible Union was again delayed until after the Indianapolis convention. Meanwhile, Massee and the Brooklyn committee forged ahead with plans for a preconvention conference. Interestingly enough, they put Van Osdel on the program and listed William Jennings Bryan as the closing speaker.[60]

Immediately before the convention, liberal pulpiteer Harry Emerson Fosdick weighed in on the fundamentalist controversy. A Baptist by ordination, he was preaching supply at the prestigious First Presbyterian Church of New York. On May 21, 1922, he delivered a sermon titled, "Shall the Fundamentalists Win?" The sermon was quickly printed and distributed by businessman Ivy Lee, who reformatted and (at the instigation of John D. Rockefeller Jr.) retitled it. The sermon swept across the country, and Fosdick became an instant sensation.

Of course, Fosdick argued that fundamentalists must not be permitted to win. He distinguished fundamentalists from conservatives: "The best conservatives can often give lessons to the liberals in true liberality of spirit, but the Fundamentalist program is essentially illiberal and intolerant." As Fosdick saw it, fundamentalists correctly perceived that a significant intellectual shift had taken place within Christian thought. Much new knowledge had recently

---

59. Oliver W. Van Osdel to J. C. Massee, February 7, 1922.

60. Van Osdel spoke on "The Constitution and Organization of the Churches—A New Testament Study," *Watchman Examiner*, April 20, 1922, 501.

come into human possession. Furthermore, he granted that liberals had not always been careful in their expression of their views. Still, liberals were the ones who were trying to reconcile the new knowledge with their Christianity, whereas fundamentalists were "out on a campaign to shut against them the doors of Christian fellowship." Fosdick thought that this agenda was where fundamentalism must not be allowed to succeed.[61]

Fosdick went further. He named several doctrines that were held as precious by fundamentalists: the reality of miracles, the virgin birth of Christ, the inerrancy of Scripture, and the substitutionary atonement. Along with these he mentioned other doctrines that fundamentalists did not always hold, such as the dictation theory of inspiration and the premillennial return of Jesus. He treated these two categories of doctrines together as the "nonnegotiables" of fundamentalism. Fosdick stated that the main liberal objection was not that fundamentalists believed these teachings, but that fundamentalists treated these teachings as fundamentals of Christianity. He continued, "Just now the Fundamentalists are giving us one of the worst exhibitions of bitter intolerance that the churches of this country have ever seen."[62]

Fosdick later characterized his sermon as "a plea for goodwill," but he admitted that "an explosion of ill will" came from it. John Roach Straton responded with a rebuttal titled "Shall the Funny-Monkeyist Win?" Straton denounced Fosdick as a Presbyterian outlaw, a Baptist bootlegger, and the Jesse James of the theological world. Presbyterian churchmen were equally incensed. Fosdick had accomplished the unusual feat of goading conservatives in two denominations at once: Presbyterians because the sermon had been delivered in one of their pulpits, and Baptists because Fosdick held Baptist ordination.[63]

The storm over Fosdick's sermon was still building as the Northern Baptist Convention met in Indianapolis. While fundamentalists bristled at Fosdick's assessment, at least some liberals must have found amusement in seeing their opponents roundly (and, on their view, fairly) denounced. The result was that the liberals approached the convention with a certain amount of momentum. The night before the convention began, about two hundred of them met at the Lincoln Hotel for a closed-door strategy session. Under the chairmanship of Cornelius Woelfkin, the liberals spent the evening mapping out a plan and

61. The sermon appeared in many publications, and the full text is available on the Internet. The version cited here is Harry Emerson Fosdick, "Shall the Fundamentalists Win?" (sermon, First Presbyterian Church, New York, May 21, 1922), accessed July 5, 2014, http://historymatters.gmu.edu/d/5070/.

62. Ibid.

63. Harry Emerson Fosdick, The Living of These Days: An Autobiography (New York: Harper and Brothers, 1956), 145, 153. For a liberal perspective on this event see Stewart G. Cole, The History of Fundamentalism (New York: Richard R. Smith, 1931; repr., Westport CT: Greenwood Press, 1971), 69–70.

appointing a steering committee. From this point forward, the liberals regularly caucused after the evening session of the convention.

The fundamentalists also held their preconvention conference, but they had no clear strategy. Their most forthright initiative was a resolution to deny convention employees (the salaried servants) the right to vote in the convention. There was some hope that the convention could be induced to appoint a committee to spend two years conferring with both the Southern Baptists and the Canadian Baptists about a common declaration of faith. The group also authorized the Brooklyn committee to continue planning preconvention conferences.

Since the conference was open to the public, liberal sympathizers were able to carry word of these initiatives to the Lincoln Hotel immediately. Before the fundamentalists could ever get a motion to the floor, the liberals already had a response in place. In addition, the liberals were able to plan a few surprises of their own.

The convention itself was held in the newly built Cadle Tabernacle, a Spanish-style auditorium of ten thousand seats located two blocks from the Indianapolis city hall. The theme was "Agreed to Differ but Resolved to Love." This theme figured prominently in Helen Barrett Montgomery's presidential address. She emphasized the gravity of the situation by stating that "our children's children will look back to this hour and judge us by what we do." Anticipating the motion for a joint confessional committee, she stated,

> There has been much talk about the necessity of issuing some Baptist statement of faith. . . . We have no body of delegates with power to impose upon our churches a confession of faith or a creedal statement. . . . Now if the Northern Baptist Convention should appoint a committee to draw up a Baptist statement of faith, we should never allow the committee to report back to the Convention, we should never formally adopt the report as our official statement. . . . For us Baptists to have an official confession of faith would come perilously near to abandoning one of our fundamental principles.[64]

The first item of business on the first morning was the report of the Executive Committee of the convention. As part of its report, the Executive Committee recommended a change in bylaws that would allow churches to send delegates only if they had contributed money to the convention or one of its subsidiaries. This was a direct slap at the fundamentalists, many of whose churches had begun supporting independent agencies. It was also the liberals' first surprise attack upon the fundamentalists.[65]

64. *Annual of the Northern Baptist Convention 1922* (Philadelphia: American Baptist Publication Society, 1922), 37–39.
65. Ibid., 28.

That afternoon Massee again put a motion on the floor to sell the *Baptist* "as soon as possible and practicable." The motion was immediately referred back to the Executive Committee, where it was of course buried. This was a defeat for the fundamentalists, but it was one that could have been anticipated.[66]

The next morning the recommendation restricting delegates from nonsupporting churches came up for consideration. It precipitated a spirited debate, and the fundamentalists quickly discovered that they would not have the votes to stop it. As a sop to them, the matter was referred back to the Executive Committee, but this event served as a warning. The liberals had anticipated the fundamentalists' strategies and were ahead of them.[67]

That night the fundamentalists met in the Palm Room at the Claypool Hotel. In spite of the Brooklyn committee's reluctance, others in the meeting wanted the convention to adopt a confession of faith. Finally, the decision was made to put the matter on the convention floor. The Goodchild Confession was dismissed as too humble, but someone had a copy of the New Hampshire Confession of Faith. Robert Ketcham recalled the episode almost twenty years later.

> Dr. Joshua Gravit, of Colorado, was asked to read the old New Hampshire Confession to us. We shall never forget that night. We question if there was a dry eye anywhere among the three hundred men present. As Dr. Gravit read, in our presence, those soul-stirring sentences which portrayed the faith of our Baptist fathers and which were also the full expression of the faith and hope of every man in that room, it seemed as though the glory of the Lord came down upon us. We had been in few meetings in our life where the presence of God was more deeply manifest.[68]

Riley was appointed to put the New Hampshire Confession on the convention floor, but it did not receive a comparable welcome there. Like Gravett on the previous night, Riley took the time to read the confession from beginning to end. When he was done, James Colgate of New York rose to remark, "So that's the New Hampshire Confession of Faith, is it? I thought Dr. Riley was reading off the back of a Western Union telegraph blank."[69]

Worse, the fundamentalists were unprepared for the liberals' response. The modernists knew that the fundamentalists would offer some kind of motion about a confession of faith. Cornelius Woelfkin was ready with a substitute motion: "The Northern Baptist Convention affirms that the New Testament is the all-sufficient ground of our faith and practice, and we need no other

66. Ibid., 106.
67. Ibid., 46.
68. Robert T. Ketcham, "Editor's Note," *Baptist Bulletin*, April 1941, 5.
69. Ibid.

statement." The debate went on for nearly three hours before the question was called. When the vote was taken, the fundamentalists lost by a margin of two to one, 637 to 1,264.[70]

No one seems to have foreseen this result. The liberals had been genuinely anxious over the apparent strength of the fundamentalists. The fundamentalists themselves seem to have assumed that the convention was so overwhelmingly conservative that it would readily vote for a statement of historic Baptist principles. The defeat was stunning.

Curtis Lee Laws later offered what seemed like an obvious explanation: Woelfkin's motion caught many fundamentalists in a double bind. "Dr. Woelfkin made the battle a choice between the New Testament and the confession." What Baptist would want to vote against the New Testament? Laws was sure that in a straight, up-or-down vote on the New Hampshire Confession the fundamentalists "would have come near winning."[71]

This explanation doubtless had the virtue of consoling the losers, but its plausibility wears thin on closer examination. The debate lasted for three hours. The issue was addressed by competent conservative voices. M. P. Boynton observed that the New Hampshire Confession contained nothing that was not in the New Testament, and declared, "There is no other authoritative declaration of Baptist principles and positions." Charles R. Brock argued that the New Testament would be sufficient except that some Northern Baptists had distorted its teachings, so a confession was necessary as an explanation of the New Testament. Massee objected that Woelfkin's substitute motion was simply a bit of parliamentary maneuvering, and he pointed out that Woelfkin himself had recently signed an "Evangelical Confession of Faith." He argued that if loyalty to the New Testament disallows further explanation, then preachers, Sunday Schools, publication societies, and ordination councils would be as superfluous as the New Hampshire Confession. The crucial question was, What do we believe about the Bible?[72]

The debate was long, the heat was oppressive, and some may have had trouble hearing in the huge tabernacle. In spite of those obstacles, the speakers were as clear as human language can be. A vote for the New Hampshire Confession was a vote for the New Testament literally interpreted. A vote for the substitute motion was to betray the New Testament into the hands of its enemies.

Also contributing to the defeat was the fact that convention employees (the salaried servants) were allowed to vote on convention business. They had been given the right of franchise in 1911, they numbered in the hundreds,

70. *Annual of the Northern Baptist Convention 1922*, 133–34.
71. Curtis Lee Laws, "Convention Side Lights," *Watchman Examiner*, June 29, 1922, 802.
72. Ibid., 814–15.

and they tended to vote as a bloc in sympathy with the liberals. Still, the most inflated estimates of their strength cannot account for a six-hundred vote difference. Even including the salaried servants, the modernists could not have numbered more than 25 or 30 percent of those voting, yet they captured 66 percent of the votes.

Another important factor in the defeat was the fundamentalists' lack of preparedness, which contrasted with the liberals' careful strategy. Laws himself admitted as much.

> We are not informed as to the plans of the liberals. At Indianapolis their organization was almost perfect. General Woelfkin put General Massee to shame when it came to the matter of mobilizing forces. The liberals fought like well trained regulars, the fundamentalists like raw recruits. For months the liberals had been planning to crush the fundamentalists, whatever their plans might be. Indeed, it was not apparent that the fundamentalists had any well defined plans. They seemed to be trusting to the righteousness of their cause. Their little skirmishes would have counted for more if they had been deliberately planned battles.[73]

All of these considerations played some role in the fundamentalists' defeat. Yet none is really an adequate explanation. The remaining factor was probably pinpointed by Charles R. Brock in an article that he wrote for the *Watchman Examiner*. Brock noted that the conflict really involved three, and not two, parties. At one extreme were the fundamentalists, who "believe that teachers of rationalism should not be tolerated in Baptist schools." At the other extreme were the liberals, who professed to believe in the New Testament, but who reserved the right to "deny the miraculous or virgin birth of our Lord, his atoning death, and his resurrection."[74]

In between these two groups was a third group. Brock designated it the "Organization Group," noting that it was made up of those who were burdened to keep the organizational machinery in operation. These individuals were most concerned with the practical situation and more likely to consider matters of policy and expediency than questions of doctrine.[75]

Brock was almost certainly correct in his observations, and this factor was crucial in the conflict within the Northern Baptist Convention. The agencies of the NBC had badly overcommitted themselves in view of the $100,000,000 drive. When resistance developed and the drive collapsed, the convention found itself in a financial crisis. In the face of the crisis, the liberals made a

---

73. Ibid., 802.
74. Charles R. Brock, "Confessions of Faith at Indianapolis," *Watchman Examiner*, July 6, 1922, 842.
75. Ibid.

concentrated effort to push for denominational loyalty, unity, and cooperation. They certainly did not want to disfellowship the fundamentalists; indeed,
they needed the fundamentalists' money. For the most part, they went out of
their way to be welcoming. For example, after defeating the fundamentalists
at Indianapolis, they hosted the fundamentalist leaders at "a delightful lun-
cheon, at which fraternity and good cheer reigned supreme."[76] This kind of
apparent magnanimity was precisely what the middle group wanted to see.

On the other hand, the fundamentalists placed themselves in the position
of aggressors. They wanted to limit the influence of the liberals and, in some
cases, to eject the liberals from the convention altogether. From the organi-
zationalist point of view, this militancy was alarming. The convention was
facing a crisis. If the fundamentalists had their way, the convention agencies
would suddenly be deprived of much of their leadership. Professors, deans,
presidents, and secretaries would be sacked throughout the Northern Baptist Convention. From the moderate perspective, the fundamentalist agenda
courted disaster.

Worse yet, the fundamentalists appeared to have no positive plan to reclaim the convention or to bolster its ministries. At best, they lacked the
forethought even to plan their own strategies (Brock admitted as much). At
worst, they seemed to be divided among themselves. Thus, while the silent
majority of convention Baptists certainly sympathized with the fundamentalist doctrine, they felt that they needed the liberals. The organizationalists,
while doctrinally conservative, were more afraid of the fundamentalists than
they were of the liberals.

Most Northern Baptists were probably conservatives, but not all conservatives were fundamentalists. The fundamentalists were militants. Their primary concern was doctrinal and their goal was for the convention to find its
unity in its doctrinal base. Other conservatives, however, were moderates.
Their primary concern was organizational peace and perpetuity, and their
goal was for the convention to find its unity in a shared work that would pre-
serve the organizational structures.

The defeat of the fundamentalists has to be explained by the difference between militants and moderates. In this instance a large center group of moderates determined the outcome in favor of an aggressive but affable minority of
modernists. These moderates were presumably conservatives who believed
in the Virgin Birth and the blood atonement, but they identified with the
modernists against the fundamentalists. Their commitment to the absolutes
of the Bible was a qualified one.

The fundamentalists were not united among themselves. From the

---

76. Curtis Lee Laws, "Sidelights 1922," 802.

beginning, Van Osdel expressed reservations about Massee's lack of militancy. Even before the Indianapolis convention he had decided to back Neighbour in founding the Baptist Bible Union. Certainly the defeat at Indianapolis did nothing to bolster his confidence in the fundamentalist conference. He was ready for an organization that would be as militant at the national level as the Michigan Orthodox Baptist Association was at the state level. He and Neighbour set to work immediately to bring it into existence.

W. B. Riley in his study at First Baptist Church, Minneapolis.

Oliver W. Van Osdel in front of the Wealthy Street Baptist Church parsonage, 1931.

4 The Baptist Bible Union

THE DEFEAT AT INDIANAPOLIS was crushing for the fundamentalists, but Robert E. Neighbour and Oliver W. Van Osdel had already prepared their next move. Van Osdel had already warned Massee that he intended to help Neighbour organize a Baptist Bible Union. After the convention voted down the New Hampshire Confession, Neighbour called for a prayer meeting in one of the hotels. An initial, informal organization came out of this meeting. Neighbour, Van Osdel, and William L. Pettingill (dean of the Philadelphia School of the Bible and pastor in Wilmington, Delaware) were appointed as an executive committee with Neighbour as the chair. Their job was to send out a call and to draft a constitution and confession of faith.[1]

By early August, the three had prepared a "Call and Manifesto." In order to gather signatures for the call, they sent a letter to fundamentalist leaders throughout the Northern Baptist Convention. Their goal was to gather fifty signatures. They ended up with 135.

One of the pastors who signed the call was J. Frank Norris, pastor of First Baptist Church in Fort Worth, Texas. Norris was a Southern Baptist, and his involvement signaled a wider Baptist Bible Union. By 1922 Norris had already built the largest congregation in the United States and had begun to establish a reputation for flamboyance and eccentricity. He edited his own paper, the *Searchlight*, which received nationwide distribution. Besides signing the call, Norris published it twice in the *Searchlight*.[2]

1. The principal treatment of the Baptist Bible Union is Robert G. Delnay, "History of the Baptist Bible Union" (ThD diss., Dallas Theological Seminary, 1963), later published in installments in the *Central Conservative Baptist Quarterly* (1964–1965), and still later as *A History of the Baptist Bible Union* (Winston-Salem, NC: Piedmont Bible College Press, 1972). Neither of the reprints included the documentation. All references will be to the original dissertation. Worth mentioning is Roland T. Nelson, "*Fundamentalism and the Northern Baptist Convention*" (PhD diss., University of Chicago, 1964).

2. One instance was in the *Searchlight*, September 1, 1922, 3. On Norris see George W. Dollar, *A History of Fundamentalism in America*, 122–234; Michael E. Schepis, *J. Frank Norris: The*

Although liberalism was not as far advanced in the Southern Baptist Convention as it was in the Northern Baptist Convention, Norris believed that it was present. He also believed that the Southern Baptist Convention had become a machine that dominated local churches. In 1922 he was protesting against liberalism, centralization, and evolution within the convention. His church would be expelled from the Baptist General Convention of Texas in 1924. Already, during the fall of 1922, he could anticipate the objections that the convention leadership would raise against the Baptist Bible Union.

> Of course we expect the powers that be to come out at once in the Baptist Standard and cry that somebody is starting a division among Baptists.
>
> We answer back and say no, it is not a division. It is simply a group of men who love the truth and who are opposed to modernism, evolution or any phase of modern infidelity and who are opposed to ecclesiastical dictation, who in the name of the Great Head of the Church are banding themselves together to declare a truceless war on these, the great evils that have afflicted Christianity in all its history.[3]

Evidently, Norris did not see the Baptist Bible Union as a separatist organization. Neighbour and Van Osdel did. Van Osdel wrote, "The Baptist Bible Union proposes a fellowship of Baptist churches, and Baptist Believers, untrammeled by unholy and unscriptural alliances." This did not mean that every pastor or church had to leave the convention, as Van Osdel made clear: "Individuals or local churches holding membership in the Union are left to their own pleasure as to maintaining other Baptist denominational affiliations." Still, the two founders clearly planned that the Union as a body would refrain from immediate participation in the affairs of the convention. Any protests it might raise or criticisms it might offer would come from outside.[4]

Norris was a rising star, and his support was not to be slighted. Before long, Neighbour prevailed upon him to join the executive committee. With Van Osdel's help, he also recruited W. B. Riley of Minneapolis. Their presence gave the Baptist Bible Union two powerful voices.

The Brooklyn committee and other supporters of the Conference on

---

Fascinating, Controversial Life of a Forgotten Figure of the Twentieth Century (Bloomington, IN: West Bow Press, 2012); Kelly David Pigott, "A Comparison of the Leadership of George W. Truett and J. Frank Norris in Church, Denominational, Interdenominational, and Political Affairs" (PhD diss., Southwestern Baptist Theological Seminary, 1993); Samuel K. Tullock, "The Transformation of American Fundamentalism: The Life and Career of John Franklyn Norris" (PhD diss., University of Texas at Dallas, 1997); Charles Lynn Walker, "The Ethical Vision of Fundamentalism: An Inquiry into the Ethic of John Franklyn Norris" (PhD diss., Southwestern Baptist Theological Seminary, 1985).

3. *Searchlight*, October 6, 1922, 2.

4. Oliver W. Van Osdel, "The Baptist Bible Union of America," *Baptist Temple News*, September 9, 1922, 1.

Baptist Fundamentals were not happy with the emergence of the Baptist Bible Union. As they saw it, the best that the new organization could do was to divide their forces. At worst, it could prove to be a rival or even an opponent. Van Osdel went out of his way to allay these fears. He insisted that the Baptist Bible Union was not "in opposition or instead of anything good." The two movements had different purposes that would keep them from coming into conflict. The convention fundamentalists were trying to purge modernism from the convention and its boards and to take control for themselves. Van Osdel stated, "This is right and no true Baptist should hesitate one moment about doing his very best to aid the Fundamentalist movement and undertaking." The purpose of the Baptist Bible Union, however, was primarily educational, "making men sufficiently intelligent to submit to [biblical] authority." Consequently, a true Baptist "may be a zealous Fundamentalist and a Bible Unionist at the same time without conflict."[5]

These words did not reassure Joshua Gravett, pastor of Galilee Baptist in Denver. Gravett was only two years younger than Riley, and was to Colorado what Riley was to Minnesota. In January 1924 he published an article in the *Baptist*, giving his reasons for refusing to join the Baptist Bible Union. Van Osdel responded in moderate tones, referring to Gravett as "a very devout man, very generally beloved by orthodox Baptists," and addressing the Colorado pastor as "our beloved brother Gravitt [*sic*]." Van Osdel conceded Gravett's right to express his opinions, but wondered why he would choose to do it in a way that provided enjoyment for the liberal publishers of the *Baptist* while injuring a movement of "men who love the Lord and are true to Him." Van Osdel then stated the reasons that he saw the Baptist Bible Union as an "imperative necessity."[6]

On January 3 the executive committee met at the LaSalle Hotel in Chicago. Apparently the executive committee meetings were rather open affairs, attended by a variety of interested leaders. The main business in Chicago was to prepare a declaration of faith, for which Norris and Riley were given the main responsibility. The committee also discussed plans for a first conference, with St. Louis as a potential meeting place.[7]

Shortly after the Chicago meeting, someone on the executive committee produced thirty thousand copies of a pamphlet, "Vital Questions and Their Answers Concerning the Baptist Bible Union of America." The document was

5. Oliver W. Van Osdel, "The Bible Union of America," *Baptist Temple News*, December 30, 1932, 2.

6. Oliver W. Van Osdel, "The Baptist Bible Union an Imperative Necessity," *Baptist Temple News*, February 10, 1923, 1–2. There are two completely different editions of the *Baptist Temple News* published under this date, both showing the same volume and number. The reason for the duplication is not known.

7. Oliver W. Van Osdel, "Bible Union Meeting," *Baptist Temple News*, January 13, 1923, 2.

evidently prepared on the initiative of Neighbour and Van Osdel. Riley had nothing to do with writing it, though his name appeared on it. The pamphlet stated that the apostasy in the denominations could not be purged. Consequently, a new fellowship separated from the apostasy must be formed. In short, the pamphlet was a clear declaration of separatist intentions by the founders of the Union.[8]

When Riley saw the pamphlet, he was horrified. He ordered the destruction of all thirty thousand copies. Charles F. Fredman managed to save a few. This episode provided the first hint that Neighbour and Van Osdel were about to be edged out by more forceful leaders. It was also an early indication that Riley could be counted on to oppose any move toward overt separation.[9]

Riley and Norris found time to meet in Keokuk, Iowa, that winter to prepare the confession of faith. Norris later recalled days "when we would walk through the snow storm, sit up all night long, hunt up Scriptures." By late February they had the confession in workable form. They presented it when the executive committee met in Toledo. The committee approved the confession and agreed that the first meeting of the Baptist Bible Union would be held in Kansas City on May 10–15. This was the week before the Southern Baptist Convention, and the plan was to allow pastors to attend both meetings.[10]

The original "Call and Manifesto" of the Baptist Bible Union had stated that the Second Advent would be "premillennial, personal, and visible." The confession that Norris and Riley prepared did not use the word *premillennial*, but it did specify that Christ would return to "rule the world in righteousness and peace for 1,000 years." This strong premillennialism led to protests, particularly in the South. It also created a problem for T. T. Shields, whom Riley was trying to bring into the leadership of the Baptist Bible Union.[11]

T. T. Shields was pastor of the Jarvis Street Baptist Church in Toronto. Like Riley and Norris, he had won renown as a pulpit orator. He would work on a sermon all week, then write it out in manuscript form on Saturday night and stitch it up into a little booklet. He would carry the booklet into the pulpit in his pocket, though he would not look at it while he preached. This technique allowed him to combine the force of extemporization with the precision of a

8. Delnay, *History of the Baptist Bible Union,* 53; 290–91.

9. Charles F. Fredman to T. T. Shields, June 1, 1929.

10. J. Frank Norris to W. B. Riley, May 4, 1929; Van Osdel, "Executive Committee Meeting of the Bible Union," *Baptist Temple News,* March 3, 1923, 1.

11. Van Osdel, "Baptist Bible Union," *Baptist Temple News,* September 9, 1922, 3; *Searchlight,* October 6, 1922, 2; Delnay, "History of the Baptist Bible Union," 286; Andrew Christopher Smith, *"'Flocking by Themselves': Fundamentalism, Fundraising, and the Bureaucratization of the Southern Baptist Convention, 1919–1925"* (PhD diss., Vanderbilt University, 2011), 100–01. On Shields see Leslie K. Tarr, *Shields of Canada* (Grand Rapids: Baker Book House, 1967); George W. Dollar, *A History of Fundamentalism in America,* 106–12; and especially Gerald L. Priest, "T. T. Shields the Fundamentalist: Man of Controversy," *Detroit Baptist Seminary Journal* (Fall 2005): 67–101.

manuscripted sermon. He did not memorize his sermons, but he knew so well what he wanted to say that the words came flowing into his mind.[12]

During the previous few years, Shields had begun a protest movement in the Canadian convention, just as Riley had in the North and Norris had in the South. Riley, perhaps concerned about the separatism of Neighbour and Van Osdel, was trying to introduce Shields into the leadership in the fledgling Baptist Bible Union. The problem was that Shields was an amillennialist who rejected dispensational theology. For Shields to feel welcome in the BBU, the premillennialism would have to go.

The only other individual who was added to the leadership was A. C. Dixon. It is not clear who recruited Dixon, but by the time the call was issued for the Kansas City meeting, he was listed as a member of the executive committee. Dixon had become a venerated figure among Baptists, especially in the South. He was almost as old as Van Osdel, and the list of his accomplishments was impressive. His name gave the executive committee an element of gravity that it might otherwise have lacked. He arrived as a latecomer, however, and never really exercised significant influence in the councils of the Baptist Bible Union. By the time of the Kansas City meeting, the initiative had really shifted to Riley, Shields, and Norris.

The Kansas City meeting was held under a big tent. During the conference, somewhere between 3,500 and 5,000 attendees found shade and shelter under the billowing canvas. These included representatives from Canada and from every state in the union. The conference opened on the evening of Thursday, May 10, with an address from Neighbour. During the next five days, more than forty speakers appeared on the platform. Every member of the executive committee addressed the crowd. So did John R. Straton, Mordecai Hamm (under whose preaching Billy Graham would later be converted), R. T. Ketcham, H. H. Savage, and Louis Entzminger. The latter three were still relatively unknown, but they would become prominent leaders in different branches of Baptist fundamentalism.[13]

The Baptist Bible Union was composed of individual members. Officers were elected by the members and all business came before the membership for approval. In Kansas City, the group chose Shields as president—an office that he would hold until the eventual reorganization of the BBU. Neighbour, the real founder, was elected secretary of the organization. The executive committee remained intact for the moment, but another layer of governance was added with an elected council. When the confession was presented, all traces of premillennialism had been expunged. The members endorsed a statement

---

12. Joseph M. Stowell Jr., interviewed by Kevin T. Bauder, June 23, 1982.
13. Joseph M. Stowell Jr., *Background and History of the General Association of Regular Baptist Churches* (Hayward, CA: Gospel Tracts Unlimited: 1949), 22.

that all Baptists, regardless of millennial views, would be welcome. The crowd also approved resolutions condemning evolution and Cornelius Woelfkin. It then pledged $30,000 to help Baptists in France.[14]

At Kansas City, the Baptist Bible Union adopted an agenda that was as definite as the plans of the fundamentalist conferences had been vague. It had a definite membership. It had definite leadership who represented the potential for a continent-wide movement. Its president articulated a definite mission: "What then shall our answer to Modernism's declaration of war be? There can be but one answer. The Baptist Bible Union is designed to mobilize the conservative Baptist forces of the Continent, for the express purpose of declaring and waging relentless and uncompromising war on Modernism on all fronts."[15]

Growth of the Baptist Bible Union

The Northern Baptist Convention opened a week after the Baptist Bible Union adjourned. The 1923 convention was held in Atlantic City, and the only prominent figure from the Baptist Bible Union was Straton. The convention had been planned as a moderates' panacea. The convention president, Frederick E. Taylor, was a well-known moderate. The convention preacher, W. W. Bustard, had been one of the signers of the call for the preconvention conference in 1920. The convention organizers had done all they could to pacify the fundamentalist faction.

Nevertheless, they had overlooked one small matter. They had invited W. H. P. Faunce, president of Brown University, as keynote speaker. Faunce was one of the most conspicuous liberals in the convention, and the only school president to refuse to reply to the questions of the investigating committee in 1920. When Faunce was introduced, Straton walked to the front of the auditorium, climbed up on a chair, and began protesting the liberal's presence on the platform. Strictly speaking, he was within his rights as a delegate to the convention. Almost immediately, however, his objections were drowned out by a storm of hissing, jeering, and calls of "Put him out!" After restoring order, Taylor ruled that, as a guest of the convention, Faunce would be permitted to speak. When Faunce finally stepped to the podium, he received an ovation from the crowd that lasted for several minutes.[16]

---

14. Oliver W. Van Osdel, "Four Great Addresses," *Baptist Temple News*, May 26, 1923, 1–3; "By-Laws and Resolutions of the Baptist Bible Union of America," *Watchman Examiner*, May 24, 1923, 662–63; Delnay, "History of the Baptist Bible Union," 56–57.

15. T. T. Shields, "Address to Baptist Bible Union," *Gospel Witness*, June 21, 1923, 1.

16. "Baptists' Convention Thrown into Turmoil by Dr. Straton's Assault on President Faunce," *Rome* [New York] *Daily Sentinel*, May 23, 1923, 1; "Baptists Hit Steam Roller," *Reading Eagle*, May 25, 1923, 1; John Roach Straton, "Why I Objected to Dr. Faunce at Atlantic

The fundamentalists attempted no new maneuvers at Atlantic City, but some old business caught up with them. At Indianapolis, the convention's executive committee had made a recommendation to deny churches representation unless they supported the convention financially. When it was clear that the motion would win, the liberals allowed it to be sent into committee. Now, in Atlantic City, the motion returned to the floor. After the fundamentalists failed to table it, the motion carried by a substantial margin—a significant defeat for the fundamentalists. Then someone moved that churches be given complete freedom to designate their giving. Massee quickly endorsed the plan and the motion carried handily. The fundamentalists claimed a victory: by designating their funds, they thought they could avoid financing liberals within the convention.[17] For the liberals, however, it was all a matter of bookkeeping. A dollar given to a conservative would free up another dollar that could go to a liberal. Designation made absolutely no difference in the long run.

The next week, the executive committee of the Baptist Bible Union met at Wealthy Street in Grand Rapids to lay plans and to conduct a conference for the church. Shields, Norris, Riley, and Neighbour all spoke. A communication from Straton proposed a merger between the BBU and his Fundamentalist League. The executive committee liked the idea. They also wanted E. C. Miller, a member of Straton's church, to join the executive committee. They talked about starting an official publication and they agreed to appeal to the BBU council for help in organizing regional and local chapters. Finally, they hired Edith Rebman, a member of Jarvis Street, to perform secretarial work for the Union.[18]

In September, Shields hosted a local Baptist Bible Union conference at Jarvis Street. With the exception of Miller, who was not a preacher, every member of the executive committee spoke. The question of an official periodical came up again and Riley was authorized to begin publication. Instead, he began his own paper, the *Baptist Beacon*. In 1926 the paper was merged with Norris's *Searchlight*, to which Riley became (temporarily) a regular contributor.

As it turned out, E. C. Miller had big plans for the Baptist Bible Union. He wanted the Union to take the initiative in building what amounted to a Baptist empire in Jerusalem. He envisioned a church, a college, a hospital, an orphanage, an asylum, and perhaps more. One can imagine how the proposal must

City," *Watchman Examiner*, June 28, 1923, 824–25; Van Osdel, "The Straton Incident," *Baptist Temple News*, August 18, 1923, 1–2; George H. Moulds, "The Conflict Between the Modernists and the Fundamentalists in the Northern Baptist Convention Since 1920" (MA thesis, State University of Iowa, 1940), 121–22.

17. For example, see "The Foreign Mission Controversy," *Watchman Examiner*, January 21, 1924, 133.

18. Stowell, *Background and History*, 22; Delnay, "History of the Baptist Bible Union," 69.

have sounded to the seasoned pastors on the executive committee, and they voted to defer action. From that moment, Miller's interest in the BBU began to wane. His antipathy was increased by a falling out with Straton, and he left the executive committee the next year.

The executive committee talked about hiring a field representative, but the one person to whom they offered the job delayed responding until they withdrew the offer. They also talked about an expanded ministry of publication. In fact, they authorized the printing and distribution of a forty-seven page booklet, *A Call to Arms*. Finally, the executive committee (probably encouraged by Van Osdel) discussed what to do about missions. Their decision was that the BBU would not start its own missionary agency, at least not for the time being. Instead, the executive committee would maintain a list of independent, Baptist agencies that would affirm the Bible Union statement of faith. This list would be supplied to all inquiring churches.

Most of the BBU leaders were aggressively involved in missions. Riley, Shields, and especially Van Osdel wanted the Union to stress the importance of missionary work. Van Osdel and Neighbour had both helped to establish the General Council on Cooperating Baptist Missions (the Mid-Africa Mission). Wealthy Street had sent out missionaries under six independent agencies. Though his official influence was eclipsed by the energy of Riley, Shields, and Norris, Van Osdel continued to work from the sidelines of the executive committee, exerting quiet pressure to promote missions.

The leadership's commitment to biblical missions was matched by a sense of outrage when modernists emerged on the mission field. Liberals were drawn to the mission field for two reasons: first, because they found in foreign fields an opportunity to pursue the social gospel and, second, because the mission field was far from home and consequently an ecclesiastically safe place to be a modernist. Conservatives had been aware of problems on the mission field for some time. Returning from a tour of foreign fields in 1917, A. H. Strong wrote,

> We are losing our faith in the Bible, and our determination to stand for its teachings. We are introducing into our ministry men who either never knew their Lord, or who have lost their faith in him and their love for him. The unbelief in our seminary teaching is like a blinding mist which is slowly settling down upon our churches, and is gradually abolishing, not only all definite views of Christian doctrine, but also all conviction of duty to "contend earnestly for the faith" of our fathers.[19]

19. Augustus H. Strong, *A Tour of the Missions: Observations and Conclusions* (Philadelphia: Griffith and Rowland, 1918), 192.

According to Strong, missionaries who accepted the new theology tended to substitute education for evangelism. With nothing positive to preach, they simply devoted themselves to teaching English. For Strong, putting such people on the mission field threatened to handicap missions and to paralyze missionary influence. Strong observed, "The preaching of the old gospel of sin and salvation seems almost a thing of the past."[20]

Strong did not say just where the liberals were. Nevertheless, fundamentalists became convinced that the Northern Baptist Convention was both redefining the task for foreign missions and sending liberals to the mission field. The problem lay in finding evidence to prove the heresy of missionaries halfway around the world.[21]

The evidence appeared rather dramatically in 1923. A member of Straton's church, Bertha D. Henshaw, had spent eight years as a missionary in China. Upon returning to the United States, she was employed by the New York office of the American Baptist Foreign Mission Society. In the course of her work she had to deal with correspondence between the society executives and the missionaries. Over a three-year period she became convinced that modernists were indeed being appointed to missionary service, and that the ABFMS office held the proof. She tried to approach the board with her concerns, but she found only resistance. Thereupon, she went to her pastor instead.

His protest against Faunce had been silenced in Atlantic City, but Straton was about to give the convention its comeuppance. Backed by a committee of thirty, he walked into the office of the foreign mission society in New York and demanded access to the documents. He specifically cited a letter from the president of a missionary college who had said, "We do not want too many conservatives here to smell out heresy." Caught by surprise, the mission board stonewalled the committee. The executives accused Straton of wanting to ransack the files. He replied that he was looking for only a few specific items that he could name. The board's response was that they had to protect the confidentiality of their missionaries' correspondence, but that they would investigate specific accusations if documentation could be provided. This was playing to Straton's strength, and he responded with names, dates, and file numbers. The board appointed an investigating committee, which eventually produced a report that Straton would call an "evasion."[22]

---

20. Strong, *A Tour of the Missions*, 193–95.
21. Robert E. Neighbour, "Modernized Missions," *Baptist Temple News*, February 10, 1923, 2–3.
22. Oliver W. Van Osdel, "Are Modernists At the Head?" *Baptist Temple News*, July 14, 1923, 1–3; Frederick L. Anderson and William B. Lipphard, "A Statement by the Board of Managers of the American Baptist Foreign Mission Society," *Watchman Examiner*, December 27, 1923, 1657; John Roach Straton and Max Schimpf, "A Statement of the Fundamentalist League of Greater New York," *Watchman Examiner*, January 3, 1924, 20–21; Anderson and Lipphard, "Statement by the Board of Managers of the American Baptist Foreign Mission Society," 82–85;

Then in November 1923 the foreign missions board announced what came to be called the "Inclusive Policy." The substance of the policy was that the foreign missions board should reflect the various theological elements that were present in the Northern Baptist Convention. The board recognized that some limits existed, but was vague about what those limits might be. A statement of the Inclusive Policy was published, among other places, in the *Watchman Examiner*. The immediate (and probably unintended) effect of the statement was to inflame criticism against the board.[23]

At just about that time, Straton's health broke. For rest, he was advised to travel abroad. Since he had been the key to pushing the missions controversy, it was set on the back burner until he returned.

The issue was still simmering as the Northern Baptist Convention prepared for its 1924 meeting in Milwaukee. Because the controversy was so important, the executive committee scheduled the Baptist Bible Union to meet in Milwaukee both before and after the convention. Massee tried to call for a general prayer meeting instead of a preconvention conference, but the Bible Union men believed that the time and place had come for a direct challenge over the missions controversy.[24] Massee went ahead with his prayer meetings, stationing underlings by the entrances to buttonhole attendees away from the Bible Union sessions.

By the time of the Milwaukee meeting, Dixon, Pettingill, and Miller had tendered their resignations from leadership of the Baptist Bible Union. Max Schimpf, a New York insurance man, was becoming more active in leadership and may have been added to the executive committee. Norris did not attend the Milwaukee meeting, leaving Riley, Shields, and Straton as the three most prominent speakers. In addition to their pre- and post-convention conferences, the Bible Union men met regularly for discussion after the convention's evening session. The spontaneous prayer meetings during these sessions could go on for hours.

For the Baptist Bible Union, modernism in missions was the biggest problem, but there were others. One was that the convention had been using the M&M Board to try to enforce standardized pastoral training, issuing a curriculum that included a significant dose of liberal theology. The Union was also concerned about the convention employees' right to vote: they foresaw

---

John Roach Straton et al, "Why Is the Foreign Mission Society's Statement Unsatisfactory?" *Watchman Examiner*, January 21, 1924, 146–49; Robert R. Mathisen, ed., *Critical Issues in American Religious History: A Reader* (Waco, TX: Baylor University Press, 2001), 469–70; Delnay, "History of the Baptist Bible Union," 74–75, 82; Moulds, "Conflict," 194–97.

23. Chester E. Tulga, *The Story of the Inclusive Policy of the American Baptist Foreign Mission Society 1923–1944* (Chicago: Conservative Baptist Fellowship of Northern Baptists, n.d.), 3–7.

24. Curtis Lee Laws, "Sidelights of the Milwaukee Convention," *Watchman Examiner*, June 12, 1924, 738.

that the hundreds of salaried servants could easily swing any decision in the direction of convention liberals.

Their main thrust, however, was to expose liberalism on the mission field and to challenge the Inclusive Policy. Their strategy focused on a foreign missionary named W. R. Hartley. The foreign board had interviewed Hartley after his return from Asia in March. When asked whether he believed in the deity of Christ, Hartley responded, "No, I do not." Nevertheless, the board had voted nine to four that Hartley was an acceptable missionary.[25]

The Hartley situation gave the Baptist Bible Union exactly what it needed: a clear, documented episode of the foreign board approving an acknowledged modernist. The first night of the convention, the men from the fundamentalist conference joined the Bible Union men for a strategy session. At that point, Massee spoke up. He had been approached by C. Wallace Petty, convention speaker and liberal strategist, with a proposal: "If you Fundamentalists will agree not to spring the Hartley matter on the floor of the Convention, we will stand with you for an investigation of the entire Foreign Mission situation."[26]

True to form, the liberals were trading away an immediate, urgent problem for a more distant one—but one that they were more likely to be able to control. Nevertheless, the prospect was too tempting to refuse, and the fundamentalists agreed to the bargain. The Hartley affair would be buried.

On Thursday afternoon, F. L. Anderson of the foreign mission society delivered his report. He explained and defended the Inclusive Policy, but then supplemented his remarks by introducing what he called the "Evangelical Policy."

> [W]e have demanded that all our officers and missionaries are loyal to the gospel. We will appoint only suitable evangelical men and women; we will appoint evangelicals, and we will not appoint non-evangelicals. And by the gospel we mean the good news of the free forgiveness of sin and eternal life (beginning now and going on forever) through a vital union with the crucified and risen Christ, which brings men into union and fellowship with God. This salvation is graciously offered on the sole condition of repentance and faith in Christ and has in it the divine power of regeneration and sanctification through the Spirit. The only reason we have for accepting this gospel is our belief in the deity of Christ in whom we see the Father, a faith founded on the trustworthiness of the Scriptures, and the fact that we have experienced this salvation in our own hearts.[27]

25. Bruce Shelley, *A History of Conservative Baptists*, 3rd ed. (Wheaton, IL: Conservative Baptist Press, 1971), 16.

26. Bruce Shelley, *Conservative Baptists, a Story of Twentieth Century Dissent* (Denver: Conservative Baptist Theological Seminary, 1960), 106.

27. "Dr. Anderson's Statement," *Watchman Examiner*, June 12, 1924, 748–49; *Shall Northern*

After Anderson's address, J. C. Massee moved that the president appoint a committee of five to inquire into the policies and practices of the foreign board. As agreed, Petty seconded Massee's motion. Unexpectedly, however, Straton offered an amendment that would have enlarged the committee to eleven members, including himself and Riley. The amendment was laughed down. Then, after some deliberation, the convention approved Massee's motion by a substantial majority. Of the five members who were appointed to the committee, however, only Massee was identifiable as a fundamentalist. No Bible Union men were included. In spite of that, the fundamentalists claimed a victory.[28]

Two other issues at the convention affected the Baptist Bible Union. The first involved the "Stockholm Message," a minimalist statement of belief that had been adopted by the Baptist World Alliance in 1923. The statement actually affirmed certain fundamentals, including the Incarnation and vicarious atonement. It also took a rather strong position in favor of the social gospel. For that reason, the Baptist Bible Union was ambivalent toward the Stockholm Message, but Massee's fundamentalists saw an opportunity to get the convention to adopt it as its own statement. Accordingly, one of the conference fundamentalists moved that the convention "accept and issue without addition or subtraction" the Stockholm Message, provided that it never be made a test of faith or service.[29]

One of the Bible Union men offered a motion that attempted to substitute a statement similar to the New Hampshire Confession. The substitution was voted down, and then the Stockholm Message was accepted by a substantial majority. Once again both sides could claim victory: the fundamentalists, because the convention had formally identified itself with a statement of faith, and the modernists, because the social gospel now had official doctrinal standing.[30]

If these were not exactly triumphs, at least the liberals were being forced to make concessions. In this atmosphere, Riley decided to challenge the attempt to standardize pastoral preparation. The convention had approved a reading course for ministers who did not have formal training. The reading course was heavily weighted with liberal theology. What Riley wanted to do was to offer an alternative reading course that emphasized Baptist orthodoxy. Unfortunately, Riley's motion was referred to the committee on resolutions, and for a time it looked as if it would never see the light of day. At that point, Max

Baptists Set up Another Foreign Mission Society? New York: American Baptist Foreign Mission Society, 1943.

28. Moulds, "Conflict," 199–200; Delnay, "History of the Baptist Bible Union," 92.

29. *Annual of the Northern Baptist Convention 1924* (Philadelphia: American Baptist Publication Society, 1924), 45.

30. Ibid., 100; Moulds, "Conflict," 70–73, 93n45.

Schimpf managed to get the matter diverted to a special committee of three, one of whom was Riley himself. That afternoon the motion was returned to the floor with a recommendation that both reading lists be published side by side. The success of this motion represented a modest victory, not only for Riley, but for the Baptist Bible Union.[31]

After the 1924 convention, both conference fundamentalists and Baptist Bible Union members could congratulate themselves upon greater triumphs than they had ever achieved before—or than they would ever achieve again. Humble as these gains were, they marked high water for Baptist fundamentalism within the Northern Baptist Convention. Over the next years the fundamentalists would put themselves through near-frenetic exertions in order to advance their agenda a bit further, but then calamity would strike.

The Decline of the Baptist Bible Union

Indeed, the misfortunes began shortly after the 1924 convention when Riley was involved in an automobile crash. Ignoring doctor's orders, he tried to continue working. The effort led to a complete collapse that put him out of commission for months. It also temporarily deprived the Baptist Bible Union of one of its most vigorous leaders. Perhaps it was his absence that prevented the Bible Union from acting on the resignations of Dixon and Pettingill—at any rate, their names were still listed on the executive committee.[32]

In July, Laws ran an editorial in the *Watchman Examiner* titled "Let Us Now Pull Together." He implied that, while the program of the Northern Baptist Convention was not perfect, it was the "best practical plan" for the immediate future. He urged fundamentalists to put their support behind the denominational program. Van Osdel, however, would have none of it. He reproduced the core of Laws's editorial in the *Baptist Temple News*, then pointed out that the real question was, "Have we a Bible?" If not, then there was no need for missions. If so, then why support modernism on the mission field? The investigative committee that had been appointed in Milwaukee was simply a waste of time. The only two possible results would be that "it tells us what we already know, or denies what actually exists." He concluded, "We have missionary money and we intend to increase it, but we insist that it must go to support men as missionaries who believe in the integrity and authority of the Bible."[33]

This was not the only time that Van Osdel disagreed with Laws. Writing

---

31. Moulds, "Conflict," 129; Delnay, "History of the Baptist Bible Union," 93–94.
32. "Illness of Dr. W. B. Riley," *Baptist Temple News*, August 9, 1924, 2.
33. Oliver W. Van Osdel, "Let Us Now Pull Together," *Baptist Temple News*, July 15, 1924, 1–2.

about Riley's illness in mid-August, Van Osdel commented, "Modernists are unable to conceal their joy that Dr. Riley has been laid aside."[34] Laws felt called upon to censure this remark. In his reply to Laws, Van Osdel offered his observations about the charity and ethics of modernists.

> Our statement was based on facts. At a recent meeting when Modernists were present in large numbers, the joy was expressed over the illness of Dr. Riley that we have described; Modernists have wrapped human excrement in copies of The Temple News and sent it to us through the mails. If the Watchman-Examiner was sufficiently out and out for the Word of God to be out and out against Modernism, they would soon learn for themselves by some actual experiences what is the real animus of Modernism. Modernists are not Christians. They do not believe the things that would make a man a Christian. Some of them may be educated gentlemen, but not all. However, educated gentlemen are not all and always Christians. Modernists are against the Bible, against the Christ of the Bible, against the blood and the plan of salvation the Bible proposes.[35]

By now, Van Osdel had simply lost patience with the entire denominational situation. Privately, he expressed the belief that the time had come for the Baptist Bible Union to capitalize on its momentum and build an independent movement of its own. He insisted that "we ought to have an organization, associations, and conventions of our own, and that we should undertake an aggressive program to advance our work, positively and directly and without reference to what the modernists may do when they get together." This move should take place "at once."[36]

He backed up his words with his own actions. In addition to supporting independent agencies like the Mid-Africa Mission, Wealthy Street was sending its own missionaries to the field. Hardly an issue of the Baptist Temple News passed without either some announcement of another missionary who was being sent or some report from a missionary who had been sent. The number of missionaries quickly exceeded the ability of Wealthy Street to support them, and funds began coming in from other churches. Wealthy Street soon found itself acting as a de facto mission board, though it would never have claimed that label.

Other churches were also following this pattern. Neighbour was sending out missionaries from Elyria, Riley from Minneapolis, Shields from Toronto, and Norris from Fort Worth. Smaller churches were also following the example of these great churches. In fact, it appears that the protest against modernism, while the most visible and public work of the Baptist Bible Union, was

34. Oliver W. Van Osdel, "Dr. W. B. Riley," Baptist Temple News, August 16, 1924, 2.
35. Oliver W. Van Osdel, "Criticized," Baptist Temple News, October 11, 1924, 3.
36. Oliver W. Van Osdel to Thomas T. Shields, October 8, 1924.

actually a secondary concern. The work of evangelism, biblical exposition, and missions was closest to the hearts of the leaders—especially leaders like Neighbour and Van Osdel. The confrontation with liberalism occurred only because liberalism blocked the ability of Baptist churches to pursue the real work of ministry in a biblical way.

Early in 1925 the Baptist Bible Union sponsored a regional conference in Chicago. The result was an unusual display of catholicity, expressed in the form of a call to believers of all denominations to unite in concerted prayer for revival. The Baptist Bible Union asked that, for the three days leading up to April 5, churches, mission halls, and other places of Christian assembly should be opened for prayer. The call was quite specific about the distinction between denominational differences and differences with liberalism: "Between Modernism and Fundamentalism, there is a great gulf fixed; but between true believers of every denomination, the unity of the Spirit still obtains."[37]

Shortly after this statement was released, A. C. Dixon shocked the Baptist Bible Union by publicly resigning both his seat on the executive committee and his membership. According to Dixon's biographer and second wife, Dixon was reacting mainly against Norris's influence and methods. In his resignation, Dixon himself wrote, "I am convinced that the Baptist Bible Union of America has fulfilled its great mission, and ought, therefore, to be dissolved." Dixon then expressed his confidence that "God will lead the Fundamentalists to ultimate victory in our beloved denomination."[38]

The resignation was published by Dixon's wife. Dixon himself was already suffering from the illness that would soon take his life. He had been incapacitated for some weeks and was gone by midyear. As soon as Dixon died, the enemies of the Baptist Bible Union tried to capitalize on the resignation, and the BBU leadership was forced to respond. With Dixon no longer able to speak for himself, Riley suggested that the rationale for the resignation came more from Mrs. Dixon than from the aging minister. Like Riley, Van Osdel believed that Dixon had been misrepresented.[39]

Shortly after Dixon's resignation, new information indicated that the investigation of the missions was in trouble. Bertha Henshaw wrote to Shields that one of the members of the investigating committee had, with her husband, attended an event honoring Ernest DeWitt Burton and the trustees of the University of Chicago. At this event "some very nice things were said about the Divinity School of that institution." Shields replied that he, Riley,

---

37. "A Call to Prayer," *Baptist Temple News*, February 7, 1925, 2.
38. Helen C. A. Dixon, *A. C. Dixon: A Romance of Preaching*, 309–10.
39. W. B. Riley, "Dr. A. C. Dixon Quits the Baptist Bible Union," *Baptist Beacon* (April, 1925), 8; Oliver W. Van Osdel, "Speaking the Truth in Love," *Baptist Temple News*, September 19, 1925, 1–2.

and Norris had about decided that the Baptist Bible Union would have to begin its own foreign missions work.[40]

The 1925 Northern Baptist Convention would meet in Seattle. Everybody expected a debate over foreign missions, but another issue suddenly emerged. This new controversy was forced on the convention by Harry Emerson Fosdick.

For years, fundamentalists and modernists had skirmished over open membership. More and more liberal pastors of Northern Baptist churches were permitting people to become church members regardless of baptism. So far, spats over open membership had been restricted to sermons and periodicals. In January 1925, however, Cornelius Woelfkin announced his retirement from the prestigious Park Avenue Baptist Church, and in March the position was offered to Harry Emerson Fosdick. Park Avenue was the church of the Rockefellers, and John D. Rockefeller Jr., insisted that Fosdick had to become the next pastor. Fosdick, however, refused to pastor a church that required baptism for membership. To Fosdick's surprise, the Park Avenue Church promised to eliminate "all sectarian restrictions on membership."[41]

Fosdick did not actually assume the pastorate of Park Avenue until that fall, but the news became public about a month before the Seattle convention. In fact, the church itself mailed a circular to ministers throughout the Northern Baptist Convention, announcing its anticipated change of policy. Open membership was no longer a theoretical issue among Northern Baptists, but a looming denominational problem. Both Frank Goodchild (of the conference fundamentalists) and John R. Straton (of the Baptist Bible Union) preached messages denouncing the decision at Park Avenue. Baptist churches and associations around the country began passing resolutions, insisting that the Park Avenue delegates be expelled at the upcoming convention.[42]

The Baptist Bible Union met in Seattle, June 25–29, at First Presbyterian Church. Pastored by Mark Matthews, this church was the largest in the Presbyterian denomination. The Presbyterians had recently managed to exclude Harry Emerson Fosdick from one of their pulpits. The Baptist Bible Union recognized a kindred spirit and even passed a resolution expressing solidarity with the Presbyterians.[43]

As usual, the meeting was planned so as to capitalize on the preaching of

40. Bertha Henshaw to Thomas T. Shields, March 16, 1925 (Toronto: Jarvis Street Baptist Church Archives); Thomas T. Shields to Bertha Henshaw, March 25, 1925 (Toronto: Jarvis Street Baptist Church Archives).

41. Harry Emerson Fosdick, *The Living of These Days* (New York: Harper and Brothers, 1958), 177–78.

42. Moulds, "Conflict," 75–79.

43. Thomas T. Shields, "Shall the Northern Baptist Convention Remain the Religious Department of the Standard Oil Company?" *Searchlight*, July 10, 1925, 1.

the leaders, especially the big three. Straton was absent. Several new members were added to the executive committee, the most significant of whom was W. B. Hinson of Portland, Oregon. The Union was at the peak of its powers and the convention was being held in a region that had a reputation as a fundamentalist stronghold. Spirits were high going into the convention.

The first clash at the convention was over the question of whether the Park Avenue delegates should be seated. The matter was referred to the enrollment committee. The committee reported and recommended that, since the church's change in membership policy would not take effect for some months, the delegates from Park Avenue were entitled to participate in the convention. The recommendation passed by a vote of 912 to 364. The next day, the convention did approve a nonbinding resolution expressing disapproval of the decision at Park Avenue Church.[44]

Neither the conference fundamentalists nor the Bible Union men were satisfied with a nonbinding resolution. Twenty-eight fundamentalist signatories from both groups presented a declaration that inserted a definition of a Baptist church into the bylaws. The key statement read, "A Baptist Church, as defined for the purposes of these By-laws, is one accepting the New Testament as its guide and composed only of baptized believers, baptism being by immersion." Since this revision to the bylaws could not be voted until the next convention, the coming year promised to be filled with controversy.[45]

The real test of strength at the Seattle convention was going to be about modernists on the mission field. All sides could anticipate how the report of the investigating committee was going to read, and the committee did not disappoint them. The committee claimed to have collected more than four volumes of testimony, and to have discovered that the overwhelming majority of missionaries were sound. No missionary had been rejected explicitly because of either liberalism or conservatism. The board had largely followed the Inclusive Policy, but in a few extreme instances had approved missionaries who did not rightly come within its limits. In one case, a liberal missionary had actually resigned in the face of questioning by the committee. The committee observed that the problem cases had likely arisen because of an overemphasis upon education in missions, and it recommended a renewed emphasis upon evangelism.[46]

The committee's report was adopted unanimously, and why not? The fundamentalists were pleased that it acknowledged the presence of some

44. Moulds, "Conflict," 79–80.
45. Ibid., 80–81.
46. Ibid., 202–03; "To All Baptists in America Who Believe the Bible to Be the Word of God," *Baptist Temple News*, November 14, 1925, 1–3; William B. Riley, "To All Baptists Who Believe the Bible to Be God's Word," *Watchman Examiner*, November 19, 1925, 1497–99.

modernists on the mission field. The liberals were happy that it stipulated no disciplinary measures. The fundamentalists, however, intended to provide those. W. B. Hinson of Portland offered a resolution that the Baptist Bible Union had adopted in its preconvention meeting. The resolution required the boards to "recall immediately every representative, whether in evangelistic or educational work, who is found on investigation to deny any of the great fundamentals of our faith." The resolution included two paragraphs that specified the fundamentals to which missionaries would have to agree.[47]

Wallace Petty tried to divert the resolution into a committee, but his attempt failed. Then a convention employee moved that the motion be printed and considered at a later time. Who could object to that? Once again, a delaying tactic gave the liberals an opportunity to strategize.

When the resolution was brought back to the floor, the modernists were ready with a substitute motion. It recognized the presence of some missionaries who did not hold to the fundamentals of the faith as commonly understood by Baptists, but made no attempt to say what the fundamentals were. It simply encouraged the foreign mission board to take "such action . . . as seems to them will best conserve our denominational interests and best serve the Kingdom of Christ." When the vote was taken, the substitute motion carried by a margin of 742 to 574.[48]

This defeat was the most bitter to date. The conference fundamentalists and the Bible Union had been united in their support for the Hinson resolution. They were in fundamentalist territory. Had it passed, the resolution would have cleansed the mission of modernists—none could have signed it honestly. Yet it lost to an insubstantial substitute motion by a margin of something less than two hundred votes. If the fundamentalists could not win in their own territory, they had little hope of ever reforming the mission society. More than that, they began to realize that their giving to the unified budget had helped the convention send about two hundred salaried servants from across the country to vote against them.

Stunned, the Baptist Bible Union met that evening in the auditorium of First Christian Church. Riley took the chair. He noted that the convention had refused to recall liberal missionaries, even though the investigating committee had found that some of them were on the field. Consequently, no alternative remained except to found a new foreign mission society, and he presented a resolution asking the executive committee to do just that. A second

47. "Dr. Hinson's Resolution," *Watchman Examiner*, July 16, 1925, 918; Tulga, *The Story of the Inclusive Policy*, 12; Shields, "Shall the Northern Baptist Convention," 1–2; Van Osdel, "To All Baptists," 3–4; Moulds, "Conflict," 203; Delnay, "History of the Baptist Bible Union," 106–07.

48. Tulga, *The Story of the Inclusive Policy*, 13–15; Moulds, "Conflict," 203–05; Delnay, "History of the Baptist Bible Union," 106–07.

resolution, adopted the following night, stated that the Baptist Bible Union intended to continue to oppose modernism from within the Northern Baptist Convention, and that the organization of a new mission society must not be interpreted as an act of separation.[49]

This decision gave the Baptist Bible Union a three-pronged strategy for the coming year. First, it had to rally the troops to vote on the amendment that would block open membership. Second, it had to do something to dismantle the voting bloc of convention employees. Third, it had to organize a new mission society.

Before anyone could begin to address these issues, however, disaster struck again. On July 10, jury selection began in Dayton, Tennessee, for the trial of John T. Scopes. A high school teacher, Scopes was being tried for violating a new Tennessee law that forbade the teaching of evolution in the public schools. Defense attorneys Dudley Field Malone and Clarence Darrow were courtroom celebrities. To counteract their influence, W. B. Riley arranged for statesman William Jennings Bryan to assist the prosecution. The trial attracted national attention, including the attention of journalist H. L. Mencken. Darrow subjected Bryan to ridicule inside the courtroom while Mencken subjected fundamentalism to ridicule in the press.[50]

Mencken's bitter wit was far more devastating to fundamentalists than any defeat they had suffered at the hands of the liberals. The journalist caricatured fundamentalism as a backwoods movement of illiterate yokels. The image stuck, in spite of the fact that people like Massee, Laws, Straton, Shields, and Riley were educated men who ministered in urban centers. The picture that Mencken painted of William Jennings Bryan and of fundamentalism was one that dominated American perceptions for more than fifty years. It has never been entirely dispelled.

The Bible Union's executive committee met at Jarvis Street (Shields's church) in September. The committee did not exactly organize a new mission board. Instead, it opened a "Missions Department" of the Baptist Bible Union. It also called for a four-day missionary convention to be held at Paul Rader's Chicago Gospel Tabernacle in November. Speakers at the Chicago meeting were to include such stalwarts as Pettingill, Shields, Norris, Van Osdel, Riley, and Straton. This meeting also brought H. H. Savage of Pontiac, Michigan, to the Bible Union platform, along with William Fetler of the Russian Gospel Mission.[51]

49. Van Osdel, "To All Baptists," 4–5.

50. Henry L. Mencken, "In Memoriam: W. J. B.," in Clifton Fadiman, ed., *Fifty Years* (New York: Alfred A. Knopf, 1965), 881.

51. Van Osdel, "To All Baptists," 5–6; "Missionary Convention Baptist Bible Union of North America Chicago, Illinois," *Baptist Temple News*, September 19, 1925, 3–4.

The convention endorsed the organization of a missions department under the oversight of the executive committee. It also authorized the executive committee to open an office in Chicago. It specified that the work of missions would be evangelism, with education operating in a subsidiary role if at all. Furthermore, at this convention the BBU acted to "adopt" the Russian Gospel Mission, provided that all officials and members would subscribe to the Baptist Bible Union confession of faith.[52]

What did it mean for the Union to adopt Fetler's mission? Apparently not that the BBU would assume ownership or oversight. Adopting the agency appears to have been equivalent to a formal endorsement. Van Osdel wrote that the action of the missionary convention was "designed to empower the Executive Committee to investigate all such fields and to endorse and recommend to our constituency such missionary organizations as desire our sponsorship and support, [and] as are found to be in harmony with our historic Baptist position." The Bible Union hoped to be able to add other agencies that it could "recommend to our constituency."[53]

The Baptist Bible Union was showing increased organization. The executive committee opened an office in Chicago on the third floor of the Monon building, a high-rise located on printing-house row. Vigorous branches of the Union were also organized in several states. Iowa's branch was active enough to hire its own field representative. Pennsylvania also had an aggressive group. In Michigan, Van Osdel's energy kept things moving, and the Michigan Orthodox Baptist Association joined the state's Baptist Bible Union as a bloc. H. H. Savage of First Baptist Church in Pontiac was chosen as president of the Michigan Union, and the organization met at his church in January 1926.[54]

The Baptist Bible Union had addressed its first concern: foreign missions. The most important issue, however, still had to be resolved: open membership. That issue would be addressed by the proposed amendment to revise the bylaws of the Northern Baptist Convention. Fundamentalists of all varieties wanted to keep the Park Avenue delegates from voting in the convention, and the amendment would do just that. Liberals understood that this decision would be equivalent to imposing a doctrinal test.

At this point, a decision of the Northern Baptist Convention's law committee completely altered the discussion. In 1911 the convention had merged with a large body of Freewill Baptists, and the properties and monies of the two organizations had been combined. The Freewill Baptists, however, had never made an issue of open membership, and some of their churches still

---

52. Van Osdel, "To All Baptists," 6–7.
53. Ibid., 7.
54. "Programme of the Annual Meeting of the Baptist Bible Union of Michigan," *Baptist Temple News*, January 16, 1926, 4; Delnay, "History of the Baptist Bible Union," 110–12.

practiced it. The law committee ruled that the proposed bylaw would expose the convention to legal action because it would exclude some Freewill Baptist churches from sending delegates. The amendment could not be allowed.[55]

The reaction of the conference fundamentalists to this news can only be described as panic. Believing that anything was better than nothing, they decided to approach the modernists in the hopes of gaining some concessions. J. Whitcomb Brougher gathered a group of seventy-five participants from both parties (including fundamentalists from both Massee's group and the Baptist Bible Union) to meet in Chicago on April 13. While personally orthodox, however, Brougher was mainly committed to denominational peace and prosperity. Through the preceding several months he had crisscrossed the country, preaching a sermon titled "Play Ball." His goal was to prod the more moderate conservatives and liberals to work together.

Brougher's meeting produced a compromise that both sides thought they could live with, though Straton (who was at the meeting) consented only provisionally. First, the convention would recognize only those churches in which the immersion of believers was acknowledged as the only Scriptural baptism. Second, only immersed members would be recognized as delegates at the convention. Of course, this compromise left open the question of whether a church could admit unimmersed members.[56]

The months leading up to the 1926 convention saw some disintegration among the leadership of the Baptist Bible Union. All were pushing themselves to the limit of their endurance. They were pastoring their own churches. They were appearing in multiple conferences with and for one another all over the country. They were writing and publishing. The constant strain was beginning to tell on them both emotionally and physically. In May, Van Osdel's health deteriorated so badly that he was forced out of active ministry for some weeks. To recover, he traveled to California where his son taught chemistry at the University of Redlands. Another member of the executive committee, W. B. Hinson of Portland, Oregon, died of a stroke on April 8. In addition to these changes, R. E. Neighbour's wife died, and he left the pastorate of First Baptist Church in Elyria, Ohio, for the Chicago Gospel Tabernacle.

The Baptist Bible Union held its 1926 meeting at the Metropolitan Baptist Church in Washington, D.C., on May 19–24. The usual figures addressed the crowd multiple times: Straton, Shields, Norris, and Riley. Savage was on the program that year, as was W. L. Walker, Neighbour's successor at Elyria. By 1926 Van Osdel was the only one of the original three still on the executive

---

55. Moulds, "Conflict," 82–83.

56. "Dr. Brougher's Amendment of the Amendment," *Watchman Examiner*, April 15, 1926, 467; John Roach Straton, "The Chicago 'Conference,'" *Watchman Examiner*, April 29, 1926, 51; Moulds, "Conflict," 83; Delnay, "History of the Baptist Bible Union," 119–20.

committee, though Shields, Riley, and Norris also counted as founders. Younger members included (among others) H. O. Van Gilder and J. J. Van Gorder. As a preaching event, the 1926 meeting probably represented the high point of the Baptist Bible Union.[57]

A committee consisting of Robert T. Ketcham, Chester E. Tulga, and W. B. Riley reported on the missions controversy. Eight liberals could be identified on the basis of the investigating report, and the committee was dissatisfied with the way these cases had been handled. The main business, however, was to articulate a response to Brougher's Chicago Compromise. The consensus within the union was that Brougher's statement really failed to exclude non-Baptistic churches from sending delegates to the convention. Riley and others later met in a hotel room to work out the wording of an amendment that they would present on the convention floor.[58]

As it happened, Brougher opened the Northern Baptist Convention in Washington with the keynote address. He argued that 85 percent of the people in the convention were fundamentalists who actually wanted to cooperate with the convention, and that most of these were ready to put the controversy behind them. Nevertheless, the controversy resumed next morning. The original (and ostensibly illegal) motion to amend the bylaws was buried by referring it to a committee. The Chicago Compromise was put on the floor as a standing resolution. Then Riley moved that it be amended to specify that immersion should not only be acknowledged, but made a prerequisite of membership for churches to send delegates to the convention. The debate over Riley's amendment was bumptious, punctuated with jeers and cheers from both sides. When the massive crowd finally voted, Riley's amendment lost by 2,020 to 1,084. The Chicago Compromise was then swept in by acclamation.[59]

The Baptist Bible Union had put its full strength into challenging open membership, but it had been outmaneuvered. Once again a Union proposal had lost by nearly two to one. This turned out to be the last great battle on the floor of the convention for twenty years. While Straton and the Bible Union leadership tried to sound encouraging, the vote was a manifest disaster—but not the last disaster of the convention.

The Union had one more trick to try. The foreign mission board still had to be elected. When the nominating committee presented its recommendations, H. H. Savage stood to offer an alternate ballot of conservatives. The ballot included both conference fundamentalists and Bible Union men, but

57. "Baptist Bible Union Programme," *Searchlight*, April 9, 1926, 6.
58. Moulds, "Conflict," 84; Delnay, "History of the Baptist Bible Union," 122.
59. Moulds, "Conflict," 84–86.

the convention's proposed ballot won by a proportion of more than three to one. This was worse than defeat: it was humiliation.[60]

Even worse was to come. Earlier in the year J. C. Massee had resigned as the head of the conference fundamentalists' committee. He was subsequently appointed to the honor of convention preacher. In his address Massee called for a six-month moratorium on controversy. Both sides, he said, should give themselves to intensive evangelism. Of course, evangelism was something that fundamentalists had already been doing, and something that modernists could only smile at. Even the conference fundamentalists were aghast at Massee's moratorium. To the Baptist Bible Union, it represented a deliberate undercutting of their efforts, a betrayal of those who were contending for the faith.[61]

By the end of the convention, every Bible Union initiative had failed. Leaders and members were reeling from Massee's betrayal. If that was not enough, Brougher was rewarded for the Chicago Compromise by being elected convention president. How could things get any worse?

The Baptist Bible Union was about to discover the answer to that question. J. Frank Norris had always been the Union's most flamboyant and controversial leader. A firm supporter of prohibition, one of the main thrusts of Norris's ministry was opposition to liquor. Opposing liquor meant opposing bootleggers, which in turn meant exposing the politicians whom they bribed. For years Norris had been at war with the political structure of Fort Worth because of its putative ties with illegal liquor. He also believed that he had discerned a link between the liquor trade and the Roman Catholic Church. Consequently, one of Norris's prime targets was H. C. Meacham, a wealthy merchant who was both a Catholic and mayor of Fort Worth.

To be fair, Norris's public opposition to liquor and other vices took some courage. More than once his life was threatened. On at least one occasion someone shot at him (and missed) from outside First Baptist Church. While some speculated that perhaps Norris had paid a marksman, it was just as possible that an irritated opponent had decided to send a warning. After all, this was Fort Worth.

In 1926 the city of Fort Worth purchased an old school from the Catholic Church. Norris alleged that the city paid over twice its appraised value. Furthermore, the property was needed to widen an alleyway into a street that would run directly to Meacham's department store. Norris denounced Meacham in a fiery sermon from the pulpit of First Baptist. As usual, the

60. Delnay, "History of the Baptist Bible Union," 128.

61. "What About the Six-Months Truce?" *Watchman Examiner*, June 10, 1926; Van Osdel, "Will the Baptists Obey?" *Baptist Temple News*, June 2 [the correct date is probably June 6], 1926, 1–3.

sermon was printed in the *Searchlight*. Norris had boys patrol the entrances of Meacham's department store, distributing copies of the paper to shoppers. Meacham retaliated by firing every employee who was a member of First Baptist Church—six altogether.

The next Sunday morning Norris interviewed each of the six from the pulpit of First Baptist Church. All testified that they had been given the same choice—either leave the church or be fired. Then Norris delivered a fiery denunciation of Meacham's character.

> Up here in Judge Bruce Young's court a few years ago it is a matter of record that H.C. Meacham had to pay one of his employees—a young lady—$12,500 and he gave the lawyers $10,000 besides to settle it. . . . [I]t is a shame on the name of Fort Worth that a man of that kind should be mayor for one minute's time. (Applause). There is no dispute about it. It is a court record, and if he wasn't as guilty as hell, why did he pay it? If he paid it, he isn't fit to be mayor of a hog pen (Applause). [62]

Again the sermon was printed in the *Searchlight* and distributed to the patrons of Meacham's department store. One of Meacham's cronies, a wealthy lumberman by the name of Dexter Elliot Chipps, made threats against Norris's life, some of them in front of police. Norris was warned by the police that Chipps was after him and that he was dangerous. On Saturday afternoon, July 17, Chipps called Norris on the phone and threatened his life. Several others heard Chipps repeating the threats.

Norris and L.H. Nutt, a First Baptist deacon, were talking in the pastor's office when Chipps burst through the door. After a verbal altercation, Norris asked Chipps to leave. On his way out the door, Chipps made what was called a "hip pocket move," and said, "All right, let's go for it." Norris reached for a revolver in his desk drawer and put multiple slugs into Chipps, killing him.

The police investigation turned up no weapon on Chipps's body. Later, in the trial, the suggestion was made that the first officer on the scene might have taken the weapon to keep it from being found. This speculation had a certain probability to it—Meacham was, after all, the mayor and in charge of the police. But the next day, all that the papers had to say was that Norris had shot an unarmed man.[63]

Norris himself insisted on an indictment, believing that the only way to

---

62. A summation of the Chipps episode that is friendly to Norris can be found in Michael E. Schepis, *J. Frank Norris*, 96–122; the citation is from 101. A more hostile account is David R. Stokes, *The Shooting Salvationist: J. Frank Norris and the Murder Trial that Captivated America* (Hanover, NH: Steerforth Press, 2011).

63. According to David O. Beale, at Norris's trial the defense produced a silver-plated revolver that it claimed Chipps had been carrying. *In Pursuit of Purity: American Fundamentalism Since 1850* (Greenville, SC: Unusual Publications, 1986), 234.

clear his name was to have all the facts come out in court. After a change of venue, Norris was tried in Austin the next January and acquitted on the grounds of self-defense. The prosecutor had been asking for the electric chair.

The Chipps shooting dramatically changed the course of Norris's ministry. It also changed the course of the Baptist Bible Union. Many of the Union leaders sent immediate expressions of support to Norris, expressing confidence in his innocence and ultimate vindication. But Norris was already a controversial figure, and the public had little sympathy for a pastor who would shoot an unarmed man. Norris immediately backed away from leadership in the Union, which only compounded the problem. The Baptist Bible Union was built on the energy of a small handful of men, and Norris was one of them.

The Chipps shooting was a disaster, but it was not the end of the Bible Union's troubles. Massee had already called for a six-month moratorium on controversy. Then in August he published a frontal attack on the Baptist Bible Union in the *Moody Monthly*. He accused the Union of being divisive and of neglecting the genuine work of the Lord while pretending to fight the Lord's battles. Riley's answer to these charges appeared in the *Moody Monthly*, in Shields's *Gospel Witness*, and in the *Baptist Temple News*. No answer, however, could remove either the sting or the stigma of being assaulted by an erstwhile ally.[64]

Michigan Baptists soon discovered that Massee was doing even worse. Since 1920 the Michigan convention had been involved in attempts to control the property of orthodox churches. The first legal battle had been over the property of the Sand Creek church. Upon the testimony of convention officials, the property was handed over to a minority of convention loyalists. Other battles had followed, with convention officials eventually trying to find some leverage to use against Van Osdel at Wealthy Street.[65]

In late 1925 Van Osdel became aware that trouble was brewing in the church at Big Rapids, Michigan. The pastor, John Ross, was a firm supporter of the Michigan Orthodox Baptist Association and the Baptist Bible Union. Most members of the church were pleased with his ministry, but a minority wanted stronger support for the state convention. Eventually the church voted to withdraw from affiliation with the convention by a substantial majority (44 to 27). The minority (which included several church officers) appealed to the convention officials, who stepped into the situation and began a public campaign against the pastor. Their most serious charge was that he was a "Van Osdelite."[66]

---

64. William B. Riley, "Letter for Rev. W. B. Riley, D.D.," *Gospel Witness*, November 4, 1926; "Dr. Riley Replies to Dr. Massee," *Baptist Temple News*, Feb 5, 1927, 1–3.

65. See chapter 2 for this story.

66. Oliver W. Van Osdel, "The Big Rapids Church," *Baptist Temple News*, December 12,

The minority exempted themselves from the services of the church and began meeting in homes. Then a convention official, John E. Smith, went to Big Rapids with a lawyer to meet with the minority. The lawyer assured them that they actually constituted the Baptist church of Big Rapids, and that the majority would have to vacate the property and turn it over to the minority. At almost the same time, Smith became involved in locking the congregation of South Baptist Church in Bay City, Michigan, out of its building.[67]

The convention based its claim in Big Rapids upon two old mortgages of $300, each dating from the 1880s. The church had received money from both the home mission society and the state convention. Consequently, the convention claimed that its financial investment provided grounds for involvement in the Big Rapids conflict. It noted that in more than a few legal cases, church property had been awarded to a minority when the majority departed from Baptist usage and affiliation.[68]

Van Osdel was only too familiar with these tactics. He had experienced some of them himself. To a questioner from Detroit he wrote,

> You ask as to what would hinder the same steps being taken anywhere, and we answer, "nothing at all." The State Convention here in Michigan has attempted to work the same racket on the Wealthy Street Church. They sent their representative here with a stenographer to take down a sermon the pastor was preaching with the expectation of getting evidence against us. Their official representative attempted to come between the Pastor and his trustees, and not satisfied with their failure a successor of the first, now the Honorable Grant M. Hudson, undertook to get between the deacons and the Pastor. If this attempt to wrest the property from the majority and turn it over to an angry minority succeeds in Big Rapids, there would be nothing to hinder their going into any of the churches or all of them and doing the same thing.[69]

In August the minority, advised by convention officials, called an ex parte council (a council that involved only one party to the dispute). Somehow Van Osdel was sent an invitation. In his response Van Osdel declared that, at best, Baptist councils were only advisory because "the majority of members of every Baptist church is sovereign over its own affairs." An ex parte council lacked even this advisory capacity: it was "destitute of all authority likewise

1925, 2–3; Van Osdel, "Facts about the Baptist Church at Big Rapids," *Baptist Temple News*, July 3, 1926, 1–4.

67. Oliver W. Van Osdel, "Persecution in Michigan," *Baptist Temple News*, June 12, 1926, 2–3.

68. Van Osdel, "Facts about the Baptist Church," 1–4.

69. Oliver W. Van Osdel to S. S. Clarke, May 17, 1926.

and amounts to nothing whatever." Van Osdel went on to encourage the minority to read some books on Baptist history and usage.[70]

At this stage in the conflict, a number of outsiders became involved, encouraging the majority either to submit to a council of members chosen by the minority, or else simply to hand over the properties to the minority. These outsiders also wrote letters to encourage the minority to fight for the property in court. Wearied by the incessant badgering, the majority finally submitted to the pressure. Ross resigned the pastorate, and the minority was given control of the building and grounds.[71]

Shortly after Ross's resignation, word leaked out that one of the outsiders who had encouraged the minority and pressured the majority was J. C. Massee. Incredulous, Van Osdel denounced Massee's conduct as "unwarranted interference" and "anti-Baptistic through and through." He went on to castigate Massee's moratorium, which (according to Massee) was supposed to lead to a revival. Van Osdel said that nobody should understand better than Massee that genuine spiritual revival was impossible among modernists: "They do not believe enough of the Bible to make a man a Christian."[72]

The situation was profoundly disturbing. For one thing, it was difficult to understand how Massee's betrayal could have been any more complete. For another, Big Rapids was only the most recent (and certainly not the last) in a string of litigations encouraged by the convention or its subsidiaries. Van Osdel was right about one thing: if the courts would take property from a majority and give it to a minority in one church, then no church was safe. Within a decade this tactic would be widely employed against churches that tried to leave the convention. From this point onward, Van Osdel began to encourage churches to do everything they could to secure the title to their property and to ensure that it was free from encumbrances.[73]

Meanwhile, the Baptist Bible Union appeared to be drifting. The executive committee met at Cleveland in October, deciding that the upcoming annual meeting would be the last one held in conjunction with the Northern Baptist Convention. The committee also thought that it might help to mend some fences if their program were to feature one of the prominent conference fundamentalists—someone like Frank Goodchild, John Marvin Dean, or Cortland Myers. In further action, the committee decided to endorse the work of the Sweet Baptist Mission to China, under the direction of Mrs. W. S.

70. Oliver W. Van Osdel to Fred A. Ashley, August 6, 1926.

71. Oliver W. Van Osdel, "Another Word from Big Rapids," *Baptist Temple News*, August 21, 1926, 1–2.

72. Van Osdel, "Another Word," 1–2; Van Osdel, "That Revival," *Baptist Temple News*, August 21, 1926, 2–4.

73. Oliver W. Van Osdel, "The Title to Your Church Property," *Baptist Temple News*, September 18, 1926, 2–3.

Sweet. Perhaps most importantly, the executive committee elected to offer the position of field secretary to W. E. Atkinson, who assumed his duties on December 1.[74]

In Toronto, Shields had been concerned about the liberalism of McMaster University. Finally deciding that no more could be done about McMaster, he opened his own seminary during the winter of 1926–27. Toronto Baptist Seminary added another responsibility to Shields's already full schedule. Inevitably, it drew him away from the work of the Baptist Bible Union.

As modernism and denominational control continued growing within the Northern Baptist Convention, Van Osdel's thoughts were never far from separation. He understood that the Baptist Bible Union was not yet ready to take that step, but he could not resist a bit of wistful reflection. "What is needed in the North is a real Baptist Convention of real Baptists. If such a movement had been launched in the year of the Buffalo meeting it would be today a large and influential body. . . . The longer Baptists delay positive aggressive action along lines in accord with New Testament teaching, the weaker they will become." The day was approaching when Van Osdel would have to guide the Baptist Bible Union through just that process, but before it arrived the Union had to experience even deeper defeats.[75]

The Baptist Bible Union planned to meet for five days immediately prior to the Northern Baptist Convention in Chicago. Norris did not appear on the platform or even attend the meeting. Shields, Riley, and Van Osdel all spoke, but this conference was remarkable for its inclusion of younger men. Some of these would go on to become significant names in Northern Baptist fundamentalism: J. J. Van Gorder, John Muntz, and R. T. Ketcham among them.[76]

By now, it was becoming evident that the Baptist Bible Union had lost its momentum. It employed both a secretary and a field representative, but by May, the Union was unable to pay their salaries. Both Atkinson and Rebman submitted their resignations. So did Shields, citing the burden of his pastorate. Van Osdel took it upon himself to announce these events publicly and to make an appeal for funds. He hoped to see enough money come in by the annual meeting in May to put the Baptist Bible Union back in business.[77]

Normally quite deferential to Van Osdel, Shields wrote to express his displeasure. On his view, the older pastor should not have made these matters

---

74. Delnay, "History of the Baptist Bible Union," 136; Van Osdel, "Bible Union Calls Field Secretary," *Baptist Temple News*, November 13, 1926, 3–4.

75. Oliver W. Van Osdel, "That Fosdick Report," *Baptist Temple News*, March 26, 1927, 1–2.

76. "Baptist Bible Union Annual Meeting at Chicago," *Baptist Temple News*, April 2, 1927, 2–3.

77. Oliver W. Van Osdel, "Shall the Bible Union Live?" *Baptist Temple News*, May 7, 1927, 2–4; Van Osdel, "The Bible Union at Its Coming Annual Meeting," *Baptist Temple News*, May 14, 1927, 2–4.

public. He was sure that Van Osdel's announcement could only hurt the Union. Van Osdel responded in a kind letter, insisting that many people already knew the situation and that the rest ought to. He gently chided Shields, "The injury the Union will suffer is not because the brethren have come to know about the situation and the plans, but from the determination agreed upon that the president, the secretary, and the field secretary would all let go of the work simultaneously in Chicago." He added, "It isn't in my heart to blame anyone for reaching this decision, but this is a fact."[78] He then appended another wistful bit of reflection.

> I hoped when the brethren met in Indianapolis to form the Bible Union that a positive program of its own would be undertaken, that it would be a regular Baptist affair, and that we would be entirely apart from the Northern Baptist Convention. There has been nothing since that time to change my judgment. The Scriptures are definite about our dealing along these lines, and I am still hoping that somehow, from somewhere, God will yet raise up men to become leaders in such a movement. Personally I am too old to undertake another movement and shall not consider it. I shall continue to do everything possible in my power to help and encourage either the work of the Union or of some other movement intended for the glory of God, but I must cease any further active operations.[79]

While Van Osdel did not actually cease his active operations, his letter appears to have offered some encouragement to Shields. There was no more talk of a resignation. Within weeks an opportunity would appear that would breathe new life into the Baptist Bible Union and take it in an entirely different direction, though again diverting it from the separatism that Van Osdel had envisioned from the beginning.

Riley's interest in the Union was also flagging. After leading the troops into so many defeats on the convention floor, he can hardly be blamed. Later, it would come out that tensions were developing between Riley and Shields, but nothing was being said publicly. Formally, Riley remained a member of the executive committee, but he was no longer an officer and his active involvement in the Baptist Bible Union had about ended.

The executive committee that was elected in 1927 indicated a shift in the Union's focus. Canadians were still represented, but not a single Southerner appeared. Max Schimpf was the only Easterner still on board. The rest of the men were from the Midwest, where a more separatistic attitude was beginning to flourish.

---

78. Oliver W. Van Osdel to Thomas T. Shields, May 17, 1927.
79. Ibid.

In previous years, some urgent issue had always determined the Baptist Bible Union's agenda. After the defeats of 1926, the urgency was gone. No one seems to have arrived in Chicago with a clear idea of what to do at the Northern Baptist Convention. During the BBU conference, however, it occurred to someone that it just might be possible to get a slate of fundamentalists elected to office. If that happened, then conservatism could begin to reassert itself in the counsels of the convention. Eight members were detailed as a committee to go through the proposed convention ballot and to list the name of a conservative in the place of every liberal or liberal sympathizer.[80]

The alternate ballot was not accepted by the Union until after midnight on the night before the convention. Once it was approved, Ketcham suggested that the convention president, J. Whitcomb Brougher, was likely to rule it out of order if the Bible Union tried to make the substitutions individually. He recommended that the alternate ballot be printed on a different color of paper so that the delegates could simply cast whichever ballot they supported. At three o'clock in the morning the group cheerfully agreed and sent Ketcham out to get the ballot printed. With the help of a police officer, he located an all-night print shop and returned to the convention hall in time for the election.[81]

The result was predictable. The alternative ballot received only 458 of the 2,297 ballots cast. This was less than 20 percent of the vote, making the situation abundantly clear. Ketcham left the platform, touched Riley on the shoulder, and said that he was never coming back.[82]

Many seem to have shared Ketcham's resolve. After 1927 the Baptist Bible Union never again attempted any direct action toward the Northern Baptist Convention. Within a few months, separatist associations had cut themselves clear of the convention in Ohio, Michigan, California, and Indiana. The leadership of the Union also changed dramatically. For practical purposes, Shields and Van Osdel were the only original founders who remained, and both of them now inclined toward separatism. This could have been the ideal occasion to turn the Baptist Bible Union into a nationwide association of its own.

The Union, however, was standing on weak legs. It needed a surge of energy, or one more hard blow would be enough to kill it. It was about to receive both the surge and the blow in the takeover of Des Moines University.

---

80. Delnay, "History of the Baptist Bible Union," 145.
81. Robert T. Ketcham, recorded interview with Robert Delnay, April 7, 1962.
82. Murray Murdoch, *Portrait of Obedience* (Schaumburg, IL: Regular Baptist Press, 1979), 116–17.

Des Moines University trustees in 1929. Front: J. H. Sperry, E. A. Roberts, J. M. Hoyt, Edith Rebman, Oliver W. Van Osdel, E. A. Brownlee; Rear: Clifford J. Loney, Max Schimpf, T. T. Shields, (unknown), H. G. Hamilton, H. C. Fulton.

5 Transition

AFTER 1927 the Baptist Bible Union and the fundamentalist conference went in separate directions. With the exceptions of some conflicts in the leadership, the members of the two organizations seem to have maintained fairly cordial relationships. Some individuals and even some leaders managed to keep a foot in both camps. Nevertheless, at the organizational level the attitudes were markedly different.

The fundamentalist conference continued to meet in connection with the Northern Baptist Convention, but the element of protest became less noticeable. The organization gave its undeviating support to the convention program. At some point the conference was taken out of the hands of the Brooklyn committee and organized as a self-standing fellowship with officers and a membership. It named itself the Fundamentalist Fellowship of the Northern Baptist Convention, and the last part of the name was just as important as the first. Earle V. Pierce of Minneapolis held the presidency for many years. This situation would only change when doubts began to increase about the Inclusive Policy during the early 1940s.

The Baptist Bible Union took a route that entailed virtual separation. It never again met in connection with the Northern Baptist Convention. Its members did their missionary work separately from the convention. In Toronto, Shields's independent seminary exemplified an increasing attitude of self-determination on the part of the Union's members and leaders.

If Van Osdel had his way, the Baptist Bible Union might have organized a completely separate association or convention after the defeats at Chicago. Formal separation, however, was delayed for some years. One reason was that too many of the Bible Union men were still involved with the convention at some level. Even Shields would stay in the Canadian convention for another year until he was thrown out. More importantly, in 1927 the Baptist Bible Union was offered control of Des Moines University.

Des Moines University

Des Moines University (unrelated to the present-day institution of that name) was founded in 1889 as Highland Park College. For a while it was under Presbyterian control. Somewhere around 1916–1921 it merged with Des Moines College and other institutions, coming under the governance of the state Baptist convention in Iowa. The merged institution occupied the Highland Park campus at Second and Euclid in Des Moines.

Leaders of the Baptist Bible Union had attempted to get a clear statement of the university's doctrinal commitments, but President John W. Million always replied evasively. By examining the required textbooks, the chapel speakers, and certain faculty pronouncements, the Union became convinced that modernism was being taught in the school. Fundamentalists stopped supporting it, and liberals could not make up the difference. The Northern Baptist Convention poured hundreds of thousands of dollars into the university, to no avail.

By 1927 the university was ready to close. Its student population had declined to around 600—smaller than some Bible schools. For a couple of years the board had been spending the endowment. Even the buildings and grounds had been pledged as collateral for the debt. The Iowa convention tried to raise $50,000 for cash flow, but only about $10,000 came in. Then the board tried to merge the school into Drake University, also located in Des Moines. Drake was willing to merge but not to accept the indebtedness, so nothing was done. Finally, the board voted to notify the university's employees that they would be jobless after June 6. As historian William H. Brackney notes, the school had ceased operations, suspended classes, and had its accounts in arrears.[1]

In a chance meeting, T. T. Shields was introduced to Frank Foulk, a trustee of Des Moines University, while he was in Chicago for the Baptist Bible Union meeting in 1927. Foulk mentioned that the Baptist Bible Union might take over the ailing university, and Shields was instantly mesmerized. Foulk provided him with a few off-the-cuff details that Shields carried to the executive committee. Eventually the parties reached an agreement: the Baptist Bible Union could have control of the school if they would assume all indebtedness (plus a $15,000 promise that the Iowa convention had made to the university) and if they could come up with $50,000 within thirty days to handle immediate operating expenses. The reaction of the Union membership was jubilant:

1. Des Moines University Minutes, October 13, 1925; Ibid., June 2, 1927. The board minutes from June 1925 through August 1929 have been preserved in the vault of Jarvis Street Baptist Church in Toronto. William H. Brackney, *Congregation and Campus: North American Baptists in Higher Education* (Macon, GA: Mercer University Press, 2008), 228; Robert G. Delnay, *"History of the Baptist Bible Union"* (ThD diss., Dallas Seminary, 1963), 180–86. See also George S. May, "Des Moines University and Dr. T. T. Shields," *Iowa Journal of History* 54 (1956): 193–232.

at the Union's business meeting on Sunday night, they gave almost half the amount in cash and pledges. Shields fired off a telegram, which Van Osdel reprinted, hoping to raise the balance quickly.[2]

Altogether, the Bible Union managed to raise about $46,000. The university board decided that was close enough. The president of Des Moines University resigned and the board elected Shields in his place. Upon the resignation of the vice president, the board elected Max Schimpf. Then the resignations continued as Baptist Bible Union members were elected in their place. Within two weeks of the initial announcement to the membership, the Baptist Bible Union had control of Des Moines University.

While Shields claimed that he had a certified audit and had taken "every precaution . . . to guard against the possibility of error in value and to guarantee absolute ownership and control by [the] Union," he cannot have dug very deeply. Nevertheless, the Baptist Bible Union did have absolute ownership and control. The old board wanted nothing more to do with the school.[3]

To move so quickly, Shields was forced to ignore good counsel. Riley wired Shields, cautioning him against taking on any debt from the old administration. He saw no reason to "pay off the debts of the Northern Baptist Convention."[4]

Shields also submitted his data to C. J. Holman, a lawyer who was a member at Jarvis Street. Holman wrote back a densely typed, four-page letter, listing nine reasons against the takeover of Des Moines University. Then Holman followed up his initial letter with at least one and possibly two more. His attitude from beginning to end can be summarized in his closing words: "I am sending you this last word of advice before you leave for Des Moines—don't—*don't*—DON'T—*DON'T*." In what probably counts as a statement about his knowledge of his pastor's character, Holman also enclosed a check for fifty dollars toward the project.[5]

The new trustees met in Des Moines on June 10. Since the old board had already dismissed the teachers, the first business was to find a faculty. The obvious place to look was to the former professors. The board established the Baptist Bible Union doctrinal statement as a datum for rehiring: any professor who could sign it would at least be considered. Many professors objected, and most of the College of Pharmacy formed a new Des Moines College of

2. "An Important Announcement," *Baptist Temple News*, June 4, 1927, 1. There is some question about how large the debt actually was. W. B. Riley listed the figure as $400,000 in "The Redemption of Des Moines University," *Christian Fundamentalist*, August 1927, 6. The *Baptist* put the figure at $330,000, with an annual deficit of $65,000 (July 2, 1927), 865.

3. Ibid.

4. William B. Riley to T. T. Shields, October 25, 1927.

5. C. J. Holman to Thomas T. Shields, June 6, 1927; Delnay, "History of the Baptist Bible Union," 189–90.

Pharmacy (now the Drake University College of Pharmacy and Health Sciences) under the leadership of Carl Weeks.[6]

The board also recognized a need for on-site management. Shields became the president of the university, but he also pastored a church and presided over a seminary in Toronto. One of the members of the new board was Edith Rebman, secretary of the Baptist Bible Union. After some discussion, the board asked her to move from Chicago and take charge of the university offices in Des Moines. She would be given full supervision: all details would be subject to her direction and advice. Her formal control over the university was, under Shields, virtually absolute. Since it made little sense to maintain a separate office for the Baptist Bible Union in Chicago, it too was moved to the university campus.[7]

The board toyed with the idea of closing the school of pharmacy, but decided to keep it open for the moment. They also talked about closing the fraternity houses and turning them into dormitories. Another conversation involved dropping athletic scholarships and suspending intercollegiate athletics. These discussions reveal that the new board had little notion of how their decisions might affect the institution. These moves could hardly have endeared the new administration to the student population. In fact, the university's alumni signed a statement recommending "a catholic attitude in the selection of teachers, suggesting the retention of both fraternities and athletics with proper moral safeguards, and calling for the maintenance of the standards of the best standardizing agencies."[8]

As it turned out, most of the faculty thought they could sign the Baptist Bible Union confession. The summer session went ahead on schedule while the board sought to fill about twenty vacancies. After interviewing around one hundred applicants, the board appointed fifteen new teachers. Under new supervision, Des Moines University prepared to face the coming academic year.

Enrollment for the fall semester was under 400 students—less even than under the old board. Most of these were continuing students who had been willing to function under a faculty that included at least some element of theological liberalism. Not only were the students from a variety of Protestant denominations, they also came from Catholic, Mormon, and Jewish backgrounds. The board seems to have given little thought to the likely

6. "Old Des Moines University, 1929," Des Moines Public Library, accessed July 15, 2013, http://www.desmoineslibrary.com/search/localhistory/olddmu.html.

7. Des Moines University Minutes, June 10, 1927.

8. Delnay, "History of the Baptist Bible Union," 193; "Alumni and Alumnae of Des Moines," *Baptist*, September 17, 1927, 1151.

consequences when this mix encountered the philosophy of the Baptist Bible Union, except perhaps to view the students as a mission field.[9]

The Bible Union launched the academic year with a conference on the campus of Des Moines University. Planned for three days at the end of September, it went into a fourth. Robert Harkness, the gospel songwriter, led the music. Aside from Shields, few of the announced speakers had national reputations. At the last moment, however, both Riley and Norris were persuaded to make an appearance. The big three were together again, probably for the last time.[10]

Some of the newer professors were also featured at the conference. In tones that were bound to appeal to the Bible Union crowd, E. C. Calloway (dean of the school of pharmacy) urged both teachers and preachers to "nail their flag to the masthead." E. O. Kaserman spoke on "The Biology of the Bible," attacking evolution as a philosophy that was, at best, incomplete and uncertain. With these phrases ringing in their ears, the members of the Baptist Bible Union left the Des Moines conference in a spirit of high optimism.[11]

Financial pressure set in almost immediately. Salaries and other bills had to be paid every month. The modernists who had not supported the old administration certainly were not going to support the new one. The Baptist Bible Union had already rejected the possibility of any denominational help. The leadership of the university quickly realized that even the conference fundamentalists were not going to give them money. In late October, Van Osdel wrote, "The institution has formidable enemies. Modernism would do almost anything to defeat the Bible Union, and unfortunately professed Denominational Fundamentalists would sit by and say 'Amen.'" He urged every friend of Des Moines University to send some amount to the secretary every week, even if only a dime.[12]

Also in late October, Shields wrote to the board and the executive committee alerting them to the need for another $50,000, asking them either to help raise the funds or to authorize a loan. Riley wrote back refusing his signature for any borrowed money. He wished the university well, but he was not going to stake his personal property on Shields's ability to raise such large sums. Still, he regularly promoted Des Moines University in his new paper, the *Christian Fundamentalist*, just as Van Osdel did in the *Baptist Temple News*.[13]

As the financial difficulties deepened, Des Moines University became

9. "Des Moines University Notes," *Christian Fundamentalist*, December 1927, 30–31; Delnay, "History of the Baptist Bible Union," 196–97.

10. "'The Beginning of Months' for Des Moines University," *Baptist Temple News*, August 20, 1927, 1–4; Van Osdel, "The Des Moines Conference," *Baptist Temple News*, October 8, 1927, 1–2; Delnay, "History of the Baptist Bible Union," 197.

11. Van Osdel, "The Des Moines Conference," 1–2; Jay A. Lapham, "Iowa Letter," *Baptist*, October 22, 1927, 1331.

12. Oliver W. Van Osdel, "A Great Opportunity," *Baptist Temple News*, October 29, 1927.

13. William B. Riley to Thomas T. Shields, October 25, 1927.

virtually the only item in the agenda of the Baptist Bible Union. The Union had been printing some Sunday School materials, but that was halted. The missions work, rudimentary as it was, began to falter. It was as if the Baptist Bible Union existed only to operate Des Moines University.

In fact, however, members of the Union still had to fight modernism on several fronts. A good example occurred in late October or early November, involving the Clarion Baptist Association of northwestern Pennsylvania. In 1925 the association, under the leadership of Baptist Bible Union members, recommended a statement of faith as part of its basis of fellowship. The statement was formally adopted in 1926, then was first implemented in 1927. Four out of twenty churches walked out of the meeting, refusing to acknowledge the statement. These four reconvened, along with a few members recruited from two of the other churches, and declared themselves to be the Clarion Association.

At this point the state convention stepped into the picture. At its meeting in Philadelphia, it voted to recognize the four churches as the Clarion Association, then made application to the Court of Common Pleas for a charter under the association's name. Three members of the majority association heard about the action and traveled to the hearing. Since they had no attorneys, they were given the opportunity to cross examine all witnesses, including the state secretaries and convention attorneys. John J. Van Gorder, one of the three pastors, was ecstatic. To J. Frank Norris he wrote, "Regardless of the decision we win hands down. As soon as we get the transcript we will be able to show the exact words of the state officials, et al. They are now out in the open.[14]

For men who were fighting such battles, Des Moines University could not become an exclusive interest, however important they may have considered it. Baptist Bible Union pastors did not abandon their local ministries, their opposition to modernism at the state and local level, or their commitment to missions. All of these interests took time, energy, and, most of all, money. For many, the university barely registered on the scale of priorities.

Back on campus, Shields preached in chapel in November. Half of the students went forward to pledge their loyalty to Christ. What no one seems to have remarked at the time was that the other half of the students did not. Of course, this reluctance was only to be expected within a religiously mixed student population. Those who did not respond to the gospel could hardly have remained unmoved. Even on Christian reckoning, preachers of the gospel are the savor of death to death and the savor of life unto life (2 Cor. 2:16). People who do not receive the gospel are often alienated by it.

14. John J. Van Gorder to J. Frank Norris, November 18, 1927. A copy of this letter was found in Van Osdel's papers.

Something like that seems to have begun with Shields's revival. Some students responded and were drawn into a deeper Christian faith. Others reacted and began to take a more dismissive attitude toward those who promoted the revival. This difference could hardly fail to produce tensions between students, or especially between some students and the administration.

Other decisions eroded the support of both students and faculty. J. E. Hampton was brought in to head up the Bible department, then quietly terminated when he was found incompetent in the classroom. The University Church that met in the chapel was given a month to vacate the premises, and the news was unfortunately delivered at a time when the pastor was sick with pneumonia. Because of this last decision, Shields was denounced in the *Baptist* for acting in "true Mussolini style."[15]

A larger issue was Shields's (and Rebman's) attitude toward the United States. The problem seems to have begun at a celebration of Washington's birthday, when Shields remarked that it was the Hessians rather than Washington who had run the British army over seventeen states. If the remark was meant in jest, it fell cold. So did Shields's disapproval of singing "The Star Spangled Banner" in chapel. So did the Canadians' refusal to stand for the national anthem when it was sung (by this time Rebman had received U.S. citizenship, but still refused to stand). Before long, rumor had it that Canadian students were being hazed. For a prank, the engineering students greased the flagpole so that the Stars and Stripes could not be lowered. Shields reportedly called the Des Moines fire department to have the flag hauled down—an act which began to embitter the city against him.[16]

In January 1928 Shields embarked on a two-month fundraising tour for the university. He traveled through the Southwest, then up and down the Pacific Coast, including into Canada, as well as traveling through the Midwest. Evidently the tour produced results. By the end of April, Shields could report that the indebtedness had been halved. Another $70,000 would wipe out the debt and pay for the rest of the school year. Beyond that, Shields estimated that $65,000 would be necessary to cover the next year's operations. He was ready to leave for the West Coast again, but had received word that he should wait.[17]

In the meanwhile, James McGinlay conducted two weeks of evangelistic meetings on campus. Many students responded, and Shields encouraged them to start a "Christian Fellowship" as a campus organization. Students began meeting before breakfast for prayer meetings. Spontaneous prayer

15. "Ejected from the Chapel of Des Moines," *Baptist*, January 7, 1928, 3.

16. Delnay, "History of the Baptist Bible Union," 203–04.

17. Oliver W. Van Osdel, "Des Moines University," *Baptist Temple News*, March 3, 1928, 3; Thomas T. Shields to the Trustees of Des Moines University, April 23, 1928.

meetings were held in dormitory rooms.[18] One result of this new society was further alienation of those who had not responded to McGinlay's invitations— and they knew better than to start a skeptics' fellowship.

During May 1928, board member J. W. Hoyt was in Iowa. He spent time in Des Moines and in Monroe, listening to what people had to say about Des Moines University. What he heard alarmed him. He wrote to Shields that he wished they could talk about what was happening: "If half what I heard is true, the situation is grave."[19]

The key to the trouble was probably that many members of the faculty, while orthodox, were moderates. They had been willing to live with modernistic colleagues and a liberal administration. Collegiality was high on their list of values. The new board and administration, however, were militants. From the beginning, they intended to use Des Moines University as a center to oppose liberalism. They saw liberals not as colleagues, but as enemies.

The difference came into focus during commencement activities. During a vespers service on the Sunday before commencement, a former student of the dean, now a Methodist bishop, was invited to preach. As the bishop commenced his remarks, Shields thought that he detected certain liberal catchphrases. After the sermon was over, Shields stepped to the podium and, speaking in behalf of the school, explained why the bishop's views were not taught at Des Moines University. Afterward, Dean Arthur E. Bennett was livid. He insisted to Shields that his former student was not a liberal, but was perfectly orthodox. Brimming with frustration, Shields took Bennett by the lapels and said, "I am not troubled about the Bishop. He is a passing stranger, but I am profoundly concerned to discover that you are unable to detect such rank poison as was served to the students today." In the evening service Shields publicly addressed the subject again, this time in front of the professors. He stated that the trustees would neither compromise nor permit the university to be used for the propagation of "such principles as had been enunciated in the afternoon."[20]

By any standard, Shields's treatment of Bennett and his tirade in the evening service was churlish. The professors (especially Bennett) must have felt as if they were being assaulted. Whatever Shields was hoping to accomplish, his conduct had the effect of permanently alienating his dean and many of his faculty. He had employed professors who shared his theology but who did not share his ethos. Now neither side was happy with that arrangement.

The school year closed with rebellion smoldering in the university, but

18. Thomas T. Shields to the Trustees of Des Moines University, April 23, 1928; Delnay, "History of the Baptist Bible Union," 205.

19. J. W. Hoyt to Thomas T. Shields, May 11, 1928.

20. Delnay, "History of the Baptist Bible Union," 206–07.

the summer break provided some opportunity for both the faculty and the administration to cool off. Focused as it was on Des Moines University, the Baptist Bible Union was still living in the larger world of theological give-and-take. While tensions had been rising within the university, events outside meant that the Union was still dogged with controversy.

Some of these controversies had been going on all year. The first was partly internal, between Oliver Van Osdel and W. B. Riley. Riley had begun publishing the *Christian Fundamentalist* as the organ of the World's Christian Fundamentals Association. As Van Osdel understood Riley's message, Riley had "hopes that out of this present great controversy, all Fundamentalists of whatever denominational name, will finally gravitate to this center and become one." Over against Riley, Van Osdel feared the development of a kind of evangelical super-denomination in which the traditional denominational distinctives would be downplayed out of deference to unity in the fundamentals.[21]

Van Osdel was too much of a Baptist to be happy with that prospect. He insisted that all of the Bible's teachings were important, and ultimate unity must come by "taking the Word of God just as it stands, believing that it says what it means and means what it says." Obviously, this did not lead him to dismiss all non-Baptists as non-Christians, but he was not willing to substitute fellowship around the fundamentals for full obedience to the Scriptures.[22]

Furthermore, Van Osdel objected to the entire course that fundamentalism had taken. He noted that fundamentalism was essentially a protest movement. From the beginning he had thought this was a mistake: "The Scriptural injunction is not to remain within the ranks of erroneous teachers and reform them, but to come out from among them and to be separate, and under these circumstances blessing is promised." While Van Osdel had done his best to support the fundamentalist agenda, he believed "there can never be complete success until the movement stands apart, unhindered by denominational harnesses and encumbering associations." In a word, the elder statesman of the Baptist Bible Union was still pushing for separation.[23]

From the beginning, Van Osdel had wanted the Baptist Bible Union to develop as an independent movement with a positive ministry, and not as a divisive movement. That purpose had been turned aside because "many of those who came into the Union have thought it the part of wisdom to make it reformatory rather than constructive." Now was the time to let "every true believer break away from every entangling alliance." Nevertheless, loyal friend that he was, Van Osdel continued to place his highest endorsement on Riley

21. Oliver W. Van Osdel, "Fundamentalism," *Baptist Temple News*, July 16, 1927, 1.
22. Ibid., 1–2.
23. Ibid., 2.

personally, and to recommend the *Christian Fundamentalist* as a publication that was "filled with good things."[24]

In March 1928 John Marvin Dean published an article in which he stated his high hopes for the conference fundamentalists at the Northern Baptist Convention in Detroit. Specifically, Dean wanted the convention to repeal the Brougher Resolution (which restricted but did not disallow open membership) and then to make other adjustments that would begin to purge liberalism from the convention. Van Osdel replied that he thought that Dean was a "good and great man," and that he shared Dean's wishes. Nevertheless, he had absolutely no hope that the fundamentalists would succeed. The reason was that fundamentalism had abandoned its initiative at the outset. Remembering the Buffalo and Des Moines conventions, Van Osdel wrote, "Those in charge of the Fundamentalist movement felt themselves so secure in their undertaking that they felt a good degree of generosity should be exercised toward the enemy, and thus they gave away their opportunity which has never returned."[25]

Van Osdel noted that the Northern Baptist Convention was about to receive a large gift from John D. Rockefeller Jr. Meanwhile, Massee was actively canvassing the country to get churches to match the gift. To repeal the Brougher Resolution would have the effect of voting Rockefeller out of the convention. Van Osdel stated that "this is about as likely to be done as that two plus two will become five." In fact, to vote Rockefeller out after accepting his money "would be a dishonest, discourteous, and unchristian thing." This was why modernistic control of the Northern Baptist Convention "will never be broken by Fundamentalists." Then, in words that could not be mistaken, Van Osdel said, "Fundamentalism has no opportunity in the N. B. C. If the historic Baptist faith is preserved at home and abroad it will be done by men who are discerning enough and brave enough to form a new Convention liberated from ecclesiasticism and true to the Word of God." While he had always favored separation, Van Osdel was becoming more explicit and more insistent.[26]

Shields also had a contentious year. Besides throwing himself into the presidency of Des Moines University, he faced an explosive situation in the Canadian convention. In 1925, Laurence H. Marshall had been appointed chair of practical theology at McMaster University. Shields was on the university's board of governors. When he received word that Marshall was a liberal, Shields requested that the appointment be delayed until a full investigation

24. Van Osdel, 3; Van Osdel, "Dr. Riley's Magazine," *Baptist Temple News*, August 6, 1927, 3–4.

25. Oliver W. Van Osdel, "Have Fundamentalists Ground for Hopes?" *Baptist Temple News*, May 5, 1928, 1–2.

26. Ibid., 2–3.

could be made. The dean rebuffed Shields's request and recommended that the appointment be confirmed. What followed was a bitter fight that terminated with Shields being ejected from McMaster's board and barred from future conventions. Then the Canadian convention took the unusual step of granting the convention leaders the authority to expel anyone who was not in harmony with its aims. Exercising this authority, in 1927 the convention officials permanently removed Shields and his followers. Separated from the convention, Shields led in organizing a new missionary and educational society as well as the Union of Regular Baptist Churches of Ontario and Quebec. All of which took place during Shields's year of presidency at Des Moines University.[27]

During the summer of 1928, however, Des Moines University was the focus of the Union's activities. Back in March, Shields had told the board that the indebtedness had been halved. Published reports from April showed that the finances were generally good. Even the *Baptist* was willing to congratulate Shields for having saved the school temporarily, and to express the hope "that the salvation may be to the uttermost." Riley called Shields a "superman." By June, however, the university needed $25,000 in order to finish the academic year in the black. Another appeal went out. With everything that was happening in Toronto, Shields must have been wondering how he could face another year as president at Des Moines.[28]

At that particular moment, the board received a ray of hope. Board member Harry Hamilton learned that the president of William Jewell College, Harry C. Wayman, had just resigned. Wayman let it be known that he had been forced out because he had fired three modernist professors. That was just the attitude that Shields was looking for. Wayman seemed like their kind of fellow, so with minimal investigation he was offered the presidency of Des Moines University.

The board held its June meeting in Toronto to coincide with the Baptist Bible Union's annual convention. The convention platform featured some old-timers such as T. T. Shields and Mordecai Hamm (Pettingill had been scheduled but did not attend). It also featured some of the rising young leaders of fundamentalism: Harry Hamilton, Howard Fulton, Robert T. Ketcham, and Earle G. Griffith. Though a Toronto meeting was convenient, it gave the board no real opportunity to get any sense of the atmosphere on campus.[29]

27. Gerald L. Priest, "T. T. Shields the Fundamentalist: Man of Controversy," *Detroit Baptist Seminary Journal* 10 (2005): 76–77.

28. "To All the Alumni and Friends," *Baptist*, May 26, 1928, 744; "Des Moines University," *Christian Fundamentalist*, June 1928, 24; Van Osdel, "Des Moines University," *Baptist Temple News*, June 2, 1928, 3.

29. "Program of the Annual Meeting," *Christian Fundamentalist*, May 1928, 15; "The Sixth Annual Meeting," *Baptist*, May 26, 1928, 745.

In addition to appointing Wayman as president, the board also formally decided to close all fraternities and sororities. These organizations would be given a year to dissolve themselves. The executive committee decided to organize a new mission and to stop endorsing independent agencies, but it failed to implement this decision. Shields, Schimpf, and Rebman were elected as officers. The executive committee now consisted of seven, three of whom were Van Osdel, Griffith, and Chester E. Tulga.[30]

Trouble broke out almost immediately after the meeting. In mid-July Harry Hamilton traveled to Iowa to deliver an ordination sermon. While he was there he tried to promote Des Moines University. Someone handed him a pamphlet written by Lewis M. Hale, accusing Wayman of claiming academic degrees that he did not actually possess. Shields quickly wrote to Hale, asking for copies of his documentation. Hale responded that the documentation had all been turned over to the board of William Jewell College, but that the pamphlet could speak for itself. Hamilton appealed to Shields to delay Wayman's installation. Shields responded that he thought the accusations were a "trick of the enemy." Even direct correspondence and further evidence from a board member at William Jewell could not change Shields's mind.[31]

For the moment, this controversy remained behind the scenes. Even so, the school year opened with mixed news. Enrollment had risen slightly, but anticipated funds failed to arrive over the summer. Consequently, the professors' salaries were in arrears. Shields wanted to throw himself into another fundraising tour, but for once the congregation at Jarvis Street would not allow it. Aware of the strain under which their pastor had been working, the church insisted that he take several weeks to rest. One evidence of Shields's exhaustion is that he agreed, spending part of September and all of October in England.[32]

In preparation for his absence, Shields wired Van Osdel asking him both to fill the pulpit at Jarvis Street and to speak at Wayman's installation in Des Moines. Van Osdel wired back that he was almost eighty-two. He added, "It would be presumptuous for me to attempt to supply your pulpit. I could not think of it. Des Moines presidential inauguration is a great occasion. Do not consider me in that connection one minute." Shields, however, would not accept this reply. "Deacons join me in urging you to come. Cannot accept refusal.... Must speak Des Moines also otherwise I won't go." Finally Van Osdel cabled back, "All right. Go ahead and fix it to suit yourself."[33]

30. Oliver W. Van Osdel, "Des Moines University," *Baptist Temple News*, June 23, 1928, 2; Delnay, "History of the Baptist Bible Union," 210.

31. Delnay, "History of the Baptist Bible Union," 214–16.

32. Thomas T. Shields to the Trustees of Des Moines University, September 15, 1928.

33. Thomas T. Shields to Oliver W. Van Osdel, telegram, ca. September 15, 1928; Van Osdel to Shields, telegram, ca. September 15, 1928.

Near the end of September, Max Schimpf (vice president of the Baptist Bible Union) wrote to Van Osdel (vice chairman of the DMU board) suggesting that the two of them try to raise funds while Shields was abroad. He suggested a letter to the constituencies of both the university and Bible Union. He was willing to sign it if Van Osdel would be willing to write it, then perhaps they could get Edith Rebman to print and mail it. Van Osdel drafted text and sent it to Schimpf for approval, copying Rebman. She wrote back that she and Wayman were already preparing a fundraising letter. Schimpf then suggested using Van Osdel's letter as a follow-up.[34]

Wayman's installation took place in November. As it turned out, Van Osdel was not the only speaker, since the event was combined with a Bible conference. Other preachers included James M. Gray of Moody Bible Institute, William L. Pettingill, Harry Hamilton, Robert T. Ketcham, W. B. Riley, and of course T. T. Shields. Wayman spoke more than once. Gray and Van Osdel were awarded honorary doctorates.[35]

While at this meeting, Riley was invited to serve on the board of trustees. He was reluctant to accept: "It seems absolutely suicidal to take on one ounce more than I am carrying. I do not believe there is another man carrying the load that I am. And yet I want Des Moines to succeed, so I am praying about it." Riley also urged that the Bible Union continue to meet separately from the Northern Baptist Convention. He believed that it needed to build up a fellowship of its own. "We are going to need it in the days to come," he wrote. "In fact, we do right now."[36]

Shields was prepared to take Riley's advice about keeping the Union away from the convention. He asked Van Osdel to try to select a date; Riley had already requested that it not interfere with the World's Christian Fundamentals Association. Then, in an uncommon demonstration of affection for Van Osdel, Shields wrote,

> We started back in 1923 together in the Bible Union work. I was a stranger, and the load, such as it was, was put upon my shoulders. You are almost the only man of the company who has stood by in any practical way, (of course you have had long experience of that kind of thing.) Neighbour dropped out, then Pettingill, then Norris and Riley, so far as any real support was concerned. But you and your church have stood by, first in the work of the Union, and then in the work of the University. . . . Not until the Lord opens His books will you have any idea of the tremendous contribution you have made to the conservation of the faith, not only in Michigan, but throughout

34. Maximilian Schimpf to Oliver W. Van Osdel, September 25, 1928; Schimpf to Van Osdel, October 8, 1928; Oliver W. Van Osdel to Minor Stevens, October 16, 1928.

35. Delnay, "History of the Baptist Bible Union," 216–17.

36. William B. Riley to Oliver W. Van Osdel, November 27, 1928.

the Continent. I at least am moved to thank God upon every remembrance of you.[37]

The spiritual emphasis on the Des Moines University campus was even more intense than it had been the previous year. In December J. Gresham Machen was on campus to preach and lecture. Shields was sufficiently impressed that he privately suggested making Machen a dean. Over Christmas break a group of male students organized a gospel team which preached and sang in churches throughout southeastern Minnesota.[38]

Correspondence from January reveals that Edith Rebman was engaged in significant organizational responsibility for both the university and the Bible Union. Others might be setting the vision, but much of the planning was up to her. From her office in Des Moines she was coordinating the annual convention of the Baptist Bible Union, trying to get Shields, Van Osdel, and others to select a meeting place (Rebman suggested Buffalo, where Howard Fulton was now pastoring). She was reporting on institutional finances and asking Bible Union pastors for donations. She was even coordinating a fundraising effort for the Sweet Baptist Mission to China, one of the independent agencies that the Bible Union had endorsed. In fact, she was acting very much like an executive officer.[39]

As president, Wayman had begun sounding like a fundamentalist. When a Baptist preachers' conference invited the Professor of Applied Christianity from Grinnell College to be their speaker, Wayman published an article denouncing the decision on the grounds that the professor was also preaching for First Unitarian Church. He concluded his article by observing that Unitarianism is the natural outcome of modernism. These words echoed sentiments that had often been expressed by fundamentalists.[40]

By most indications, Wayman was an affable chap who quickly ingratiated himself to the faculty. His organizational skills, however, appear to have been less than sterling, and he did not demand accountability. Given Rebman's precision, she and Wayman were virtually destined to clash. Worse, the lines of authority were not clear. Wayman was president of the institution, but Rebman was an officer of the board. At the outset, the board had given her complete oversight on campus—and this may well have included oversight over Wayman, no doubt to his surprise.

37. Thomas T. Shields to Oliver W. Van Osdel, December 21, 1928.

38. Edith Rebman to Oliver W. Van Osdel, January 7, 1929; Delnay, "History of the Baptist Bible Union," 217; Harry G. Hamilton, "The Des Moines University Gospel Team in Minnesota," *Baptist Temple News*, January 19, 1929, 4.

39. Edith Rebman to Oliver W. Van Osdel, January 7, 1929; Rebman to Van Osdel, January 8, 1929; Rebman to Baptist Bible Union Pastors, January 8, 1929; Mrs. W. S. Sweet to Rebman, February 5, 1929.

40. Harry Wayman, "Which Way Are the Iowa Baptists Going?" *Baptist Temple News*, January 19, 1929, 3.

Rebman was giving orders to the dean and perhaps even to the president. She was accused of operating a network of campus spies (historian William Brackney called it "academic espionage"). And no one had forgotten her refusal to stand for the national anthem. By about March, she had become the most despised person on campus.[41]

While Wayman later attempted to portray himself as a neutral mediator, he probably felt as irritated with Rebman as anyone else. At any rate, he was about to feel some pressure of his own. Both Shields and Riley had recently denounced the practice of claiming cheap doctorates, and now Shields was getting pressure about Wayman's degrees. In late April or early May, Shields told Wayman that they would need to clear up the controversy once for all.

Wayman was tired of questions about his academic background (he would later charge that accuser L. H. Hale had "determined to hound me for life"). Most likely, he also had something to hide. Ketcham, who was a university trustee, later claimed that Wayman had admitted to the board that he was guilty of claiming degrees he did not have. Either way, he knew that his presidency at Des Moines University was in danger, and he decided to take the offensive.[42]

He quickly found that he had allies. One of them was an Iowa pastor, later identified as Warren Steeves, who had been denied a board membership at Des Moines University and who was looking for retribution. Evidently, Shields, who was taking the train through Des Moines, met Rebman to discuss business over breakfast in a Des Moines restaurant. As it happened, the restaurant was located on the ground floor of a hotel, and the university's coach witnessed Shields and Rebman leaving the hotel together. This provided enough evidence to start a whispering campaign accusing the two of adultery.[43]

Animosity fueled the rumor. Steeves told the hotel clerk that he wanted to take pictures of some hotel rooms. Given permission, he found two rooms with a connecting door and snapped a photo with the door open. This snapshot was offered as proof that Shields and Rebman had spent the night together. So strong was the vindictiveness against the two that few paused even to question the flimsy evidence.

At this point, the deans wrote to the trustees requesting that Shields and Rebman be removed from office. Wayman talked specifically with trustee

41. Delnay, "History of the Baptist Bible Union," 218–19; Harry Wayman, "The Trouble at Des Moines University," typescript sent to Oliver W. Van Osdel, May 16, 1929; Brackney, *Congregation and Campus*, 229.

42. W. B. Riley, "The Dishonor of Literary Titles," *Christian Fundamentalist*, August 1927, 28–29; Wayman, "The Trouble at Des Moines University;" Ketcham, recorded interview, April 7, 1962; Delnay, "History of the Baptist Bible Union," 209, 220–21.

43. Ketcham, interview.

Minor Stevens. Stevens went to two fellow-trustees and repeated Wayman's accusations, stating that he could prove them. Acting on Stevens's assurances, the trustees, James H. Sperry and Frank E. Foulk, joined Stevens in demanding that Rebman call a special meeting of the trustees "to consider requesting the resignations of Dr. T. T. Shields and Miss Edith Rebman from all official connections with Des Moines University."[44]

By this time the situation was out of control, and the board was called together for an emergency meeting. Most of the trustees arrived on the campus on May 9. They found that someone had printed poster-sized copies of Shields's photograph with the caption, "Is he Edith's Ormiston?" The caption was a reference to a recent scandal in which female evangelist Aimee Semple McPherson was accused of running off for a fling with colleague Kenneth Ormiston. Somebody had taken the posters and used paper hanger's paste to cover every building on campus, as high as a person could reach. Van Osdel wrote, "It was evident upon the arrival of the board that everything was in readiness for a riot, and the deans and the president seemed to have no disposition to in any way quiet or hinder the prevailing mob spirit."[45]

The board began its meeting on Friday, May 10. Most of the day was spent hearing the evidence against Shields and Rebman. As it turned out, Minor Stevens had nothing to say. The accusations turned out to be nothing but character assassination. Faced with these findings, the board completely exonerated both Shields and Rebman.[46]

At this point the deans, speaking for the faculty, demanded that Shields and especially Rebman be fired because of their heavy-handed administration. This was probably their strongest complaint, but after hearing such scandalous false accusations, the board was in no mood to listen. To them, the deans' complaints were merely evidence of disloyalty. Even Van Osdel had little sympathy: "For the deans to assert that they could not get along with Miss Rebman is to indict themselves of childish weakness, and an expression of a fear that their own work would not stand inspection."[47]

The board was beginning to believe that Wayman and the faculty were guilty of sowing dissatisfaction among the students. Shields had a solution ready: just fire them all. At the end of the semester, every position in the university would be declared vacant. Anyone who wished to resume employment in the institution could apply to Edith Rebman. Four of the trustees dissented, but Shields's motion passed.[48]

44. Minor Stevens, James H. Sperry, and F. E. Foulk to Rebman May 2, 1929.
45. Ketcham, interview; Van Osdel, "Des Moines University," *Baptist Temple News*, May 25, 1929, 2.
46. Delnay, "History of the Baptist Bible Union," 223–25.
47. Van Osdel, "Des Moines University," *Baptist Temple News*, May 25, 1929, 2–3.
48. Oliver W. Van Osdel, "The Des Moines Situation," *Baptist Temple News* (8 June 1929),

The board, however, had badly misjudged the students. Already while the board was meeting on Friday morning, a freshman, I. Cedric Peterson, passed himself off as the student body president and gathered the others in the chapel for a fiery address. In response to his charge that the board was about to fire seven professors, the students drafted resolutions of confidence for the whole faculty. Professors who were in the building did nothing to dispel this meeting. That afternoon the students wore small American flags as an act of defiance. On Saturday morning, the board reached its decision to fire all of the university's employees—an action that exceeded anything that even Peterson had suggested.

The trustees called for the students to meet that afternoon, planning to announce the results of the board meeting. It was too late. The word was already out. Students from the college of engineering drove to a local hatchery and asked to buy some rotten eggs. The manager refused to sell any, but, with a wink, told the students where the rotten eggs were kept while awaiting disposal.

At lunchtime Shields left the building a bit ahead of the others. Suddenly, students began to converge on his path and a cab pulled up to the curb. Fearing that Shields was about to be kidnapped, one of the trustees rushed out and pulled him back into the building. The trustees called the police, who sent a couple of officers. The officers fraternized with the students for a while and then left. The board did not take advantage of this opportunity to vacate the campus, but went on with its meeting.

About 7:30 in the evening, rotten eggs began sailing through the open windows. When the windows were pulled shut, the eggs were replaced with stones. As windows shattered, the board retreated from room to room. Then hundreds of eggs and stink bombs came whizzing through the windows. A call to police was not answered for forty minutes.

During that forty minutes, the students mobbed the administration building. The board retreated into a washroom and then into a closet. All the while there were cries of "Get Shields!" and "Beat him up!" Both observers and rioters subsequently agreed that if the mob could have found Shields, they would probably have murdered him.

After the rioters dispersed, the board members emerged from hiding. They found everything covered in broken glass, rotten eggs, and unhatched chicks. The police refused to protect the building and stated that they could only guarantee the board members' personal safety by taking them to the police station. The board, still technically in session, passed a resolution closing the university until further notice, and then left in police cars. Once they arrived

---

1–2; Delnay, "History of the Baptist Bible Union," 225.

at the station, the police refused to protect the board members anywhere outside the station itself. Shields was in the most danger, so he quickly traveled to his hotel, packed his bags, and left by the 11:00 p.m. train.[49]

The following Monday several students got an injunction halting the board from formally closing the school before the end of the academic year. Classes did not resume, but Wayman and the faculty held a graduation and handed out diplomas. Those diplomas did not bear the signature of the chairman of the board.

Just a week later, the Baptist Bible Union held its annual convention in Howard Fulton's church, First Baptist of Buffalo, New York. According to reports, Riley had been scheduled to preach, but after the riot he refused to appear. Dr. French Oliver happened to be in Buffalo and was invited to deliver three addresses. Shields also spoke. The Des Moines University board also met.

Professor Callaway appeared as representative of the faculty and students. Accounts of his treatment at the meeting differ. According to the *New York Times*, Callaway was interrupted by repeated badgering from Shields until he finally said, "I think I've taken this browbeating like a sport, haven't I?" at which point he left the meeting to applause and cries of "yes you have." According to Van Osdel, however, Callaway "was given opportunity to say everything that he would, and when he had said all that he cared to say he was urged to say more. In addition, after he had left the platform he was urged to return and make additional statements if he cared to do so, but he refused." Van Osdel stated that the entire convention then voted without dissent to support the board.[50]

Wayman, Stevens, and Foulk were removed from the board and several new members were added. Shields, Van Osdel, and Rebman were all reelected to their positions as board officers. The board voted to open a College of Biblical Theology—the equivalent of a seminary—to offer graduate courses in theology. It also chose a committee to appoint faculty members and stipulated several new requirements for professors.

In an important resolution, the board voided all certificates and diplomas that were awarded by Wayman and the faculty after the riot. It agreed to exchange authorized diplomas for the unauthorized ones, except in the case of

---

49. Shields later wrote a full report of the incident and printed it as a special, 48-page edition of the *Gospel Witness*. He printed 75,000 copies with the intention of sending them to every Baptist minister in the world. The total cost of producing the special issue was about $8,000. Thomas T. Shields, "Des Moines University Riots," *Gospel Witness*, May 23, 1929; Oliver W. Van Osdel, "The Gospel Witness," *Baptist Temple News*, June 1, 1929, 3; Delnay, "History of the Baptist Bible Union," 227–31.

50. Delnay, "History of the Baptist Bible Union," 233; Van Osdel, "Des Moines University," *Baptist Temple News*, May 25, 1929, 2.

students who were known to have participated in the riot. Permanent records and transcripts would be handled as normal. The board also authorized a committee to oversee the administration of all these matters.[51]

Des Moines University never reopened. In August the corporation went into receivership. The academic records were taken to Sioux Falls College. For years the buildings stood vacant, equipment set up in the laboratory, library books in shelves or on tables. During the early 1940s the property was purchased by Alfred Lawson, who opened what he called the "University of Lawsonomy." Ten years later Lawson sold the property to a developer and moved his "university" to a farm near Racine, Wisconsin. The developer razed most of the old buildings and replaced them with the Park Fair Shopping Center.[52]

The irony is that, up until the riot, Des Moines University was doing better under the Baptist Bible Union than it had for years. The decline in student population had been halted and even reversed. While cash was still tight, the indebtedness was being paid down. The school had at least restored its credit with local merchants. To all appearances, graduates were in demand. What miscalculations could have brought such a precipitous end to such an auspicious beginning?

In brief, the differences had been too great. In America's heartland Shields came across as an arrogant foreigner. He further miscalculated the difference between the militants and the moderates. The board was made up of militants, but most of the professors were religious moderates—and the board alienated even the militants among them. Another problem was that Shields was an outsider to academics. He had no college experience, either as a student, teacher, or administrator, nor did most of the board members. He seems to have thought of himself as the pastor of the school, and to Shields that vision involved a peculiar kind of pastoral authority. Accordingly, his administration came with built-in misunderstanding between him and the whole school. Neither side more than barely knew what the other was talking about, but each seemed to think that the other side perfectly understood what it was saying. Granting Edith Rebman almost carte blanche authority could only aggravate this situation, and her manner of confrontation made things worse. Given these mistakes, a collision was inevitable.

51. Oliver W. Van Osdel, "Action of the Des Moines University Board," *Baptist Temple News*, June 29, 1929, 1–4.

52. The alumni association continued to meet almost every year for another sixty years. Regular Baptist professors Robert Delnay and George Houghton attended the last two meetings during the fall of 1988 and 1989. The aging remnant met for lunch at the Fort Des Moines Hotel and shared their memorabilia and memories. The clear impression afterward was that not an alumnus there had any idea of the forces that had actually closed their school. What to them was a lark was to the Bible Union a matter of profound gravity. Shields may have been guilty of heavy-handed leadership, but he was certainly innocent of the charges that Steeves leveled.

The Low Ebb

In retrospect, the Washington convention was probably the high-water mark for the Baptist Bible Union. Even then fissures were beginning to open within the organization. For all of its work and for all of its protests, the Bible Union did not have one clear victory to show.

By the following year, 1927, the militants came to realize that there was no hope of retaking the convention. Despite the perception that most of its 11,000 churches were conservative, the modernists had the NBC totally under their control. Furthermore, increasing numbers of its missionaries were coming out of modernistic schools. The only seminaries that were not under direct liberal control were Northern (founded in 1913), Central in Kansas City (1920), and Eastern (1925), all of which had been established in reaction against modernism. All of the older schools had gone modernist: Newton, Crozer, Colgate, Rochester, Chicago, and Berkeley. All of the colleges were teaching evolution in their science departments and none was taking a literal view of the Bible.

One need not look far for other evidences of modernistic control. Of all the state conventions, only two were ever retrieved by conservatives: Arizona and Minnesota. By 1930 nearly every downtown "First Baptist" had a modernist for its pastor. Only the neighborhood churches and the small towns still heard the gospel according to Paul.

Still reeling from the debacle of Des Moines University, the leaders and members of the Baptist Bible Union could see the trends pretty clearly. The question for them was what to do next. For five years they had acted as a protest movement in connection with the Northern Baptist Convention. Then for two years they had focused most of their institutional energy on a failed university. Whatever happened, the future of the Baptist Bible Union was going to look very different from the past.

Part of the answer was determined by brute circumstances. On September 4 prices in the stock market began to fall. Then on October 29 came Black Tuesday and the Great Depression. John Roach Straton died of a heart attack that same day. The world was changing.

Shields had been reelected president of the Baptist Bible Union. Vice presidents were John J. Van Gorder and Edward A. Roberts. Schimpf, Van Osdel, and Earle G. Griffith were members of the executive committee, but the others were virtually unknown. While nominally president, Shields began to retreat into his work in Canada, while Riley wanted nothing more to do with Shields or the Baptist Bible Union.

Tension had arisen occasionally between Riley and Shields, but they had managed to maintain a publicly cordial relationship. As recently as the previous November, Shields had tried to recruit Riley for the board of Des Moines

University. Riley begged off, pointing to his responsibilities with First Baptist Church, Northwestern Bible School, and the World's Christian Fundamentals Association. More was at stake than Riley stated, however. He had begun to entertain serious misgivings about Shields's leadership. More than that, the two were on different trajectories. Shields had been thrown out of the Canadian convention and had organized a separatist convention of Baptist fundamentalists. Riley was headed back toward the Northern Baptist Convention, where he would remain until the year of his death. He was throwing himself more and more into interdenominational fundamentalism.

After the Des Moines riot, the differences between the two leaders erupted into open hostility. Riley withheld his moral support, and in fact leveled criticisms against both Shields and Rebman. Shields responded indignantly. Then Riley accepted an invitation to preach from the platform of the Northern Baptist Convention in Cleveland, sharing the responsibility with Harry Emerson Fosdick. To Shields, this decision was indefensible—and he said so publicly.

Very quickly, the relationship turned ugly. Someone drew Shields's attention to a paragraph in Riley's paper, the *Christian Fundamentalist*, and told him that the paragraph was about him.

> There is an essential difference between a sane contention for the faith and an acrimonious spirit that can walk with no one. There are men with whom you must agree to the last jot and tittle; whose deliverances you must accept even to the semicolons and commas, or else come under their anathemas. Such men make poor material for successful evangelical movements, and they even doom the same when they assume leadership.[53]

Shields's remark was, "If that be so, I am glad to be informed of it, for I had no idea I was such a tyrant." He reciprocated with sentiments that were as hard as Riley's: "I have met with not a few disappointments in our Bible Union fellowship. I fear Dr. Riley is not a Baptist in any true sense, and is just now displaying a spirit which is difficult to understand."[54]

Over the next months the situation continued to deteriorate between the two leaders. Riley responded heatedly to Shields's criticisms. When Van Osdel attempted to intervene, Riley wrote,

> Do not forget that I did not start this controversy but Shields made a vicious attack upon me, which I answered privately to him in a way to silence him; and publicly in as mild a manner as I thought I could. I do not need to tell you anything, you know perfectly well, or as well as any body living why I did not, and why I could not back Shields

---

53. Quoted by Thomas T. Shields to Oliver W. Van Osdel, May 8, 1930.
54. Shields to Van Osdel, May 8, 1930. Shields sent copies of this letter to the whole executive committee.

in the Des Moines affair, and down in your secret soul you admired me for refusing to put myself in the breech that would have required falsification on my part.[55]

In his reply, Van Osdel affirmed his esteem for Riley: "I have not ceased to hold you in the very highest regard, and to hope that our friendship reaching over many years may continue to the end." Nevertheless, Van Osdel clearly thought that Riley was wrong in both his attitude and actions toward Shields. He blamed the Des Moines debacle on Wayman, Steeves, and Stevens.

> The one unfortunate step was the choice of Dr. Wayman as President. I have known quite a number of liars. Dr. Wayman was one of the worst I ever met. He had Steeves of Iowa, and Stevens of Des Moines, put their heads together and deliberately determined to ruin Dr. Shields. Dr. Wayman made a trip to Minneapolis and told you his invented story. I am afraid you believed him. You thereupon made a demand upon Dr. Shields and Miss Rebman which they regarded as an attack. . . .
>
> Personally, if I had been attacked as Dr. Shields was, I would defend myself, and I would hope that my friends would stand by me. I certainly think you ought to settle this matter with Dr. Shields and be on friendly terms with one of the biggest and best men that ever lived.[56]

Riley would have none of it. He denied that Wayman ever came to Minneapolis or told him anything. On the contrary, he believed that the problem arose from Rebman and Shields themselves.

> I shortly discovered the imperiousness of [Shields's] secretary, and on both occasions when I was chosen as a member of the Board of the University, I told him that she would wreck the university and I refused to serve in view of that certainty. Edith is very talented, but not at all fitted for teamwork.
>
> Dr. Shields' attack upon me in consequence of my decision to appear at Cleveland [for the Northern Baptist Convention] was absolutely unjustifiable and in view of his immediate past, most amazing. I regarded him a mental giant, but I am very sorry that I have not seen in him the Christian courtesy toward men from whom he happened to dissent even on small matters, that would have eventuated in his success as the leader of the Union; in fact, that would have given him a permanent victory in Canada itself.
>
> It is my conviction and always has been that we are to hold the truth steadfastly, unequivocally, and we are to hold it in love. Not to speak of the incidents that really brought the crash at Des Moines, this lack of ordinary courtesy toward those who would not sign on the

55. William B. Riley to Oliver W. Van Osdel, September 10, 1930.
56. Van Osdel to Riley, September 18, 1930.

dotted line every opinion held by the Doctor has been his undoing, and I have not apology to make to him or to any other man.[57]

Shields could be just as intransigent as Riley. A year later, Van Osdel tried again to make peace between the two men. Shields replied,

So far as I can judge, Riley is now about the worst enemy of Baptist Fundamentalism.

Dr. Riley's course, to me, is most tragic. He shows all the bitterness that characterized Massee and others in his opposition to those who were once his colleagues. I have lost all confidence, not only in his profession, but in his manhood. Norris from time to time continues to eulogize him, but to my certain knowledge he has betrayed Norris as he has betrayed everybody else who has ever trusted him.[58]

The friction between Riley and Shields could easily be seen as a case of pigheadedness between two embittered leaders. Undoubtedly, stubbornness and bitterness did have a role to play. More was at stake than personal pique, however. Now that the protest of the Baptist Bible Union had failed, they had taken different paths. Both men were separatists of a sort, but each held a vision of separatism that differed from the other. Riley still hoped to find a way to purge the convention or, failing that, to recover some resources that had been captured by the liberals. Shields, however, had become convinced that the conventions were beyond purging—in fact, the Canadian convention had pointedly truncated his efforts by separating from him. Consequently, Shields had become what was called a "come-outer." He was committed to abandoning the institutions that were under liberal control and starting over again. Shields could not help seeing Riley as hopelessly compromised, while Riley necessarily perceived Shields as an extremist.

Van Osdel was definitely on Shields's side of the argument. Because of his close and longstanding friendship with Riley, however, the Minneapolis pastor was willing to tolerate some rebukes from Van Osdel that he would not accept from Shields. For his part, Van Osdel remained committed to Riley, even though he sometimes felt personally affronted by Riley's attacks upon "come-outism."

Van Osdel had been a "come-outer" since 1909, when he led in founding the Grand River Valley Baptist Association. When it renamed itself the Michigan Orthodox Baptist Association in 1920, the entire group was thrown out of the Michigan Baptist Convention. In April 1928 Van Osdel was one of the leaders who transformed the state Baptist Bible Union in Michigan into a separatist Regular Baptist Convention of Michigan. The Michigan Orthodox

---

57. Riley to Van Osdel, September 22, 1930.
58. Thomas T. Shields to Van Osdel, August 29, 1931.

Baptist Association—now consisting of thirty-four churches—joined the new convention as a body. This move meant that Van Osdel had pioneered "come-outism" at the state level as well as the local level.[59]

About 1926 Shields began to use the name *Regular Baptist*, and Van Osdel borrowed it from him. Van Osdel offered a brief definition of a Regular Baptist in 1928, specifying that they were Regular because, "we are holding to the faith in every detail that has come down to us from our historic people." In context, Van Osdel was contrasting Regular Baptists with the irregular beliefs of theological liberals. It would appear, therefore, that the term *Regular Baptist*, as Shields and Van Osdel used it, simply means an orthodox, conservative, or biblicist Baptist.[60]

Neighbour and Van Osdel had originally envisioned the Baptist Bible Union as a "come-out" organization. That intention was diverted by Riley, Shields, and Norris, but Van Osdel never abandoned the vision. After the 1927 Northern Baptist Convention in Chicago, the BBU began to go its own way. Even as it focused on Des Moines University, Van Osdel continued to press for separation.[61]

At the same time, Van Osdel was becoming cooler toward Riley's interdenominational involvement. He expressed these reservations as early as July 1927. The issue came up again in June 1929, when Riley ran an article urging membership in the World's Christian Fundamentals Association. Part of Riley's sales pitch was to question the legitimacy of independent movements. Van Osdel took these words personally, retorting that Riley's interdenominationalism amounted to compromise. [62]

A month later, Van Osdel wrote that he wished for a more definite label than *fundamentalist*. He noted that "a great variety of people whose beliefs are very widely separated are valiantly and vociferously declaring themselves Fundamentalists." He asked for some "ingenious Baptist" to invent a term "completely expressive of a Regular Baptist who stands true to Christ and His Word, without confusing himself with pedo-Baptists." In short, he preferred to be known as a Baptist rather than by the "promiscuous word Fundamentalist."[63]

These remarks must be placed in context. On the one hand, Van Osdel

---

59. *Twentieth Annual Meeting of the Grand Rapids Association of Regular Baptist Churches* (Grand Rapids: Grand Rapids Association of Regular Baptist Churches, 1928), 29; Van Osdel, "The Coming Associational Meeting," *Baptist Temple News*, August 25, 1928, 1–2; Van Osdel, "Are Baptists Done?" *Baptist Temple News*, September 15, 1928, 4.

60. Van Osdel, "The Coming Associational Meeting," *Baptist Temple News*, August 25, 1928, 1.

61. Van Osdel, "Are Baptists Done?" *Baptist Temple News*, September 15, 1928, 4.

62. Van Osdel, "Fundamentalism," *Baptist Temple News*, July 16, 1927, 1–3; Van Osdel, "International and Ancient Fundamentalism," *Baptist Temple News*, June 8, 1929, 4.

63. Oliver W. Van Osdel, "Fundamentalism," *Baptist Temple News*, July 6, 1929, 2–3.

had paid a severe price to become a Baptist. He was reared in the home of a Methodist class leader, and when he submitted himself for baptism, his whole family ostracized him. On the other hand, his opposition to interdenominationalism was hardly as extreme as these words sound. He sent students and money both to Moody and to Northwestern. He brought non-Baptists into the Wealthy Street pulpit. At this particular point in time, however, Van Osdel saw the need for an explicitly Baptist fellowship to engage in work that could not be done by an interdenominational group. He was not willing to surrender all parachurch ministry to interdenominational organizations. Most importantly, he was determined to rescue the Baptist Bible Union.

The Union certainly needed rescuing. After June 1929 activity virtually came to a halt. M. E. Hawkins offered his church in Mishawaka, Indiana, for the 1930 convention, but no one seems to have made any plans. Writing to the executive committee in May 1930, Shields admitted that the Union had been "practically out of business for a year." In fact, the only reason some of the committee wanted to hold another annual meeting was to avoid the appearance that the Des Moines riot had killed them off.[64]

In the middle of February, Rebman wrote to the executive committee that they would meet in Mishawaka on March 6 and 7 to decide on the future of the Baptist Bible Union. No help was available for expenses because the treasury was empty. This was her last official communication as secretary of the Union. She was preparing to embark for China as a missionary.[65]

Once they saw Mishawaka, the executive committee decided that it was definitely not the place to hold the convention. Of course, this left some uncertainty about just where the Baptist Bible Union would meet. A few of the men suggested going back to a preconvention conference format with the Northern Baptist Convention, which was meeting in Cleveland that year. After a bit of discussion, the executive committee agreed with the suggestion. There was also a strong feeling that the time had come to change the organization's name. The old name was too closely associated with the debacle at Des Moines University. Most of the committee also wanted a name that would denote the positive program of the Union: perhaps something with the word *missionary* in it.[66]

Van Osdel had been prevented from attending the Mishawaka meeting. When he heard about the decision to go back to the Northern Baptist Convention, however, he was incredulous. As far as he was concerned, that was a huge step in the wrong direction. Harry Hamilton expressed much the same

---

64. Thomas T. Shields to the Baptist Bible Union executive committee, May 9, 1930; Maximilian Schimpf to Thomas T. Shields, April 25, 1930.
65. Edith Rebman to Oliver W. Van Osdel, February 15, 1930.
66. Maximilian Schimpf to Oliver W. Van Osdel, March 29, 1930.

opinion. Shields and the executive committee, however, seemed to be too fatigued to develop an alternative. It was now the end of April, and time was running out for the Baptist Bible Union.[67]

Others besides Hamilton shared Van Osdel's view. One example is Chester Tulga of North Platte, Nebraska. In the middle of the discussion over a meeting place, he wrote to Van Osdel,

> The battle is hard but compromising with the enemy isn't one of my failings so I keep on. However, I am through cleaning up the denomination. Hereafter the Convention meetings will neither be adorned or marred by my presence. I have become a come-outer. I am through with the Northern Baptist Convention. I write this with regret but I see no other way for me but that. My church here is with me. We are free from convention control and will remain so. I have no place to hang my hat, ecclesiastically speaking, for I stand practically alone here. But I am going to hang in mid air awhile I suppose. Outside the camp alone is preferable to the camp.[68]

Finally, Van Osdel decided to take matters into his own hands. On April 29 he sent a letter to the executive committee offering to host the Baptist Bible Union at Wealthy Street on June 11 and 12. He said that he hoped to use the meeting to reorganize the Baptist Bible Union into some kind of separatist fellowship with a positive agenda. Shields polled the executive committee, then wired Van Osdel that his offer was "unanimously and heartily" approved. In fact, Van Osdel could arrange the program to suit himself. The executive committee would send him their suggestions.[69]

Under normal circumstances, Van Osdel preferred to leave leadership to others, but these were not normal circumstances. The Baptist Bible Union had lost its secretary. The mailing lists were badly out of date. No planning committee had been appointed. Everything was up to him, and he was well past eighty years old.

He rose to the occasion. He immediately prepared a tentative program and sent it to the executive committee. While waiting for their approval, he began contacting speakers: getting men to agree on such short notice would not be easy. He also wrote up a call for the meeting, had it approved by the executive committee, and published it in the *Baptist Temple News*.

The call is an interesting document. While it acknowledged that "ostensibly this is to be a meeting of the Baptist Bible Union of North America," it clearly indicated that the purpose of the meeting was to form a separatist

---

67. Maximilian Schimpf to Thomas T. Shields, April 25, 1930.
68. Chester E. Tulga to Oliver W. Van Osdel, April 26, 1930.
69. Thomas T. Shields to Oliver W. Van Osdel, May 8, 1930; Thomas T. Shields to the Baptist Bible Union executive committee, May 9, 1930.

organization. Furthermore, the call specified that those who attended should be authorized as representatives or delegates by their churches. The Baptist Bible Union had been a "very loose form of organization," but now the time had come to form "some tangible form of organization consonant with Baptist principles."[70]

Shields reprinted the call in the *Gospel Witness*, and both he and Van Osdel continued to promote the meeting in print. For Van Osdel, however, a printed call was insufficient. He sent personal letters of invitation to many pastors, probably at his own expense. He specifically encouraged Michigan pastors to bring their congregations to the meeting.

When the meeting convened at Wealthy Street, about ninety delegates from churches showed up (Van Osdel noted that this was three times the number who had founded the American Baptist Foreign Missionary Society). At Shields's suggestion, Van Osdel had left the daytime sessions open for discussion and planning. The result was a complete overhaul of the organization—indeed, the establishment of an altogether new organization. It would be named the Missionary Union of Baptist Churches of North America. As the name implied, it was to be a fellowship of churches rather than individuals.

Howard Fulton of Buffalo was elected as president of the new organization. Several vice presidents were chosen by region. Shields became the first vice president, representing Canada. Other regional vice presidents were chosen, then the new organization also appointed a committee of five to draft a constitution and statement of faith and to organize the next year's meeting. The committee included Fulton, Shields, Schimpf, Ketcham, and D. R. Walkinshaw.

Instead of attending the June meeting of the Baptist Bible Union, Riley appeared at the Northern Baptist Convention in Cleveland, where he shared the platform with Harry Emerson Fosdick. For the Bible Union men, this decision seemed like a betrayal. Probably stung by criticisms from Shields, Riley ran an article in the *Christian Fundamentalist* defending his decision and taking a swipe at those who had been expelled from the denomination. He probably never paused to consider that this reproach would also fall upon his old friend Oliver Van Osdel.[71]

While Van Osdel took no personal offense (as he put it, "we have known Dr. W. B. Riley all his ministerial life"), and while he continued to express esteem and even admiration for Riley, he felt bound to reply. He stated that by preaching with Fosdick, Riley had put a stamp of approval upon the Inclusive Policy of the convention. Riley had claimed that he wanted to stay in the

70. "A Call to All Real Baptists Everywhere," *Baptist Temple News*, May 17, 1930, 1–4.
71. W. B. Riley, "My Cleveland Appearance," *Christian Fundamentalist* (June 1930), 688.

convention to try to recapture some of the resources, but Van Osdel observed that the resources did not amount to that much. Besides, Scripture itself "has always insisted everywhere on the people of God separating themselves from all contaminating influences." [72]

Van Osdel went on to criticize Riley's interdenominationalism (again). This time he deployed a new argument.

> All our lives we have opposed Christian people in any endeavor to distinguish between essentials and non-essentials in the Word of God. For anyone to say that the Word of God contains matter that is not essential, is to disparage the inspiration and revelation and the Author of the Bible itself. . . . We believe that the Bible is inspired from the first word to the last. It is all essential and all Fundamental, or the Holy Spirit would not have dictated it. . . . To be sure there are doctrinal portions, prophetic portions, and historical portions, but every part is essential to the fully developed Christian life, or God would not have placed these particular things in His Word.[73]

While Van Osdel's criticism of Riley's participation in the convention was cogent, his objections to interdenominationalism are puzzling. For one thing, Van Osdel certainly did not believe in a dictation theory of inspiration, though he sounds like he did here. For another, the aged pastor did not treat all doctrines as equally important. He disagreed with Shields over eschatology and covenant theology, but the two regularly exchanged pulpits and worked together in the Bible Union. He held peculiar views on women's ministry (more on this later), but he did not cut off fellowship with people who disagreed. He had brought the Methodist evangelist Bob Jones into his pulpit, and he had been willing to have the Presbyterian J. Gresham Machen in the pulpit of Des Moines University.

What could Van Osdel have meant by denying the distinction between essentials and nonessentials? The key probably lies in the expression "essential to the fully developed Christian life." Fundamental doctrines are normally understood to be those doctrines that are essential to the gospel. Interdenominational institutions like the World's Christian Fundamentals Association could come close to sounding as if the fundamentals were sufficient for faith and life. That was what Van Osdel denied. More was necessary for the fully developed life of faith. By themselves, the fundamentals were not sufficient for fully obedient Christianity. For example, Van Osdel would have argued that believer immersion was essential for obedience, though not for salvation.

Riley responded in the next issue of the *Christian Fundamentalist*. He

---

72. Oliver W. Van Osdel, "A Very Great Sorrow," *Baptist Temple News*, June 28, 1930, 1–2.
73. Ibid., 2–3.

insisted that his appearance in Cleveland did not endorse the Inclusive Policy, but was an opportunity to put the fundamentalist cause in front of the convention. He disclaimed any attack upon those who had been expelled from the convention, wishing only to keep them from insisting that everyone else had to leave with them. He pointed out that, unlike Van Osdel in Michigan, he had actually won in Minnesota. He asked why, if the biblical commands really required people to come out of the conventions, had Van Osdel and others stayed in until they were thrown out?[74]

Van Osdel continued the controversy in the *Baptist Temple News*, stating, "The Northern Baptist Convention is permeated with modernism from center to circumference." By appearing in this environment, Riley could only strengthen the position of the liberals—an endorsement of the inclusive nature of the convention was unavoidable. Van Osdel also reminded Riley that the Grand River Valley Baptist Association actually had withdrawn from the Grand Rapids Baptist Association. It had ceased support of the state convention and was attempting to "oppose the sway of Modernism" at the time it was thrown out of it. He reiterated his arguments against interdenominationalism, then said, "We wish that Dr. Riley with his great ability and his wonderful powers of leadership was completely lined up with Regular Baptists who have been compelled to declare their independence for truth's sake."[75]

Instead of publishing another article, Riley wrote directly to Van Osdel. He stated that he was not going to answer Van Osdel again, for two reasons. First, "I love you and always will, and on that account do not care to keep up what others could interpret as a controversy." Second, "I feel that all these attacks on one another discredit fundamentalism in every form in the eyes of the enemy, . . . and I do not wish to provide them pabulum." Then he added,

> In starting fundamentalism I did not give up my views of baptism, or any other biblical doctrine but I did feel that I could join with believing Presbyterians, Methodists and Congregationalists in opposing the common enemy. And if I had it to do over again, notwithstanding the fact that it caused me much time and anxiety I certainly would organize afresh the identical movement, the World's Christian Fundamental Association.[76]

For his part, Van Osdel reassured Riley that he held him in the highest regard. He intended to say no more about the matter, and would have said

74. W. B. Riley, "The Criticism of Beloved Brethren," *Christian Fundamentalist* (August 1930), 48.

75. Oliver W. Van Osdel, "A Great Sorrow Intensified," *Baptist Temple News*, September 6, 1930, 1–4. Van Osdel reproduced the relevant portions of Riley's article verbatim.

76. William B. Riley to Oliver W. Van Osdel, September 10, 1930.

nothing at all except "for what seemed to me to be a slur upon those who were out of the Denomination." The matter seemed to be closed.[77]

Then came the October issue of the *Christian Fundamentalist*. Defending his presence at the Cleveland meeting, Riley referred to the Northern Baptist Convention as "his own convention." This was more than Van Osdel could bear. He wrote back to Riley, "This was somewhat startling to me, for the Northern Baptist Convention possesses all the Modernists who are masquerading under the name of Baptists including the notorious Fosdick." Van Osdel pointed out that the Michigan convention was about to meet in Wishart's church—an unqualified endorsement of his infidelity. Yet many Michigan Baptists stayed in the convention because they saw themselves standing just where Riley was. Van Osdel wished that he could have Riley's support. He concluded, "Dr. Curtis Lee Laws has announced that he serves a composite denomination, and for you to claim ownership of the Northern Baptist Convention is certainly startling."[78]

If Van Osdel was disappointed in Riley, the news that he received from Chester Tulga did nothing to cheer him. Tulga wrote on New Year's Eve to announce that Earle V. Pierce had invited him to become the Nebraska representative for the convention fundamentalists. This would require a reversal from Tulga, who only a short time before had written that "outside the camp alone is preferable to the camp." Evidently, occupying a prestigious position within the camp was preferable to either: "After some hesitation I have consented. I have never thought a great deal of the movement but at the present time it is the best thing for me in my situation." As for the Bible Union (especially in Ohio), they were "a fine lot but they haven't displayed any great leadership as far as I can see." He had planned to lead his church into the "new convention" (the Missionary Union of Regular Baptist Churches), but he was "not in that mood now." Tulga was afraid that "it will peter out and become another fundamentalist failure."[79]

Tulga probably spoke for more than a few conservatives. At one time, the Baptist Bible Union had attracted thousands. Now it could draw only ninety messengers, and its problems were still not over. Like Tulga, many were doubtless tired of standing alone. Earle V. Pierce's Fundamentalist Fellowship was about the only alternative—even if it was still inside the convention.

So far, the committee of five had accomplished nothing. Perhaps Tulga's letter goaded Van Osdel into writing, "We are hoping the committee . . . will plan a meeting of Regular Baptists to be held in some center early in the year

77. Van Osdel to Riley, September 18, 1930.

78. W. B. Riley, "The Riley Apostasy," *Christian Fundamentalist* (October 1930), 131; Oliver W. Van Osdel to William B. Riley, October 8, 1930.

79. Chester Tulga to Oliver W. Van Osdel, December 31, 1930.

1931. We should be glad to do our part to encourage such a meeting." He also offered further explanation of the expression *Regular Baptist*. "A Regular Baptist is a Baptist who has refused to take on any of the vagaries borrowed from the pedo-Baptists or Roman Catholics, or the world, or the flesh, or the devil." He further suggested that the expression *Regular Baptist* was meaningful enough that the word *Missionary* could be dropped from the name of the new group.[80]

On the one hand, people like Pierce (and now Tulga) found solace by clinging to the convention. On the other hand, some who had come out of the convention were so badly wounded that they wanted no other organization at all. Van Osdel also had to respond to this perspective. While he strongly defended the autonomy of the local church, he also believed that Regular Baptists had to organize or they were destined for oblivion. Without organization there could be no cooperation, and without cooperation, much work (especially the work of missions) would remain undone. Churches that would not organize for cooperative work "cannot become active agents in aggressive undertakings along Pauline lines." He reiterated, "If Regular Baptists are to live under present conditions they must organize."[81]

At the first of the year, the committee had still accomplished nothing. Van Osdel was not the only one who was concerned. John J. Van Gorder had been pushing Walkinshaw for action since October. In January he wrote to Fulton to express his concerns. He noted that several of the Pennsylvania churches had come out of the convention, but if a pastor left, the convention officials would step in to try to pull the church back in. Van Gorder worried that "if there be no organization to which they may turn for help and fellowship many of them will not survive the strain." Then he pressed Fulton as hard as he dared.[82]

Besides writing to Fulton, Van Gorder also sent a letter to Van Osdel, saying that he was "sick over the whole affair." He had been talking to the Pennsylvania pastors. They all agreed that if the committee of five could not get the job done, it would be up to the "Michigan brethren" to take up the task.[83]

Fulton replied that he thought the Regular Baptists needed more state organizations before they planned a national one. That remark put Van Gorder almost beside himself with frustration. He wrote to Van Osdel in mid-April that the pastors of the Clarion Orthodox Association were unanimous: if the

80. Oliver W. Van Osdel, "The Union of Regular Baptists in Canada," *Baptist Temple News*, November 8, 1930, 3–4.

81. Oliver W. Van Osdel, "Shall the Regular Baptists Have a National Organization?" *Baptist Temple News*, December 27, 1930, 1–2.

82. John J. Van Gorder to Howard Fulton, January 13, 1931. A copy of this letter was found in Van Osdel's papers.

83. John J. Van Gorder to Oliver W. Van Osdel, January 13, 1931.

committee did not act soon, then Van Osdel must be the one to head the movement for national organization. He also remarked, "I see more and more of the wisdom of the name you suggested of "Regular" if for no other reason [than] to confuse courts."[84]

At that point, Van Osdel wrote to Shields, urging him to prod the committee. Shields wrote back that "Brother Fulton has written me saying that he is waiting for me, but I sent him, and the other members of the committee, my best judgment in the form of a Constitution." No one even acknowledged receiving it. Shields said that he had made a few revisions to the draft and would now send it out again (including a copy for Van Osdel), hoping to provide a starting place for conversation. Shields was not sure what else he could do.[85]

At eighty-five years, age weighed heavily on Van Osdel. Furthermore, the Depression had hit Wealthy Street hard. In spite of its name, it was a working-class congregation, and unemployment was high. He had even been forced to cut the *Baptist Temple News* back to a monthly publication—and even then it appeared sporadically. The veteran pastor could hardly have welcomed the additional responsibility that was being thrust upon him, but he refused to let go of the dream of a nationwide fellowship. Once again he decided to take the matter in hand.

He began by writing letters to the other members of the committee. One reply particularly surprised him. Robert T. Ketcham responded that he was seeing more and more danger in a national organization. The Northern Baptist Convention had grown to be an oligarchy, and he did not wish to risk another. He had decided that he could not participate in planning the new fellowship. He was prepared to let the matter die.

Van Osdel wrote back rather coldly that "you have utterly misconceived what you were appointed to do." He continued, "[I]t was never intended that your committee decide to disband the Baptist Bible Union." The older pastor argued that the Northern Baptist Convention did not become an oligarchy: it was organized that way and had never been anything else.

> All the dangers that you enumerate will stare you in the face in any organization whether it is small or large. The devil isn't dead, but my conception of Christianity is not for it to lie down before its difficulties, but to overcome them and go forward with energy and faith. If the Regular Baptists had organized five years ago they might today be carrying on a vigorous evangelistic program and be sending missionaries to the foreign field.[86]

Fulton sent Van Osdel a similar response. He expressed less concern than

---

84. John J. Van Gorder to Oliver W. Van Osdel, April 14, 1931.
85. Thomas T. Shields to Oliver W. Van Osdel, May 28, 1931.
86. Oliver W. Van Osdel to Robert T. Ketcham, June 17, 1931.

Ketcham about the problems of centralization and oligarchy, but he was just as clear that no national organization was necessary. In any case, planning a meeting was difficult, especially without a secretary. His committee had decided not to plan the meeting after all, but if Van Osdel wanted to do something himself, then he was welcome.

Fulton had pastored for several years in Grand Rapids and knew Van Osdel well. The two had a warm relationship, but Van Osdel's reply was icy: "Now that the committee has prepared the whole movement for burial you graciously offer the corpse to me to do what I please with it." Van Osdel refused to accept this conclusion. Fulton needed to get his committee together and plan a meeting for the fall if at all possible.[87]

The reply from D. R. Walkinshaw was better. Walkinshaw claimed that he had gone through Shields's constitution, annotated it, and returned it to him. He had been waiting for Fulton to call the committee together. All he had received so far was a copy of Ketcham's letter to Van Osdel, and "his position is entirely untenable and his words do not express my attitude as a member of the committee." Walkinshaw continued, "I join with you in the complaint that this committee has been silent and inactive." Now it was time for Fulton, "in honor and due fidelity to his brethren," to call the committee together or else to resign his position.[88]

Shields saw his role on the committee as merely advisory. Schimpf was not a pastor. Walkinshaw was an outsider. That left Fulton and Ketcham, and the two of them had apparently decided to bury what was left of the Baptist Bible Union. Van Osdel's letters must have stung, and perhaps they provided some necessary motivation. Even so, the committee was not able to prepare a meeting for the fall as Van Osdel had suggested.

Furthermore, in spite of Van Gorder's continued pleading, Van Osdel was not in a position to plan or call another meeting. Throughout the fall he had to deal with a laggard committee at home. Then, in August, further controversy erupted with Riley.

Writing in the *Christian Fundamentalist*, Riley devoted a six-page editorial to attacking "come-outers" such as Van Osdel. He accused them of desertion and of "taking the part of least resistance." He pointed to Scriptures that commanded courage and steadfastness, insisting that manly Baptists would stay in the convention and fight rather than beating a retreat. He denied that 2 Corinthians 6:14–17 was relevant, just as it would not be relevant for a wife who discovered that her husband was unsaved. Northern Baptist institutions had been built with fundamental money, and fundamentalists should not

87. Oliver W. Van Osdel to Howard Fulton, June 23, 1931.
88. D. R. Walkinshaw to Oliver W. Van Osdel, June 28, 1931.

simply give them up to liberals without a fight. Riley pointed to Minnesota, where the state convention was largely under fundamentalist control, and argued that "it is impossible that modernism should continue in the saddle in the Northern Baptist Convention." True courage permitted no easy surrender or personal escape. Even if fundamentalists were in the minority, and even if they had been beaten repeatedly, they could win if only they would come back to fight again and again.[89]

Because the *Baptist Temple News* had gone to monthly publication, Van Osdel could not reply immediately. In either his August or September issue, however, he printed an article that could be seen as a refutation. He again attacked interdenominational fundamentalism, but now he also took aim at convention fundamentalism. He stated that convention fundamentalists declared their own orthodoxy while continuing as "ardent supporters of the inclusive policy and Modernism in its rankest and most radical forms." In Van Osdel's judgment, "The pre-Convention Baptist Fundamentalist movement is a huge joke, has never had the slightest influence, and never can have the slightest influence." On the other hand, the Bible Union movement had a meaning. It "never compromised with Modernists or extended to Modernists the hand of fellowship." Van Osdel concluded,

> There was no meeting of the Bible Union this year. This has afforded the enemies of this movement an opportunity to announce its death, but if the friends of the movement live and our Lord does not come to take them away, there will be a strenuous endeavor made another year to hold a meeting, with an invitation to all lovers of truth and righteousness and defenders of the faith to participate. Our latch-string is out. We invite all men of courage and faith to come in with us.[90]

In October, Van Osdel specifically responded to Riley's editorial on the "come-outers." While still speaking personally of Riley in warm terms, Van Osdel stressed the points of disagreement. He wrote that Riley's editorial really meant "that he is under conviction, but doesn't want his friends to know about it." Van Osdel insisted that the teaching of 2 Corinthians 6:14–17 was obvious: "Every man of God knows definitely that he has no business yoking up with unbelievers in the Northern Baptist Convention or anywhere else." Modernists had organized the convention and controlled it from the very beginning. Riley "knows that Modernism is here to stay, and cannot be dislodged by any man living, great or small." Anyone who claimed that he might be able to recapture the resources of the convention was "either afflicted with a cloudy mind or throwing dust in the air to hide himself from the deep

89. William B. Riley, "The Come-Outers," *Christian Fundamentalist*, August 1931, 46–51.
90. Quoted in William B. Riley, "Fundamentalism and Fundamentalists," *Christian Fundamentalist*, October 1931, 123–24.

convictions which must press upon any one whose mind is open to the Spirit of God."[91]

The articles by Riley and Van Osdel were like letters crossing in the mail. Each replied to the other in October. In his response to Van Osdel, Riley continued to profess the deepest affection for Van Osdel, yet his rebuttal was about as unsparing as any he made.

On the issue of interdenominational fundamentalism, Riley simply revisited the old arguments. What really stung him, though, was Van Osdel's treatment of convention fundamentalism. Van Osdel had said that convention fundamentalism was a huge joke that never had or would have any influence. Riley jibed that this statement, "coming as it does from the now defunct Baptist Bible Union representative, creates a joke beyond dispute." In response to Van Osdel's observation that Bible Unioners never compromise, Riley took a jab at Shields: "The late lamented president of the Bible Union won some victories in Canada against modernism, but by lack of generalship and considerate treatment of even confederates, finally lost out entirely." Riley ridiculed Van Osdel's hope of a future for the Baptist Bible Union as "pathetic." Then he added these paragraphs:

> We are sorry for the good men connected with that movement who now have to read such an epitaph to the same; but, in the language of a brother of mine, *"They did it themselves, or at least backed up their leaders while they discredited and destroyed the movement."*
>
> In the blow-up of Des Moines University, the death-sentence of the Bible Union was written. We knew the blow-up would come from the day of its foundation, and told the president the ground on which it would occur. Two years later we repeated our warning, but it was unheeded, and the result was inevitable.[92]

Perhaps other relationships would have been ruined by such strong words, but the friendship between Riley and Van Osdel endured. Later that month, Riley wrote to the Wealthy Street pastor, "With all my faults I love you still and I thank God for your fellowship in the faith. The fact that we do not both take the same position in our attitude toward denominational fellowships does not in the least debar me from appreciation of the staunch belief in the great fundamentals of God's Word that you entertain and that we hold in common."[93] They had been friends for forty years or more, and each freely forgave the other his faults as men of God should. Still, they had taken different paths, and their collaboration was over.

Furthermore, Riley had written what he had written. There it was in cold

91. Oliver W. Van Osdel, "Come-Outers," *Baptist Temple News*, October 3, 1931.
92. Riley, "Fundamentalism and Fundamentalists," 125.
93. William B. Riley to Oliver W. Van Osdel, October 27, 1931.

print, personal considerations notwithstanding. The Baptist Bible Union was dead, and no less a figure than W. B. Riley had undertaken to write its obituary. As Van Osdel wryly noted, the committee of five had given the corpse to him to do with as he pleased. The question was whether, at eighty-five years of age, in the midst of the Great Depression, Van Osdel would be able to do anything at all.

Des Moines University president's office after the 1929 riots.

Belden Avenue Baptist Church, Chicago.

Dissolution of the Baptist Bible Union and first meeting of the GARBC, Belden Avenue Baptist Church, 1932.

6 The GARBC

At the end of 1931, the Depression was still deepening. In October, Al Capone was sentenced to eleven years for tax evasion. The George Washington Bridge opened to traffic between Manhattan and New Jersey. Salvador Dali completed his painting "The Persistence of Memory" with its images of melting watches. In fundamentalist churches, pastors were warning their flocks against movies, especially James Whale's new version of *Frankenstein*. Factories lay idle, rail cars and engines stood rusting, and the remaining trains that were operating carried few passengers.

Hard times are times of spiritual searching, and they often turn out to be times of fruitful ministry. During the Depression, evangelism reaped a harvest of souls that became difficult to remember a generation later. H. H. Savage of First Baptist Church in Pontiac once remarked that it took about four times the prayer and energy to get a soul saved during the 1960s as it took during the 1930s. Savage was qualified to offer an expert opinion.

In Grand Rapids, Oliver W. Van Osdel was trying to pick up the pieces of the Baptist Bible Union. He remained convinced that some nationwide organization of Regular Baptists was absolutely necessary. He grounded his reasons not only in mutual work, but also in mutual defense.

The one principle that remained within the Northern Baptist Convention was the principle of institutional loyalty. According to abundant testimony, the agents of the convention rarely appealed to churches and pastors on the grounds of biblical or spiritual considerations. Their appeals were based primarily upon loyalty and a resulting pragmatism. Hypothetically, all Baptist churches were independent and autonomous, but autonomy was allowed in practice only as long as a church did not come into conflict with the convention. Once that happened, the establishment found it necessary to maintain control, whether with promises or threats.

Convention officials had many ways of enforcing loyalty. To pastors they could promise choice pulpits when they became vacant. To churches they emphasized the sense of security that came from being connected with a large organization. As long as they were loyal, both pastors and churches could place their confidence in state secretaries who would care for their interests.

When a young minister wanted to be ordained, the custom was for him to be reviewed by the local association's ordination committee first. Then he came before the state convention's committee. If he was approved, then his church could call a council. Sometimes he was required to sign a statement that if he ever left the convention, he would turn in his ordination certificate to the state office. Should he attempt to extricate his church from the convention, he could expect a visit from the state secretary, probably with a lawyer, to threaten him both with a lawsuit over the building and with the prospect of being turned out.

The machinery operated smoothly. It was not unknown for state secretaries to send out questionnaires with pointed queries about the preacher's loyalty to the convention. Convention agencies would sometimes offer gift mortgages to churches, promising with a smile that they would never be collected. Officials would suggest to deacons that for safekeeping it might be a good idea to entrust the church deed to the office of the state convention.

Then there was the M&M Board, the convention's retirement program. The plan had been well researched, and it was one of the best in the nation. After years of both his money and his churches' money going to his account, a retiring pastor or missionary could count on income for the rest of his life. If he were called to, say, a Southern Baptist church, he would be given a paid-up policy, and at his retirement he would get a pension on the basis of the years he and his churches paid in. Presumably he would have a similar pension, perhaps somewhat reduced, from the Southern Baptist Annuity Board. He could still hope to retire comfortably.

But what if he left the convention to take a separatist church? He could expect to be mailed a check for the 2 percent of his income that he himself had contributed. All the money that his churches had paid in would be forfeited. He would receive an explanation that the fund had to make many outright grants to pastors who were in desperate need and had never been able to afford any part in the program, and the church contributions were needed for them. Depart in peace.

Many men chose not to depart in peace. They preferred not to depart at all.

Van Osdel knew all of this. For years he had watched the convention officials using these tactics to enforce denominational loyalty. He hated it. From his perspective this kind of control was anti-biblical and anti-baptistic. Individual churches and ministers found the pressures almost impossible to withstand. He was determined to create some nationwide structure that could provide for mutual defense as well as mutual ministry.

A Growing Network

By the beginning of 1932 the Baptist Bible Union, now tentatively renamed the Missionary Union of Regular Baptist Churches, had almost completely collapsed. It had, however, given birth to a movement that was larger than the organization itself. Over the nine years of its existence the Baptist Bible Union had attracted many talented and energetic people. They had established a variety of organizations that identified more or less closely with the ideals for which the Union stood. These organizations were a resource upon which a resurgent national organization would be able to draw.

Throughout the country, Bible Union members had been establishing separatist associations. For example, when John J. Van Gorder encouraged Van Osdel to call for a national organization, he spoke for an entire association of churches—the Clarion Orthodox Baptist Association—whose pastors agreed with him. This fellowship, located in northwestern Pennsylvania, had been formed when courts delivered the assets and name of the old Clarion Baptist Association to a tiny handful of convention loyalists. The new association adopted the Baptist Bible Union confession and identified itself with the Union.

In Ohio a group of Bible Union pastors presented their state convention with a list of concerns, mainly focused on the denominational schools. The state convention refused to get involved in the controversy. These pastors met at Central Baptist Church of Columbus in 1928, leading several churches to separate from both the Ohio and the Northern Baptist Conventions. These churches then organized the Ohio Association of Independent Baptist Churches.[1]

By 1928 several churches in California had separated from the convention. G. Rector Dye began visiting these pastors and argued persuasively that all of their churches would be strengthened if they would form a Regular Baptist association. Meeting in Modesto, five pastors issued a call for organization. By 1930 the association had a complete structure. It chose J. Carlos Derfeldt of Ceres as moderator and G. Rector Dye of San Diego as secretary. For a treasurer, the association elected the elderly A. B. Whitney, an 1881 graduate of Newton Theological Institution. Whitney was one of only two men (Galusha Anderson was the other) who had voted against the organization of the Northern Baptist Convention in 1907. Whitney was delighted that Van Osdel

---

1. Joseph M. Stowell Jr., *Background and History of the General Association of Regular Baptist Churches* (Hayward, CA: Gospel Tracts Unlimited, 1949), 29.

had called an organizational meeting, and wrote to express his full sympathy. He added, "When the present president of Newton Theo Inst. wrote about endowment I replied that, while I retained love for the Old Newton . . . , I had lost confidence in the new Newton."[2]

The oldest of the regional associations was the Michigan Orthodox Baptist Association, founded as the Grand River Valley Baptist Association in 1909. By 1928 Van Osdel was becoming impatient with the label "Orthodox Baptist." When he announced the association's annual meeting in the *Baptist Temple News* he opined that the time had come to change the name. His argument made sense to the association, which began to call itself the Grand Rapids Association of Regular Baptist Churches.[3]

In April 1928 the state Baptist Bible Union in Michigan reorganized itself into a convention. The Michigan Orthodox Baptist Association had joined as a bloc. How many other churches were involved is not certain, but probably not many. One of the leaders was H. H. Savage of First Baptist Church in Pontiac. As the Baptist Bible Union languished, however, so did the state Regular Baptist convention. Perhaps part of the problem was that Savage, its most energetic leader, was lured back into the old state convention when he was placed on the nominating committee. That happened in late 1928, and no record appears of a Regular Baptist state convention after that time.[4]

Early in 1931 Regular Baptists from across Michigan met in St. Johns to organize a statewide association. The assembly elected a president and an executive committee, charging them with the responsibility of drafting a constitution and plan of organization. After the meeting, however, the president changed his mind and persuaded the executive committee simply to hold a conference rather than to create an organization. This decision created a practical problem: the assembly had also agreed to hire a missionary to help plant and reclaim Michigan Baptist churches. Without a definite organization behind him, this missionary quickly found himself facing financial embarrassment.[5]

Once again Van Osdel took the matter in hand. He drafted a "Call for Organization," summoning messengers to meet on October 13 at the Baptist church in Byron to "consider the advisability" of forming a statewide association. Seven other pastors signed the call along with Van Osdel. He then mailed the call to as many churches and pastors as he thought would be interested.[6]

2. A. B. Whitney to Oliver W. Van Osdel, June 6, 1930.
3. Oliver W. Van Osdel, "The Coming Associational Meeting," *Baptist Temple News*, August 25, 1928, 1.
4. *Twentieth Annual Meeting of the Grand Rapids Association of Regular Baptist Churches*, 29; Henry H. Savage to Oliver W. Van Osdel, November 7, 1928.
5. Oliver W. Van Osdel to Gerard Knol, September 10, 1931.
6. Oliver W. Van Osdel, "A Call for Organization," mimeographed document, September

During the interim before the Byron meeting, Van Osdel traveled to Hazel Park to help start an association on the east side of Michigan. Even though Hazel Park was in Savage's backyard, there is no indication that he attended the event. Interestingly enough, T. T. Shields was one of the speakers. On October 6 and 7 the Eastern Michigan Association of Regular Baptist Churches was organized.[7]

The next week, messengers from both eastern and western Michigan met in Byron. The resulting organization was called the Union of Regular Baptists of Michigan, and C. R. Peterson was selected as home missionary for the new fellowship. In addition to church planting, his responsibilities included representing the association and publishing a monthly paper.[8]

Altogether, Van Osdel spent twenty-five years as the pastor of Wealthy Street Baptist Church. During that time he gave himself to the work of Baptist churches in Grand Rapids and around the state. One of the young pastors who came up in the shadow of his influence was Joseph M. Stowell Jr. When asked about Van Osdel's influence in Michigan, Stowell remarked, "He is the reason that Regular Baptist churches outnumber convention churches in Michigan today."[9]

In addition to establishing church fellowships, Regular Baptists were also founding educational institutions. California had one of the earlier Regular Baptist associations; unsurprisingly, it also established one of the early schools. Los Angeles Baptist Theological Seminary was organized in that city's downtown in 1927. The leading figure in its establishment was William A. Matthews, who would also serve as its president for years to come. During the mid-1940s, theologian Henry C. Thiessen would serve briefly as its president.[10]

By early 1932 a second Regular Baptist school was in the planning stages. Pastor Richard Murphy of First Baptist Church in Johnson City, New York, saw a need for Baptist ministers to be trained in Baptist institutions. Over time, this vision came to be shared by theologian Emery H. Bancroft and three other professors from the nearby Practical Bible Training Institute. In 1932 Murphy's church agreed to house the institution, and the Baptist Bible Seminary was formally launched that summer. The fall semester opened with forty students in class. Subsequent pastor-presidents included Harold T. Commons and Earle G. Griffith.[11]

Regular Baptists had already been organizing missionary agencies for more than a decade. Many churches (like Wealthy Street) sent out their own missionaries. Others used the interdenominational faith mission boards.

9, 1931.

7. "Eastern Michigan Association," *Regular Baptist Missions*, November 1931, 2.

8. *Regular Baptist Missions*, November 1931, 1.

9. Joseph M. Stowell Jr., interview with Kevin T. Bauder, June 23, 1982.

10. Stowell, *Background and History*, 52.

11. Ibid., 53.

Increasingly, however, Baptist churches wanted to send Baptist missionaries to the field through Baptist agencies. In view of the Inclusive Policy of the Northern Baptist Convention, their only real alternative was to erect new organizations.

The oldest of these agencies was organized by veteran missionary William Haas. For a decade Haas had been ministering in the heart of Africa. The convention's foreign mission board failed to support him, and the interdenominational agencies could not provide all of the help that he needed. To complicate matters, he recruited a number of missionaries from the United States, only to discover that he could not coordinate their work through their disconnected churches. He needed a formal missionary agency. With help from R. E. Neighbour and Oliver W. Van Osdel, he called several Baptist leaders to the First Baptist Church of Elyria, Ohio, in 1920. There they organized the General Council of Cooperating Baptist Missions of North America. Since Haas's vision was for the interior of Africa, the agency was frequently called the "Mid-Africa Mission." As it expanded into other fields, it perpetuated Haas's goal of reaching people in the interior of their countries. Eventually, the organization was renamed Baptist Mid-Missions.[12]

Less formally organized but nearly as old was the Sweet Baptist Mission to China (later renamed the East China Baptist Mission). It was named for W. S. Sweet, a physician who had been sent to China in 1893 under the American Baptist Foreign Mission Society. When his health deteriorated in 1914, he and his wife were forced to resign from the board and to return to the United States. After Dr. Sweet died in 1917, Mrs. Sweet wanted to return to China, but the foreign mission board rejected her appeals. She went anyway, and over the years she built up an organization in the United States for coordination and support of her ministry. By the late 1920s she had a number of younger missionaries under her care. The Sweet Baptist Mission was the agency under which Edith Rebman left for Hangchow in 1930. Harry Hamilton provided a main point of contact for the mission.[13]

Another new mission was formed in the wake of the 1927 Northern Baptist Convention in Chicago. Present in the meeting was Raphael C. Thomas, a physician who had also studied theology at Newton. He had served in the Philippines since 1904 under the foreign mission board. Now he was deeply concerned about the Inclusive Policy. Even worse, the foreign mission board was pressuring him to abandon evangelism and stick to medicine. In 1927 he

12. The history of Baptist Mid-Missions has been written by Polly Strong, *Burning Wicks* (Cleveland, OH: Baptist Mid-Missions, 1984); see also William J. Hopewell, *The Missionary Emphasis of the General Association of Regular Baptist Churches* (Chicago: Regular Baptist Press, 1963), 40–41, 61–66; Oliver W. Van Osdel, "Mid-African Mission," *Baptist Temple News*, November 6, 1920, 1–2.

13. Hopewell, *Missionary Emphasis*, 41–42.

appealed to the board for a hearing about the situation in the Philippines, but his appeal was rejected. The situation then came to the attention of Mrs. Henry W. Peabody, a former missionary to India who had served on several Northern Baptist boards. Three months later, at Peabody's behest, the Association of Baptists for the Evangelism of the Orient was organized to support the work of Thomas and others who could no longer work with the convention boards. This agency was later renamed the Association of Baptists for World Evangelism.[14]

The next year still another mission came into existence. Joseph McCaba wanted to go to French West Africa as a missionary, but knew of no existing board that could assist with his work. In September he met with Pastor Edward Drew and six members of the Madison Avenue Baptist Church in Paterson, New Jersey. That night they established Africa Christian Missions (later renamed Evangelical Baptist Missions), an organization that would for many years be one of the most successful Regular Baptist agencies.[15]

Not all missionaries travel halfway around the world. During the 1920s Leonardo Mercado pursued missionary work in Mexico with the Northern Baptist Convention. Disturbed by the convention's modernism, he withdrew in 1930 and founded the Mexican Gospel Mission. With offices in Phoenix, Mercado's agency worked in the southwestern states and in Mexico. It developed a significant work among the Tarahumara in the high canyons of the Sierra Madre. A visionary and strong promoter, Mercado traveled through the northern states raising Regular Baptist support for the work.[16]

The field of home missions was represented by the Interstate Evangelistic Association. Harold Strathearn originally established the organization to help churches look for pastors. Too often, convention secretaries would swoop down upon a pastorless church, persuading the church that independence was the road to disaster, then urging the church to call a pastor from a list of convention loyalists. Strathearn saw that Regular Baptist churches needed somewhere to turn when they lacked a pastor, just as pastors needed somewhere to turn when they were without a congregation. Besides pastoral placement, the Interstate Evangelistic Association coordinated preachers for evangelistic campaigns and engaged in publishing work.[17]

The Baptist Bible Union had begun a movement. Even though the organization had collapsed, the movement had not. A network of missionary agencies, educational institutions, and both state and local associations was continuing to grow, even in the absence of a strong national voice. The people

14. The history of ABWE has been written by Harold T. Commons, *Heritage and Harvest* (Cherry Hill, NJ: Association of Baptists for World Evangelism, 1981); see also Hopewell, *Missionary Emphasis*, 52–61.
15. Hopewell, *Missionary Emphasis*, 42, 66–70.
16. "News Items," *Baptist Bulletin*, July 1934, 4; Hopewell, *Missionary Emphasis*, 42.
17. Hopewell, *Missionary Emphasis*, 41.

who operated these institutions were aware of each other. They felt a sense of commonality and even camaraderie. They shared the same repudiation of the convention, the same devotion to Baptist ideals, and the same commitment to the Lord's work. Thanks to Van Osdel, they were increasingly claiming the same name: Regular Baptist. They only needed something—some organization—to bring them together in a coordinated effort.

The Birth of the GARBC

Through the autumn of 1931 Van Osdel's attention was drawn to the needs of Michigan Baptists. He invested a fair amount of energy in guiding the Grand Rapids Association of Regular Baptist Churches, in helping to organize a Regular Baptist association in eastern Michigan, and in setting up a statewide association for Michigan. He did not forget the need for a national fellowship, but he was trusting the committee of five to lead that undertaking.

The California Regular Baptists held their associational meeting that October. Many of these pastors wished that they could fellowship with a national association, but they had no leader with the stature to step forward and call an organizational meeting. After deliberation they authorized G. Rector Dye to send a letter to Van Osdel in their behalf, asking Van Osdel to take the initiative and to convene a meeting. [18]

A letter from Max Schimpf in early December hinted that the committee of five still lacked direction. Schimpf agreed that an organization had to be created. He was particularly concerned for churches that had separated from the convention fearing that "when the next pastor comes, the machine officials are able to bring the church back into the organizational fold." [19]

The committee's problem consisted in trying to decide what sort of organization to set up. Schimpf noted that in some states these churches were too widely distributed to organize into local associations and too few to organize into state fellowships. Often they were too poor to participate in a nationwide meeting. He noted that Shields's group in Canada had just adopted a constitution that was even more autocratic than the convention's had been, and many potential participants were concerned that the same thing might happen if an organization were established in the United States. Schimpf himself personally favored a loose form of organization that could be used for fellowship, encouragement in the Christian life, maintenance of the pure faith, and stimulation of missionary work. He closed, "I feel that we have been negligent in not doing something about this Bible Union matter. There are a large group

---

18. "Inspiring Fellowship of Calif. Churches," *Baptist Bulletin*, January 1936, 10.
19. Max Schimpf to Oliver W. Van Osdel, December 4, 1931.

of young ministers in our denomination who are waiting for some leaders to take the initiative.[20]

Schimpf had put his finger on the difficulty: leadership. No member of the committee was willing to exercise the leadership to call an organizational meeting. Schimpf was an insurance man, not a pastor, and felt in no position to be the leading light. His letter was effectively an appeal for Van Osdel to take charge.

The lack of leadership was not necessarily due to opposition or even lethargy. Some leaders were facing personal transitions. Howard Fulton, chairman of the committee of five, was in the process of moving from Buffalo, New York, to take the pastorate of Belden Avenue Baptist Church in Chicago. Harry Hamilton had candidated and been called to a church in Vancouver, but then declined and moved from Austin, Minnesota, to Buffalo. Hamilton was one of the more separatistic leaders in the Bible Union, and his ministry in Austin had been fraught with obstacles. Since W. B. Riley was trying to gain control of the Minnesota convention, he found Hamilton's separatism distasteful. Hamilton claimed that Riley was interfering directly in the Austin congregation, trying to influence members against separation.[21]

Overseas, another situation was developing that was a portent of problems in the future, though it raised few concerns in the short term. In late 1930 Edith Rebman had gone to Hangchow to work under the East China Baptist Mission (the Sweet Baptist Mission). In October 1931 Mrs. Sweet invited J. Hudson Taylor's grandson to conduct a Bible conference with the missionaries. Rebman believed that Taylor was teaching perfectionism and the eradication of the sin nature. She voiced her objections to Sweet, who thought that Taylor's teaching was within the bounds of toleration. When Taylor was asked to spend another week, Rebman sent Sweet a list of terms under which they could continue to work together. She also expressed her concerns to her coworkers. In response, Sweet put out a letter to the whole mission explaining why she thought Taylor's ministry was vital to the organization. She also sent a note to Rebman stating, "I am sure you will get your things packed up, and get away as soon as possible. The Lord will bless and use you in some other corner of this great land."[22]

Rebman had no choice but to leave China. She returned to Vancouver, then to Toronto where she took a commercial office job. When she lost the commercial job, she suffered an emotional breakdown from which she probably never fully recovered. Perhaps in view of Rebman's known style of

20. Ibid.

21. Edith Rebman to Oliver W. Van Osdel, November 17, 1931. Hamilton was in correspondence with Rebman; she was relaying news to Van Osdel.

22. Edith Rebman to Oliver W. Van Osdel, October 31, 1931; Rebman to Van Osdel, November 7, 1931.

confrontation, or perhaps in view of the breakdown, questions were never raised about her treatment within Sweet Baptist Mission. Within a few years, however, Regular Baptist leaders would have their hands full responding to intransigence from this mission's leadership.

Van Osdel was also encountering his share of distraction. After investing a huge amount of time helping to organize Regular Baptists in Michigan, he left for a month at his son's home in Redlands, California, where he stayed over the holidays and well into January. While he was in Redlands, he was paid a visit by Theron Wood, an energetic pastor in that state's Regular Baptist association. Wood pressed him to take the lead in planning a national organization. By the time Van Osdel returned home, he had made up his mind. Although he preferred to let others lead, he would take the initiative.[23]

In late January or early February he wrote to Howard Fulton, chairman of the committee of five. He suggested that, since the committee seemed unable to agree on a plan of organization, perhaps the members should simply call a meeting and let the messengers work out a plan. Fulton was just settling into the pastorate of Belden Avenue Baptist Church in Chicago, and Van Osdel suggested meeting in his church sometime in June. Simultaneously, Earle G. Griffith of Emmanuel Baptist in Toledo wrote to Fulton volunteering to hold a meeting at Toledo in May. Fulton, Griffith, and Van Osdel conferred, then decided that they would split the difference. The meeting would be held at Belden Avenue, but it would be held in May.[24]

Van Osdel might reasonably have expected that the committee would now take over. That was not to happen. Fulton wrote back almost immediately to unburden himself about the severe financial difficulties that Belden Avenue was facing. He begged Van Osdel to write a call, set the dates, outline the program and get the publicity out. In effect, Fulton was giving the whole project to Van Osdel to plan as he wished.[25]

Van Osdel decided to follow an old Northern Baptist custom and to hold the meeting during the week of Pentecost. He wrote up a call for May 15–18, then sent a copy to Fulton. The two agreed on the dates, and somehow Van Osdel persuaded Fulton to begin writing the other members of the committee for suggestions about the program.[26]

This was the first that the other committee members had heard of the proposed meeting. They had not yet even seen the call, so Fulton asked Van Osdel to send a copy to every member. He did, telling them that he had agreed to

23. Theron Wood to Oliver W. Van Osdel, February 24, 1932; Edith Rebman to Van Osdel, January 15, 1932.

24. Howard Fulton to Oliver W. Van Osdel, February 9, 1932.

25. Howard Fulton to Oliver W. Van Osdel, February 23, 1932.

26. Oliver W. Van Osdel, "A Proposed Convocation," typed draft, n.d. but March 1932.

act as secretary for the committee of five. That was the truth, even if it was not the whole truth. During the same month, he also put a notice in the *Baptist Temple News* so that people could begin planning for the date. J. Frank Norris saw it and replied, asking Van Osdel to discuss the matter with a young evangelist named John R. Rice, who was hoping to develop contacts in the North.[27]

Shields's response to the call represents his formal departure from the Baptist Bible Union. He offered a couple of suggestions for clarifying the call, but pointed out that Van Osdel had called for a nationwide association. He took this to mean that "no delegates from Canada would be expected," but offered the pages of his paper to publicize it. [28]

Shields was politely backing away from the new organization, but Ketcham flatly withheld his endorsement.

> I regret that I find it necessary to return, unsigned, the call to the Chicago meeting. As you know, I am not convinced of the advisability of another nation wide organization. . . . I am heartily in favor of a meeting in Chicago on the proposed dates and for the purpose of getting together for prayer and fellowship, and even to discuss such a proposed organization, but for me to sign a statement which says that I already have in mind such an organization when at present my mind is exactly in the opposite direction would be for me to mistate facts.[29]

A short time later, Ketcham further explained his hesitancy in a letter to Max Schimpf. The core of his objection was that a national organization capable of doing anything would almost certainly lead to overhead control.

> No doubt you noticed the absence of my name from the call signed by the committee. I wrote Dr. Van Osdel stating it was impossible for me to sign it because of the paragraph in the same committing the committee, at least, to a nation-wide organization. I am full-length for a national gathering at least every two years, as a place of fellowship and interchange of ideas, but absolutely no overhead board or convention which heads up a nation-wide missionary program which must be brought back to the churches and sold to them cold. It would be an almost exact duplication of the principle of the Northern Baptist Convention only in the hands of Fundamentalists, and how long even that would be safe guarded is doubtful.[30]

Van Osdel sent a kind note back to Ketcham, expressing his understanding of Ketcham's position. Ketcham was not alone, however. About the same time,

27. J. Frank Norris to Oliver W. Van Osdel, March 17, 1932.

28. Thomas T. Shields to Oliver W. Van Osdel, March 23, 1932.

29. Robert T. Ketcham to Oliver W. Van Osdel, March 28, 1932.

30. Robert T. Ketcham to Max Schimpf, May 3, 1932. A copy of this letter was in Van Osdel's papers.

Max Schimpf wrote to Howard Fulton expressing some of the same concerns. He was particularly alarmed by the way that Shields's group had organized in Canada. According to Schimpf, the Canadian group's constitution forbade the churches to support any missions work except that of their own official organization. This was exactly the kind of dictatorial attitude that Schimpf feared. He also doubted that his non-pastoral opinion would count for much in the discussion at Belden Avenue, so he was seriously thinking about staying away from the meeting.[31]

By mid-April the program was set. The call was sent out early in the month, then printed with the program in the *Baptist Temple News*. Since at least three members of the committee had some sort of reservations about the meeting, the call was published without signatures. The absence of signatures contrasted sharply with the columns of names that had appeared with the call for the pre-convention conference in 1920 and the call for the Baptist Bible Union in 1923.

Perhaps this noticeable contrast was what led Ketcham to write that he was "sorry I could not fix my signature to the call for the Chicago meeting. I think you understand that my objection is not to the meeting, but to the paragraph in the call for the same which commits us, as a committee at least, to the proposition of a nation-wide organization."[32] Given the amount of disagreement within the committee of five, it is surprising that Van Osdel decided to hold the meeting at all.

One encouraging word arrived from James M. Gray, president of Moody Bible Institute. Gray would not be able to attend the meeting, but he wrote to express his personal support. He also offered to feature the meeting in the *Moody Monthly*, then suggested that the institute might be able to help entertain the attendees at a low cost. In the middle of the Depression, Gray's offer provided a welcome solution to a significant logistical problem.[33]

Shields made it clear that he would not attend the Chicago meeting and asked to be removed from all correspondence about it. Schimpf also decided that he could not attend. With the meeting less than two weeks away, Ketcham wrote to both Schimpf and Van Osdel that he could not be there unless something changed. Ketcham told Schimpf that he wished he could be present to "lay out before the brethren the objections which I see to the proposed nation-wide organization, but I do not see how I can afford the trip just now." He assured Van Osdel of his love and prayers, "no matter how much you may misbehave at Chicago!!!!"[34]

---

31. Max Schimpf to Howard Fulton, March 22, 1932. A copy of this letter was in Van Osdel's papers.

32. Robert T. Ketcham to Oliver W. Van Osdel, April 12, 1932.

33. James M. Gray to Oliver W. Van Osdel, April 7, 1932.

34. Howard C. Fulton to Oliver W. Van Osdel, April 21, 1932; Robert T. Ketcham to

Did Ketcham make it to the Belden Avenue meeting? The answer to this question is not clear. As an old man, Ketcham claimed to have been there. The record does not list his name, however, and Joseph Stowell once commented that Ketcham's son-in-law would likely say that he was not. Ketcham certainly attended the next meeting in 1933, and he figured prominently every meeting for decades after. He preached at Belden Avenue on many occasions and was later a member of the church for many years. He knew all of the men who were there, and he heard their stories over and over again. Even if he was not present, his familiarity with the setting and the stories may have produced such a vivid impression upon his imagination that he felt as if he recalled the meeting.

The last meeting of the Baptist Bible Union convened on Sunday, May 15, 1932, at the Belden Avenue Baptist Church. Approximately thirty-four messengers from twenty-two churches attended (accounts vary). Howard Fulton's keynote address, delivered on Sunday morning, was titled, "What Old Fashioned Regular Baptists Stand For." Van Osdel preached on Sunday evening. Other speakers during the conference included Clyde E. Wood of Grand Rapids, Earle G. Griffith of Toledo, Isaac Van Westenbrugge of Grand Rapids, John Muntz of Forestville, New York, E. E. Shields of Chicago (he was T. T. Shields's brother), Harry G. Hamilton of Buffalo, M. E. Hawkins of Mishawaka, Indiana, and John J. Van Gorder of Butler, Pennsylvania. Van Osdel was scheduled to close the conference with a second sermon, but he yielded his place to D. J. Davies of St. Paul, Minnesota. The meeting was first and foremost a preaching conference, with sessions for business and discussion scheduled on Monday through Wednesday.[35]

The first order of business at the Belden Avenue meeting was to elect officers for the coming year. Harry Hamilton was chosen as president, with Earle G. Griffith of Toledo as vice president. John Muntz of Forestville, New York, became the secretary-treasurer. Vice presidents were also chosen for six states. Except for Van Osdel, none of the speakers or officers was widely known outside of Regular Baptist circles. This represented a distinct shift in philosophy from the early days of the Baptist Bible Union, when the leaders would use celebrity preachers to attract huge crowds. After its experiences with big name preachers, the Regular Baptist movement seems to have quietly repudiated the leadership of Great Men. In this sense, it was unique within fundamentalism. Other versions of fundamentalism, such as interdenominational fundamentalism, Southern Baptist fundamentalism, and, later on, the

Oliver W. Van Osdel, May 2, 1932; Ketcham to Maximilian Schimpf, May 3, 1932. A copy of this letter was in Van Osdel's papers.

35. Stowell, *Background and History*, 30–31; "Convocation of Regular Baptists," *Baptist Temple News*, April 30, 1932.

Conservative Baptist movement, all gravitated toward powerful personalities. Perhaps because of Van Osdel's example of leadership, however, the Regular Baptist movement welcomed little men (men who did not have powerful positions or prestigious reputations) into its leadership. The tendency to distance itself from Great Men became characteristic of the Regular Baptists.[36]

The minutes of the 1932 meeting record that a committee was appointed to draft a constitution or to revise the Baptist Bible Union constitution, but no names were listed. The absence of these names occasioned some confusion after the meeting—many of the messengers could not even remember appointing this committee. Fulton later clarified that this duty was assigned to the "executive committee," by which he seems to have meant the elected officers. The minutes do note that the assembly held a general discussion of the constitution which resulted in suggestions for change.[37]

The record also shows that the Regular Baptists were very concerned with the effects of the Depression. J. E. Conant drafted a resolution to be sent to the President of the United States, requesting that he call a "day for national humiliation, penitence and prayer to God, Divine intervention, to relieve the distress." The resolution passed unanimously.[38]

Both home and foreign missions were a central concern of the Belden Avenue meeting. The convocation took a first step toward organizing home missions by passing a resolution commending the work of the Interstate Evangelistic Association. The attendees also heard several reports about activity on foreign mission fields. The assembled messengers appointed a committee to investigate Baptist missionary societies and to advise churches that wanted information about Baptist missionary activity.[39]

The most important decision of the Belden Avenue meeting was to change the name. By now, no one was talking about the Missionary Union of Regular Baptist Churches. Several had objected to the word *Missionary* as part of the name. The growing prejudice of Schimpf against Shields's organization was probably shared by others, and it may have led the group away from the word *Union*. At the same time, nobody wanted to call the new organization a convention. Somebody remembered that early Baptists used to refer to large fellowships of churches as *General Associations*. That is the name that stuck, and the organization was renamed the General Association of Regular Baptist Churches. The executive committee was instructed to ensure that the name

---

36. Minutes of the Convocation of Regular Baptists held in the Belden Avenue Baptist Church, Chicago, Illinois, May 15–18, 1932, 2.

37. Harry Hamilton to Howard Fulton, June 17, 1932; Fulton to Oliver W. Van Osdel, n.d. but after June 17, 1932; John Muntz to Harry Hamilton, June 17, 1932; Minutes, GARBC, 1932, 2. Copies of all letters were in Van Osdel's papers.

38. Minutes, GARBC, 1932, 3.

39. Ibid., 3–4.

would be changed in such a way that the new association would be the legal successor of the Baptist Bible Union.[40]

From the very beginning, the GARBC organized as an association of churches. This structure was another contrast with the Baptist Bible Union, which had been a fellowship of individuals. During the Belden Avenue meeting, some attendees wanted to accommodate individuals who were sympathetic with the association but whose churches were not. This was a problem that would have to be solved when the constitution was finally adopted.[41]

The newly named GARBC received invitations from churches in three cities to host its next annual meeting: Grand Rapids, Buffalo, and Toledo. The gathering tentatively accepted the invitation from Toledo. The assembly also passed a motion to reprint Fulton's sermon, "What Old Fashioned Regular Baptists Stand For." David Gillespie of Western Springs, Illinois, suggested that each state vice president should appoint a secretary-treasurer for that state "to assist in carrying out of the detail work so that it will be satisfactorily accomplished." The meeting closed with brief words of encouragement from Fulton, Hamilton, and Muntz.

The meeting hardly seemed auspicious: thirty-odd messengers from twenty-some congregations attracted no newspaper headlines. Nevertheless, the Belden Avenue meeting represented a turning point in Baptist fundamentalism. With this meeting, separatists began to construct both the superstructures and an infrastructure that they would need if they were going to survive outside the convention. The GARBC grew rapidly, and within a decade it had become one of the most important organizations within Baptist fundamentalism. It still is.

The First Controversy

The newly elected president, Harry Hamilton, threw himself into the work of promoting the General Association of Regular Baptist Churches. Simultaneously, Earle G. Griffith and the missions committee began to push hard toward fulfilling their task. Before the GARBC fairly got off the ground, however, its existence was threatened by the eruption of a controversy within its ranks. This time, Van Osdel was at the center of the conflict.

Actually, the conflict was not a new one. It had flared up at intervals since 1928. It concerned the role of women preachers in general, and the preaching ministry of Amy Lee Stockton in particular.

As a teenager in California, Stockton had been asked to deliver an address

40. Ibid., 4–5.
41. Ibid., 4.

for a youth night at a Baptist associational meeting in Santa Clara. After the meeting, one of the pastors asked whether she ever did evangelistic preaching. She never had, but she agreed to make the attempt. He scheduled her for a week of meetings in a downtown mission. That week she saw her first conversions. A short time later she was sent by her pastor to fill the pulpit in a small church whose pastor was ill. After hearing her preaching, the deacons asked her to stay on for a series of evangelistic meetings that stretched over weeks. By 1911 she was preaching regularly, though only a recent high school graduate.[42]

During the early years of fundamentalism, female preachers were not uncommon. Eva Ludgate, Grace Saxe, and Uldine Utley all preached at the Winona Bible Conference. Utley also preached regularly at Calvary Baptist Church in New York under Straton's pastorate. Amy Lee Stockton became one of the foremost of these female fundamentalist preachers.[43]

After high school, Stockton attended the University of the Pacific, then took her Bachelor of Arts from the state college in her hometown of San Jose. She continued preaching while she attended college. After receiving her diploma, she became a youth evangelist with the California Baptist Convention. John Marvin Dean had been her pastor in San Jose, and he was always something of a hero to her. Now Dean was pastor of Second Baptist Church in Chicago. He was about to establish Northern Baptist Seminary, and he recruited Stockton as his first student. The two maintained a cordial relationship until his death in 1935.[44]

After graduating, Stockton teamed up with Rita Gould, who became her musician, song leader, and vocalist. For years the two women criss-crossed the nation, preaching not only in youth meetings and rescue missions, but in camps, conference centers, and local churches. One of their engagements took them to the University of Redlands. There they met Edgar Van Osdel, son of Oliver Van Osdel.[45] Edgar was the one who introduced the women to his father.

Oliver Van Osdel was very much a traditionalist when it came to women preaching. He saw the practice as unbiblical. Early in 1923, however, he came across a book titled *The Prophesying of Women* by George F. Wilkin. As he studied it, he became convinced that it was the best book on the subject of women preaching. He even gave it a public recommendation in the *Baptist Temple News*. Wilkin placed a qualified endorsement upon women preaching,

42. Amy Lee Stockton, "Unfinished Autobiography of Amy Lee Stockton" (unpublished typescript, 1979), 12–15. Courtesy of Northern Seminary Archives.
43. The most extensive work on female preachers within early fundamentalism and evangelicalism is Janette Hassey, *No Time for Silence: Evangelical Women in Public Ministry around the Turn of the Century* (Grand Rapids: Zondervan, 1986).
44. Warren Cameron Young, *Commit What You Have Heard*, 25.
45. Stockton, "Unfinished Autobiography," 35.

and his arguments evidently led Van Osdel to rethink his opinions. By 1928 he was ready to open his pulpit to Stockton for evangelistic services.[46]

Stockton preached in many different venues. She conducted union meetings and campaigns in nondenominational churches, but she was personally a Baptist. Given a choice, she preferred ministering to Baptist congregations. Whether Baptist or not, her campaigns were rarely as short as a week. She preferred to work in the same location for a month or more. Besides preaching for Van Osdel, she also held meetings for such notables as T. T. Shields, J. Frank Norris (at Temple Baptist Church in Detroit), and H. H. Savage. After she made Savage's acquaintance, he began to schedule her as a regular preacher at the Maranatha Bible Conferences near Muskegon, Michigan.

According to reports, Stockton's style was earnest and aggressive. One eyewitness recalled that she had a voice "like a gravel crusher." Her preaching was unquestionably effective. Hundreds of people might make public decisions during a single campaign.

Not all of her effectiveness was due to her pulpit delivery, however. Stockton was a strong organizer and she knew exactly how to plan her meetings for maximum effect. Weeks before a campaign she would contact the host pastor. He would be tasked to organize bands of members throughout the congregation for prayer and visitation. He would prepare a list of prospective converts. Church members would pray over this list and personally call upon every individual whose name appeared. Someone had to keep records of every prayer uttered and every call made. The church would have to order special hymnals for the campaign. Under Stockton's direction, an organization for personal workers would be formed, then its members would be trained to deal with people who made decisions during the meetings.[47]

Once the campaign began, the preaching services were only the slightest part of Stockton's duties. She would get the pastor to arrange noontime speaking engagements at business clubs, temperance organizations, or even factories and railroad shops. She and Gould knew how to use their femininity during these meetings. Dressed in white, they would enter some grimy factory during the workers' lunch break. Gould would sing and play the vibraphone, then Stockton would follow with a few words of exhortation, closing with an invitation to the service that evening. The technique succeeded: men came in droves, and they brought their families with them.

Stockton and Gould also added the feminine touch to their services. They

46. George F. Wilkin, *The Prophesying of Women* (Chicago: Fleming H. Revell, 1895); Oliver W. Van Osdel, "The Prophesying of Women," *Baptist Temple News*, March 10, 1932, 3.

47. John Marvin Dean reported more than four hundred decisions in a union campaign in Portland, Oregon. *Baptist Temple News*, March 24, 1928, 4. Stockton had a reputation for special effectiveness with young people.

would hold a special service for children and their parents; it was always a crowd-pleaser. The highlight of every campaign was the "Pink Rose Service," during which the church auditorium would be crammed with roses and decorated in pink and green. Stockton would tell the story of "The Bluebird of Mulberry Bend," interspersing it with vocal and instrumental solos from Gould. This was more than evangelism: it was often the best show in town.

While Stockton's methods drew criticism from such noteworthies as M. R. DeHaan and Donald Gray Barnhouse, the popular audiences jammed the services. Stockton dismissed the criticisms as "cheap talk, without anything to back it up." Of DeHaan she commented, "I don't see that he has set Grand Rapids on fire or accomplished enough to make us want to follow his methods."[48]

That comment was illustrative. While Stockton knew how to capitalize on her femininity, she was never passive or weak-willed. She was a hardheaded professional who knew her work and who held strong opinions. She had enough confidence in both her calling and her competence to excoriate the occasional pastor who failed to give adequate support to her evangelistic meetings. She was not afraid to appeal to a church board to overturn the decision of a pastor. On at least one occasion she flatly refused to preach during a weeknight meeting when the pastor insisted upon altering the plan of the service to fit his radio broadcast. She canceled the service instead.[49]

Stockton also held strong theological views, though her associations tended to be wider than her doctrine might indicate. She was a committed Baptist and premillennarian. She called the Victorious Life Conferences at American Keswick "heaven on earth."[50] She held a deep interest in the activities of the Baptist Bible Union, especially the doings of Van Osdel and Shields. Her hatred of modernism nearly matched her passion for evangelism.[51]

Stockton and Gould conducted their first campaign at Wealthy Street during the spring of 1928. They immediately became Van Osdel's favorites, and he invited them to return every year until he retired from the pastorate. In July 1930 the two evangelists were received as members at Wealthy Street, where they were immediately licensed as ministers. They were listed as licentiates in the yearbook of the Grand Rapids Association of Regular Baptist Churches at least until 1935. The two women were provided with clergy credentials to use in obtaining rail passage.

The initial invitation of Stockton and Gould to Grand Rapids in 1928 raised a storm of controversy. Both privately and publicly Van Osdel found himself forced to defend the team's ministry and, by extension, the legitimacy of

48. Amy Lee Stockton to Oliver W. Van Osdel, September 20, 1932.
49. Stockton to Van Osdel, February 26, 1931.
50. Stockton to Van Osdel, July 16, 1928.
51. Stockton to Van Osdel, May 19, 1928.

female preachers. He published his first defense of women preaching the week after Stockton began her campaign at Wealthy Street.[52] The essay provoked a flood of correspondence, much of which expressed disagreement. A month later, Van Osdel printed another defense of women preaching.[53] The response to Van Osdel's original essay had been heated. The response to the second was worse, and it led Van Osdel to publish yet a third defense.[54]

By the third essay, the tone of Van Osdel's argument was becoming more strident. He was using words like *prejudice* and *blindness* for his opponents. Not surprisingly, the next batch of mail brought more angry letters. These led to a fourth defense of women preachers, which read more like an attack upon his opponents.[55] By now the element of charity had largely vanished from the conversation. As Van Osdel dug in his heels, his opponents became increasingly shrill. One example comes from an exchange with the ultra-dispensationalist pastor John O'Hair of Chicago. O'Hair offered Van Osdel the following observations.

> It seems that the most pleasant pastime of "Fundamentalist" brethren today is to judge one another. I have heard such cruel criticism of you by Baptist "fundamental" brethren who have called you a czar, a Baptist Pope, a dictator etc. The most recent criticism was your most unscriptural action in having two bobbed-hair women preachers in your church and thus endorsing one of the most abominable practices of this apostate age. One charitable brother forgave you because of your dotage. I refrain from calling you a traitor because you went wholly contrary to the plain, clear, unmistakable teaching of God's holy book.[56]

O'Hair was right about one thing: the controversy was indeed divisive. Van Osdel continued to invite Stockton and Gould to appear at Wealthy Street. Whenever they came, he would use the *Baptist Temple News* to promote their meetings. The controversy began to escalate again at the very time when the GARBC was brought into existence. Harry Hamilton had thrown himself into the task of promoting the GARBC, but he discovered that the organization's growth was hampered by several controversies. The greatest of these was Van Osdel's defense of women preachers.[57]

52. Oliver W. Van Osdel, "Let Your Women Keep Silence in the Churches," *Baptist Temple News*, April 7, 1928, 1–4.
53. Oliver W. Van Osdel, "That Woman Question Again," *Baptist Temple News*, May 5, 1928, 3–4.
54. Oliver W. Van Osdel, "I Suffer Not a Woman to Teach—Let Your Women Keep Silence in the Churches," *Baptist Temple News*, May 12, 1928, 1–3.
55. Oliver W. Van Osdel, "That Woman Preacher," *Baptist Temple News*, August 18, 1928, 1–2.
56. John C. O'Hair to Oliver W. Van Osdel, September 18, 1928.
57. "Notes," *Baptist Temple News*, August 1932, 4 (by this time the periodical had shifted

The situation was aggravated when, in August 1932, Van Osdel used the *Baptist Temple News* to announce that he was bringing Stockton and Gould back for more meetings at Wealthy Street. In November Hamilton gave vent to some of his frustration in a lengthy letter (Hamilton was never much of a typist or proofreader—all grammar and spellings are true to his original).

> The Baptist Temple News at hand—I have read everything with interest, but I am more than sorry that you keep waving that red flag in the faces of Regular Baptists who may not see eye to eye with you in regard to Womans ministery.
>
> Dr. Shields even to your dissatisfaction delights to rave against the Scofield Bible. I have taken time to write to several of the brethren to find out if possible their reaction, and I am frank to say it is terrible. I had hoped that we could invite Dr. Shields to Toledo for a great closing address, but now I know any such attemp would be suicidal to our cause. Remember I am not debating with Dr. Shilelds that he is wrong. I do maintain he has all the right in the wold to his own opinions, but the least said in print on these debatable questions at such a precarious time as this the better. And what is true in realation to the Scofield Bible and our cause is also true in relation to Woman's ministry.
>
> Surely our Regular Baptist Association has a much bigger task these days than stirring up such questions that are non-essential. As for myself I regard both. I own and use an Scofield Bible and I am even guilty of the unpardonable sin in the eyes of Dr. Shileds as to be a subscriber to Our Hope published by Dr. Gaebelin. And I even had a woman in the pulpit of this church a few weeks ago.
>
> The last paragraph on page four. "It is time to get together but Satan will stir up some devises" Why blame the stirring up on the devil when we are guilty of the misdemeanor ourselves Three years ago Dr. W. B. Riley said to me "Hamilton dont waste your time trying to organize that crowd, they will never stick" I have been skeptical of his idea, but untill now and I am about persuaded that he is right.[58]

Unless Hamilton was being disingenuous, the real issue for him was not whether women's ministry could be justified biblically. He was willing (at least for the sake of the discussion) to concede that it could. The real issue was damage control. Secondary arguments such as dispensationalism and women's ministry threatened to tear the Regular Baptist coalition apart and to block the growth of the new association. He pleaded for Van Osdel to stop "waving the red flag" so that the Regular Baptists could unify around the most important things.

Van Osdel, however, was not easily deterred. An extended illness in early 1933 left him incapacitated for several months, but by July he was feeling well

---

from a weekly to a monthly publication).

58. Harry Hamilton to Oliver W. Van Osdel, November 10, 1932 (entire citation *sic*).

enough to begin writing a booklet that he would title *Should Women Preach?* When the pamphlet was complete, he had it printed and advertized it in the *Baptist Temple News*. He also sent a free copy to each Regular Baptist pastor in Grand Rapids.

Hamilton's response to Van Osdel's booklet is particularly illustrative of its effect upon the Regular Baptist movement. Hamilton was no longer president of the GARBC, but he was still the editor of the *Bulletin*, the official Regular Baptist publication. When Van Osdel requested space to advertise his booklet in the *Bulletin*, Hamilton flatly refused. He wrote to Van Osdel, "To raise the controversy of Woman's Ministry on top of our already great issue would undoubtedly veil the purpose of the policy of The Bulletin and throw a monkey wrench into the effort." Actually, Hamilton considered printing a refutation of Van Osdel's argument. He even prepared a rough draft, which he sent along with his letter. Hamilton was not usually one to back away from a controversy, but he never published his refutation. Here was a clear decision that it was better to bury the issue than to debate it.[59]

Van Osdel was old and his health was failing. The *Baptist Temple News* had already dropped from weekly to monthly publication, and it would soon cease to appear at all. Not long into 1934, Van Osdel asked Wealthy Street Baptist Church to begin looking for his successor. Though he did not leave the pastorate for several months, his infirmities greatly diminished his activity. When he died on January 1, 1935, the women's ministry controversy in the Regular Baptist movement was laid to rest for the next fifty years.

Stockton and Gould remained members at Wealthy Street after Van Osdel's death, and for at least a while they continued as licentiates of the church. Their ministry was even commended as "enjoying much blessing from the Lord," in the *Baptist Bulletin*, the renamed publication of the GARBC.[60] Their new pastor, David Otis Fuller, seems not to have supported their work as enthusiastically as Van Osdel, so they eventually relocated their center of operations. After World War II, fewer and fewer pulpits were open to them within Baptist fundamentalism. Neither woman ever married, but both gave their lives completely to the ministry of evangelism. Northern Baptist Seminary eventually conferred a doctorate upon Stockton, and she kept up a cordial relationship with the school until her death. Both women retired to Stockton's family home in Fremont, California. Gould died in 1982. Stockton never really recovered from the loss, living alone until her death six years later.

Though some pastors stood with Van Osdel at the time of the controversy,

59. Harry Hamilton to Oliver W. Van Osdel, November 24, 1932.
60. "Evangelist Amy Lee Stockton," *Baptist Bulletin*, November 1934, 4.

his was a minority position even then. Many found his views offensive. Hamilton and others implied that his writings on female preachers had hurt the growth of the GARBC. If they are right, the situation was ironic. On the one hand, the GARBC probably would never have come into existence without Van Osdel's leadership. On the other hand, his idiosyncratic defense of women in the pulpit posed a significant obstacle to its development. Perhaps the wisest move he made was to distribute influence and leadership among the younger organizers. Because the GARBC was not tied to his personality, it could survive his peculiarities.

Never again would Van Osdel take the initiative in Regular Baptist leadership, though he would still play one more important role. For the time being, leadership had shifted to men like Harry Hamilton, Earle G. Griffith, Clyde Wood, John J. Van Gorder, David Gillespie, G. Rector Dye, and Robert T. Ketcham. Whether Ketcham attended the founding of the GARBC or not, he was clearly present in 1933 and in every year after that until his health failed. No one could have guessed it at Belden Avenue, but Ketcham was about to emerge as the most competent, vigorous, and articulate leader that the GARBC would ever follow.

The Infancy of the GARBC

Objectively, not much had changed at the Belden Avenue meeting. The organization had a new name: the General Association of Regular Baptist Churches. Nevertheless, it was still operating under the bylaws of the old Baptist Bible Union. Its statement of faith was still the old Bible Union confession.

Nevertheless, two important subjective changes had taken place. First, the delegates (they would soon reject the term *delegate* for the term *messenger*) now viewed themselves as part of a new organization. They had put behind them both the good and the bad of the old Baptist Bible Union. Second, the group was beginning to develop self-awareness as an association of churches. This is one point at which Van Osdel's influence probably counted heavily. The call to the 1932 meeting was a call to delegates appointed by local churches. Although the association would go through at least one debate before this policy became official, it was already the unofficial consensus.

The newly appointed missionary committee of the GARBC went to work immediately. The three members were Earle G. Griffith, Howard Fulton, and Clyde E. Wood. Within days they developed an application blank for mission agencies that were interested in receiving endorsement. Griffith sent copies to any parties that he thought might be interested. By July the committee endorsed two agencies: The General Council of Cooperating Baptist Missions (the Mid-Africa Mission) and the Lithuanian Mission Association. Only two months into its existence, the GARBC had already made as much progress on missions as the old Baptist Bible Union ever had.[61]

Hamilton began gathering names and addresses to compile a mailing list. He wanted to include anyone who might be in sympathy with the program of the GARBC and any person of influence who might be interested in receiving literature. In early June he sent out his first form letter on the newly printed associational letterhead. He included a report of the Belden Avenue meeting and a reminder that the association had agreed to meet at Toledo the next year. He emphasized three points about the shared vision of the GARBC. First, it would maintain a testimony for the supernaturalism of Christianity and against modernism. Second, it would promote foreign missions in all lands. Third, it would promote home missions, including both education and evangelism. He pointed to the Interstate Evangelistic Association as a beginning.[62]

A bit of good news arrived in June. Hamilton was notified by a lawyer from Kansas City that someone had left a legacy to the Baptist Bible Union. The only question was whether the Union was still in existence. Hamilton had been able to point the lawyer to publications that affirmed the continued existence of the Baptist Bible Union under the new name. In 1932 the Depression was approaching its depth, and the GARBC was broke (though according to the treasurer funds were beginning to trickle in), so the bequest would provide needed funds.[63]

In September Ketcham moved from First Baptist Church of Elyria, Ohio, to Central Baptist Church of Gary, Indiana. Central Baptist was still nominally connected to the convention, though Ketcham made it clear that he intended to lead them out. Somewhere during his first months at Gary, Ketcham's attitude toward national organization began to change. Whether the change was due to Van Osdel's influence, to the counsel of other friends, or to Ketcham's own observations is uncertain. What is clear is that by the time of the next year's meeting, he had become a believer in the GARBC.

Also in September the Interstate Evangelistic Association held a large conference in Atlantic City. To everyone's surprise, Earle V. Pierce and Curtis Lee Laws showed up. Pierce and Laws were two of the most noteworthy leaders among those fundamentalists who had chosen to stay in the convention. Pierce asked Harold Strathearn, president of the Interstate Evangelistic Association, for permission to speak at the conference. Hamilton, who was present, warned Strathearn against it.

---

61. Earle G. Griffith, form letter, n.d. but late May 1932; Oliver W. Van Osdel, "The Regular Baptists," *Baptist Temple News*, August, 1932, 1–2.

62. Harry Hamilton, form letter, June 3, 1932.

63. Harry Hamilton to Oliver W. Van Osdel, June 17, 1932; John Muntz to Van Osdel, June 29, 1932.

Also present was Mrs. Henry W. Peabody, the key founder of the Association of Baptists for the Evangelism of the Orient. She had reason to feel some irritation with Pierce: in his defense of the convention mission board, he had come perilously close to implying that some of her missionaries were liars. When she heard that he was at the meeting, she hunted him down and publicly took him to task for his words. Pierce and Laws left the conference unhappy with their reception.[64]

In December messengers from seven churches met in Buffalo to try to organize a Regular Baptist association in western New York. The meeting hit a snag over an issue that was destined to trouble the GARBC for some years, and the organization of the fellowship was actually delayed. Hamilton summarized:

> The pain of the evening came when poor old Brother Muntz and his pussey footing son began to raise innumerable difficulties. Again he emphasized that the G.A.R.B. was not a come out movement for that was not touched upon at Chicago, and he feels that there are many good brethren who are not quite ready for such a movement, I tried hard to remain silent and Keithley made a good job of answering his temerity. The problem of church property loomed large and that was one thing that he re-emphasized again and again a 100% denominational official could not have aided the cause better.[65]

As far as Hamilton was concerned, the GARBC was exactly a come-out organization, and he knew that Van Osdel agreed with him. Evidently, Howard Keithley did as well. All parties recognized, however, that there would be some pastors who, while not wishing to cooperate with the Northern Baptist Convention, were still trying to get out. Because of their situation, the question was whether the Regular Baptists ought to require separation from the convention to formally enter fellowship with the GARBC. This issue would be debated for some years before a definite decision was made.

In January 1933 influenza spread across the United States and then into Europe. One of the victims of this pandemic was Oliver W. Van Osdel. He was knocked completely out of public ministry for several months. By mid-February his recovery had become doubtful. He managed his correspondence only by dictating to a stenographer. He could not preach, he could not even write the *Baptist Temple News*. Only in July did the little paper resume publication. One of the results of his sickness was that Van Osdel was not able to attend the GARBC meeting in 1933.

---

64. Harry Hamilton to Oliver W. Van Osdel, October 24, 1932.
65. Howard Keithley to the First Baptist Church, Buffalo, New York, November 25, 1932. A copy was in Van Osdel's papers. Harry Hamilton to Oliver W. Van Osdel, December 10, 1932. As usual with Hamilton, spellings and punctuation are *sic*.

Also in January the GARBC launched its own publication, the *Bulletin*. Hamilton was the editor. The first issue gave notice of a regional Bible conference for separatists in Minnesota. The conference was organized by young pastors who were critical of the Northern Baptist Convention. Hamilton reported that a "prominent fundamentalist pastor of Minnesota" had made this threat to the pastors, "If you young men decide to continue with this conference, ... you will soon find yourselves out of a Baptist church and it will be difficult for you to get another." Hamilton never actually named Riley, but nobody doubted whom he meant.[66]

The first issue of the *Bulletin* also included a report on the Interstate Evangelistic Association and another report on the Mid-Africa Mission. It contained news of pastoral changes and church events. Hamilton also used the *Bulletin* to promote the upcoming conference which, he said, would still be held at Toledo even though Earle G. Griffith had accepted a pastorate in Erie, Pennsylvania.

The Depression was still deepening. It hurt most people, but pastors who had separated from the convention were among the hardest hit. One example is C. R. Peterson, who had been the association missionary for the newly established Michigan association. When the association could no longer support him, he found a temporary job in a sugar beet factory. When that ran out, his only income was provided by occasional pulpit supply. In mid-March he wrote,

> Last week I was compelled to do the most humiliating thing I have ever been forced to do. I had to go to the poor commissioner of the county to get the necessary food for my family. I have tried in vain to get work of some kind. . . . Do you know of any opening anywhere, either a church or any other kind of work? I have had a number of contacts with churches, but it seems that churches are not calling pastors at all these days. These contacts have been in a number of states. Naturally in this state it would be difficult for me to get a church, outside of a very limited number.
>
> I have offered my car and some household furniture for sale, but you can't get a buyer for anything these days. Do you know where I could borrow some money for a time? Naturally the repayment of it would have to be at such a time as I again enjoyed the income. There is no one in this small town [St. Louis, Michigan] who can help me out.[67]

Peterson's situation was what many pastors feared. Denominational officials could capitalize upon that fear. They could use their influence to stir up a group that would fire a pastor. They could blackball an uncooperative

66. Harry Hamilton, "The Regional Bible Conference of Minnesota," *Bulletin*, January 1933, 1.
67. C. R. Peterson to Oliver W. Van Osdel, March 14, 1933.

minister and ensure that he stayed out of ministry. Apparently this was what the Michigan convention officials did with Peterson. No wonder that many pastors were reluctant to commit to overt separatism, even if their hearts were with the Regular Baptists.

Hamilton was doing his best to dispel these fears. In late April he sent out a letter announcing that the year's meeting was being moved from Toledo to the First Baptist Church of Buffalo, New York. Then he promoted the GARBC as an organization of "Simon-Pure, Bible Believing, Non-Compromising Baptists." He encouraged churches to send their pastors as delegates, noting that the Northern Baptist Convention "with its inclusive policy of Modernism has robbed Christ of His Deity, the Bible of its Inspiration, and the Atonement of its Efficacy." He admitted that "this is not an hour for easy optimism; the clouds hang darkly," but he insisted that "in those clouds our Lord may come." In 1933 such words were still thought to mean something.[68]

Hamilton put out his letter just in time. Many were wanting to know what was going to be done about the meeting. For example, Max Schimpf wrote from New York that he had heard the meeting was being moved, but did not know any details—though business was bad and he probably could not attend anyway. Ketcham and Fulton wrote to say that they could not afford to go to Buffalo. Hamilton responded that they would absolutely have to be there. Both Clyde Wood and Isaac Van Westenbrugge had become critical of Hamilton's leadership and it was not clear whether the GARBC could count on their support.[69]

As circumstances developed, Ketcham did attend the Buffalo meeting, held on May 16–18, 1933. Years later David Gillespie affirmed that he took Ketcham there in his six-cylinder Essex. Although illness kept Van Osdel at home, T. T. Shields was invited to come over from Toronto to deliver an address. The messengers were also delighted to hear R. E. Neighbour deliver the closing sermon. One wonders what Neighbour thought as he saw what had become of his dream.[70]

The executive committee had prepared a constitution for the Buffalo meeting, and it was presented by John Muntz. G. Rector Dye moved its adoption, but no one would second the motion. The problem was that "when the first draft of the Constitution was presented it provided for almost all of the machinery of the old Northern Baptist Convention." Finally, Ketcham stood up and expressed his reservations about the proposed form of organization. On

68. Harry Hamilton, form letter, April 28, 1933.
69. Max Schimpf to Harry Hamilton, May 3, 1933. A copy was in Van Osdel's papers. Harry Hamilton to Oliver W. Van Osdel, May 5, 1933.
70. David Gillespie, interview with Robert Delnay, June 1962.

David Gillespie's motion, the constitution was tabled, to be taken up again later in the day. It never was.[71]

Dissatisfaction with Hamilton's leadership had been growing, and it was expressed at the Buffalo conference. People were upset for several reasons. In the first place, Hamilton had a rather aggressive style of leadership, and not just about issues. For example, he had prepared and published the program without first consulting all of the people whose names he had listed. Among those who were named without being asked were Clyde Wood and Isaac Van Westenbrugge of Grand Rapids. Both simply skipped the conference, and Van Westenbrugge never even bothered to respond to Hamilton.

Another who was named without being asked was J. Irving Reese of the Interstate Evangelistic Association. Over the past couple of months, Hamilton had grown cold toward the work of the IEA, and he had stopped promoting it. Hamilton's coolness provoked the organization's founder, Harold Strathearn, and now the annoyance had spread to Reese. Why should they be presumed upon by a man who would not even support their work?[72]

Others were probably concerned about Hamilton's commitment to a more convention-like structure. For example, he questioned whether Hawkins's Mid-Africa Mission and Peabody's Association of Baptists for the Evangelism of the Orient should be seen as genuinely Baptist institutions. As far as Hamilton was concerned, they "are not Baptist Missionary Societies until the Churches sponsor them." These words hint at a replaying of the old debate between the associational model and the service organization model. Baptists had deliberated this question for a century. Hamilton was on one side of the debate, and he had supporters. Hawkins and Peabody were on the opposite side of the debate, and they, too, had supporters.[73]

Most serious was the question of separation. In his presidential address, Hamilton pressed hard for the instant and complete severance of all ties to the convention. When he made these demands, he knew that he had opposition within the auditorium. He and Muntz had clashed over this very issue earlier in the year. After his address Earle G. Griffith took him aside and told him that he was trying to rush things and that perhaps a complete break with the convention should not come immediately. Griffith pointed out that Ketcham had accepted the pastorate of a church in Gary that was nominally in the convention. Furthermore, he himself was in a new pastorate, and John Muntz was also inclined to move more slowly. Hamilton replied that they "had been going very slow for sixteen years and I venture to say that John Muntz will

71. Ruth Ryburn, "The Outworking of Obedience," *Baptist Bulletin*, March 1966, 11; "Minutes," *Bulletin*, June 1933, 3.

72. Harry Hamilton to Oliver W. Van Osdel, June 19, 1933.

73. Hamilton to Van Osdel, May 12, 1933.

not be any more willing to break after sixteen more than he is now, and he has a son that is coming on and he likes to mingle with both groups so there you are."[74]

The next morning the association held its elections. Given the dissatisfaction with Hamilton's leadership, it is not surprising that Earle G. Griffith was chosen as president. More surprising is the election of Robert T. Ketcham as first vice president. This position would give Ketcham a substantial voice in framing the future shape of the organization. John Muntz was reelected as secretary-treasurer, and a full slate of state vice presidents was chosen. Hamilton was asked to continue as editor of the *Bulletin*.[75]

As the 1933 meeting of the GARBC came to a close, many issues remained unresolved. Three were particularly important. Could the fellowship truly function as an association of churches without either reproducing the convention machinery or falling into individual membership? Would separation from the convention become a requirement for fellowship with the GARBC? In the absence of a convention structure, would the GARBC be able to find an effective way to promote missions and other cooperative work?

Even with these questions unanswered, the GARBC was beginning to take shape. It now had a recognizable constituency, an identifiable mission, and an attractive publication. Perhaps most importantly, a key individual had been inserted into a position of leadership. Robert T. Ketcham would no longer be able simply to point out the problems. He would now be expected to solve them.

Organization

When Van Osdel heard about the results of the Buffalo meeting, he was overjoyed. He remarked that "the work is evidently putting on strength and taking form for continuance." He believed that the success of the GARBC was vital to the future of Baptist principles. The convention fundamentalists had become an "ornamental appendage to the Northern Baptist Convention." Even the modernists thought they were a joke. Van Osdel was aware of complaints about the idiosyncrasies of some Regular Baptists, but he reminded his readers that these complaints were most likely propagated by convention officials who were looking for ways to pry church properties away from separatist congregations. Consequently, Van Osdel argued for unity among Regular Baptists just as he argued for separation from the convention.[76]

Harry Hamilton was no longer the president of the GARBC, but he was

---

74. Harry Hamilton to Oliver W. Van Osdel, June 19, 1933.
75. "Minutes," *Bulletin*, June 1933, 4.
76. Oliver W. Van Osdel, "The Meeting of the General Association of Regular Baptists," *Baptist Temple News*, July 1933, 2–3.

still the editor of the *Bulletin*. The little paper was already performing an important role in forming the identity of the GARBC. It had become the chief means of publicizing and coordinating events that involved churches, pastors, and institutions. Hamilton also regularly used the paper to denounce liberalism in the Northern Baptist Convention. He further used it to confront fundamentalists like Earle V. Pierce who, though conservative in their beliefs, claimed to be able to support the Inclusive Policy. When Pierce raised objections to Hamilton's methods, Hamilton replied,

> Dr. Pierce would not regret to see modernism with all its filthy blasphemy of God's dear Son driven from the Convention but he does not like our method of doing so. We are not sticklers for method, any method that will work will suit us, but we know that after trying for twelve years by night and day to drive modernism out by remaining in and supporting the program will never accomplish results. True and faithful Baptists over the North land feel that Dr. Pierce is lending a great help to the modernists by his effort to uphold and cooperate with an organization wholly given over to the inclusive policy. Modernists themselves are bold to declare that their God is not the God of Dr. Pierce; why then should Dr. Pierce think that he is aiding the cause of our Lord Jesus Christ while advocating cooperation with a pagan God.[77]

This paragraph exhibits the ambivalence and frustration that the Regular Baptists felt with the convention fundamentalists. On the one hand, they recognized a community of belief and a commonality of purpose: both groups affirmed the fundamentals and both groups wanted to see modernism defeated. At the same time, the Regular Baptists were convinced that modernism had a death grip on the convention. Consequently, any further cooperation with the convention program was merely giving aid and comfort to the enemy. Needless to say, the convention fundamentalists continued to participate because they nourished a hope of capturing at least some part of the denominational machinery and resources for themselves. They saw the Regular Baptists as radicals whose tirades tended to alienate conservatives and to undermine attempts to reclaim convention resources. While people in the two groups generally remained friends, the element of exasperation tended to dominate their public interaction.

Hamilton returned to the theme of separation in the next issue of the *Bulletin*. He republished on the front page a part of Harry A. Ironside's book, *Holiness, the False and the True*. The excerpt was titled "Ecclesiastical Sanctification." Hamilton set one section in bold type. "But this brings in responsibility.

---

77. Harry Hamilton, "Secretary Lerrigo of the N.B.C. Struggle Hard to Explain," *Bulletin*, August 1933, 3.

I am not to go with evil—protesting, perhaps, but fellowshipping it still—though it be in a reserved, half-hearted way. I am called to separate from it. In so doing I may seem to be separating from dear children of God and beloved servants of Christ. But this is necessary if they do not judge the apostate condition." With the Muntzes and even Griffith wavering, Hamilton was pushing separation as hard as he could.[78]

The new fellowship was gaining attention, some of it from young, new pastors. One of them was a recent graduate of Wheaton College who had just taken the pastorate of a small church in Michigan's Keweenaw Peninsula. His name was Joseph Stowell Jr., and he would later play a significant role in the history of the GARBC. For the moment, however, he simply announced his presence in upper Michigan and asked for prayer for the souls in "copper country."[79]

The officers of the GARBC were less visible than Hamilton had been, but they were busy behind the scenes. In January Harold Strathearn offered to let the GARBC take over the mailing list of his *Inter-State Baptist Believer*. When Hamilton balked, Griffith told him to do it anyway. The move substantially enlarged the number of individuals who were receiving the periodical, and in March it was renamed the *Baptist Bulletin*. By late February Griffith was lining up speakers for the May meetings. Ketcham offered to hold the meetings at Central Baptist in Gary, and the executive committee agreed on the dates of May 15–17. Most importantly, in early March Ketcham proposed a draft constitution to the executive committee. This was better planning and organization than the group had seen for years.

By late April the executive committee had finished work on the proposed constitution. It was published in the May edition of the *Baptist Bulletin*. It included bylaws and seventeen articles of faith.

The GARBC confession is not simply the old New Hampshire Confession with a premillennial ending. During the winter of 1922–23 Riley and Norris drew up the BBU Confession of Faith, which was a considerable revision of the New Hampshire. Their original version had premillennialism written into it. When Shields came into the Baptist Bible Union, they revised the last article to accommodate amillennialists among the members. Now in 1934 the executive committee began with the BBU confession and modified it again. Among other changes they strengthened the statement on inspiration, relaxed the Calvinism, and added the words *premillennial* and *millennial* to the final article (though making no mention of the Rapture). The new

---

78. Harry A. Ironside, "Ecclesiastical Sanctification," *Bulletin*, September 1933, 1.
79. Joseph M. Stowell Jr. to Oliver W. Van Osdel, February 14, 1934.

confession excluded any modernist from signing, but it remained relatively broad in some other areas.[80]

The 1934 conference proved to be decisive for the direction of the GARBC. The meeting attracted 251 registered messengers, considerably more than the thirty-some who had attended in 1932. The association dealt with two of its most important questions at this conference. The first was the question of what to do about missions. The second was the constitutional question: What type of organization would the GARBC become?

Van Osdel brought up the problem of missions in his address during the second session of the conference. Much of the address was a retelling of Northern Baptist history, from the old "May Meetings," down through the Northern Baptist Convention and its apostasy, to the ineffectual protests of the convention fundamentalists. Decades later, Joseph Stowell Jr. remembered Van Osdel making the statement that "if the GARBC ever goes liberal, I'll leave it, too."[81] John Muntz's handwritten minutes then record that,

> Dr. Van Osdel expressed the hope and made an earnest plea that this year, this convention will take steps to form a missionary society with a treasurer which shall be a channel through which missionary work can be done. Dr. Van Osdel spoke of a number of people ready to go to the field—but after having applied to some faith boards—but cannot go forth, on account of lack of money. . . . Dr. Van Osdel spoke with much effort and great feeling.[82]

From Muntz's record, Van Osdel seems to have favored the creation of a GARBC mission board, more or less comparable to the convention board. The difference would be that the Northern Baptist Convention operated with a unified budget, whereas the Regular Baptist board would guarantee that every penny given to missions went to missions. Everyone was impressed with Van Osdel's earnest commitment to missions. Stowell later reflected that Van Osdel's greatest contribution to the GARBC may have been its missions emphasis.[83]

Late that afternoon Robert T. Ketcham led a discussion titled "What Shall We Do about Missions?" He began by stating that he would speak only for

80. "Constitution, By-Laws and Articles of Faith," *Baptist Bulletin*, May 1934, 2–4. Joseph Stowell Jr. was asked during a 1982 telephone interview why the executive committee did not simply use the original BBU statement on eschatology. He replied, "Probably none of them had a copy." The only copy of the original BBU confession known to have survived was in the files that Riley left at Northwestern Schools.

81. Joseph M. Stowell Jr., interview.

82. Minutes of the Third Annual Convocation of the General Association of Regular Baptists in the U.S.A., Held in Central Baptist Church, Gary, Indiana, May 15–17, 1934. The official, typed minutes are supplemented by John Muntz's handwritten minutes. The citation is from the handwritten minutes, 10–11.

83. Joseph M. Stowell Jr., interview.

himself, but that he believed there was a great danger in organizing a mission-ary board. To do so would be a duplication of the Northern Baptist Conven-tion. Nevertheless, he was deeply committed to the idea that the group must take some step to crystallize its missionary efforts. Faith mission boards were not enough: the GARBC needed Baptist missions. He wondered whether something might be done with the existing agencies like the Association of Baptists for the Evangelism of the Orient or the Mid-Africa Mission.

After Ketcham had finished his remarks, several others participated in the discussion. Specifically, Harry Hamilton suggested that one or two rep-resentatives from the GARBC could be added to the boards of Mid-Missions (this name was coming into use for the Mid-Africa Mission) and the ABEO. Mrs. Peabody replied that such representatives would be welcome. Van Osdel spoke again and pleaded for leadership, after which Ketcham summarized what he considered to be the consensus at that point. He then moved that the president appoint a committee to bring a recommendation to the association on the next morning. The motion passed, and Griffith made sure to put both Ketcham and Van Osdel on the committee.[84]

The next morning the committee presented its recommendation in the form of a resolution. The core of the resolution contained two elements. First, by election of two members to each council, the GARBC would establish official relations with the Association of Baptists for the Evangelism of the Orient, Mid-Missions, and with any other Baptist missionary agency that met the approval of the missionary committee. Second, the missionary committee would be responsible to present the work of these approved agencies to the churches.[85]

This recommendation was essentially a compromise. The GARBC would not organize its own mission board, but it would establish formal relations with existing agencies and commend them to the churches. With both Van Osdel and Ketcham agreeing to the compromise, its adoption by the associa-tion was virtually guaranteed. This compromise, which became known as the approval system, served the GARBC for sixty years.

The missionary committee for 1934 consisted of Howard Fulton, H. W. Jones, and Clyde Wood. They put their approval upon the Association of Baptists for the Evangelism of the Orient, the Lithuanian Missionary Asso-ciation, the General Council of Cooperating Baptist Missions, and the Inter-state Evangelistic Association. Except for ABEO, these missions had all been approved the previous year.[86]

---

84. Minutes, GARBC, 1934, 14–16. MS by John Muntz.
85. Ibid., 3–4. The text of the minutes reads "Cooperative Baptist Missions" instead of "General Council of Cooperating Baptist Missions."
86. Minutes, GARBC, 1934, 5.

Having decided its policy for missions, the GARBC now needed to adopt a form of organization. The Baptist Bible Union had been an organization of individuals, and some still favored making an allowance for individual membership. The proposed constitution, however, called for a fellowship of churches.

> Any Baptist Church in the United States which subscribes to our Constitution and Confession of Faith, contained herein, and signifies in writing its desire to find fellowship with the Association, may upon such written application be received by a majority vote of the Association. . . . Each year every voting messenger shall subscribe to the Constitution and Articles of Faith of the Association prior to taking his seat in the annual meeting.[87]

The newly adopted missions policy meant that the GARBC would not erect a convention-like structure. By itself, however, this provision was not adequate assurance for people who, like Ketcham, feared that the GARBC might become another domineering organization. Consequently, the constitution inserted one more provision: no salaried servant of the association would be entitled to vote.

Once the constitution was put on the floor, it provoked surprisingly little discussion. Gerard Knol of Grand Rapids moved that the constitution be adopted for one year, then revised from year to year as necessary, until it was completely satisfactory. Muntz, who was meticulous about recording debate, put nothing in his minutes about a discussion over the constitution. Apparently the association simply voted in favor of Knol's motion.[88]

The association then elected Robert T. Ketcham as its next (and, had they known it, last) president. The first vice president was H. O. Van Gilder and the secretary-treasurer was Raymond F. Hamilton. As in previous years, vice presidents were selected for each state in which Regular Baptists had a presence: ten states altogether. The GARBC had achieved full organization. Years later, historian Calvin Odell wrote,

> The GARBC was born amid poverty and has remained largely conservative in its economic outlook. It was salvaged from the demise of the old BBU, which may somewhat explain a defensive and cautious attitude. It did not attempt to begin new institutions because of its poverty and the failure at Des Moines University. Its membership was to be churches, because individuals had not given stability and support to the old BBU. It paid no leaders for over ten years lest executive secretaries might gain control as they had in the NBC. It shunned organization through fear of convention machinery. It adopted the faith mission principle in aversion to a unified budget controlled by liberals.[89]

87. "Constitution and By-Laws," *Baptist Bulletin*, July 1934, 1–2.
88. Minutes, GARBC, 1934, 27. MS by John Muntz.
89. Calvin Odell, *The General Association of Regular Baptist Churches and Its Attendant*

The 1934 meeting at Gary was a milestone for the General Association of Regular Baptist Churches. In one sense, the association began more at Gary than it had at Chicago. The organization received its name at Belden Avenue, but it was defined at Central Baptist. The missionary policy that was adopted in 1934 also became a template for the educational and social work of the fellowship. Perhaps most importantly, momentum had finally been established. After the Gary conference, President Robert T. Ketcham would write, "Regular Baptists can now go forward."[90]

Movement (Salem, OR: Western Baptist Bible College Press, 1975), 11.

90. Robert T. Ketcham, "Regular Baptists Can Now Go Forward," *Baptist Bulletin*, July 1934, 1.

Robert Ketcham, 1930.

Amy Lee Stockton and Rita Gould on the grounds of Maranatha Bible Conference, Muskegon, Michigan.

GARBC Council of Fourteen with Robert Ketcham (center at desk), 1938.

7 Growing Pains

To 1934 THE LEADERS of the General Association of Regular Baptist Churches were preoccupied with simply bringing the organization into existence. Van Osdel's influence was critical during the years after the Des Moines University riot and the collapse of the Baptist Bible Union. In 1934 the initiative in leadership shifted to Robert T. Ketcham. Under his presidency, the next four years brought growth and definition. They also forced the GARBC to hold its own in the world of ecclesiastical criticism and controversy.

Controversy began soon after the 1934 conference. The July issue of the *Baptist Bulletin* carried the full text of the new constitution, bylaws, and articles of faith. It also carried the text of the missionary resolution that had been passed at Gary. In its justification of the GARBC missionary policy, the resolution declared the convention mission board to be permeated with modernism.

One person who read the resolution was Earle V. Pierce, leader of the Fundamentalist Fellowship and a member of the convention's foreign mission board. Relations between the convention fundamentalists and the Baptist Bible Union had been strained for some time. Pierce's view of Regular Baptists had further deteriorated because of his experience the year before at the Interstate Evangelistic Association conference, where he had been denied the opportunity to speak and had been publicly lectured by Lucy Peabody. Now he found the GARBC resolution deeply offensive. He wrote to Ketcham immediately.

> I do not believe that you wish, knowingly, to violate the ninth commandment. I enclose to you a brief pamphlet stating the evangelical policy of the Foreign Mission Board. . . . If you will read this carefully you will see that there is no basis for the statement so often made in Dr. Hamilton's paper *The Baptist Bulletin* and otherwise that

the Foreign Mission Society or the Northern Baptist Convention as a whole is committed to an inclusive policy which means the sending out of modernists as well as sound missionaries.

I feel that the organization of your association is a very unfortunate division of our conservative portion. The liberals stand together. If we could only get the conservatives also to stand together, we could do anything that we wanted or that was necessary in the Northern Convention. It has been the sin of schism that has weakened our conservative forces so that liberals have had whatever power they have manifested. But when it is stated that our Foreign Mission Society is sending out modernistic missionaries, the person who makes that statement is either ignorant or mendacious.[1]

From Pierce's perspective, the GARBC was schismatic and posed a hindrance to the fundamentalist mission of recapturing the structures and resources of the Northern Baptist Convention. He questioned either the intelligence or the veracity of the association for passing the missionary resolution. His viewpoint would continue to define the attitude of the Fundamentalist Fellowship toward the GARBC for at least the next eight to ten years.

During the waning months of 1934, the GARBC also faced a different kind of test. Van Osdel had earlier announced his intention to retire and asked Wealthy Street Baptist Church to begin looking for his replacement. Eventually the congregation called David Otis Fuller, a young pastor from Atlantic City, New Jersey. When Fuller arrived at the Grand Rapids train station in September, Van Osdel was there, leaning on his cane, to greet him. It was the only time the two men met.

Van Osdel intended to go live with his son, but that never happened. His health was already failing when he retired. In December his family was notified that the end was near, and Edgar traveled from California to be with his father. As he entered the room where the elder Van Osdel lay, Edgar said, "Father, you should have retired." The aged pastor replied, "I was just going to."

Oliver Willis Van Osdel died on New Year's Day, 1935. He was eighty-eight years old. He had spent twenty-five years as the pastor of Wealthy Street Baptist Church and sixty years in ministry. The GARBC would quickly forget his name, but it would bear witness to his values for decades to come. While he never occupied any high office in the association, he molded its structure and shaped its policies. Perhaps his greatest achievement was to ensure that the fellowship was in the hands of capable leaders before he passed from the scene.

1. Quoted in Robert T. Ketcham, "The Northern Baptist Situation," *Baptist Bulletin*, November 1943, 2.

Issues and Changes

At its 1934 meeting in Gary, Indiana, the GARBC positioned itself as an association of churches rather than either a convention or a preachers' fellowship. This distinction required clarification for a number of reasons. One was that some people were concerned (as Ketcham had been) that an association might turn into a convention and try to dictate to the churches. Another was that the Northern Baptist Convention tried to present itself as the Baptist denomination, implying that leaving for some other group was, in effect, to cease to be Baptist. Many Baptists accepted the convention's dictum without giving the matter much thought.

Ketcham knew that these misperceptions were going to have to be addressed before the GARBC could grow. One of his first tasks as president of the fledgling association was to begin educating Baptists about their own polity. Ketcham saw the *Baptist Bulletin* as the ideal vehicle for doing this kind of work.

The first step was to clarify the procedure for entering the fellowship of the GARBC. Ketcham explained that all a church had to do was to subscribe to the association's constitution and articles of faith, then to notify the association by letter of its desire to be counted in the fellowship. Of course, the letter had to be acted upon by the association, but once that was done the church would be qualified to send messengers in numbers proportionate to its membership.[2]

Next, Ketcham published a front-page article in the *Baptist Bulletin* titled, "The Status of a Regular Baptist Church." In this article he answered the question, "Just what is the relation of a local Baptist Church to the various other organizations which go to make up what is commonly called the Denomination?" As a platform for his remarks, Ketcham appealed to Edward Hiscox's *New Directory for Baptist Churches*, which was at that time being distributed by the American Baptist Publication Society. Relying upon Hiscox, he made the point that an association does not consist of churches and that a church cannot be a member of an association. Instead of being received into associational membership, churches are received into fellowship and cooperation. Fellowship with an association is voluntary, so a church is free to withdraw its fellowship at any time "for any reason sufficient to itself without prejudice either to its evangelical or denominational standing." Ketcham clarified, "It does not cease to be a Baptist church simply because it chooses its own Baptist companions."

---

2. Robert T. Ketcham, "Regular Baptists Can Now Go Forward," *Baptist Bulletin*, July 1934, 1.

For Ketcham, the distinction between membership and fellowship was an important one. Membership implied some limitation upon the church's autonomy, while fellowship did not. Ketcham reasoned that if a church was not a member of an association, then it could not be subjected to the control of the other churches with which it chose to fellowship. He concluded that "any regular Baptist Church which no longer wishes to fellowship [with] a Convention or Associational program can withdraw their fellowship without damaging their reputation as Baptists."[3]

These were themes that Ketcham would repeat over the next three decades. He would drill them into the fellowshipping churches of the GARBC. He would teach them to churches that were deciding whether to leave the Northern Baptist Convention. Furthermore, he would deploy them as weapons against convention officials who tried to interfere in the business of local congregations. On more than one occasion, Ketcham would even carry these ideas into courtrooms when he defended separatist churches against convention lawsuits.

If Ketcham was eager to thwart predatory convention officials, he was equally eager to prevent the GARBC from ever becoming a convention. He wrote that the GARBC, "stands for the minimum of organization and the maximum of fellowship." He insisted that "there shall never again be among us, any kind of an overhead organization to which allegiance must be ascribed." Rather, the GARBC was a place for independent Baptist churches to come together for prayer, Bible study, and missions.[4]

Ketcham derided the idea that the Northern Baptist Convention was equivalent to the Baptist denomination. He observed that the normal sense of the term *denomination* was completely foreign to Baptist usage. The only proper sense in which the word could be applied to Baptists was as a label to "denominate us from other Christian bodies." Thus understood, the Northern Baptist Convention could not constitute "the denomination," for somehow the denomination had to include the Southern and Canadian Baptist Conventions, not to mention the British Baptist Union. By the same token, churches that left the Northern Baptist Convention and placed their fellowship with the GARBC had not left the denomination. He noted that the number of these churches was increasing throughout the country.[5]

While Ketcham was clarifying the ideas upon which the GARBC was founded, the organization also had to clarify its procedures. For example,

3. Robert T. Ketcham, "The Status of a Regular Baptist Church," *Baptist Bulletin*, November 1934, 1–2.
4. Robert T. Ketcham, "Baptists at Grand Rapids," *Baptist Bulletin*, April 1935, 3.
5. Robert T. Ketcham, "The Break-up in the Northern Baptist Convention Continues," *Baptist Bulletin*, April 1935, 3.

under the newly adopted constitution of the GARBC, each fellowshipping church had the right to send messengers to vote on the association's business. The number of messengers was proportioned to the church's membership. Each church could also designate one of its messengers to serve as a member of the nominating committee. This pattern of organization required the officers of the GARBC to develop a way of recognizing who the messengers from each church were. They published a short form in the *Baptist Bulletin* that would allow a congregation either to apply for fellowship in the association or to designate its messengers.[6]

These organizational matters represented one of the great concerns of the GARBC leadership. A second great concern was how the churches of the GARBC could be related to the Northern Baptist Convention. The question here was whether the association would permit dual affiliation or whether it would require separation from the convention.

Harry Hamilton, still the editor of the *Baptist Bulletin*, definitely favored complete separation. In February 1935 he wrote an article reviewing the career of W. B. Riley. Hamilton was complimentary about Riley's giftedness, his personal virtues, and his influential ministry. He expressed disappointment, however, that Riley had not seen fit to lead pastors out of the convention. Indeed, Riley "has been content for the time being to be a mere cog in the wheel of an apostate religious organization." Nevertheless, Hamilton expressed hope: "Baptists of the Northland are looking for a leader who will lead them out of the slough of apostasy back to the faith of our Fathers, we still think that leader can be, William B. Riley."[7]

Even though Belden Avenue Baptist Church was the host church for the founding of the GARBC, it remained in the convention. Its pastor, Howard Fulton, was a separatist, but he recognized that an orderly separation took a certain amount of preparation. On February 20, 1935, Belden Avenue formally severed its ties with the Northern Baptist Convention. Belden was one of the largest Baptist churches in Chicago, and the news made the *Chicago Daily Tribune*. Delighted, Hamilton reprinted the article from the *Tribune* on the front page of the *Baptist Bulletin*.[8]

As the 1935 meeting of the General Association of Regular Baptist Churches drew near, Hamilton emphasized the importance of separation.

> Let it be known that the General Association of Regular Baptist Churches in the United States is a fellowship movement among Baptists, who can no longer find a free fellowship in the Northern Baptist

6. "Suggested Credentials Blank," *Baptist Bulletin*, May 1935, 4.

7. Harry Hamilton, "Dr. Riley in Buffalo," *Baptist Bulletin*, February 1935, 3.

8. John Evans, "Belden Baptists Quit Convention in Fight on Reds," *Baptist Bulletin*, April 1935, 1–2.

Convention and its subsidiary organizations. The fellowship of the Association is made up of churches who are either actually or nominally separated from the old Conventions. According to the present Constitution a church may fellowship with the Association without voting to withdraw fellowship from the old Convention circles, but it ought to be frankly and honestly said, that no Baptist or no Baptist church who still feels at home in the Modernistic atmosphere of the old Conventions, would feel very much at home in a meeting of the Association of Regular Baptists. Distinctly, primarily, and fundamentally, this association is a fellowship of Baptists who have lost all heart in the fellowship provided by the Northern Baptist Convention.[9]

Separation was bound to become a key issue for the General Association of Regular Baptist Churches. When Belden Avenue left the convention, however, the church introduced a new element into the discussion. The church claimed to be reacting, not only against modernism, but also against communism.

Less than twenty years before, the Bolsheviks had taken control of Russia. With its avowal of atheism and its rejection of all religion, communism was viewed with alarm by many people of faith. When President Franklin Roosevelt extended diplomatic recognition to communist Russia, fundamentalists reacted in disbelief. In its 1934 conference the GARBC even passed a resolution denouncing Roosevelt's "madness in recognizing dishonest and atheistic Russia."[10]

Then in December, communist soldiers in China abducted and brutally murdered American missionaries John and Betty Stam. Fundamentalist alarm over communism soared. Stringent opposition to communism would become a principal feature of most versions of fundamentalism until near the end of the 1980s.

Shortly after Regular Baptists heard about the killing of the Stams, they also discovered that the American Baptist Home Mission Society had decided to allow communists to hold meetings in one of its buildings in Hammond, Indiana. Fundamentalists believed that this episode exposed a direct link between the Northern Baptist Convention and communism.[11]

The rise of communism and socialism gave the GARBC a new issue in its relationship to the Northern Baptist Convention. Hitherto, the main concerns had been liberalism and what was called "conventionism," or the abuse of power by convention officials. After 1935 Regular Baptists would raise all three issues in their criticism of the Northern Baptist Convention.

In addition to these issues, a change occurred in early 1935 that would

9. Harry Hamilton, "On to Grand Rapids," *Baptist Bulletin*, May 1935, 1.
10. John Evans, "Belden Baptists Quit Convention," 1; "Resolutions," *Baptist Bulletin*, July 1934, 4.
11. RoberT. T. Ketcham, "Strange Bed Fellows," *Baptist Bulletin*, April 1935, 3.

have far-reaching consequences for Regular Baptists. Until the early 1930s train travel dominated the transportation industry in the United States. The automobiles of the Roaring Twenties were not suited for long trips, and the highways were rudimentary. Air travel was dominated by the Ford and Stinson Trimotors which, while reliable, were decidedly uncomfortable even for short flights. In the middle of the decade, however, air travel challenged the dominance of railroads for the first time. Boeing introduced its 247 in 1933; then Douglas brought out the DC-2 in 1934. These were all-metal, low-wing aircraft capable of transporting passengers for longer distances in relative comfort. Most importantly, these new airliners cut travel times dramatically.

In 1934 E. J. Rollings of Detroit's Metropolitan Tabernacle invited J. Frank Norris for a weeklong evangelistic campaign. The meetings were held in a huge tent. Norris preached to thousands every night. Among those who attended the meeting were four men from the Temple Baptist Church, who asked Norris to return in December to preach to their congregation.

After the Chipps trial in 1926, Norris's influence in the North had plummeted. While Northern leaders remained nominally his friends, fewer and fewer pulpits were open to him. The meetings in Detroit represented an opportunity for Norris to reestablish himself in the North. Not surprisingly, he preached some of his best tried-and-true sermons.

Temple Baptist had just lost its pastor, Albert Johnson, to Hinson Memorial Church in Portland, Oregon. Johnson was an Englishman whose polished preaching style stood in marked contrast to the extemporized pyrotechnics of the Texas Tornado. The church loved Norris from the first moment they heard him. Both leaders and congregation were certain that he should become the next pastor.

Norris, however, told the Detroit congregation that he had no intention of leaving First Baptist Church in Fort Worth. Consequently, the creative minds in Detroit went to work, and before long they came up with a solution. Norris could pastor both churches simultaneously, traveling back and forth. He could even select his own right-hand man to administer the work at Temple in his absence.

A decade earlier, this kind of dual pastorate would not have been physically possible. With the advent of air travel, however, it seemed just feasible. Norris was intrigued by the potential: Temple was a prominent congregation. The thought of simultaneously pastoring two important churches, one in the North and the other in the South, was tempting.

Temple Baptist was still in both the Northern and the Michigan Baptist conventions. When word got out that Norris was preaching at Temple Baptist in December, the convention officials tried to step in to block his meetings. When they heard that the church had called Norris to its pastorate, convention officials applied even more pressure. In their efforts they overlooked one factor: J. Frank Norris loved a fight. Conflict was his most important tool for drawing a crowd. If the convention had wanted J. Frank Norris in Detroit, there would have been no better way to invite him than to pick a quarrel. In January he became the pastor of Temple Baptist Church.

After the Chipps shooting, Norris had largely dissociated himself from the Baptist Bible Union. He had continued to offer the pages of his paper (now renamed the *Fundamentalist*) free of charge to promote the Union and then the GARBC. Nevertheless, geography kept him from active participation. The BBU (and later, the GARBC) was focused upon Baptist work in the North, while Norris was in Texas. The pastorate at Temple, however, put him squarely in the center of Regular Baptist territory. From Detroit, any point from Milwaukee to Buffalo was an easy day's travel.

In January Ketcham found himself sharing a platform with Norris at Jackson, Michigan. The next day the two traveled to Grand Rapids, where they appeared together again. Ketcham was convinced that "the coming of Dr. Norris to the leadership of the Temple Baptist Church, Detroit, could mean much to the fellowship of the Association of Regular Baptist Churches." He and Norris discussed this relationship for hours, and Norris intimated that the South had its own Baptist movement that was nearly identical with the Regular Baptists of the North. Ketcham suggested that leaders from the two movements ought to meet for a couple of days for prayer and talk.[12]

On January 22 and 23, 1935, sixteen men joined Ketcham at Central Baptist in Gary. One result of the conversation was an agreement that each group would exercise a kind of comity with respect to the other. Each group would remain within its own geographical region while retaining a sense of joint, continent-wide fellowship. In token of this agreement the GARBC included the word *North* as part of its name for several years. What this agreement left unclear was the role of Norris. By virtue of his dual pastorate, he was now ministering in both territories. That was going to lead to problems for the GARBC, but for the moment Ketcham was thanking God for Norris's ministry.[13]

In May the General Association of Regular Baptist Churches returned to Wealthy Street Baptist Church in Grand Rapids. In this setting, the absence of Van Osdel was felt keenly, and the youthfulness of his successor was highlighted by the contrast. Nevertheless, David Otis Fuller was undaunted. Fuller was converted as a boy of thirteen and baptized by I. M. Haldeman at the First Baptist Church of New York City. He was a descendant of Elisha Otis, inventor

---

12. Robert T. Ketcham, "The Recent Important Conference," *Baptist Bulletin*, February 1935, 4.
13. Ibid.

of the braking system that made commercial elevators possible. Backed by the Otis family's fortune, he graduated from Princeton Seminary where, like other students, he developed a friendship with J. Gresham Machen. Confident to the point of brashness, even in his younger years Fuller was never a retiring character.

More than three hundred messengers and visitors registered for the 1935 conference, not counting registrants from the city of Grand Rapids. Over one hundred of them were pastors, missionaries, evangelists, or other preachers. Four other Grand Rapids churches worked with Wealthy Street to provide free lodging for as many messengers as possible. The conference was the earliest so far, meeting on April 30 through May 2.

Among those who attended was J. Frank Norris, accompanied by his associate Louis Entzminger. One of the first items of business was a discussion of the constitution that the messengers had adopted the year before. Norris took an active part in this discussion. Finally, some slight changes were made in the article dealing with ministerial changes. The constitution was then adopted for another year.[14]

In his presidential address, Robert T. Ketcham outlined the threefold purpose of the GARBC. First, he said that the association provided "a fundamental fellowship for churches which are opposed to the program of the Northern Convention." Second, the GARBC would offer a way to maintain independent, orthodox Baptist missions. Third, it was "an agency for the dissemination of authentic information on conditions in the Northern Convention." This last purpose contained an implicit criticism of the convention fundamentalists (now called the Fundamentalist Fellowship). If the GARBC needed to disseminate "authentic information," then the information coming from the Fundamentalist Fellowship was probably inauthentic. Ketcham emphasized this point, stating that the GARBC had to engage in a program of "militant publicity" to inform the churches that were still in the convention of the "true state of affairs."[15]

Robert T. Ketcham was reelected as president of the association, and David Otis Fuller was chosen as vice president. Ray Hamilton, Ketcham's associate at Central Baptist, was reelected as secretary and treasurer. Fuller was also made editor of the *Baptist Bulletin*, which the association decided to expand and to turn into a subscription periodical (until then, it had been sent free of charge).

14. Minutes of the Annual Meeting of the General Association of Regular Baptist Churches, held at Wealthy Street Baptist Church in Grand Rapids, Michigan, April 30–May 2, 1935. The official, typed minutes do not mention who took part in the discussion. The unpaginated, handwritten draft, which is in Ray Hamilton's script, indicates that along with Norris, the conversation involved Knol, Fulton, Muntz, Lyons, and Fargo.

15. Minutes, GARBC, 1935; R. T. Ketcham, "The Three-Fold Purpose of the Association," *Baptist Bulletin*, June 1935, 7.

During its Thursday afternoon session, the fellowship observed a memorial service for Oliver W. Van Osdel. David Otis Fuller spoke of Van Osdel's reputation and his stand for truth. Then J. Frank Norris spoke as one who had known Van Osdel. He kept his remarks brief, but spoke about Van Osdel's faithfulness and courage. Norris remarked, "I didn't grieve for him. When he went home, I said, 'Hail, victorious soldier.'"[16]

The GARBC took no dramatic actions at its Grand Rapids meeting. Now that he had been replaced as editor of the *Baptist Bulletin*, Hamilton's involvement with the Regular Baptist movement declined significantly. Norris's sudden presence in the North and his appearance at the Grand Rapids conference marked the beginning of a new stage in the association's development. Many observers must have wondered how rapidly he would rise to leadership within the fledgling GARBC. In any event, the mood following the Grand Rapids meeting was clearly optimistic.

Controversy and Conflict

In his 1935 presidential address, Ketcham had promised that the GARBC would become "an agency for the dissemination of authentic information on conditions in the Northern Convention." This heightened exposure of the convention began in the August 1935 issue of the *Baptist Bulletin*. Ketcham used the magazine to show that James H. Franklin, the newly elected president of the Northern Baptist Convention, was a modernist. In a separate article Ketcham exposed the convention's Home Mission Society for allowing communists to meet in one of its facilities—a problem that he said was ongoing. David Otis Fuller, writing as editor of the *Baptist Bulletin*, reported how convention officials had tried to block an independent ordination in Michigan. In the future this negative coverage of the NBC would become a staple of the Regular Baptist reading diet.[17]

Ketcham also expressed his unhappiness with the Fundamentalist Fellowship. Even though they were ostensibly trying to clean up the convention, he noted that not one of them protested Franklin's election as convention president. Ketcham admitted that they could not have defeated Franklin, but "it would be refreshing at least to have heard the voice of some Fundamentalist raised in objection."[18]

The Fundamentalist Fellowship also came in for criticism over another

16. Minutes, GARBC, 1935.
17. Ibid.; Ketcham, "The Three-Fold Purpose," 7; Ketcham, "The New N.B.C. President," *Baptist Bulletin*, August 1935, 1, 7–8; Ketcham, "The Case against the American Bap. Home Mission Society," *Baptist Bulletin*, August 1935, 2, 10–12; "Courageous Pastor Ordained," *Baptist Bulletin*, August 1935, 1, 5–6.
18. Ketcham, "The New N.B.C. President," 1.

matter. In 1934 the Northern Baptist Convention had authorized a Commission on Christian Social Action. The commission brought back a report in 1935 that most conservatives found alarming. It strongly favored a pacifist approach to international relations, making little or no allowance for just war. Conservatives thought that its treatment of economic problems tilted toward socialism. When the report was presented at the 1935 convention in Colorado Springs, a conservative pastor from California actually sent children racing through the crowd to distribute fliers titled "CHOICE BETWEEN REDS AND GOD FACES BAPTISTS." Yet when the report was brought to a vote, not a single fundamentalist spoke against it. A compromise had already been hammered out. The report was received by the convention, but it would only be distributed to those churches that requested it. The Fundamentalist Fellowship then claimed this vote as a victory "without compromise." Astonished, the editor of the *Baptist Bulletin* accused the Fundamentalist Fellowship of "busily congratulating themselves on a victory" while "blinding themselves to the facts."[19]

The attitude of Regular Baptists toward the Fundamentalist Fellowship was not entirely negative. The two groups still recognized a commonality of belief and commitment, and could still sometimes engage in "cobelligerency." For example, when W. B. Riley denounced the Northern Baptist Convention as "Bloodless, but Red," the *Baptist Bulletin* thanked him and reprinted the sermon. Still, the dominant tone between these two groups was one of frustration. When the fundamentalist leader James Whitcomb Brougher of Tremont Temple was invited to speak at Will Rogers's funeral, he failed to mention the gospel. Regular Baptists were appalled. The editor of the *Baptist Bulletin* observed, "The last time we listened to Dr. Brougher in Tremont Temple we left with a sad heart. We almost felt like saying without bitterness or sarcasm, 'Dr. Brougher, how much better it would be if there was less clown and more Christ.'"[20]

Regular Baptist leaders were further scandalized when Earle V. Pierce, leader of the convention fundamentalists, accepted a position as representative of the Northern Baptist Convention to the Federal Council of Churches. The Federal Council was founded in 1908 as an organization of church groups. Its purpose was to represent the interests of the mainline denominations in America. Like the Northern Baptist Convention, it had never been conservative, but included modernistic leaders from the very beginning. If anything, the FCC was even more pronouncedly liberal than the convention.

19. *Annual of the Northern Baptist Convention 1935* (Philadelphia: American Baptist Publication Society, 1935), 161–85, 241–42; "Worldlings See Thru Subterfuge," *Baptist Bulletin*, August 1935, 9.

20. "Bloodless—But Red," *Baptist Bulletin*, October 1935, 1, 6–7; "A Tragedy Within a Tragedy," *Baptist Bulletin*, October 1935, 4.

David Otis Fuller wrote to Pierce expressing his objections to the FCC. He also mentioned his concerns about the convention's apparent endorsement of a socialistic and even communistic program. When Pierce replied that this charge was "an absolute falsehood, if not worse," Fuller pointed him to Riley's "Bloodless, but Red" speech. In defense of the Federal Council of Churches, Pierce sent Fuller a pamphlet that was supposed to illustrate the council's evangelical commitment. Pierce even said that he had personally voted for the publication of the pamphlet.

Fuller, however, spotted ambiguous terminology in the pamphlet that seemed to call the gospel into question. He responded, "I say it kindly, Dr. Pierce, but I say it plainly, and that is that there is but one thing you need, and that is to wake up to the facts which you refuse to face." He accused Pierce of "running along with the prophets of Baal," and stated that Pierce's presence in the convention did "more harm than any ten outspoken Modernists who have no use for the blood of Christ, His resurrection, and the other great Fundamentals of the faith." Fuller then published this letter in the *Baptist Bulletin*, adding, "We do not accuse Dr. Pierce of not being a fundamentalist, but we do accuse him of being totally lacking in spiritual discernment in a matter in which a child could see the difference." This language was not likely to promote greater harmony between the two groups.[21]

Exposing the liberalism of the Northern Baptist Convention became an important item on the agenda of the GARBC, followed closely by pointed disagreement with the leadership of the Fundamentalist Fellowship. At the same time, the GARBC tried to encourage the pastors and churches that were leaving the convention. Hardly an issue of the *Baptist Bulletin* passed without reports of and applause for churches that were pulling out. Each issue of the *Bulletin* also ran congratulatory reports about ministers who were receiving ordination outside the convention structures.

One noteworthy story was about the Temple Baptist Church in Detroit. Fuller opened the report with praise for the new pastor of Temple Baptist.

> Hundreds of Baptists all over Michigan have followed with increasing interest the great work that Dr. J. Frank Norris is accomplishing in the city of Detroit since his call to the pastorate of the Temple Baptist Church at the end of last year. We praise God for this mighty testimony raised in such a needy city. His radio and tent campaign, in spite of the cold and rainy weather, has gone on with great success. Souls have been saved at every service in the tent, and the best is yet to come.[22]

21. David Otis Fuller, "We Feel the Facts Should Be Known," *Baptist Bulletin,* January 1936, 9.

22. "North Baptist, Flint; and Temple Church, Detroit, Sever Relations with Convention," *Baptist Bulletin,* August 1935, 3.

According to the article, Temple was the largest Baptist church not only in Detroit, but in Michigan. Now it had withdrawn entirely from the Northern Baptist Convention. The church's reasons included the convention's modernistic and communistic leadership.[23]

The GARBC did not yet require separation from the convention as a test of fellowship. Nevertheless, virtually every edition of the *Baptist Bulletin* proved that the leadership of the association had become strongly separatist. The importance of separation was emphasized by excoriation of the Northern Baptist Convention, by criticism of fundamentalists who deliberately stayed in the convention, and by celebration of churches and pastors who took the step of separation. In contrast to the woes of the convention, the GARBC put itself forward as an association with a minimum of organization and a maximum of fellowship.[24]

This claim was no mere boast. The GARBC paid no employees, but it was the center of a strong and growing movement. Besides coordinating pastoral placement, the Interstate Evangelistic Association had just opened a conference ground on the shores of New York's Lake Canadigua. Throughout the North, state and local Regular Baptist associations were doing much to strengthen churches and to assist with pastoral exchange. Two schools (Los Angeles Baptist Theological Seminary and Baptist Bible Seminary) were providing education for future generations of Baptist workers.[25]

Most important was the work of missions. The GARBC saw itself as a coordinating channel through which local churches could send their missionary dollars. Churches could designate money for particular agencies or even specific missionaries, and the GARBC would ensure that every penny reached its destination. Undesignated funds were distributed entirely among the approved missions, and nothing was kept for the association's costs.[26]

The approved agencies received regular promotion in the *Baptist Bulletin*. The heaviest coverage went to the Interstate Evangelistic Association, though the Association of Baptists for the Evangelism of the Orient also knew how to take advantage of the publicity. Mid-Missions, the Mexican Gospel Mission, and the Sweet Baptist Mission to China were mentioned less often, but they still maintained a presence.

In one of its boldest initiatives, the Regular Baptist movement actually began to send ministers back into old convention churches to try to reclaim them. Sometimes these churches had grown weary under the ministry of

23. Ibid.

24. Ray F. Hamilton, "How We Operate," *Baptist Bulletin*, June 1935, 1.

25. "The Tabernacle on the Lake," *Baptist Bulletin*, June 1935, 1; "Schools of the Prophets," *Baptist Bulletin*, November 1935, 12.

26. "Clearing House for Fundamental Baptist Missions Established. Money 100% for Mission Fields," *Baptist Bulletin*, November 1935, 1.

modernists. Other times, the churches had simply lost vigor and were in danger of collapsing. Such pulpits could often be occupied by Regular Baptist pastors, who would reinvigorate the church, instruct the people, and ultimately lead the congregation to separate from the convention.[27]

Regular Baptists and convention fundamentalists had different ways of justifying their existence. The GARBC defended its program of separation by arguing that the Northern Baptist Convention was irretrievably under the control of modernists. The Fundamentalist Fellowship legitimated its course of remaining in the convention by appealing to what they saw as a reasonable hope that the liberals could be thwarted. Due to this difference, the GARBC kept exposing liberalism, and the convention fundamentalists kept downplaying its influence.

In January 1936 the *Baptist Bulletin* introduced a two-part series by Franklin G. Huling titled "The Devil's Game Today." Writing satirically, Huling used his first article to list the excuses given by convention fundamentalists for continuing to support the old structures. Point by point he refuted these excuses and argued for separation. Huling insisted that "the time is long past when any pastor can plead ignorance of his fellowship and support of Modernism when he supports the denominational missionary budget." He continued, "[E]very child of God who knowingly goes on supporting Modernism by contributing to the denominational budget, will suffer the loss of God's approval and reward."[28]

The next month Huling continued by attacking the notion that fundamentalists should clean up the convention from the inside—the very thing that the Fundamentalist Fellowship claimed to be doing. Regular Baptists typically conceded that if liberals could be purged out of the convention, then there would be no need to come out. The disagreement lay in whether it was possible to purge the liberalism from the convention. Huling answered the question in the negative.

> That sounds well, but the facts are that the Fundamentalists started out with that program some years ago, and, finding it impossible, have been obliged to give it up. Instead of succeeding in expelling the Modernists, the Fundamentalists have seen that if they did not "quiet down," they themselves were likely to be expelled! They found they could not "purge out the old leaven," (I Cor. 5:7), and therefore they should do what they can do, namely, "Be ye not equally yoked together with unbelievers" (II Cor. 6:14). Fearful havoc is being wrought by the

27. "Miracle is Wrought in Kalamazoo," *Baptist Bulletin*, August 1935, 2; "The Need of the Hour! To Reclaim Modernist Baptist Churches for the Lord Jesus Christ," *Baptist Bulletin*, October 1935, 1.

28. Franklin G. Huling, "The Devil's Game Today," *Baptist Bulletin*, January 1936, 5.

unequal yoking together of believers with unbelievers in supporting
Modernism by means of the denominational missionary budgets.[29]

That same month Robert T. Ketcham ran a front-page article answering
the question, "Is There Modernism in the N.B.C.?" He offered several evidences for the affirmative. First was the willingness of the American Baptist
Home Mission Society to allow communists to meet in one of its facilities.
Second was the 1935 report of the Commission on Christian Social Action
(here Ketcham also mentioned the "everlasting shame" of the fundamentalists who agreed to the compromise in receiving the report). Third was the
liberal president of the convention, James H. Franklin, who was now going
around the country and asking Baptist youth conferences to vote approval of
the commission's report—a clear violation of the compromise under which
the report had been received. Fourth was Albert W. Beaven, past president
of the convention and now president of Colgate Rochester Divinity School,
who had lent his signature to a document calling upon Franklin D. Roosevelt
to push liberal social policies even further. Having offered this indictment of
the Northern Baptist Convention, Ketcham concluded that separation was
unavoidable.[30] Ketcham's article was reprinted as a pamphlet titled "Facts for
Baptists to Face," and distributed all over the country.

To a later generation of churches that have experienced peace and freedom from outside interference, the attitudes of Regular Baptists may seem
difficult to understand. These leaders saw the fundamentals as essential to
the gospel and the gospel as essential to Christian fellowship. Denying the
fundamentals entailed a denial of the gospel and put one outside of any legitimate sphere of Christian fellowship. More than that, the Regular Baptists
were reacting against threats from within the convention itself. Even before
1910 the liberals were trying to marginalize strict conservatives. Before 1920
they were intruding into churches, stirring up opposition against pastors, pit-
ting minorities against majorities, and maneuvering in the courts to seize the
buildings, properties, and bank accounts of orthodox churches. The liberals
had won the battle in the convention, and now they were also regularly winning battles against pastors and churches. Regular Baptists like Ketcham saw
the liberals as bullies, and they were determined to stop them in the only way
that bullies understand.

Separation and exposure were not the GARBC's reason for existence, but
they were a necessary prelude to the positive work that the Regular Baptists
wanted to do. As the *Baptist Bulletin* put it,

29. Franklin G. Huling, "The Devil's Game Today," *Baptist Bulletin*, February 1936, 10.
Spellings and punctuation *sic*.

30. Robert T. Ketcham, "Is There Modernism and Apostasy in the N.B.C.?" *Baptist Bulletin*, February 1936, 1, 11.

This is primarily a Fellowship. Organized, yes, but with an absolute minimum of organization.

We are not seeking a fight; we are seeking fellowship. But that does not mean that we "soft-pedal" or "crawl in our shells" when blatant error, and soul-shriveling apostasy parade in open garb and daring denial.

People will misunderstand our motives. They have already. That is to be expected. We are sorry, but we certainly do not intend to cry "Quits" just because the devil has his scouts and henchmen busy. Above all things PRAY that the Lord our God, even Jesus Christ our Sovereign King, may be glorified, and souls strengthened in "the Faith once for all delivered unto the saints."[31]

Immediately before the 1936 annual meeting of the GARBC, the Walnut Street Baptist Church in Waterloo, Iowa, voted to leave the convention. This was important news, and it made headlines in the *Baptist Bulletin*. Walnut Street was at that time the largest Baptist church in the state of Iowa. Its loss would be a severe blow to both the Iowa and the Northern Baptist conventions. It was unimaginable that these conventions would let the church go without a fight.[32]

In fact, the convention secretaries immediately issued a series of challenges over the church's right to separate, each of which was answered by the young pastor P. B. Chenault. Then convention officials demanded a private meeting in Waterloo, to which Chenault would be permitted to bring others in support of his position. Chenault agreed to the meeting and chose Ketcham, Strathearn, and Norris to stand with him. When the three sent word that they would appear, the officials quickly canceled the meeting, stating that the three advisers were in "ill repute."

Strathearn and Norris turned aside to help a church in Aurora, Illinois, while Ketcham continued to Waterloo. The church held a public meeting on a Monday evening in which Ketcham went through a seventeen-page letter from one of the convention secretaries. Line by line he refuted the convention's arguments. Then the church actually retook the vote to withdraw from the convention. Hundreds of members stood to their feet in a unanimous affirmation of the original vote, and the crowd of observers broke out into loud and sustained applause. The only unhappy people were two convention pastors, both Colgate Rochester graduates, who had come to see the spectacle.[33]

For its 1936 conference the GARBC returned to the place of its founding,

31. "Pray, Plan & Prepare for the Coming Fellowship of G.A.R.B." *Baptist Bulletin*, April 1936, 3, 12.

32. "Largest Baptist Church in Iowa Severs All Connections with Northern Baptist Convention!" *Baptist Bulletin*, May 1936, 2, 7; "Walnut Baptist Leaves Group by 148 to 20 Vote," *Baptist Bulletin*, May 1936, 2, 5.

33. "The Lord God of Elijah Still Lives," *Baptist Bulletin*, June 1936, 7, 8.

Belden Avenue Baptist Church. This meeting was viewed as primarily a preaching event. Of course Ketcham spoke, as did Griffith, Fulton, and Fuller. Other speakers, such as William Headley from Grand Rapids, M. E. Hawkins of Baptist Mid-Missions, and Harold T. Commons of ABEO, had become well known in Regular Baptist circles. The pastor of Walnut Street Baptist Church, P. B. Chenault, was given a place on the program—he had suddenly become something of a celebrity in the Regular Baptist movement. Invited guest speakers included T. T. Shields and Louis Entzminger (J. Frank Norris's associate). The conference also featured Ralph Neighbour, son of R. E. Neighbour—but not as a speaker. Neighbour astonished the crowd with an exhibition of musical whistling.[34]

The conference organizers received a bit of a surprise when a representative of the *Watchman Examiner* showed up at the meeting and, without asking anyone for permission or direction, set up a table and began to take subscriptions. When the matter was brought to their attention, Fulton and Ketcham went to the representative and explained that they could not approve of subscriptions being taken for the *Watchman Examiner* at the GARBC conference. The *Baptist Bulletin* later published a report of the event, adding that the GARBC had been founded to repudiate the very Inclusive Policy that Curtis Lee Laws and the *Watchman Examiner* were willing to tolerate. The report was clear: the GARBC did not believe "that there is any hope whatever" of cleaning up the convention from the inside. It concluded, "It is time—and high time—for Baptists to get their eyes open to such a deadly policy and procedure which has been carried on by fundamentalists within the convention."[35]

Ketcham was reelected for a third term as president of the association, in spite of his own protests. He was becoming concerned that the GARBC could be perceived as a one-man organization. The nominating committee and the messengers, however, were enthusiastic about his leadership. In the end, he agreed to serve as president, but put the nominating committee on notice that he would not serve more than four terms. This left the committee with the option of nominating him only once more in 1937.[36]

At the 1936 conference another event occurred that would have far-reaching consequences. Since J. Frank Norris had taken the pastorate of Temple Baptist Church near the beginning of 1935, he had experienced a cordial relationship with the GARBC. He spoke twice during the 1935 annual conference and entered into the discussion on the floor. His associate, Louis Entzminger,

34. "Conference Speakers," *Baptist Bulletin*, May 1936, 10; "Conference Close-Ups," *Baptist Bulletin*, June 1936, 2.

35. "The Best Thing—A Frank Explanation," *Baptist Bulletin*, June 1936, 2.

36. Robert T. Ketcham, "Concerning the Presidency," *Baptist Bulletin*, May 1937, 11.

was on the platform in 1935 and again in 1936. He had worked with Regular Baptist leaders on projects such as the defense of Walnut Street Baptist Church in Waterloo. Now he and Entzminger came to the 1936 meetings with credentials that identified them as messengers from Temple Baptist Church.

Nevertheless, Norris's relationship to the GARBC had another side. Norris had earned a checkered reputation through the years. On the one hand, he was viewed as one of the champions of fundamentalism, an acknowledged leader whose flamboyance and personal magnetism could sway large groups of people. On the other hand, he was also seen as a verbal pugilist who could be unsparing and even unscrupulous when attacking opponents. He had for years engaged in verbal sniping at W. B. Riley. Shortly before the 1936 conference he wrote to Ketcham, "I excuse him on the ground of age. I can't understand it on any other basis. It sometimes occurs in the last stage of senility, that a man gets over jealous. I know this is true of old bulls out on the ranch, when they can't do anything except lean up against a mesquito tree with a curl in their tails and bellow."[37]

The Regular Baptists certainly had their share of disagreements with W. B. Riley, particularly over the issue of separation. Nevertheless, they recognized Riley as a comrade in arms who had been one of their main leaders during the fight within the convention. Ketcham held Riley in esteem and even affection. Norris's malicious comments did not sit well, and they probably revealed more of Norris's character than he had intended.

The leaders of the GARBC had good reason to treat Norris's credentials cautiously. The problem was exacerbated by the fact that Temple Baptist had sent no application indicating its desire to be recognized as part of the GARBC's fellowship. Consequently, the messengers were not asked to vote on receiving Temple Baptist into the fellowship in 1936. Norris and Entzminger were not recognized as messengers. Evidently, Norris was absent during that particular business session and did not realize until sometime later that Temple Baptist had no standing within the GARBC.

Subsequently, Ray Hamilton (the secretary-treasurer of the GARBC) carried on correspondence with both Entzminger and Norris, trying to get an application for fellowship. Eventually, Hamilton received two different versions of the church clerk's minutes from Temple Baptist, leading him to suspect that neither was authentic. In view of these inconsistencies, Ketcham contacted an old friend who was a member of Temple Baptist Church. As the facts emerged, Ketcham realized that neither the deacons nor the church membership at Temple knew anything about an application for fellowship with the GARBC. The church had never voted to seek fellowship. In early 1937,

37. J. Frank Norris to Robert T. Ketcham, May 8, 1936.

when the credentials committee met in Johnson City, New York, Ketcham shared this information and suggested that Norris's messenger credentials be treated as a forgery. The committee agreed. This was the point at which the relationship with Norris began to sour.[38]

In the meanwhile, Norris continued in good graces with the Regular Baptist movement. In September 1936 the Interstate Evangelistic Association held its annual rally and prophetic conference at the First Baptist Church in Johnson City, New York—a church that had by now become a Regular Baptist capital. Ketcham received top billing as a conference preacher. He was joined by William Ward Ayer (one of Straton's successors at Calvary Baptist Church in New York City), Harry Hamilton, J. Palmer Muntz (son of Richard Muntz), and, of course, Harold Strathearn. Norris had not been scheduled to speak, but when he dropped into the meeting unannounced, he was given two services by popular acclaim. This may have been the last time that Ketcham and Norris appeared together on the same platform.

For their part, the GARBC leadership pressed ahead with the organization's work of coordinating missions, exposing liberalism in the convention, and assisting churches. Much as the leadership insisted upon a minimum of organization and a maximum of fellowship, they were beginning to realize that their efforts were going to take more organization and funding than they could afford. In June 1936 the GARBC began to ask churches to add the association to their missionary budgets, arguing that the association was a legitimate missionary agency and was worthy of confidence and support.[39]

Authorized by a resolution from the Belden conference, Ketcham appointed a committee to begin planning a Sunday school curriculum that would cover the entire Bible for all age groups. This decision meant developing a children's curriculum, something with which the association had no experience. The committee met in July and asked Louis Entzminger to take charge of the project. He was given authority to select a competent staff of writers and to begin issuing a New Testament course by April 1937. All materials were to be reviewed by the committee before publication, after which the copyrights would be held by the Interstate Evangelistic Association.[40]

The GARBC launched a new line of attack when the Northern Baptist Convention featured the liberal Japanese evangelist, Toyohiko Kagawa. Orphaned as a child, Kagawa had been reared by American missionaries. He studied in the very conservative Princeton Theological Seminary, but rejected the

38. Ray F. Hamilton to Kevin T. Bauder (n.d. but ca. April 20, 1981); Murray Murdoch, *Portrait of Obedience: The Biography of Robert T. Ketcham* (Schaumburg, IL: Regular Baptist Press, 1979), 148–49.

39. "Resolutions Passed at G.A.R.B. Fellowship," *Baptist Bulletin*, June 1936, 4.

40. Louis Entzminger, "Wonderful Progress in the New Whole Bible Lessons," *Baptist Bulletin*, October 1936, 7.

orthodoxy that he was taught there. David Otis Fuller (himself a Princeton alumnus) accused Kagawa of advocating evolution, of doubting the resurrection, and of denying the unique deity of Jesus Christ. Never deeply interested in the details of doctrine, Kagawa's focus had shifted toward social activism by the 1930s. The *Baptist Bulletin* claimed that Kagawa's Christ was simply an antichrist.[41]

In October 1936 the full executive committee met at Central Baptist in Gary. Seventeen leaders spent two days thoroughly evaluating the position and strength of the GARBC. Several old issues were revisited and some new ones were raised. During the meeting, the executive committee reaffirmed the intention of the GARBC to operate as a fellowship of churches, not a fellowship of individuals. The members reaffirmed the approval system as the best way to handle missions, but recommitted themselves to do more. Editorial and policy changes were approved for the *Baptist Bulletin*. The executive committee voted to approve a change in the name of the organization to the Association of Independent Baptist Churches in the U.S.A., but this change was never implemented. The committee also discussed ways in which the fellowship could help churches, especially in the area of pastoral exchange.[42]

The greatest concern at the meeting, however, was to find a way to promote the GARBC before the churches. The committee was aware that many churches had either left the convention or were about to. The minutes read, "Recognizing that the churches of like faith and order need to fellowship together as much as do individuals, it, therefore, behooves us to show these churches the advantages of this new fellowship." Ketcham estimated that the number of prospective churches might be a thousand or more.[43]

This discussion raised the problem of fundamentalist churches that were not yet ready to leave the convention. Here, the committee members were not thinking so much of people like Earle V. Pierce and others who aggressively promoted involvement in the convention program. Rather, they recognized that "many are in hard places; many are 'on the spot' with the machine. Some of course willfully blind themselves, but these are in the minority we believe."[44] Finally the sense of the committee was summed up in these words.

> It was the sentiment of the committee that we should deal kindly and patiently with the brethren who have not yet separated from the N.B.C. even though they believe as we do. Every consideration and help shall be extended to those whose fundamentals are the same as

41. "The Antichrist Kagawa Advocates," *Baptist Bulletin*, August 1936, 7.
42. Minutes of the Executive Meeting of the GARBC, held at the Central Baptist Church, Gary, Indiana, October 1936.
43. Minutes of the GARBC Executive Meeting, October 1936; "Progress and Mutual Understanding at Meeting at Gary," *Baptist Bulletin*, December 1936, 5, 7, 12.
44. "Progress and Mutual Understanding at Meeting at Gary," 5, 7, 12.

ours, but for reasons which they know best they have not taken their churches out of the apostate N.B.C.[45]

Many separatist churches knew nothing of the GARBC. Others were ill-informed. To reach these churches, the association needed someone to put the cause of the association in front of them. By this time, Robert T. Ketcham had become recognizable as both the face and the voice of the fellowship. The executive committee agreed to petition Central Baptist Church to release Ketcham from pastoral duty for three months. He would be authorized to tour the nation in behalf of the GARBC, speaking not only to local churches, but also in specially arranged conferences located in strategic centers.[46]

While Central Baptist weighed this decision, the GARBC continued to push ahead, especially in the pages of the *Baptist Bulletin*. Immediately after the executive committee met, Ketcham published an open letter to W. B. Riley. This was a letter that had been simmering for a while, and it arose directly out of the misperceptions that some held of the GARBC. Riley had evidently played a role in perpetuating those misunderstandings through his writings in the *Pilot* (his publication through the Northwestern Bible School).

In January 1936 Riley had addressed the deepening liberalism of the Northern Baptist Convention, and he knew that he had to respond to the question of separatism. To his "come-out brethren" he stated, "I would as soon be the subject of an old rift as a new one." Then in March he had made the statement that,

> Unfortunately there has broken out in the ranks of the Regular Baptists a very heated and much to be regretted scrap over the subject of divine healing. It looks as though the American Regular Baptists might go the way of the Canadian Regular Baptists, and there might be two or three bodies of them in the near future. This is what I meant in my article . . . published in the January issue of the Pilot when I said . . . I would as soon be the subject of an old rift as a new one.[47]

Riley was already doing his best to oppose Regular Baptists in Minnesota, arguing that he had virtually cleaned up the Minnesota state convention. Now he was publicly stating reasons for continuing in the fellowship of an admittedly liberal Northern Baptist Convention. On top of that, he was attacking Regular Baptists for false doctrine and schism.

Ketcham responded in a letter to Riley, enclosing a copy of his pamphlet, "Facts for Baptists to Face." In the letter—parts of which he published in the *Baptist Bulletin*—he stated that Riley already knew the situation was worse even than Ketcham had documented. Then he argued that cleaning up the

45. Minutes, GARBC Executive Committee, October 1936.
46. Ibid.
47. Robert T. Ketcham, "An Open Letter to Dr. W. B. Riley from Dr. R. T. Ketcham," *Baptist Bulletin* (November 1936), 3–4.

Minnesota convention was a hollow victory as long as the state group was simply "the provincial agent for the promotion of the program of the Northern Baptist Convention."

The main issue, however, was Riley's ongoing connection with the NBC. Ketcham pointed out that hundreds of young preachers were trying to lead their churches out of the "awful situation" in the Northern Baptist Convention, but many church people were more willing to trust Riley's example than they were to trust their own pastor's leadership. Ketcham challenged Riley to reverse his example by coming out of the convention and to exert his leadership in the opposite direction. Ketcham admitted: "It is true that a great man and a great church like you and your church, can fairly well paddle your course through these waters. So could I. So could scores of others with great and good churches back of them. But what about these hundreds of smaller churches and pastors who are constantly under the club of this spiritually murderous outfit?" Ketcham went on to discuss specific episodes in which convention officials were using their power to throttle fundamentalist churches and pastors, then suggested that Riley's example consistently worked against those who were being wronged. Of course, Ketcham thought that he had the Scriptures on his side, citing 2 John 1:9 and 2 Corinthians 6:14.[48]

In the conclusion of his letter, Ketcham tried to clarify that he was not attacking Riley's character. "We desire and shall always strive to be the best of friends and brothers beloved in the gospel." But Ketcham immediately continued, "I want to take this opportunity also to state frankly, that I shall not hesitate to preach the doctrine of separation from the Northern Baptist Convention and all of its auxiliaries, and that this presentation shall be made as strongly in the state of Minnesota, if the Lord opens the doors for it, as anywhere else." In his final words, Ketcham argued that Riley needed to respect the consciences of those men who were leaving the convention. This was a clear reference to Riley's interference in the ministries of separatist pastors in Minnesota.[49]

While Ketcham's letter was respectful and cordial in tone, the implications were pretty clear. Riley had a duty, not only to separate from the convention, but to lead a separatist movement in Minnesota. If he would not, then Ketcham intended to bring the separatist message right to Riley's doorstep, and he expected Riley to keep his hands off the separatist pastors and churches in Minnesota. Ketcham was drawing a line in the sand, and he was doing it publicly.

The same issue of the *Baptist Bulletin* carried an editorial in which David Otis Fuller contrasted three approaches to the convention. One approach was

48. Ibid.
49. Ibid.

to deny that anything was seriously wrong with the convention, and to follow "without so much as a peep of protest or dissent." Fuller stated that this view was "ridiculously impossible."[50]

The second approach was one that Fuller characterized as "Don't give up the ship." Those who held this approach admitted that the liberalism, communism, and infidelity of the convention were serious wrongs, but believed that they could still save the property and interests of the convention for orthodoxy. They thought that they could do more good in the convention than outside it. Fuller responded that the convention was a "derelict adrift on a sea of stagnant compromise" in which the "crew are drunk with their own importance and are utterly incompetent" to address spiritual matters. Those who stayed in the convention might be sincere, but they were nevertheless doing evil in order to accomplish good. Fuller conceded that this evil might be unwitting, but insisted that "it is NOT and NEVER COULD BE God's will, by the wildest stretch of the imagination for any of his servants to be wittingly linked up with such an apostate, communistic, modernistic organization as the Northern Baptist Convention." As far as Fuller was concerned, "the ship's sunk." No excuse could justify remaining in the NBC. The time had come to declare "whole-hearted allegiance to Jesus Christ," and that allegiance could only be proven by "severing all 'entangling alliances' with apostate Christendom." [51]

The leadership of the GARBC had always tended toward separatism, but the October meeting of the executive committee seems to have been a turning point. After that meeting, the public pronouncements of the Regular Baptist leaders became more confrontational and more insistent, even though the fellowship itself had yet to take a formal position on separation. Technically, the GARBC still permitted dual affiliation. Churches could still enter its fellowship while retaining their connection with the convention. Nevertheless, the overall direction of the Regular Baptist movement was plain to see. Regular Baptists who took pastorates in convention churches did so in order to lead them out, as Harry Hamilton did with the First Baptist Church of Buffalo in the summer of 1936.[52]

The Regular Baptist leadership was constantly encouraging pastors to lead their churches out of the convention. As already noted, Regular Baptist pastors would even take convention churches in order to lead them out. Not surprisingly, this tactic led to cries of foul play from convention officials, who saw it as unethical. In response to their objections, the *Baptist Bulletin* adopted a

50. David Otis Fuller, "Don't Give Up the Ship? The Ship's Sunk!" *Baptist Bulletin*, November 1936, 8.
51. Ibid., 8, 16.
52. David Otis Fuller, "Good News from Buffalo," *Baptist Bulletin*, August 1936, 4.

derisive tone: "For a modernist to raise the cry of 'Unethical!' almost borders on comedy, if it were not so tragic. For it is modernism that we can thank for tearing to shreds every vestige of ethics in the Christian ministry." Far from being unethical, the editor of the *Bulletin* thought that every pastor had a "solemn duty under God" to warn his church against apostates and modernists, using his influence to draw the church away from the convention.[53]

By February 1937 the GARBC executive committee was already advertising the annual conference, to be held on May 10–13 at First Baptist Church in Johnson City, New York. Shortly after the publicity began to appear, J. Frank Norris wrote to Ketcham, stating that he had a conflict on these dates and requesting that they be changed. Ketcham replied that missionary speakers had already made arrangements and that the dates could not be changed. Norris then traveled to Gary in person to try to persuade Ketcham to change the dates, but Ketcham still refused. When the executive committee next gathered, Norris invited himself to the meeting and made his request to the whole group. The entire committee declined to alter the dates. Two weeks later, Norris again wrote to Ketcham, stating that he had changed his schedule and would plan to speak at Johnson City. In reply, Ketcham pointed out that Norris had not been invited to speak. These events indicate that a gap was widening between J. Frank Norris and the Regular Baptist leadership.[54]

During the first part of 1937, the Regular Baptist movement continued to consolidate is missionary work. Baptist Mid-Missions had sent about twenty missionaries to the field during the previous year, and about twenty more were ready to go. With around sixty missionaries in active service, the agency found that it needed a full-time administrator and field representative. The position went to M. E. Hawkins of Mishawaka, Indiana. The Association of Baptists for the Evangelism of the Orient was already being led by Harold Commons. The Sweet Baptist Mission to China had placed Fred S. Donnelson in a comparable position. Regular Baptist missionary activity was increasing at the very moment when the convention's mission board was being forced to bring scores of missionaries home from the field—a fact that Regular Baptist leaders were quick to trumpet publicly. They insisted that the collapse of the convention's mission work was the result of Baptists' refusal to support the Inclusive Policy.[55]

The conference in Johnson City took place just as planned. To everyone's surprise, Max Schimpf and his wife attended the meeting. Evidently, Norris

53. David Otis Fuller, "Concerning Ministerial Ethics," *Baptist Bulletin*, January 1937, 6.

54. "Gathering of Bible Believing Baptists (G.A.R.B.) Set for May 10, 11, 12, 13," *Baptist Bulletin*, February 1937, 3; Murdoch, *Portrait of Obedience*, 149–50.

55. Robert T. Ketcham, "Foreign Missionaries Flocking to the Foreign Field," *Baptist Bulletin*, March 1937, 4.

did not. Both Howard Fulton and Earle G. Griffith preached on the second coming of Christ. No one was surprised when Ketcham was reelected president for a fourth year. His presidential address, titled "Hebron," included a strong defense of separation.

Reorganization

The GARBC adopted its first constitution in 1934. The next three years were a rough-and-tumble period of leadership transition, organizational consolidation, opposition to liberalism and communism, controversy with convention fundamentalists, increasing separation from the convention, and the beginnings of a breakdown between the Regular Baptist leadership and J. Frank Norris. Several prominent leaders had come to the fore of the new movement: Howard Fulton, Earle G. Griffith, David Otis Fuller, and especially Robert T. Ketcham. Now serving his fourth term as president of the GARBC, Ketcham sensed that organizational stability would require several important decisions and changes. These came into focus during the year between the 1937 conference in Johnson City and the 1938 conference at Walnut Street Baptist Church in Waterloo, Iowa. The 1938 conference would prove to be one of the most important in Regular Baptist history.

Coming out of the Johnson City conference, one of Ketcham's greatest concerns was for the office of president. He was serving his fourth term, and had already stated that he would not accept another. To the Regular Baptist fellowship he wrote, "I have a tremendous fear that by carrying a president over too many years, this association shall get the name of being a one man affair. The day that the Association becomes a one man affair, my interest is utterly gone in it, even though some folks think that one man was myself."[56] Ketcham admitted that the GARBC was still facing critical days. To prevent confusion during the crisis, he was willing to serve one final year. Nevertheless, he was convinced that others could do the job just as well. In phrases that would be repeated for years to come, Ketcham wrote,

> If I thought for one moment that either the Nominating Committee or this body was naming me to the presidency because they honestly felt that I was the only man that could fill this position, you would have my resignation instantly. There are many who are as worthy and capable as I can ever hope to be. If I thought you were naming me as the president of this Association because you think I am a great man, I would walk from this platform now. I have said, and been honestly sincere in the saying of it, that there are no great men among us. We are all little men with a great God. The moment any one of us in this

56. Ketcham, "Concerning the Presidency," 11.

> Association feels that he is a greater man than the rest of his brethren, that moment his services can well be dispensed with.[57]

The association needed Ketcham for more than the presidency. In late 1936 the executive committee had asked Central Baptist Church to allow Ketcham three months to travel and represent the GARBC. The church, which was deeply involved in planting new mission works in northwestern Indiana, could not see its way clear to grant this request. The longer it waited, however, the more it was bombarded with appeals from both churches and individuals. During the Johnson City conference, the association as a whole appealed to Central Baptist "to release your Shepherd to us for at least six months to engage in general field work on behalf of this association."[58]

Faced with this appeal, the church finally agreed to make the sacrifice. Its members understood that hundreds of churches around the country felt betrayed by the Northern Baptist Convention. Ketcham had proven himself capable of helping these churches find their way out of the convention and often into the GARBC. Central Baptist Church agreed to grant Ketcham a paid leave during the first half of 1938 in order to give himself to this task.

As Ketcham's attention turned more and more toward the concerns of the association, he began to sense that a structural change was needed. He was deeply concerned about the risk that the GARBC could be dominated by a single, vigorous personality. This concern was almost certainly underlined by J. Frank Norris's near success in gaining standing as a messenger on the basis of forged credentials. Ketcham set himself to devise both a leadership structure and an associational process that would thwart the possibility of any one individual controlling the Regular Baptist movement.

Other institutional deficiencies were appearing at the same time. One was the process for approving missionary and educational institutions. By 1937 the GARBC had approved six mission agencies: the Interstate Evangelistic Association, the Association of Baptists for Evangelism in the Orient, Baptist Mid-Missions, the Sweet Baptist Mission to China, the Lithuanian Mission Association, and the Mexican Gospel Mission. It had also approved two educational institutions: the Los Angeles Baptist Theological Seminary and the Baptist Bible Seminary in Johnson City, New York. Just before the conference in 1937, the GARBC leadership was approached by J. Oliver Buswell, president of Wheaton College, about the possibility of a new seminary.

As a rule, the GARBC was interested only in Baptist institutions. Wheaton was interdenominational and Buswell was a Presbyterian, but he was offering to include a Regular Baptist professor on the faculty of the new seminary.

57. Ibid.
58. "God Bless Baptist Bible Seminary," *Baptist Bulletin*, May 1937, 14.

Furthermore, Wheaton would allow the GARBC to select qualified lecturers to teach church history, Baptist polity, and Baptist theology. When the leadership brought Buswell's offer before the association at Johnson City, the excitement was palpable. The GARBC passed a resolution encouraging Regular Baptist churches to open their doors to Wheaton, and appointed Fuller, Strathearn, and Ketcham to oversee the interests of the GARBC as the new seminary was organized.[59]

The plan had only one flaw: Buswell's offer had not been approved by the Wheaton board. When the board met in June, they decided that funds for a seminary were not available. They supported the idea of a seminary, but refused to move ahead. Buswell was forced to communicate this news to the leadership of the GARBC, after which a correction was published in the *Baptist Bulletin*.[60]

This embarrassing episode underlined the rather haphazard nature of the approval process. The GARBC was committed to the idea of approving independent agencies, but its policies and procedures were sketchy at best. Little or no investigation had been done before Wheaton was brought to the association. The truth is that little investigation was done for any of the approved agencies. The idea was sound, but the process needed to be tightened up. The GARBC, however, would not get around to revising the process for another decade.

The other lingering problem for the GARBC was the issue of separation. While the association had clearly identified itself as separatistic, the fellowship had never specifically disallowed dual affiliation for churches that were still in the Northern Baptist Convention. Given the ambivalent relationship between the Regular Baptists and the Fundamentalist Fellowship, this was a situation that needed to be rectified sooner rather than later.

In spite of their differences, Regular Baptists still recognized significant commonality with both convention fundamentalists and with churches that had separated from the convention but not yet affiliated with the GARBC. Leaders from these three groups could even collaborate in some areas. No area was more important to all three than missions. In the middle of 1937 events in the convention's foreign missions board underlined the importance of developing a missions program separately from the Northern Baptist Convention.

As the Depression deepened, the convention board was experiencing severe financial hardship. Consequently, it began to consolidate some of its fields. For many years it had operated a medical station at Tondo in the Belgian Congo. The board now decided to relocate all of the Tondo missionaries

59. "Bible Baptists Accept Gracious Offer of Wheaton College," *Baptist Bulletin*, May 1937, 15.

60. "Correction and Explanation," *Baptist Bulletin*, July 1937, 7.

to a medical school in Sona Bata. Tondo Station would be given to a sister society in the unlikely event that one wanted to take it. Failing that, it would be closed.

H. H. Savage heard about the proposed closing. At one time Savage had been very involved in the Baptist Bible Union and had helped to organize its work in Michigan. After being elected to office in the Michigan convention, however, he had backed away from the BBU. His church, First Baptist Church of Pontiac, was still in the convention. Still, Savage had more sympathy for Regular Baptists than some. Now he thought that he saw an opportunity to recover part of the convention's mission work for fundamentalists.

Savage approached the foreign mission board with a proposal. He would gather a group of Baptists who would commit themselves to support the Tondo Station. He was confident that he could find enough Baptist fundamentalists not only to keep the work open, but to make it flourish. The only requirement was that a creedal test would be imposed upon all personnel who would work at the station. The churches that supported the Tondo work would be given the information to assure them that they were supporting Bible-believing missionaries.

Officials from the foreign board responded favorably to the plan, and Savage began to recruit individuals and churches to support the Tondo Station. Eventually he rallied between thirty and forty churches for the project. Using amateur radio, he also established direct contact with the missionaries on the field. From them he was surprised to learn that the foreign board had decided to send a new missionary to Tondo. The board had given him no information about the new missionary, nor had the supporting churches received any opportunity to review the missionary's doctrine.

When Savage confronted the foreign mission board, its members simply ignored him. Then, in January 1937, it placed a series of restrictions upon Savage and his supporters. They would not be allowed to promote the Tondo work separately from the promotional activities of the foreign board, and they would have to destroy all of the promotional materials that they had prepared. All statements about the Tondo work would have to be approved in advance by the foreign board. In particular, no creedal statement could be circulated. The supporting churches would not be permitted to communicate with the missionaries about administrative matters on the field, except through the offices of the foreign mission board. Savage would no longer be permitted to pursue radio contact with the missionaries. The foreign board also placed limitations upon the extent to which the Tondo Station could be developed, regardless of the funds that became available.

These restrictions amounted to a complete repudiation of Savage's efforts. The foreign board would be happy to take his money, but it was not willing to give him any say in the operation of the station that he had offered to fund. The board's intransigence led Savage to wonder whether the board ever meant to act in good faith. From this point onward, he became convinced that no part of the foreign mission board could be reclaimed for biblical Christianity.[61]

Like most Baptist fundamentalists, Savage was intensely interested in missions. If the denominational board was unworkable, he would find another way to support missionary activity. Nevertheless, he was not prepared to separate from the convention, much less to identify with the GARBC. He would develop his own alternative.

Savage called for a two-day conference on missions to be held at Pontiac on May 17 and 18, 1937. These dates came immediately after the GARBC annual conference in Johnson City. Savage aimed to include Regular Baptists as well as convention fundamentalists and unaffiliated Baptists. To his surprise, members of almost one hundred churches attended the meeting. ABEO, Mid-Missions, and the Interstate Evangelistic Association were represented, as were other groups. W. B. Riley thought the meeting was so important that he skipped the Northern Baptist Convention in order to deliver the closing address. [62]

As a rally for missions, the meeting was a definite success. The consensus was that everyone wanted to do more for the cause. The assembly appointed a committee of seven (H. H. Savage and David Otis Fuller were its most recognizable members) to explore ways of helping churches promote and coordinate the work of missions. When it came to actually deciding what to do, however, the committee was baffled. They decided not to establish another new mission board, but to poll the churches about their missionary interests. Aside from that, the committee could only speak in vague terms about working through the established agencies—but these were mostly agencies with which the GARBC was already working. Indeed, it is difficult to imagine anything that the committee might propose that the Regular Baptists were not already doing.[63]

Then why bother? Why not just use the mechanisms that the GARBC already had in place? The most likely answer to this question is that separatism was still the biggest issue. Even though he had broken with the foreign board, Savage still wanted to retain his connection with the convention. Technically, Savage's church could still have sought fellowship with the GARBC, but the constant drumbeat of separatism among Regular Baptist leaders did not sit well among those who preferred to stay in the convention. More than that,

61. H. H. Savage, "Tarry—Go," *Baptist Bulletin*, July 1937, 9–11.
62. A. O. Odegaard, "Conference at Pontiac," *Baptist Bulletin*, July 1937, 13.
63. "Pontiac Conference Committee of Seven Meet At Lansing," *Baptist Bulletin*, July 1937, 5–6.

the Fundamentalist Fellowship retained a veneer of sophistication and re-spectability that had never characterized the Regular Baptist movement. To identify with the GARBC would be a significant step down for someone of Savage's denominational and social standing.

Still, Regular Baptists supported Savage's conference. The committee of seven called for a second conference to meet at North Baptist Church in Flint, Michigan, on November 2–4. Once again, members of over ninety churches attended. Nearly thirty missionaries were featured at the meeting. The infor-mal fellowship ended up endorsing ABEO, Mid-Missions, the Detroit Hebrew Mission, the School for Mountain Preachers, the Interstate Evangelistic As-sociation, the Russian Missionary Service, and the French Bible Mission. It also encouraged support for needy Michigan pastors.[64]

Although no organizational effort came out of Savage's meetings, it was significant. First, it showed that various stripes of Baptist fundamentalists could be led to rally together if the cause was important enough. Second, it underlined and heightened the already intense missionary fervor that was shared by virtually all Baptist fundamentalists. Third, it was a portent of con-flict to come. Convention executives reacted badly to these meetings, leading to public confrontations. The foreign board retrenched its position against imposing a doctrinal test upon missionaries, and it reaffirmed its rejection of any church interference with its decisions on any field, regardless of the church's financial support. In fact, the situation with the foreign board began to worsen by the year. Within five years, convention fundamentalists would be forced to deal with this problem once for all, and within a decade they would find themselves virtually excluded by the convention. Savage's clash with the foreign mission board was only a skirmish in what was about to become an all-out denominational war.[65]

While Savage was fighting the foreign mission board, Earle V. Pierce was accepting the presidency of the Northern Baptist Convention. Pierce was the pastor of Lake Harriet Baptist Church in Minneapolis. He taught inter-mittently for Riley at the Northwestern Bible School, and was president of the Fundamentalist Fellowship of the Northern Baptist Convention. When he was elected as convention president in 1937, Regular Baptists shook their heads in disbelief. David Otis Fuller wrote that "we have lost all confidence in *Dr Pierce* and his leadership."[66]

In fact, the relationship between Pierce and the GARBC leadership had

64. John West, "Great Meeting of Baptist Missionary Fellowship," *Baptist Bulletin*, De-cember 1937, 5–6.

65. "We Are Back Where We Were Six Years Ago," *Baptist Bulletin*, August 1937, 5–6.

66. David Otis Fuller, "The Last Desperate Move of NBC Modernists," *Baptist Bulletin*, July 1937, 8, 11.

been strained for quite some time. He accused them of misrepresenting the extent of liberal influence within the foreign mission board, while they thought that he had "irreparably injured his Christian testimony" by serving as the convention's representative to the Federal Council of Churches. For Pierce to accept the convention presidency was another step of compromise, especially at a moment when Savage and others were exposing the obstinacy of the foreign board. To Regular Baptists, Pierce's presidency signaled that he "has proven himself to be unfitted for leadership among fundamentalists, or worthy of one iota of their confidence."[67]

In fact, as Regular Baptists saw the situation, the modernists were the ones who had elected Pierce, because the modernists controlled the entire elective process of the convention. Why would the modernists elect a fundamentalist? Regular Baptists had an answer. "They are alarmed—and rightly so—because of fundamentalists within the convention whose eyes are being opened, and who are refusing wholesale to cooperate in any way whatever." Savage exemplified this noncooperative spirit, whereas Pierce was undermining it. He was a useful tool for the modernists to employ against fundamentalists who were getting too close to separation. Pierce and Savage were both still part of the Fundamentalist Fellowship, but they had developed different ideas of loyalty to the convention and differing attitudes toward separation.[68]

Of course, neither was as separatistic as the Regular Baptists had become. For the GARBC, separatism was about to become a test of organizational fellowship. By late 1937 its churches were either out of the convention or rapidly heading out. When they left, they did not leave quietly. They publicized their complaints and tried to persuade others to separate. They were quick to help churches against convention opposition, and they were ready to exploit situations that would help them expose the modernism and heavy-handed tactics that were increasing within the convention. Two episodes from the latter half of 1937 illustrate this point.

In the first, Pastor Maynard Rogers of Farmington, Iowa, had begun to inform his congregation about the situation in the Northern Baptist Convention. After the 1937 convention he withdrew his personal membership from both the NBC and the Iowa convention. He stated his reasons in a letter to the convention secretary in Iowa. The following Sunday he happened to be ministering in another church, and in his absence the chairman of the deacons announced that the convention secretary would be conducting a business meeting on Friday night. Rogers heard the news on Monday, then on Tuesday drove to Des Moines to seek counsel from Regular Baptist pastors who were

67. Ibid.
68. Ibid.

holding a youth camp. At his request, three of the GARBC pastors, includ-ing P. B. Chenault of Waterloo, drove to Farmington to testify at the Friday business meeting. The convention secretary arrived in Farmington early and stopped first at Rogers's home, where he recognized Chenault's car in the driveway. He immediately backed out of the driveway and spent the next half hour at a service station before driving to the church. When he reached the church, the convention secretary discovered that Rogers himself intended to chair the meeting. Faced with the three Regular Baptist pastors, each armed with a large briefcase, the secretary stated that he was not on trial, that he did not have a speech, and that he did not intend to make one up. Rogers allowed him half an hour to present his concerns, then gave comparable time to each of the three Regular Baptist pastors. By the end of the evening, the Farming-ton church had gained a pretty clear idea of the situation in the convention.[69]

The second instance involved the ordination of Winthrop Hudson at the First Baptist Church of Lansing, Michigan. Six convention churches sent mes-sengers to the council, which was also attended by William S. Ross of the South Baptist Church in Lansing. Ross stated that he was not attending as a messenger, but the council permitted him to ask Hudson a few questions. During his examination, Hudson denied ever having been regenerated. He insisted that the resurrection of Christ was only spiritual and that the writers of the New Testament contradicted each other in their accounts. He ducked a question about inerrancy, then expressed uncertainty as to how the atone-ment might have worked. In response to a question about the blood of Christ, Hudson stressed that the example of the life of Christ was what kept people from sin. In spite of the objections of at least one pastor, the council voted to ordain Hudson. At that point, Ross spoke up, pointing out that Hudson could not even be received as a member at South Baptist. The moderator insisted that Ross take his seat, which he did—but he later published an account of the ordination.[70]

As the year drew to a close, Robert T. Ketcham began to prepare for his six months of travel representing the GARBC. His assistant pastor, Ray Hamilton, would guide Central Baptist Church during his absence. He began to adver-tise his availability for conferences and meetings. Once the new year began, however, he was forced to confront an unforeseen problem, one that would precipitate the most threatening crisis that the Regular Baptist movement had yet faced.

For more than a year the relationship between J. Frank Norris and the

69. "A Penetrating Glance into the Character of Dr. Anderson State Secretary of Iowa Bap-tist Convention," *Baptist Bulletin*, August 1937, 7.

70. William S. Ross, "Details of Another Modernistic Ordination," *Baptist Bulletin*, Oc-tober 1937, 6.

GARBC had been deteriorating. In 1936 Norris had arrived at the GARBC conference with forged credentials. In 1937 the executive committee refused to alter the dates of the meeting to suit him, and then denied him an opportunity to speak. For a while he lapsed into a kind of silence about the Regular Baptists and concentrated on his own work in Fort Worth and Detroit—and that work was flourishing. Norris claimed that his paper, the *Fundamentalist*, was read by hundreds of thousands every week. He was also one of the pioneers of Christian radio, and he had developed a continent-wide radio ministry.

Norris did not need the Regular Baptist movement. He pastored two of the largest churches in the world. He was also the key power in the Premillennial Baptist Missionary Fellowship, which had been organized in 1933. This organization was a loose fellowship of pastors. The two presidents of the organization, C. P. Stealy of Oklahoma City and Robert White of San Antonio, had both been appointed by Norris. In early 1938 Norris would fire White from the presidency, reorganize the fellowship, and move the offices to Chicago. Both before and after the reorganization, the group represented a substantial bloc of preachers and churches that looked to Norris for leadership. Through this fellowship Norris was also responsible for annual conferences in Detroit and Fort Worth (he called them his "Bible Schools").[71]

More than once during the latter half of 1937, Norris published that "there is no organization among Fundamental Baptists, and there needs to be none." This statement is puzzling in the light of Norris's own Premillennial Baptist Missionary Fellowship. It probably reflects his personality-driven style of leadership. Norris was notoriously impatient with planning meetings and administrative details. The main problem, however, was that by saying "there is no organization among Fundamental Baptists," Norris was deliberately slighting the Regular Baptists. Less than a year before, he had been only too eager to connect with the GARBC. Now, like a jilted teenager, he was acting like it did not even exist.

Ketcham was not about to let that pass. In January 1938 he wrote an editorial taking issue with Norris's statements. Ketcham was careful to keep the tone respectful and cordial, referring to Norris as "our good friend" and stating that he wanted to "good naturedly . . . take exception" to Norris's remarks. Nevertheless, he emphasized that "there never has been and never will be a time when Baptist churches scattered here and there will just suddenly decide to all congregate at a certain place for a certain number of days for fellowship

71. Billy Vick Bartlett, *A History of Baptist Separatism* (Springfield, MO: Baptist Bible Fellowship, 1972), 25–29.

purposes." Whenever two or more churches were going to cooperate, organization was always necessary.[72]

As evidence, Ketcham pointed to Norris's own Bible schools "from which infinite blessing is derived by the hundreds who attend." Ketcham noted that these conferences did not just happen. Someone had to publicize them, select the speakers, and arrange the details. Ketcham pointed out that this was indeed organization—"a one man organization." If Norris himself did not oversee these events, they simply would not occur. Ketcham insisted that he was not criticizing Norris: "More power to him, and may his gatherings for fellowship here and there all over the country increase." Nevertheless, the fact that these meetings had a single individual behind them "spells 'organization' boiled down to one man."[73]

On the other hand, Ketcham noted that the GARBC also publicized meetings, invited speakers, and arranged details. The difference was that these responsibilities rested with a group of fifteen or twenty people who were chosen by the churches whom they served. The continuity of the fellowship did not depend upon one person, but upon the combined responsibility of a whole group. He insisted that the GARBC was not a machine and that it was so constituted that it could never become one. Nevertheless, it did possess a very simple form of group organization that could facilitate the association's goals without ever foisting anything upon the churches.[74]

The editorial closed with a surprisingly concessive paragraph. Ketcham stated that "there is room in this great country for both kinds of organization—that which is publicized, propagated and perfected by one man, and that which is publicized, propagated and perfected by a responsible group of men chosen by the churches themselves." He suggested that each individual and church could choose as they wished.

Ketcham published the article in the February edition of the *Baptist Bulletin*. He also sent a copy to the *Beacon* (Riley's paper) and to the *Fundamentalist*. He wrote to Norris, "Would be glad to have you publish it with or without comment." Norris wrote back, "Go ahead and publish it in the 'Bulletin' and 'Beacon'. There are many erroneous statements in your article." This cryptic response might have prepared Ketcham for the reaction that was to follow.[75]

Later that same day Norris sent a second and longer letter. He claimed that he had shown Ketcham's editorial to several young ministers and that they considered it a "deep, though veiled attack." Norris accused Ketcham of "whispering about me and my work," and of never saying a kind word about

72. Robert T. Ketcham, "Baptists and Organization," *Baptist Bulletin*, February 1938, 2.
73. Ibid.
74. Ibid.
75. J. Frank Norris to Robert T. Ketcham, February 3, 1938. First letter.

his ministry (a charge that was demonstrably untrue). He called Ketcham's article a "declaration of war," and stated that he was "well prepared to take care of any attack."[76]

After pausing to boast about his own work, Norris stated that he had been Ketcham's "friend and booster." He continued, "Your attack on my work may be the first one in thirty years to make a dent on it, but many very powerful combinations and persons have tried it and there are two lesser fry here in Texas who tried it by circularizing the mails and are in pitiable plight in their own churches." Norris was implying that criticism of him would lead to disaster within Ketcham's own ministry—and as events developed, Norris would do his best to ensure that this prediction came true.[77]

Specifically, Norris critiqued Ketcham's role in the GARBC. Ketcham had written about Norris's work being organization "boiled down to one man." Norris responded that the GARBC "is a one man proposition and you are perpetual president of it, though that is no concern of mine." Norris insisted that he was not a president of anything within his fellowship, and he would not be.[78]

Norris said that he would submit the whole matter to a public referendum in the pages of the *Fundamentalist*. He would not do the writing himself—"I am sending your article, to a group of the brethren and they will reply." Neither they nor Norris would name Ketcham personally, but "your attack will be thoroughly taken care of," for "you have elected to declare war and with my name and so that is your privilege."[79]

Ketcham might have anticipated a hostile reaction, however genially his editorial was worded. He should have guessed that calling Norris a "one man organization" would be construed as a criticism. Only six months earlier Ketcham himself had written, "I have a tremendous fear that by carrying a president over too many years, this association shall get the name of being a one man affair. The day that the Association becomes a one man affair, my interest is utterly gone in it, even though some folks think that one man was myself."[80]

Norris had already given Ketcham reason to suspect his ethics. Even so, Ketcham could hardly have foreseen the intensity of his reaction. Norris's response was completely out of proportion to the offense, even if offense had been intended. Ketcham waited a full week before replying to Norris's letter, knowing that his response was going to shape the future relationship between those Baptists who followed Norris and those who aligned with the Regular Baptist movement.

76. Norris to Ketcham, February 3, 1938. Second letter.
77. Ibid.
78. Ibid.
79. Ibid.
80. Ketcham, "Concerning the Presidency," 11.

Ketcham's reply was quite direct. He first denied that his editorial could be read as a declaration of war, even "by the wildest stretch of one's imagination." He insisted that no criticism of Norris's work was intended or implied. His purpose was merely to answer questions that were raised by Norris's statements in the *Fundamentalist*, and Ketcham said that he "simply took the best natured way I could possibly think of to answer them."[81]

As Ketcham saw it, Norris's response proved one thing, namely, "that you were waiting for the slightest possible thing which you could interpret as an overt act, to give you an excuse to turn your guns upon an individual and a group of individuals whom you could not dominate." Ketcham implied that he had files of documentation that could discredit Norris if they were released, but stated that "there is no use going into endless detail and useless controversy." Consequently, Ketcham supposed that he would "have to pay the penalty of public crucifixion in the Fundamentalist which others of your erstwhile friends have had to pay."[82]

Ketcham rejected Norris's offer to avoid calling his name. He said that he was not in the habit of doing things that he would not want the world to see and know. "You will, therefore, please do me the favor of naming the object of your attack." Ketcham granted that Norris was fully able to crucify anyone upon whom he turned his attacks. Then he concluded,

> All I desire to say is go ahead, dear brother, and crucify. Do a good, thorough job of it, and when you are all through, I will trust the God of resurrection to take care of His servant.
>
> If you can afford to attempt to rip and tear to pieces life long fellowships, and thoroughly established Independent Baptist movements, all for the mere satisfaction of attempting to vindicate yourself from the charge of being a one-man organization, then I can afford to be crucified at your hands.

By this time, Norris was already laying plans to reorganize his fellowship. The president of the Premillennial Fellowship was Robert White. Norris accused White of misappropriating funds by using the fellowship's money to buy himself a hat. Removing White from office, Norris filed papers registering the World Fundamental Baptist Missionary Fellowship as a Michigan corporation. The first board of directors consisted of Norris, G. Beauchamp Vick (administrator at Temple Baptist), Ralph Jackson (a staff member at Temple Baptist), Howard Fulton, and Harry Hamilton. Future directors were to be elected annually by the membership of Temple Baptist Church.[83]

81. Robert T. Ketcham to J. Frank Norris, February 11, 1938.
82. Ibid.
83. "Articles of Incorporation," World Fundamental Baptist Missionary Fellowship, April 7, 1938.

Fulton and Hamilton may not yet have known about the conflict that was brewing between Norris and Ketcham. As the conflict became evident, Fulton quickly backed away from Norris. Hamilton, however, continued to serve as a director of the World Fundamental Baptist Missionary Fellowship. In fact, Hamilton would back Norris in later disruptions and would eventually become the dean of Norris's school in Texas.[84]

Early in 1938, Fred Donnelson, director of the Sweet Baptist Mission to China, came to the United States on a furlough. At some point he met J. Frank Norris, who in April suggested that Donnelson allow the mission to be taken over by the World Fundamental Baptist Missionary Fellowship. One of Donnelson's supporting churches was Walnut Street Baptist in Waterloo, Iowa. Pastor P. B. Chenault was deeply concerned about what the takeover might mean for the mission. Chenault and the deacons decided that if the Sweet Baptist Mission lost its independence, they were going to drop Donnelson's support. Later in April Donnelson was at Waterloo for a conference in which Ketcham was also participating. In private conversation Ketcham told Donnelson what had happened with Norris. Donnelson, however, still wanted to put the Sweet Baptist Mission under the World Baptist Fellowship. Even though Chenault and the church were ready to revoke their support, Ketcham encouraged them not to take this step, but to give the situation time to work itself out. As events developed, Donnelson went ahead and placed the mission and all its resources under the auspices of the World Baptist Fellowship.[85]

This maneuver supplied Norris with a recognized mission that he could add to his empire. More than that, it created confusion among the ranks of Regular Baptists. The Sweet Baptist Mission to China was one of the approved agencies of the GARBC. Now it was owned by Norris's WBF, but Norris was at war with the president of the GARBC. The relationship between these institutions suddenly became very ambiguous.

By April Norris was making good on his promise to "take care" of Ketcham. Through pamphlets and articles in the *Fundamentalist* he began to attack, not only Ketcham, but the entire GARBC. His main criticism echoed his letter to Ketcham, that is, that the GARBC "is a one man proposition and you are perpetual president of it." Given the wide circulation of the *Fundamentalist* and the number of Norris's friends who would repeat this accusation, it was soon raising questions throughout the Regular Baptist movement.

The accusation was full of irony, given Ketcham's reluctance to serve a fourth term as president of the GARBC. When he had accepted the office, he

84. Harry Hamilton to J. Frank Norris, June 6, 1951. Courtesy of Earl K. Oldham Library at Arlington Baptist College, Arlington, Texas.

85. Deacons of Walnut Street Baptist Church, "The Facts in the Donnelson Case," mimeographed report, February 7, 1944.

had clearly stated that he would not serve another term. He had even said, "I have a tremendous fear that by carrying a president over too many years, this association shall get the name of being a one man affair. The day that the Association becomes a one man affair, my interest is utterly gone in it, even though some folks think that one man was myself."[86] He had insisted that the GARBC should not be led by great men, but by little men with a great God.

Now Ketcham's fears were being realized. The GARBC was being attacked as a one-man organization, and he himself was being depicted as someone who wanted to be a great man. While he felt the injustice of the attacks, he also felt concern that the current structure of the GARBC left the association liable to the perils of authoritarian and idiosyncratic leadership. He wanted to find some way to protect the GARBC by preventing any leader—himself included—from gaining too much power. Because he was convinced of the centrality of the local church, he wanted to put as much of the association's actual authority into the hands of the churches as he possibly could. He believed strongly in the original vision of the GARBC: it was a fellowship of churches and not simply of pastors.

Working with the executive committee, Ketcham devised a plan to reorganize the GARBC. The plan had two parts. First, the old offices and the executive committee would be abolished. The association would have no president or vice presidents. Instead, it would elect a council of fourteen members, each serving a two-year term, with seven to be reelected each year. This Council of Fourteen would select a chairman, but only for parliamentary purposes. The whole Council of Fourteen would serve as the executive to carry out the wishes of the association.

Second, the old nominating committee would be abolished and the election system would be revised. The fellowshipping churches would nominate people to the council directly. Each church could nominate whomever it wished, and as many as it wished. The fifteen names that received the greatest number of nominations would appear on the ballot. Each church would designate two of its messengers to serve on the association's elections committee. The members of this committee would vote on the fifteen nominees. The seven receiving the highest number of votes would serve on the Council of Fourteen for the next two years.

In some ways, the plan was sheer genius. One of the greatest concerns of the Regular Baptist movement had been to keep the GARBC from ever becoming another convention. In one stroke, Ketcham's plan eliminated virtually all of the residual convention structure from the GARBC's operation. It evened out the disparity between large churches and smaller churches. It

---

86. Ketcham, "Concerning the Presidency," 11.

promised to thwart the machinations of anyone who hoped to be able to manipulate the structure. Most of all, it placed as much of the decision-making process as possible into the hands of the churches.

To adopt Ketcham's plan would require a major revision to the constitution—indeed, it required virtually a new constitution. At the time, the process of revision was relatively simple. The original constitution had been adopted for a single year, to be revised and reapproved annually. After six years it was still subject to annual revision and reapproval. If the messengers could be convinced, the new constitution could be adopted at the annual meeting in May.

The meeting was held at Walnut Street Baptist Church in Waterloo, Iowa. With the Belden Avenue meeting of 1932 and the Gary meeting of 1934, it was one of the most important gatherings in the history of the GARBC. Three issues were openly and publicly addressed at the conference. The first was the constitutional revision. As Ketcham moved its adoption, he said,

> There has been widespread criticism that this organization is a one-man outfit. While that is not true and could not be true, . . . if the constitution of the Association is changed to eliminate the lifting up of one man to the headship of the organization as president, and instead provides for the establishment of a properly elected council of fourteen men, independently nominated by the individual churches prior to the convening of any annual gathering of the Association, then the public will begin to realize what we have long contended, namely, that there are no big men in the General Association but only many little men with a big God.[87]

Once the messengers understood what they were being asked to vote on, they granted their approval surprisingly quickly—and unanimously.

The GARBC addressed a second organizational issue in 1938. The experience with Norris had revealed that the procedure for receiving new churches into fellowship was far too flimsy. The fellowship expected a church to vote into the Regular Baptist fellowship, but how was the church's decision to be communicated? What constituted a legitimate application for fellowship? Norris had nearly succeeded in bringing Temple Baptist Church into the GARBC without even having presented the decision to the congregation.

The solution to this problem was actually fairly simple, and completely in keeping with Baptist usage. Typically, communications between Baptist churches (such as calling church councils or sending church letters) do not come from the pastor, but from the church clerk. At Waterloo, the messengers decided to apply this principle to associational fellowship. Henceforth, applications from pastors would not be accepted. Since only the church itself

---

87. "Truly a Glorious Fellowship," *Baptist Bulletin*, May 1938, 3–4.

could vote to fellowship with the GARBC, only the church clerk's record of the vote would be accepted.[88]

The third organizational issue at the Waterloo meeting was the question of separation. The GARBC was avowedly a separatist organization, yet separation had never been instituted as a requirement for fellowship. The 1934 constitution had simply not addressed the issue. The question of dual affiliation apparently came to a head at the 1938 meeting. It was faced squarely on the floor, where men spoke from deep conviction on both sides of the issue. Ketcham later recalled that nearly a day and a half was spent in prayer and Bible study over the issue.

In the end, the messengers decided that no ties to the Northern Baptist Convention could be tolerated. The constitution was amended to read: "Any Baptist Church in the North which is no longer in Fellowship or cooperation with the Northern Baptist Convention and/or its auxiliaries . . . may . . . be received into the Fellowship by a majority vote of the Association." The issue was settled—dual affiliation would not be permitted.[89]

While the 1938 GARBC conference addressed these three major organizational issues, the conference was not primarily a business meeting. Its main focus was on missions, and most of the speakers were either missionaries or representatives of mission organizations. Even Fred Donnelson was given a session to present the work of the Sweet Baptist Mission to China (or, as it was now known, the East China Baptist Mission).

One issue that was not publicly addressed in Waterloo was the relationship with J. Frank Norris. Not that Norris neglected the Waterloo conference. Without naming Norris, the *Baptist Bulletin* told how "a brilliant preacher with dazzling personal magnetism" had shipped a thousand copies of "a certain fundamentalist publication" to Walnut Street Baptist Church for distribution to the messengers. Also enclosed were several hundred copies of "a recent pamphlet by the editor of this publication." The *Baptist Bulletin* noted that all of the material was returned to the owner, collect.[90]

The attitude of the fellowship toward Norris was also reflected in a thinly

88. "Important Changes at Waterloo," *Baptist Bulletin*, July 1938, 7. Later, favorable action from a recognition council of messengers from Regular Baptist churches would become necessary.

89. Robert T. Ketcham, recorded interview with Robert Delnay, April 7, 1962; "Important Changes at Waterloo," 7. Both Ruth Ryburn and Murray Murdoch present this debate as having taken place in 1934. Yet the constitution published in 1935 did not require separation, and pronouncements in the *Baptist Bulletin* acknowledged that churches could come into the GARBC fellowship without leaving the convention. None of the surviving minutes reference this action, but the revised constitution of 1938 is the first to institute separation as a condition of fellowship. One possibility is that the debate took place in an earlier meeting (perhaps 1934), while the final decision was delayed until 1938. See Ruth Ryburn, "The Outworking of Obedience," *Baptist Bulletin*, March 1966, 11–12; Murdoch, *Portrait of Obedience*, 133.

90. "Conference Closeups and Sidelights," *Baptist Bulletin*, May 1938, 7.

veiled reference that Ketcham made when discussing the constitutional revision. He wrote,

> There has never been any desire or attempt on the part of any individual in connection with the General Association to use the Association as an arena for the display of selfish ambitions. Two or three individuals looked the Association over for a year or two, and when they found that it was just a group of old-fashioned Baptists with no personal axes to grind and no desire to perpetuate the idea of somebody being "a great man," they immediately decided that this Fellowship was not a proper field from which the fly their personal kites, and so with much noise and clatter, they passed on to other fields.
>
> The Association is sold out to the one proposition that Jesus Christ is the only One worthy of prominent mention, and that there are no "great men among us." We are all little men with a great God.[91]

This attitude is one of the principal features that distinguished the Regular Baptist movement from other groups within Baptist fundamentalism. Most groups tended to rely upon one or more "great men" (as Ketcham would put it) in order to attract a crowd, establish the vision, set the agenda, and enforce loyalty. That spirit was almost entirely absent from the GARBC for the first several decades of its existence. One of the effects of the experience with Norris was to solidify the Regular Baptist commitment against the "great man" style of leadership.

With the 1938 conference in Waterloo, the GARBC adopted the form of organization under which it would operate for more than half a century. Minor adjustments would be made, but no other significant alterations would be introduced until the 1990s. Under the leadership of Van Osdel, Ketcham and others, the Regular Baptist movement had done more than to erect an organization. It had nurtured an ethos that would survive the generation of the founders. That ethos can be summarized briefly.

First, the GARBC was an association of churches rather than a fellowship of individuals. The experience of the Baptist Bible Union, and especially of Des Moines University, had left Regular Baptists distrustful of individual membership. They believed that the local church was central to God's plan in the New Testament. The constitutional revisions of 1938 aimed to place as much organizational authority in the hands of the churches as possible.

Second, Regular Baptists had seen enough of "great men" in the Baptist Bible Union. They had grown weary of individuals who used fellowship as a platform for personal advancement or the promotion of their own agendas. Ketcham was the one person who could have led as a "great man," and he refused to do

---

91. "Important Changes at Waterloo," 7.

it. Instead, he placed a strong emphasis upon the preeminence of Christ as the One worthy of all loyalty. He led the association to adopt a form of organization that spread out leadership over a larger body of fourteen (eventually eighteen) people, all of whom were ultimately accountable to the churches.

Third, the Regular Baptist movement inherited an intense interest in evangelism and missions. These interests reflected the stamp of Van Osdel's persona, but they were held almost universally among Regular Baptists. The principal churches of the GARBC practiced strong outreach within their own communities, and they experienced remarkable growth. At the national level, the work of missions was the primary emphasis of the GARBC. Missionaries were the heroes of the association, and there was a strong sense that the GARBC existed primarily to provide a meeting place for churches and missionary agencies.

Fourth, the GARBC approval system provided an ingenious solution to the debate between the associational model and the service-organization model of Baptist collaboration. Van Osdel had wanted the GARBC to establish its own mission board, while Ketcham had wanted to use only independent agencies. The approval system provided a way in which service organizations would become at least indirectly accountable to the churches while not surrendering their own autonomy. It gave the churches significant assurance that an approved mission or school had been examined and found worthy of support.

Fifth, Regular Baptists committed themselves to a strongly separatist position. This had been Van Osdel's goal from the beginning, and it was shared by Harry Hamilton, Howard Fulton, Earle G. Griffith, Robert T. Ketcham, and other leaders. From 1938 onward, the association would require separation as a condition of fellowship. This position meant that the association would separate (at the level of associational fellowship) from churches that did not separate from the liberal convention. Later the requirement was expanded to include separation from "any national or local convention, association, or group which permits the presence of modernism or modernists."[92] This position came to be called "secondary separation," and it has been a hallmark of the GARBC.

The Regular Baptist movement represents a distinct and identifiable variety of Baptist fundamentalism. It is not, however, the only variety. While the various branches of Baptist fundamentalism do exhibit certain commonalities, they also display significant differences. The next chapters will explore the development and ethos of three other significant branches within Baptist fundamentalism.

---

92. "Constitution of the General Association of Regular Baptist Churches," May, 1951, Article IV, Section 1.

J. Frank Norris in a First Baptist Church publicity photo from the 1920s.

8 The Norris Legacy

ONE OF THE FIRST real religious celebrities, J. Frank Norris stood in a tradition of Christian showmanship that reached from Charles G. Finney through Billy Sunday. He loved to preach to crowds, and he would go to extraordinary lengths to attract one. At some point during his early ministry, he discovered that people love to watch a fight. Much of his ministry was characterized by conflict as he picked one fight after another.

Something of Norris's character is revealed by an episode that occurred in 1936. Tragedy descended upon one of the pastors in his fellowship when a church member was shot dead on the steps of the church building. Shaken, the pastor wrote to Norris, asking for counsel in shepherding the congregation through the calamity. What Norris sent back was not counsel but congratulations; he assured the pastor that he would have a full auditorium the next Sunday.[1]

When Robert T. Ketcham penned his editorial on "Baptists and Organization," he had not meant to launch a public campaign against J. Frank Norris—but it was an opportunity for Norris to pick a fight. By the time of the GARBC's 1938 conference in Waterloo, the conflict between these two leaders had become a public spectacle. The leaders of the GARBC never hesitated to side with Ketcham. The first test came when Norris sent copies of the *Fundamentalist* and of his pamphlet against Ketcham to Waterloo for distribution. Returning these at Norris's expense was a bit of a dig, but it was also a clear message that his interference was not welcome. As the new Council of Fourteen would soon discover, however, Norris was not a man to accept a rebuff gracefully.

He soon launched attacks against other leaders of the GARBC. Besides

---

1. The episode is narrated by Billy Vick Bartlett, *A History of Baptist Separatism* (Springfield, MO: Baptist Bible Fellowship, 1972), 29n65.

Ketcham, two special targets were Harold Strathearn and David Otis Fuller. He also attacked the GARBC fellowship as a whole, attempting to spread confusion and dissention within the ranks. Decades later, Fuller would recall,

> Yes, J. Frank attacked us and <u>ALL</u> who would not knuckle under and bow to his dictum. He was a dangerous man if you disagreed with him. Genius? Certainly but the time came with me, and plenty of others, when I saw I could no longer go along with him and his methods which a [*sic*] at times were unethical <u>to say the least</u>. If I cannot trust a man I let him alone; that has been my policy up until now and it will continue to be and I have never regretted it.
>
> At first Norris was all gungho for the GARB in its infancy but when he saw he couldn't "run the show" and have everyone bow and kowtow to him then he began to act nasty and I have never known anyone who could act nastier than J. Frank. But then I think of the little couplet, "To live with saints in heaven above; is endless bliss and glory. To live with saints on earth below—is quite another story."[2]

The Initial Conflict

Norris's attack upon Regular Baptists took several forms. One of his stratagems was directed toward the missionary work of the GARBC. His newly incorporated World Fundamental Baptist Missionary Fellowship had recently taken ownership of the Sweet Baptist Mission to China, now renamed the East China Baptist Mission. Confusion arose from the fact that the mission was also an approved agency of the GARBC. Fellowshipping churches might well have wondered whether this approval now extended to Norris's fellowship. The confusion was exacerbated by the organizational form of the WBF itself. The control of the fellowship was firmly in Norris's own hands. Though he did not hold any office, the board of directors had to be elected directly by the membership of Temple Baptist Church, of which Norris was pastor. His control of the fellowship was as certain as his control of the church. To join the fellowship, one merely sent financial support to its missions office. Any contribution to the World Fundamental Baptist Missionary Fellowship made one a member of the organization.[3]

Many Regular Baptist churches had been supporting Fred Donnelson in his work under the Sweet Baptist Mission to China. One example was the Walnut Street Baptist Church of Waterloo, Iowa, which was sending

---

2. David Otis Fuller to Kevin T. Bauder, December 11, 1981. In his old age, Fuller typed his own letters and then corrected them by hand, creating individual pages that must be seen to be appreciated.

3. Deacons of Walnut Street Baptist Church, "The Facts in the Donnelson Case," mimeographed report, February 7, 1944, 1–2; Bartlett, *A History of Baptist Separatism*, 30n68 confirms that "membership was achieved by beginning to support a Fellowship missionary."

Donnelson $40 per month—a respectable figure during the Depression. Pastor P. B. Chenault insisted that this support was to be treated as a direct gift to Donnelson, but since the mission had been placed under the World Baptist Fellowship, Donnelson forwarded the money to the parent organization. The result was that on at least two occasions, Norris listed Walnut Street Baptist Church as a contributor to the World Fundamental Baptist Missionary Fellowship. The church became very concerned that it, or its pastor, would be listed as a member of the World Baptist Fellowship because of these contributions. The church authorized its pastor to investigate this situation, but Chenault was killed in a car crash before he could pursue it. There the matter stood until late 1939, when Robert T. Ketcham was called to the Walnut Street pastorate.

Meanwhile, tensions had arisen within Baptist Mid-Missions. Some missionaries and members of the council (the Mid-Missions board) were expressing unhappiness with certain aspects of M. E. Hawkins's leadership. Years later, Mid-Missions personnel would recall that the problem centered on Hawkins's wife, who became more actively involved in running certain aspects of the mission than some believed to be appropriate.[4]

The council (of which Ketcham was a member) began to work with Hawkins toward solving the problem. Somehow Norris got wind of what was happening. In October 1938 he began to use the *Fundamentalist* to insinuate himself into the situation. Positioning himself as a defender of the Mid-Missions president, Norris published that Ketcham was trying to fire M. E. Hawkins and to seize the presidency for himself. He wrote directly to Ketcham:

> And now it is out everywhere that you are trying to fire Hawkins and you will not succeed. You want to run Mid-Missions. The missionaries are laughing at it. It was discussed at Hamilton. Quite a number discussed it at Butler where you was former pastor and where you can not go and preach now. . . . I am going to publish what your scheme is to fire a great and good man like M. E. Hawkins.[5]

Ketcham saw Norris's tactic not only as a personal attack, but as an attempt to drive a wedge between Baptist Mid-Missions and the GARBC. In a letter to Regular Baptist pastors, Ketcham charged that Norris's "only reason for the creation of such a wild story is that he is determined to bring Mid-Missions under the control of his own missionary interest, and is setting about

---

4. This story was repeated to Kevin T. Bauder by missionary Jim Garlow and by former Mid-Missions missionary and president C. Raymond Buck.

5. J. Frank Norris to Robert T. Ketcham, October 1, 1938. Grammar and spellings in the Norris correspondence are sic.

to accomplish it by the creation of a disturbance within Mid-Missions itself." Ketcham insisted that he still supported Mid-Missions and that he supported Hawkins in particular.[6]

Norris's tactic placed Hawkins in a position that was especially difficult. He had no desire to be drawn into the conflict, especially since his missionaries received support from both Regular Baptist churches and World Baptist Fellowship churches. Yet if he tried to remain silent, he ran the risk that Regular Baptists would construe his silence as support for Norris's attacks. Ketcham came to his rescue, pleading with the churches not to let Norris "disturb your support of, and confidence in, Mid-Missions." Ketcham noted that anything Hawkins could say would alienate supporters of Mid-Missions. Furthermore, "If Dr. Hawkins should answer this statement of Dr. Norris, then Norris would make another which would require another answer and so on far into the future. . . ." Hawkins's silence was the course of prudence, but "Mid-Missions is not part of the World Baptist Missionary Fellowship, and by virtue of its organic set up, can never be anything other than an independent Baptist Missionary agency." Ketcham argued that Hawkins was making an honest and sincere attempt to do what was best for Mid-Missions, and he pled with Regular Baptist churches not to diminish their support for the agency.[7]

On occasion, Ketcham took the offensive against Norris, particularly when Norris published falsehoods. One example goes back to the founding of the World Fundamental Baptist Missionary Fellowship. Among the founders were two GARBC leaders: Harry Hamilton and Howard Fulton. Seeking to avoid the accusation that the fellowship was a one-man organization, Norris promised that the new fellowship would be placed under the leadership of three hundred directors, that their names would be published in the *Fundamentalist*, and that Fulton would read the list of names at the fellowship's first meeting in Detroit.

At the Detroit meeting Norris gave Fulton a list of three hundred names, and Fulton read them. The list did not appear in the *Fundamentalist*, however. The only place that the list appeared in print was on the back of the fellowship's letterhead. After the meeting, one of the World Baptist Fellowship state chairmen commented to Ketcham that Fulton had not actually read the names of the list of directors. This comment roused Ketcham's curiosity, and he sent letters of enquiry to thirty-two of the men whose names had been listed. Twenty-six of them responded indignantly that they had no knowledge of their names being used, and another two indicated that their names appeared without their consent. Only three of the thirty-two said that they

6. Robert T. Ketcham to the pastors of Baptist churches in fellowship with the General Association of Regular Baptist Churches and interested friends, October 18, 1938.

7. Ibid.

had agreed to be listed as directors of the fellowship. Before long, several of these men forwarded to Ketcham copies of letters in which Louis Entzminger apologized for including their names on the list. The list was subsequently removed from the back of the fellowship's letterhead.[8]

While the conflict with Norris was deepening, Ketcham sent circular letters to Regular Baptist pastors to keep them informed of the situation. In one letter he pointed out that Norris had not made good on his promise to list three hundred directors for the World Baptist Fellowship. In response, Norris republished Ketcham's letter and accused Ketcham of lying. He insisted that Fulton had read the names of the directors at Detroit. In October 1938 he sent Ketcham a special delivery letter, saying,

> Among the large crowd of preachers at Butler—and they were there from all surrounding regions—they had your latest ebullitions and were all roaring with laughter. One of them said you wrote 4,000 words, trying to get out of the falsehood that you circulated about the names not being read at the Bible School.
>
> It is pitiful to see a man so brand himself and be published throughout the world as a deliberate falsifier, and on a most essential issue. How true is the old Latin phrase, "falsum omnibus. . . ."
>
> These circular letters must cost you a good deal of money and time, and more than three hundred,ooo [*sic*] people—preachers in France and England and all over the world—reading your own false statements and Howard Fulton and hundreds of others knowing that you are a deliberate falsifier.
>
> Your feet will be held to the fire on this one issue and all the dust that you throw in the air will not hide it. . . .
>
> Everybody is laughing at you—life long friends. Men who have known you are pitying you.
>
> I was loathe to come to the conclusion that you are a deliberate falsifier. . . . Nothing discredits a man like cowardice, and deliberate falsifying.
>
> There you stand branded, published, photostatic copy, as a deliberate falsifier and that record will remain, for you haven't sense enough and religion enough to reverse your gears and remit and confess your sins.[9]

This was one of Norris's tactics. Caught in a lie, he would respond by repeating the lie and accusing his accuser of being a liar. He used every accusation as an opportunity to raise the stakes in the game, and he had the temperament and resources to outlast most opponents. He was a master of the Big Lie. He could publicize his accusations faster and send them to more people than

8. Robert T. Ketcham to J. Frank Norris, October 6, 1938.
9. J. Frank Norris to Robert T. Ketcham, October 1, 1938.

virtually anyone could answer them. He wrote to Ketcham, "Why don't you have as much sense as W. B. Riley. He has admitted that he got cut all to pieces and he has called his dogs off."[10]

Norris saw conflict as something like total war, and he was willing to do virtually anything to demoralize an opponent. Even his opponents' families were not off limits. For example, Ketcham's daughter and son-in-law, Lois and Don Moffat, had gone as missionaries to Brazil. Far up the Amazon, Lois had been stricken with the thyroid condition known as beriberi. As her health plummeted, she lost over seventy pounds in six weeks. She was evacuated by ship from Brazil, but no one believed that she could survive without immediate medical care. The United States Navy actually flew a doctor to her ship, saving her life. In September 1938 she was still bedridden, too weak to stand, and Ketcham himself was providing much of her care. Ketcham began sending out a prayer letter to about fifty family friends.

No weakness was too personal for Norris to exploit. While Ketcham's daughter was still lingering near death, he wrote:

> [M. E. Hawkins's] daughter is one of the greatest missionaries of this age and he has not exploited the fact that his daughter went to Africa. She went over there and had a baby, then came back home, travelled and raised money and I was happy to raise two fine offerings for her. Did it myself without being asked.
>
> I am going to raise money to send her a car. Dear Brother Hawkins has not exploited his daughter, nor has he sought to get cheap sympathy. Men don't have to do that unless they want to alibi for either their failures or their lying.[11]

A few days later, Norris alluded to Lois Moffat as a missionary who "went to the field on a honeymoon and a romance, and when the honey ran out and the moon went down she came running home to her father." He again implied that Ketcham had used the episode for "cheap sympathy."[12]

Norris attacked Ketcham at every level. He was not above stooping to personal abuse. He tried to find ways to insult every aspect of Ketcham's ministry and his personal bearing. This abuse was punctuated by Norris's boasting about his own ministry.

> No wonder you are mad and mad at yourself more than anybody for being caught on your petard. . . .
>
> You were fired at Waterloo [when the GARBC adopted the Council of Fourteen] and they let you down easy by discontinuing the office— they did like I saw a crowd do to a smart Alex at a country dance

---

10. Ibid.
11. Ibid.
12. Robert T. Ketcham to Robert D. Ingle, June 3, 1952.

when I was a boy. They slipped the chair out from under him and his caboose hit the floor.

You are mad and you are going to be madder. . . .

In your asinine conceit—and most big-bellied men are conceited—you thought I needed a favor from you. Why would a man need a favor from a man whose work is on four flats?

My crowds are greater than ever before. Baptizing more people today than I ever did in my life. . . .

You fellows remind me of a little flea-bitten fice dog jumping up in a wheat field to see which way the rabbit went. . . .

You are mad and you are going to get madder, and you just as well understand you will have to stand up and take it. . . .

You have ruined the G. A. R. B. . . .

You think you are a great preacher and there are a thousand others just as good, many of them better.

You run your hands down in your pockets and strut up and down the stage and folks laugh at you.

The only time you had a big crowd was at Harvey Morrison's when our crowd went there, and most of them went to sleep while you were scraping the star dust and nobody understood it, and you yourself did not know anything about it.

When I was up at Shields not long ago, he was laughing at your conceit.

When a man is conceited, he should have something to be conceited about. I am writing you with the hope that I can make you mad enough to send out some more letters. . . .

Everybody knows that your jealousy is measured by your large waist band and they are all laughing about it.

May the God of all Grace pity you. . . .

P.S. If you knew some of the wonderful things that have come into my work, of the men who are backing me, you would just bust your belly-band with the worst case of envy, even worse than the envy that caused Saul to go to the witch of Endor.[13]

When the conflict began, Ketcham had written to Norris that he knew Norris had the machinery to crucify him. He had said, "All I desire to say is go ahead, dear brother, and crucify. Do a good thorough job of it, and when you are through, I will trust the God of the resurrection to take care of His servant."[14] This was a suggestion that Norris mocked time and again.

You have been hollering and squawking about me trying to crucify you. You have crucified yourself. . . .

I stopped a bunch of crows once from eating up my watermelons once by putting some horse hairs an inch long in some grains of corn and soaking it over night, then scattering the swollen grains with the

13. J. Frank Norris to Robert T. Ketcham, October 1, 1938.
14. Robert T. Ketcham to J. Frank Norris, February 11, 1938.

hairs over the watermelon patch, and I sat under a tree watching the crows gather up the corn, and in a few minutes they cut their craws and the earth was strewn with dead crows. They "crucified themselves."[15]

Most of the foregoing quotations come from a single, special delivery letter that Norris sent to Ketcham in October 1938. It was timed to arrive at Central Baptist Church just before Ketcham stepped into the pulpit on Sunday morning. At the same time, Norris was sending comparable letters to David Otis Fuller, Harold Strathearn, and, to a lesser degree, other Regular Baptist leaders. He challenged Ketcham to meet him and Entzminger at the World Baptist Fellowship offices in Chicago. He planned to have a stenographer present (as he often did) who would record the conversation word for word. Norris believed that he could make Ketcham look foolish in a face-to-face confrontation, and if he had succeeded, he almost certainly would have published the whole conversation in the *Fundamentalist*. Ketcham, however, responded differently than Norris had hoped.

> Your communication was a very evident attempt to make me so mad that I would lose my head and rush into a conference with you, where I would lose my head even more, and be at your mercy forever after. You might be interested to know that your letter had exactly the opposite effect. I could not get mad at a man who could write such a letter; I can only pity him and pray for him.[16]

Idea by idea Ketcham went through Norris's letter and responded to each of the main points. He demonstrated factually that Fulton had never read a list of three hundred bona fide directors of the World Baptist Fellowship, for the simple reason that three hundred directors had not agreed to serve. He emphasized his ongoing support for M. E. Hawkins. He insisted that even Norris must know that he had gone too far in attacking his daughter: "I believe that even you are sorry that you penned such a statement." He explained that he himself had written the new constitution that was approved at Waterloo. In the process he concluded, "So, Dr. Norris, after all if there has been any falsifying, it looks to me as though it were on the other side."[17]

Ketcham also thought that Norris's letter was virtually self-incriminating. If it were shown to any fair-minded man, "it will mean the end of your influence over him." Ketcham considered the epistle to be a disclosure of Norris's character.

> Your letter is a shocking revelation of the fact that in spite of your public profession of loyalty to Christ, you can in private, resort to such

15. J. Frank Norris to Robert T. Ketcham, October 1, 1938.
16. Robert T. Ketcham to J. Frank Norris, October 6, 1938.
17. Robert T. Ketcham to J. Frank Norris, October 6, 1938.

vile and coarse expressions as would not be resorted to even by men of the world. In fact Dr. Norris, while it grieves me greatly to say it, I am of the opinion that your letter to me last Sunday was such a letter as the Holy Spirit would not permit any Christian to write, the Holy Spirit indwelling and controlling that Christian. . . .

I tell you again, Dr. Norris, I am sorry beyond words to express, that such a man as yourself with tremendous talents for leadership and ability to organize and carry great pieces of work, should in his insane desire to crush men who disagree with him in the slightest, make such a sorry spectacle of Fundamentalism. Truly, Dr. Norris, I care not one bit for myself, what you may say about me, or what you do about me. The Lord's blessing is upon me and upon my work in power and that is all I need to be concerned about so far as I am personally concerned. But my heart is truly broken as I see this awful spectacle of slam and bang, mud-slinging, innuendo, insinuation, vituperation, throat-cutting and crucifying, going on in your Fundamentalist with men who you have set out to ruin because they would not consent to bow down before your image.

In one of his letters concerning you, Dr. Entzminger once said that any man coming into contact with you must "either bow or burn." I cannot bow to this cruel, unkind and un-Christian attitude of yours, neither can I associate myself with your great program of make-believe and super-inflation. Therefore, I suppose I shall have to burn.[18]

As he was attacking Ketcham and the GARBC, Norris was also assaulting Harold Strathearn and the Interstate Evangelistic Association. Strathearn had actually broken with Norris during the summer of 1937. For a year Norris threatened to write Strathearn up in the *Fundamentalist*. Early in 1938 Strathearn began to return Norris's letters unopened. Finally, Norris made good on his threat, accusing Strathearn in the *Fundamentalist* of misappropriating funds by refusing a receipt for a $250 donation from First Baptist Church in Buffalo, New York (Harry Hamilton's church).

Strathearn's first step was to have Palmer Muntz, the treasurer of the Interstate Evangelistic Association, write to the treasurer at First Baptist of Buffalo for a complete statement of the church's donations to the association. Having obtained this list, Muntz gave a complete accounting of the donations, matched by receipts issued to the church. The donation that Norris said was misappropriated had never even been made, and neither First Baptist of Buffalo nor its pastor, Harry Hamilton, had ever requested a receipt for it.[19]

Strathearn printed the documentation in a letter that he sent to supporting pastors of the Interstate Evangelistic Association. The letter was also sent to

18. Ibid.
19. Harold Strathearn, form letter, n.d. but early October 1938.

other interested pastors. Norris had made other accusations, and Strathearn included a promise:

> You will receive, Brother Pastor, in due time, a printed document in which every one of Dr. Norris' malicious falsehoods will be answered with factual evidence. I send this brief statement on to you to-day that you may be informed. Dr. Norris, through the use of falsehoods, can make a white man look very black. Experience has taught me that Dr. Norris rules men by fear. Harold Strathearn knows no fear of any man; save the fear of the Lord.[20]

One cringes at Strathrearn's response, but one thing is clear. The man had been unfairly attacked, and he intended to hit back. In fact, he soon began a campaign to try to get people to cancel their subscriptions to the *Fundamentalist*.

Strathearn was less vulnerable than Ketcham. Ketcham was simply a local church pastor. Strathearn, however, had formed a strong friendship with the wealthy businessman R. G. LeTourneau. As long as he had LeTourneau's financial backing, he could afford to boast that he feared no man—he had the resources to get into a long-term conflict. Ketcham's response was the more temperate and thoughtful. Both men felt that they had to answer Norris's slanders, but Ketcham seems genuinely to have been concerned about the state of Norris's soul.

After the exchange in October 1939 Ketcham completely withdrew his personal fellowship from Norris. By his own testimony, he only ever wrote to Norris twice again, and then only a brief paragraph. While Ketcham would no longer write to Norris, however, the opposite was not true. Quite the contrary: Norris continued to batter Ketcham in print for years. Just three days after Ketcham mailed his long last letter, Norris responded with a telegram: "You are pitiful and the laughing stock of the limited number who know you. You will faint when you see the full write up of my continent-wide tour, radios, newspapers, auditoriums, and backing. Mission Fellowship going too rapidly for any doodlebug like you to stop it."[21]

A week after Ketcham sent his last letter to Norris, the GARBC's new Council of Fourteen met at First Baptist Church of Elyria, Ohio. In one of its first actions, the Council agreed that the *Baptist Bulletin* would be the only periodical presented on the platform of the national meetings. The approved missions could feature their periodicals as part of their displays. Any other periodical would have to be approved by the Council before being exhibited anywhere at the conference. This measure was probably a reaction

---

20. Ibid.
21. J. Frank Norris to Robert T. Ketcham, October 9, 1938.

to Norris's attempt to deluge the previous conference with copies of the *Fundamentalist*.

The Council also withdrew its approval from the East China Baptist Mission (formerly the Sweet Baptist Mission to China). Donnelson was taking money that was being sent to him personally and turning it over to the World Baptist Fellowship. The Council saw this as a breach of trust. They also disapproved of the World Baptist Fellowship's method of operation and of the fact that Donnelson had transferred all the mission's assets to the fellowship. Furthermore, the East China Baptist Mission had not reapplied for approval since it was reorganized.

The Council also discussed the problems in Mid-Missions. Specifically, the members reviewed the correspondence between Ketcham and Hawkins relative to Norris's accusations. According to the minutes, "After much discussion in regard to same, the council concluded that every effort must be made to prevent Norris from driving a wedge between Mid-Missions and the G.A.R.B.C., and that the Regular Baptist Churches should be encouraged to continue their support of Mid-Missions."[22]

Another topic of discussion was the Interstate Evangelistic Association, and Harold Strathearn in particular (Strathearn was not a member of the Council, but his right-hand man, J. Irving Reese, was). For some reason the Council was unhappy with some of the speakers that Strathearn had been inviting to his meetings. It asked him to exercise greater care in selecting speakers in the future. The Council also sought to discourage Strathearn from "carrying out his campaign for cancellations of subscriptions to the Fundamentalist, as being unwise at the present time." Otherwise, the Council expressed its confidence in Strathearn and the IEA, suggesting that the organization receive "an encouraging write up" in the *Baptist Bulletin*.[23]

Over the next few months, Norris's assault upon the GARBC and its leadership continued and increased. The Council of Fourteen held its next meeting on March 21–24, 1939, at Temple Baptist Church of Portsmouth, Ohio. Once again the Council discussed Norris's attacks. The minutes contain the following declaration.

> The slanderous and libelous attacks of Mr. J. Frank Norris upon the G.A.R.B. and men associated, were thoroughly gone into, and while it was agreed there was sufficient unimpeachable evidence in our files which, if published, would brand Mr. Norris forever and evermore as a man utterly devoid of Christian ethics, common courtesy, and trustworthiness, it was decided to follow the policy

22. Minutes of the Meeting Held by the Council Members of the GARBC in the First Baptist Church of Elyria, Ohio, October 11–13, 1938, 2–3.

23. Ibid., 3.

of silence as far as any published answer to his attacks is concerned, and commit Mr. Norris to the judgment of "HIM WHO JUDGETH RIGHTEOUSLY", Who hath said "VENGEANCE IS MINE, I WILL REPAY, saith the LORD."[24]

Ongoing Attacks

After March 1939 references to J. Frank Norris vanished from the literature and public discussion of the GARBC. Officially, it was as if the man did not exist. Unofficially, however, Ketcham kept careful files to document the ongoing abuse. Occasionally he would allow someone to view these files.

On April 1, 1939 P. B. Chenault was killed in a car crash. Walnut Street Baptist Church was left without a pastor. One item of business that Chenault's death left unfinished was the investigation into Fred Donnelson and the World Baptist Fellowship. Donnelson had adopted the pattern of forwarding his support to the World Baptist Fellowship. While the church wanted to support Donnelson, Chenault did not want the support to go to the WBF. Consequently, for five months the church had been accumulating his support rather than sending it.

When Chenault was killed, the deacons voted to forward the accumulated support and to begin sending monthly support until after the church called a new pastor. In September the church called Robert T. Ketcham. Once Ketcham arrived in Waterloo, the church's leadership apprised him of the Donnelson situation and asked for his counsel. In return, he asked whether the church was aware that Donnelson had transferred all of the assets of East China Baptist Mission to the World Fundamental Baptist Missionary Fellowship. They did not know, but the news did help them to make their decision.

> The Board immediately took the position that though they loved Mr. Donnelson, that this action had automatically put him where they could no longer conscientiously support him. The Board was not willing to invest $40.00 a month in the work of an individual, when the ULTIMATE ACCRUEMENT of that individual's work in building up a great mission center would become the property and possession of ANOTHER mission agency in which the board did not have confidence. It was therefore voted to discontinue the $40.00 a month and at the Annual Business Meeting of the Church, the Church unanimously approved the new budget.[25]

---

24. Minutes of the Meeting of the Council of Fourteen Held in the Temple Baptist Church of Portsmouth, Ohio, March 21–24, 1939, 2.
25. "The Facts Concerning the Donnelson Case," 3.

For the next several years, Norris continued to promote the World Baptist Fellowship as an independent organization, not under the control of any one individual or church. Year by year, a nominating committee would be appointed and the committee would recommend seven individuals to serve as directors of the WBF. These seven would then be voted into office in open session. The problem was that the articles of incorporation placed sole authority for selecting directors with Temple Baptist Church in Detroit. The three original incorporators had been Norris (pastor at Temple), G. Beauchamp Vick (superintendent at Temple), and Ralph Jackson (business manager at Temple). In other words, the election of the seven supposed directors was merely for show. The legal control of the organization remained in the hands of Norris, Vick, and Jackson—Temple Baptist had not elected any other directors.[26]

Howard Fulton and Harry Hamilton were also listed as directors of the World Fundamental Baptist Missionary Fellowship under its articles of incorporation, but the three from Temple Baptist constituted a voting majority. Furthermore, a majority of the directors could exercise absolute control over the fellowship and all of its resources. This was the real objection that Walnut Street voiced against Donnelson deeding over the properties of East China Baptist Mission. Legally, the directors "if they should so choose, could mortgage the property in which Brother Donnelson has given his life to build, WITHOUT HIS KNOWLEDGE OR CONSENT." Even if this was not what Norris intended to do, it is what he had a legal right to do. That was reason enough for Walnut Street to withdraw its support of Fred Donnelson.[27]

Evidently, this termination of support continued to be a sore spot with Donnelson into the 1940s. On December 11, 1943, Donnelson wrote to the deacons of Walnut Street Baptist Church, challenging them to meet with him and Norris. Ketcham presented Donnelson's challenge to the church's deacons, together with his request that Norris be allowed to attend the meeting. The deacons passed a resolution that they were "more than desirous of meeting with Rev. Fred Donnelson, but having a full regard for the truth will under no consideration meet with Dr. J. Frank Norris." By now the matter had become public, so when Donnelson failed to accept these terms, the deacons published a seven-page report on what they called "the Donnelson Case," detailing their reasons for withdrawing support. They sent this report to every church in the fellowship of the GARBC.[28]

Both Ketcham and the church continued to speak graciously about Fred

26. Ibid., 3–4.
27. Ibid., 4.
28. Ibid., 4–5; Deacons of Walnut Street Baptist Church, Waterloo, Iowa to Fred Donnelson, December 21, 1943; Deacons' Minutes, Walnut Street Baptist Church, Waterloo, Iowa, December 20, 1943; Deacons' Minutes, Walnut Street Baptist Church, Waterloo, Iowa, February 7, 1944.

Donnelson. Their complaint was not with the missionary, but with Norris and the structure of the World Baptist Fellowship. Ketcham continued to write to Donnelson until, in May 1944, a letter was finally returned unopened. It was marked, "Further private correspondence useless."[29]

The Donnelson controversy went on for years, and it gave Norris an excuse to redouble his personal attacks upon Ketcham. Hardly had Ketcham settled in Waterloo when he received a letter that said, "I find in the limited sphere of your acquaintance that the fellows pity you and understand your motive. It amuses me when I hear that you think I wanted your help and needed your introduction when I came north." In another letter he wrote, "You are an amateur in controversy. You can wave your arms the fastest and holler the loudest, and say the least—well, people are laughing. . . . Well, you have spent most of your thirty years and have built nothing."[30]

From every indication, Norris was trying to break Ketcham's will and to drive him out of ministry. During 1943 and 1944 he began to send long telegrams that were delivered just as Ketcham was about to enter the pulpit. Ketcham later cited a sample of the wording: "You put your hands down in your pocket and strut up and down the platform and think you are a great preacher. The people laugh at you but you think they are laughing with you."[31]

Eventually, Ketcham began refusing telegrams signed by Norris, so the telegrams started arriving with names like Wilson Connell and H. C. Willoughby. The contents made it clear that Norris was still the author. Then Norris began sending penny postcards filled with the same insulting, demoralizing language. The postcards were timed to arrive on Saturday or Sunday morning. When Norris needed more than one postcard, he would number them. On one occasion he filled four postcards with vitriol. When Ketcham refused to respond, he again shifted tactics, as Ketcham would later recall.

> [H]e succeeded in getting from someone a list of nearly 200 of my members and sent his FUNDAMENTALIST into my membership, which every week carried a scurrilous, slanderous attack concerning me. He had me "burglarizing" other men's homes and offices. He had me staying all night with Sunday School teachers in other cities and in general I was an all-around undesirable citizen.[32]

The list was probably provided by Don Miller, a member of Walnut Street who had publicly expressed dissatisfaction with Ketcham. The deacons had

29. Deacons' Minutes, Walnut Street Baptist Church, Waterloo, Iowa, May 4, 1944.
30. J. Frank Norris to Robert T. Ketcham, April 17, 1939; J. Frank Norris to Robert T. Ketcham, October 28, 1943.
31. Robert T. Ketcham to Robert D. Ingle, June 3, 1952.
32. Ibid.

wanted to disfellowship Miller, but Ketcham interceded in his behalf, hoping for some turnaround in Miller's attitude. Instead, Norris got Miller to employ a stenographer to take down at least one of Ketcham's sermons, which Miller then forwarded to Norris. Miller had also written to Norris to express his complaints with Ketcham, several of which Norris repeated in his attacks upon Ketcham. Eventually, the deacons proceeded to recommend that the church disfellowship Miller.[33]

Miller's complaints gave Norris a tool he could use. He wrote to the deacons at Walnut Street, challenging them to confront Ketcham in his presence about the complaints. Ketcham indicated to the deacons that he would be quite willing to submit to such a meeting, but the deacons wanted nothing to do with it. The minutes read, "The board after reviewing the evidence on hand wanted to go on record as not wanting to meet with Dr. Norris or to even as much as answer his letter."[34] The deacons did, however, begin to pray for Norris in their meetings.

As the attacks continued into 1944, the Walnut Street deacons finally reached the limits of their tolerance. They offered to place all the resources of the church at Ketcham's disposal if he would sue Norris for slander and libel. The offer seems to have caught Ketcham by surprise, but he quickly informed his deacons that what they were asking was impossible. Ketcham then offered an explanation.

> One day in 1939 I walked into my daughter's sickroom in Gary, Indiana, and as I saw her frail little body lying on the bed where it had been for many months, I asked her if she would like to try sitting up in a big, overstuffed chair. She nodded her assent. I picked her up, sat her in the chair, and turned to the bed for a pillow. When I turned back she was in a heap on the floor. As I picked her up and laid her back in the bed, and saw her flutter between life and death, a fury of hatred swept through my soul for the man who had slandered her in his paper. As I realized what was taking place, I became terribly frightened. I called Mrs. Ketcham to take care of Lois and I locked myself in a room alone. Kneeling down I told the Lord that I would not and could not leave that room until I could pray in love for Dr. Norris. For over an hour the battle raged. At last in sheer exhaustion I slumped to the floor and said, "Dear Lord, I can't." It was then that the dear Lord said to me, "Son, that is what I have been waiting for you to say. I know you can't but I can, and if you want Me to, I will do it through you." Before I knew what had happened I was pouring out my soul in prayer for Dr. Norris. Both my wife and I have prayed for

33. Deacons' Minutes, Walnut Street Baptist Church, Waterloo, Iowa, February 9, 1943; Deacons' Minutes, Walnut Street Baptist Church, Waterloo, Iowa, February 14, 1943; Deacons' Minutes, Walnut Street Baptist Church, Waterloo, Iowa, October 15, 1943.

34. Ibid., October 15, 1943.

him literally hundreds of times since. There is no bitterness or hatred. There is absolutely nothing personal in any of these issues. That was settled, thank God, that day.[35]

Ketcham declined the church's offer to back a lawsuit in 1944. At about that same time, Norris seems to have tired of the conflict and turned his attention elsewhere. The reason is not clear. Perhaps Norris thought that he had made his point. Perhaps he became absorbed in other conflicts. For whatever reason, however, his brutalization of the GARBC leadership decreased and then ceased. The old wounds would be opened only once more, and that only shortly before Norris's death. Before the final episode, however, Norris would begin to pay a price in his personal relationships and organizational influence.

Norris Unravels

Power changes some people, and within his small circle J. Frank Norris held nearly absolute power. His personal magnetism could sway crowds of adoring followers, and it was rare for his admirers to challenge him. If they did, he was capable of ruining nearly anyone just as he had tried to ruin Ketcham. It is difficult to say exactly when Norris understood the extent of the power that he held over people or the degree to which he could get away with lies and outrageous actions. By the 1940s, however, he was clearly transgressing the boundaries of public decency, let alone biblical morality.

Three men were the original incorporators of the World Fundamental Baptist Missionary Fellowship: J. Frank Norris, G. Beauchamp Vick, and Ralph Jackson. Eventually Norris would break with both of the others. The break with Jackson came when Jackson's wife publicly accused Norris of sexual harassment.

Dorothy Jackson released a letter in June 1940 accusing Norris of multiple attempts to initiate a sexual relationship with her. Specific allegations involved several episodes, beginning in 1935. Jackson alleged that in the last episode Norris attacked her in an empty room in the Sunday School building at First Baptist of Fort Worth, tearing her clothes and attempting to force her into a sexual encounter. She fled, and she claimed that she could produce reliable witnesses to the condition of her clothing, just as she could produce a witness to the circumstances of previous incidents. Her closing paragraph stated,

> I challenge Dr. J. Frank Norris to face me before the Board of Deacons of the Temple Baptist Church at which time I can produce the witnesses to certain of the accusations set forth above, and at the same time bring before the Board other women, who have been similarly approached.[36]

35. Robert T. Ketcham to Robert D. Ingle, June 3, 1952, 5.
36. Dorothy Jackson, mass letter, June 14, 1940. A copy was in Ketcham's papers.

Are Dorothy Jackson's accusations credible? One of the people who received her letter was W. B. Riley of Minneapolis. He wrote to her husband, Ralph Jackson,

> [T]he statement signed by your wife, at hand. Her testimony is in perfect line with what some of us have long known to be a custom with this gentleman. If I were making a rough guess, I should say that she is only one of possibly a hundred. I base that, however, upon absolute knowledge on some occasions, and suggestive appearances in many others. I have been expecting for years that some man would give him the same dose that he once administered to Chipps. . . .
>
> I thank God for the steps you have taken, and the fact that you have discovered his perfidy sooner than I was able to do. And I admire your wife that she was willing to take the courageous step she has in uncovering his conduct. I am sure it is one of the most difficult things that a woman has to do, but there are times when for the salvation of her sisters, a woman becomes a heroine in doing it. I think throughout the length and breadth of this land that truly Christian people will appreciate and applaud her conduct.[37]

Dorothy Jackson's testimony is also corroborated by similar testimony from others. One woman who had been a student at Norris's school in Fort Worth offered her recollection. "When we girls would leave our dormitory room in the morning, we would lightly sprinkle powder in front of the door. When we came back, if we saw a man's footprint we wouldn't go into our rooms. We knew that Dr. Norris was inside waiting for us."[38]

More corroborating testimony comes from G. Beauchamp Vick. After Norris and Vick split in 1950, Vick had the deacons at Temple Baptist Church invite Norris to tell his side of the story. In preparation for this meeting, Vick gathered considerable documentation of improprieties in which Norris had been involved. Vick later recalled, "And I also had two, had, ah, had one girl that Norris had tried to get fresh with sitting outside the entrance of the door so I could call her if necessary, and that kind of jolted him when he saw her sitting out there, and I had an affidavit from another one that he tried the same thing with—a signed affidavit." As it turned out, Vick did not use this evidence of Norris's sexual improprieties in that meeting. The only occasion upon which he did use it was in a meeting at Lackland Road Baptist Church, where Vick presented affidavits from multiple women.[39]

People encouraged Vick on more than one occasion to publish this evidence against Norris, but, as Vick recalled, "I said I don't want the world to know about that. But I knew that as long as Norris knew I had it, it would sure put a

---

37. W. B. Riley to Ralph W. Jackson, June 27, 1940. A copy was in Ketcham's papers.
38. Ann Hauser, interview with Kevin T. Bauder, April 26, 1984.
39. G. Beauchamp Vick, recorded interview with Robert Delnay, 1962.

crimp in him. . . . I'm telling you, he was scared to death in this thing." What happened to those affidavits? Years later, Joseph M. Stowell Jr. claimed that he had talked to the man who cleaned out Vick's office after his death. As Stowell told the story, this man said that he had found a bundle of material implicating Norris in multiple cases of immorality. Since Vick and Norris were both dead, and the evidence was of such a devastating nature, the man burned it all.[40]

In view of these and other witnesses, Dorothy Jackson's accusations are at least credible. At the very minimum, Norris was indiscrete in his conduct toward women. More likely, as he learned the true extent of his power over others, he engaged in repeated sexual harassment. If that is the case, then he was neither the first nor the last religious leader to use his power to gratify sexual temptation. Unfortunately, no record of a public confrontation between Dorothy Jackson and J. Frank Norris has surfaced for this history. That, too, is in keeping with Norris's ways of operating. He could usually count on his loyal followers to bury or at least minimize the embarrassing and scandalous episodes.[41]

Only a few years after the Jackson incident, Norris even fell out with his own son, George. In 1944 Norris decided that it was time to retire without retiring. He selected George as his successor at First Baptist of Fort Worth—without asking either the church or George. He simply told the church that he was making his son the head pastor. He made it clear to George, however, that he was to do exactly as his father told him.

The arrangement lasted only about a year before George revolted. Leading many members out of First Baptist Church, he went across town to start Gideon Baptist Church. The elder Norris was incensed. He accused his son of dishonoring his parents. He told George that he ought to repay the money that the elder Norrises had put into his education. He charged George with having stabbed his parents in the back. He threatened to accuse George's friends of criminal activities. He called him a fool. In one of his most poisonous moments, Norris told his son that he would happily pay the fees to have George's last name legally changed.[42]

The greatest fracture that Norris had to endure, however, lost him most of his following. The conflict revolved around the Fundamental Baptist Bible Institute, founded in 1939 at First Baptist in Fort Worth. Technically owned by the World Fundamental Baptist Missionary Fellowship, the institute had Louis Entzminger for its first president. In 1944 the school was renamed

40. Ibid.; Joseph M. Stowell Jr., interview with Kevin T. Bauder, June 23, 1982.
41. See the exchange below involving Robert D. Ingle and Luther Peak.
42. This conflict is summarized in Barry Hankins, *God's Rascal: J. Frank Norris and the Beginnings of Southern Fundamentalism* (Lexington, KY: University of Kentucky Press, 1996), 128–130.

the Bible Baptist Seminary. Norris took the presidency himself, moving Entzminger to the office of dean.

The school was not what would now be considered a seminary, that is, a graduate school for pastoral training. Indeed, it was hardly even a Bible institute like Moody or Northwestern. Teachers had little academic preparation. The schedule was flexible. Students would congregate daily in one of the church's halls (typically the John Birch Hall, named for one of the fellowship's first missionaries), where they would listen to basic teaching from the King James Bible. Sometimes Norris himself would interrupt the schedule to treat the students to a display of his platform technique. After three years, students would be awarded an academic degree: a master's degree if Norris knew and liked them, or a bachelor's degree if he did not.[43]

While Bible Baptist Seminary was formally owned by the World Baptist Fellowship, all of the finances ran through First Baptist Church. By most reports, little effort was made to keep separate accounts. Funds that ran into the church could be diverted in several directions, some of which benefitted Norris personally. One never knew where one's gift actually went. For example, Norris had talked about putting up a building for the seminary. He gathered the fellowship's pastors and broke ground for the building. The pastors gave an offering, which disappeared into the financial maze of First Baptist Church. The next year they gathered at the same hole and the same thing happened all over again. The seminary was running debts all over Fort Worth, leaving the fellowship with $250 thousand in red ink.

For more than a decade, G. Beauchamp Vick had been Norris's right-hand man at Temple Baptist in Detroit. Officially he was the church's general superintendant, but in practice he pastored the church during Norris's absences. Over time, the church came to see Vick as their real pastor, and in early 1948 he was formally made co-pastor of the church. Norris had chosen Vick because of his administrative skill, and Vick had proven more than capable. Now Norris wanted Vick to take the presidency of the financially beleaguered Bible Baptist Seminary in Fort Worth.

Initially, Vick was concerned that he might have to give up the co-pastorate of Temple, but Norris agreed to let him do both jobs. In fact, Vick's main responsibility would continue to be the pastorate at Temple Baptist. He would be permitted to install his own right-hand man over the seminary in Fort Worth. Vick further insisted that he be given real authority over the seminary and that the finances of the seminary be completely severed from those of First Baptist Church or other organizations operating out of the First Baptist facilities. Vick was specific in his reasoning:

43. Bartlett, *History of Baptist Separatism,* 34–35.

> I feel that all of this is very vital inasmuch as a year or so ago you and I tried to get from the Seminary records the total amount of money that the Temple Baptist Church had given to the Seminary within a certain year. You will recall that we got three different sets of figures, widely divergent and none of them correct. Where one person receives the money and deposits it, another person acknowledges it and another person keeps the records, it is absolutely impossible to hold any one individual responsible for the efficiency and correctness of financial records. Neither by correspondence nor by personal inquiry a few weeks later when I was down there at a Fellowship meeting, could I get heads or tails of their records.[44]

The problem was not just one of how the funds were recorded, but of how they were appropriated for use within the institution. According to Vick, on one occasion Norris had to make a trip for the seminary, so he purchased a new Buick Roadmaster out of seminary funds. After the trip, the car was his to keep. Consequently, Vick insisted that he and the seminary trustees would go over the books every month, reviewing every financial item. Furthermore, he required a monthly financial report be sent to the directors of the World Baptist Fellowship.[45]

At the 1948 meeting of the World Baptist Fellowship, Norris moved that Vick be elected to the presidency of the seminary. Before the motion could be voted, Vick stood and announced that he was not eager to become the president. Then he turned to Norris and said, "Dr. Norris, if I become the president of the seminary, then you will not be." As it turned out, this was exactly what the Fellowship pastors had been waiting to hear. Vick was swept into office.[46]

Though Vick had no background as an educator, his common-sense administrative skills quickly reversed the financial woes of the institution. He negotiated a loan to pay off the school's immediate debts. His insistence upon rigorous accounting blocked many of the financial leaks in the seminary. He noticed that some professors were teaching an extremely light load, that some were poorly qualified, and that all were underpaid. He dismissed the worst-qualified, increased the remaining professors' teaching load, and gave the entire faculty a substantial raise in salary. The net effect was an increase in both productivity and satisfaction from the professors, combined with a substantial net savings for the seminary.[47]

Academically, Vick divided the curriculum and insisted upon separate classes by year. The school still focused upon teaching the English Bible, but

44. G. Beauchamp Vick to J. Frank Norris, April 9, 1948; cited in G. Beauchamp Vick, "Separation from WFBMF and the organization of the Baptist Bible Fellowship and Baptist Bible College: The Real Issues Involved," *Baptist Bible Tribune*, June 23 1950, 1.
45. Vick, interview; Vick to Norris, April 9, 1948.
46. Vick, interview.
47. Ibid.

now it had a specific plan that appealed to prospective students. From all over the World Baptist Fellowship, students began gravitating toward the seminary, and churches multiplied their giving. Not only was the seminary meeting its current expenses, but the institutional debt, which had been over $250 thousand, was reduced by more than half.[48]

As the second year of Vick's presidency drew to a close, the school was more stable than it had ever been. Enrollment was up, the finances were good, and morale was high. With the institution doing so well, Norris decided to reclaim control for his own purposes. To do that, he needed to invent some occasion to use against Vick. He found his raw material in a suggestion that Vick had made concerning Louis Entzminger's salary.

Now aged seventy-four, Entzminger was still teaching at Bible Baptist Seminary. The conditions of his employment stated that, in addition to his regular salary as a professor, he would receive a significant bonus as long as he brought a certain amount in donations to the seminary. For some years he had failed to produce these donations, but he continued to receive the bonus. Vick suggested that it might be time to rethink the bonus.

From this small suggestion, Norris manufactured a story that Vick was trying to fire Entzminger from the seminary. Supposedly Vick had verbally assaulted the elderly professor so badly that Entzminger's health was wrecked and he was now bedridden. On April 3, 1950, Entzminger telegraphed Vick, "Since Reg informed me you intended to reduce my salary, I could not retain my self respect and continue with the Seminary." At the same time Vick was reading the telegraph in Detroit, professor Frank Godsoe was reading it to the students of the seminary in Fort Worth. After both Godsoe and Norris ranted against Vick, the students voted to send another telegraph to Detroit: "We the student body of the Bible Baptist Seminary by unanimous vote emphatically reject the resignation of Dr. Louis Entzminger and move he be retained as professor at not less than present salary for life."[49]

After receiving the two telegrams, Vick tried repeatedly to call Norris. Norris refused to take Vick's calls, but busied himself trying to arrange a meeting of the seminary's trustees. The only two trustees who could be gathered, however, were Norris and Godsoe. Norris tried to persuade others to wire him proxy votes, but they refused. Meanwhile, Entzminger, who was supposed to be bedridden, took the seminary's business manager to lunch and announced that Norris was reappointing him dean of the seminary. Finally, Vick was able to get the business manager on the phone and, using one of the school's transcriptionists, dictated a long message to Norris. The message concluded,

48. Ibid.; G. Beauchamp Vick, "Separation from WFBMF," 1, 5.
49. Ibid., 5.

I repeat, I consider the whole affair foolish and stupid, and calculated to harm me, and that as a result, it will harm both the Seminary and the Fellowship.

I had no desire to become president of the Seminary. You repeatedly urged that I do so. But as long as I am president, I intend to exercise all prerogatives of that office."[50]

The incident remained unresolved. Over the next month Norris, Entzminger, and Godsoe repeatedly attacked Vick before the students of the seminary. The annual meeting of the World Baptist Fellowship was fast approaching, and in preparation for it Norris went in front of the students and read a new set of bylaws for the seminary. He also went on a rant against Vick, declaiming, "I'll be the cock of the wall or there will be no wall!" Then he put the bylaws to a vote by the students. First, those in favor of the new bylaws were asked to stand, and almost everyone did. Then those who were not in favor were asked to stand. About fifteen or twenty students—mostly from Temple Baptist in Detroit—stood.[51]

The students who would not support the new bylaws were informed by Godsoe that they were being expelled from the institution. They were told to vacate the dormitories immediately. One of them managed to get a call through to Vick, who told them to stay put and that he would be on campus on Monday. Then Vick learned that the business manager, R. O. Woodworth, had also been fired and told to vacate the property immediately. Vick immediately sent a strongly worded telegram to Norris, ending with the words, "I'll meet you at Philippi," a reference to the great battle in which Octavian and Mark Antony fought for control of Rome against Brutus and Cassius. Monday was the beginning of the fellowship's annual meeting, and Vick's words were a threat of open warfare on the floor of the conference.[52]

Many prominent leaders would gather for the fellowship meeting. Among them were Wendell Zimmerman (pastor of the Kansas City Baptist Temple), Fred Donnelson (World Baptist Fellowship missionary, recently returned from China), Noel Smith (editor of Norris's paper, the *Fundamentalist*), Luther Peak (pastor of Fundamentalist Baptist Tabernacle in Denton, Texas), Robert Ingle (pastor of Berea Baptist Church in Jacksonville, Florida), and W. E. Dowell (pastor of High Street Baptist Church in Springfield, Missouri, and the elected president of the World Baptist Fellowship). Dowell, Vick, and Zimmerman all arrived in Fort Worth at about the same time, where they were met by Woodworth and the expelled students from Temple Baptist.

Meanwhile, events had transpired in Fort Worth that caught Norris's opponents by surprise. Norris had arranged to have a few of his supporters in town

---

50. Ibid., 6.
51. Hauser, interview.
52. Bartlett, *History of Baptist Separatism*, 37–39.

on Monday morning. At 9:00 this small group came together and declared that they were meeting as the World Fundamental Baptist Missionary Fellowship. In the absence of opposition, they formally adopted the new bylaws for the seminary, which gave Norris virtually dictatorial authority. Then they voted to fire Vick and to install the Scottish evangelist Jock Troup as new president of the seminary. Later, at the evening service, Norris circulated handbills that accused Woodworth of misappropriating $10,000 in seminary funds.[53]

The next morning was "Seminary Day," and Norris had arranged to have Godsoe in the chair. The first event of the day was to be a sermon by Norris, after which Vick was supposed to deliver the seminary report. Norris, however, had rearranged the schedule to have Godsoe introduce Luther Peak (a Norris supporter) instead of Vick. Before Godsoe could announce the speakers, however, W. E. Dowell stepped to the platform and took the pulpit. Dowell reminded the crowd that he was the elected president of the fellowship and that he ought to be chairing the meeting. From behind, Norris sputtered that it was Seminary Day. Dowell quietly put the matter to a vote, and Norris was overruled by a margin of about four to one. Dowell then pointed out that there was a public controversy of which Norris would give one side. He asked the crowd whether they thought it would be fair to hear from both sides and to give Vick a chance to state his case. This time the margin was even larger, probably because even Norris's supporters wanted to see the fight. Consequently, Vick again replaced Peak as the second speaker.[54]

Norris spent his time attacking Vick personally and mostly in generalities. When Vick's turn came, however, he carried his large briefcase into the pulpit with him and began a well-documented response to the charges that Norris had raised. Citing Norris's own words, Vick cleared himself of the accusation that he was persecuting Entzminger. Then he turned his attention to the new, "cooked-up bylaws," as he repeatedly called them. He pointed out over and over again that the bylaws gave absolute control of the seminary to one church, then repeatedly added, "And you might as well say one man." He stated that any church that wanted to send money to such an organization was well within its rights to do so, but those who did not want to support it were also within their rights. Then he ended his remarks by formally resigning from the presidency of the Bible Baptist Seminary.[55]

As soon as Vick had finished, Zimmerman moved that the fellowship reject the resignation. In his remarks, Zimmerman also asked some very pointed questions about the legality of the new bylaws. Then Robert Ingle, a Norris supporter, offered a substitute motion: instead of rejecting Vick's resignation,

53. Ibid., 39–40; Vick, interview.
54. Bartlett, *History of Baptist Separatism,* 40–41.
55. Vick, interview.

the group would appoint a committee with representatives of both parties to investigate the legality of the new bylaws. At that point Norris interrupted the proceedings. It was his church, he said, and there was not going to be a vote on either Vick's resignation or on Ingle's committee. Instead, he and Vick would go to lunch and work out a solution.[56]

At lunch Norris asked Vick for his conditions. Vick stipulated three terms for settling the conflict. First, the students from Temple Baptist would be reinstated at Bible Baptist Seminary. Second, since Vick was resigning from the seminary, Norris would resign the co-pastorate of Temple Baptist Church. Third, Vick and his supporters would establish a new school at Springfield, Missouri, and both schools would operate within the constituency of the World Baptist Fellowship. Each church could decide which school it would support. Norris agreed to all three stipulations.[57]

The terms of this agreement were announced that afternoon. The next day Vick's supporters met in the ballroom of the Texas Hotel. There they organized Baptist Bible College, to be opened in Springfield, Missouri. Some thought they ought to go further and establish a new fellowship as well, but Vick was determined to keep the fellowship intact. Debate over this question was cut short when someone arrived to announce that Norris's crowd had just voted to move the fellowship headquarters from Springfield to Fort Worth, and that Norris was again using his meeting to denounce Vick. Given this breach of faith, the assembly immediately voted to establish the Baptist Bible Fellowship and to start a paper, the *Baptist Bible Tribune*, with Noel Smith as editor. The paper was considered necessary in view of the attack that Norris would surely launch in the *Fundamentalist*.[58]

Vick, Dowell, Smith, and Zimmerman were Norris's most public antagonists in the conflict, but many other pastors had become tired of the Texan's domineering attitude and destructive attacks. Among these was Fred Donnelson, whose influence helped to guarantee a strong missionary emphasis for the newly organized Baptist Bible Fellowship. The BBF promptly adopted all the missionaries of the old fellowship and sent them notice of this fact.[59]

The new Baptist Bible Fellowship also moved quickly to launch the Baptist Bible College. Almost immediately after the Fort Worth meeting, the new fellowship purchased a vacant acreage in Springfield, Missouri. With Vick as the president, the trustees decided to erect a dormitory as their first building. It was ready for use when the school opened in September.

56. Bartlett, *History of Baptist Separatism,* 44–45.

57. Vick, interview; Bartlett, *History of Baptist Separatism,* 45–46.

58. Vick, interview (1962); Bartlett, *History of Baptist Separatism,* 47–50.

59. Fred S. Donnelson, "What Happened at Fellowship at Fort Worth," *Baptist Bible Tribune,* June 23, 1950, 2.

The largest remaining problem was the relationship of J. Frank Norris to Temple Baptist Church. He had been pastor since 1935 and co-pastor with Vick since 1948. Part of the lunch-table agreement between the two men was that Norris would resign his co-pastorate at Detroit, but he had no intention of keeping his word. Vick had been the church's real pastor for several years, however, and the deacons were ready to go ahead and vote Norris out of the church. Vick was the one who slowed them down, insisting that Norris should have the opportunity to come to Detroit and tell his side of the story. On Vick's strong recommendation, the deacons extended an invitation to Norris, and on Thursday evening, June 1, he came to Detroit to meet with the deacons and to present his claims.

Vick knew of a young woman whom Norris had tried to seduce, and she agreed to testify before the deacons. Vick positioned this woman outside the door of the meeting room so that Norris would see her when he entered. According to Vick's later recollection, Norris was visibly shaken. Then, at the beginning of the meeting, the chairman of the deacons told Norris that he should stick to the facts and not engage in personal attacks against Vick or others. Norris, however, quickly strayed into invective, only to be interrupted by deacons and reminded to stick to the facts. After the third interruption, one of the deacons stood and moved that, since Dr. Norris appeared to have no facts to present, they proceed with the vote. Norris immediately replied, "I see that you already have your minds made up. I'll not be party to any secret meetings." He then gathered his hat and stalked out of the room. Altogether, he had taken only about ten minutes. Of the twenty-six deacons present, twenty-five voted to recommend that the church immediately sever its connections with Norris. The remaining deacon, whose son was a friend of Norris's son Jim, abstained.[60]

That Sunday, the deacons placed their recommendation before the church at the close of the morning service. The crowd numbered well over three thousand. As soon as the deacons put the motion on the floor, seconds came from all over the auditorium. The question was determined by a standing vote. Virtually the whole church arose in favor of the motion. While an exact count could never be tabulated with precision, all parties agree that over three thousand members voted to expel Norris from the pastorate and membership. It was easier to count those who opposed the motion: there were only seven.[61]

Norris was not a man to take defeat graciously. As he had with the GARBC leadership a decade earlier, he launched a smear campaign against the founders of the Baptist Bible Fellowship in the pages of the *Fundamentalist*. He

60. Vick, interview; Vick, "Separation from WFBMF," 7.
61. Ibid.

accused his opponents of conspiring to overthrow him, then added accusations of fraud, theft, adultery, homosexuality, and other offenses. This time, however, he had badly misjudged both his opponents and his supporters. Even his supporters knew that his charges were false and driven by spite, while his opponents were quite prepared to defend themselves in public. During its first year or so of operation, the *Baptist Bible Tribune* regularly answered the charges that Norris brought against Smith, Zimmerman, Dowell, Vick, and others. Still, Norris's constant accusations could be exasperating. On one occasion Zimmerman happened to be passing through Detroit, and he told Vick, "If you don't go down there and shoot him, I will!"[62]

One more bizarre episode followed the split between Norris and his former associates. About three weeks after the break, the founders of the Baptist Bible Fellowship began to receive telegrams from Norris threatening to sue them for slander. Then Norris, on his personal initiative, announced that he was going to hold a hearing at First Baptist Church. To make the event appear more like a legal proceeding, Norris announced that he would have a court magistrate present at the hearing. Then he issued his own subpoenas to the men whose character he intended to attack. Since the hearing had no legal standing at all, they either ignored the subpoenas or else responded that they did not intend to appear.

The day before the hearing, however, Dowell, Woodworth, and Vick were meeting with Zimmerman in Kansas City. On the spur of the moment, they decided that they would drive to Fort Worth for the meeting after all. While they drove, Zimmerman's secretary called around to the Baptist Bible Fellowship pastors within driving distance of Fort Worth. By the time of the meeting, about seventy-five preachers had assembled at the Blackstone Hotel.

First Baptist Church was only about three blocks from the Blackstone, so the throng of pastors walked the distance. The whole group arrived about fifteen minutes after Norris had launched his opening attack. Norris was in the middle of denouncing his opponents as cowards for not attending the hearing, when in they walked, backed by their crowd. Suddenly deflated, Norris asked, "You come to testify, Beauchamp?"

"That's the general idea," Vick boomed.

The auditorium was packed. Unable to find another seat, Vick strode to the platform and pulled up a chair. He was facing the lectern from about four feet away on the edge of the platform. Later he would remark, "If I was going to hear my funeral preached, I wanted a good seat." One suspects that he may have enjoyed having the upper hand on Norris for a change.

After the first witness testified against Vick, he was denied the right to

---

62. Bartlett, *History of Baptist Separatism*, 57–59.

cross-examine. When Vick pointed out that Norris had promised to follow courtroom legal procedure, Norris launched into a tirade about how it was his church and he would do as he pleased. Vick responded that he had not really expected Norris to keep his word.

For eight hours, Norris brought witness after witness to accuse Vick and the others. Finally, he announced the end of testimony for the day. Vick shouted that Norris had to give his men an opportunity to present their side. Norris tried to delay their testimony until the next day, but Vick pointed out that Norris had promised a one-day hearing. Norris responded, "That's no concern of mine," at which point Vick stood, shook his finger in Norris's face, and exclaimed, "You're the biggest coward I ever saw!" John Rawlings stood up on the mourners' bench and began to yell, while Noel Smith shouted while standing on a chair. Looking at Smith, Norris began to mock, "Know-all Smith! Know-all Smith!" From somewhere in the auditorium, W. E. Dowell hooted, "Three thousand to seven! Three thousand to seven!" Norris ordered a couple of seminary students to throw Dowell out of the building, but Dowell faced them down and dared them to try it. Finally Vick, perhaps sensing the disgrace that the meeting had become, called his followers together and exited the building.[63]

This was the last personal confrontation between Norris's forces and Vick's forces. Norris had made Jock Troup the president of the seminary. Troup, a Scottish evangelist, was largely unfamiliar with the situation. He was in the United States on a visitor's visa and was not allowed to receive a salary. He told this to Norris, who replied, "I'll take care of it." Troup thought that Norris, who had considerable political pull, had arranged the matter with the federal immigration officials. Norris had done nothing of the kind. After about six months, Troup became suspicious of Norris's ethics and began to hesitate over some of the things that Norris wanted him to do. Norris simply called the immigration agents and reported Troup for a violation of his visa. Troup was arrested and deported from the country. Troup believed himself to be disgraced. While he was able to return to the United States, his ministry was never the same. He died a couple of years later.

Norris offered the presidency of the World Baptist Fellowship to Harvey Springer, pastor of First Baptist Church of Englewood, Colorado. Springer was a tall man, a converted drunkard, and a cowboy preacher. Under his pastorate, First Baptist of Englewood had become famous for holding an annual rodeo in the church building. He used to go incognito to the National Western Stock Show in Denver to work as a bull fighter (in those days called a *rodeo clown*, and by any name a dangerous avocation). He had been greatly used to

63. Vick, interview; Bartlett, *History of Baptist Separatism*, 53–55.

start churches all over eastern Colorado. From First Baptist, Springer built an empire that included Silver State Camp and Silver State Academy. Springer had been only marginally active in the World Baptist Fellowship and probably did not know what the issues were at the time. He simply accepted the presidency from Norris and went forward from there.

Reconciliation Attempted and Failed

In 1941 Carl McIntire led in the formation of the American Council of Christian Churches, a story that must be told elsewhere. As the ACCC grew, both the GARBC and the World Baptist Fellowship became constituent members. When McIntire learned about the tensions between Norris and the leadership of the GARBC, he wanted to help make peace. He met with Ketcham and Robert D. Ingle, one of Norris's closest associates, in late April 1952. He asked what would have to take place in order for Norris, Ketcham, and the GARBC to establish fellowship and stand together in a united testimony for Christ.[64]

Ketcham gave the matter some thought, and then said that Norris needed to come out in the *Fundamentalist* with a confession that his attacks upon Strathearn, Fuller, and others, as well as the attacks upon the GARBC itself, were "deliberate falsehoods uttered with malicious intent to hurt and crush." Norris would further have to state that he wanted to confess his guilt and be forgiven. If Norris would do those things, Ketcham said, then he would be the first to get on a plane to Fort Worth and extend his hand of fellowship to Norris. Ketcham clearly stated that he needed no personal confession or apology from Norris. If Norris would make things right with the others he had hurt, then Ketcham would overlook the personal wrongs against him.[65]

McIntire asked Ingle if he thought that Norris would agree to these requirements. Ingle replied that he was sure Norris would, but he would not do it in just that way. He would probably write an article saying nice things about the GARBC and its leadership, and that article would prove that he held no animosity or ill will. Ketcham responded that such an article would only constitute another insult against the men whom Norris had deeply wronged. He and the other leaders of the GARBC were not about to go rushing to Fort Worth and to take Norris in their arms for a few crumbs of "nice things" said about them in the *Fundamentalist*.

On May 16 the *Fundamentalist* ran an article headed, "A Review of the History of the GARB, the World Baptist Fellowship, the Regular Baptists of

64. Robert T. Ketcham to Robert D. Ingle, June 3, 1952.
65. Ibid.

Canada and Other Independent Baptists." Most of the article was a rambling and error-filled narrative of the development of Baptist fundamentalism. Buried in the article was the statement, "I would like to correct any statement of mine issued in past years that might be interpreted as being calculated to destroy or injure the testimony or character of any of those men herein named, or any others connected with the GARBC work."[66]

Ketcham found the statement to be completely unsatisfactory. In his response to Ingle he wrote,

> Dr. Norris comes forward and says that if he has said anything which could be INTERPRETED as harmful to anybody, he would like to correct it. My dear brother, when I look at this stack of telegrams, letters, postal cards, and editorials lying here on my desk, and when I think of the same which one day laid on the desk of such men as Strathearn, Fuller, Riley, and others, this shallow, meaningless statement instead of correcting anything, simply adds another Norrisian stunt to the collection.[67]

Even worse, Ketcham suspected that Norris had not even written the article. He speculated that Ingle had written it with Luther Peak, and then the two of them had published it in Norris's name. Ketcham concluded his letter to Ingle by stating, "When Dr. Norris, on his own, from the depths of a broken heart, under the impress of the Holy Spirit, dictates and publishes his own confession, we shall be happy to be the first to re-establish fellowship."[68]

Ingle replied to Ketcham, expressing his disappointment. He admitted that he and Peak had written the article for the *Fundamentalist*, but he insisted that Norris had approved it. Furthermore, he thought that Ketcham did not know Norris well enough to judge him properly. He insisted that Norris, though a ruthless fighter, left his conflicts completely behind when he was through with them. That had already happened with Ketcham.

> In the case of his controversy with you . . . I believe he absolutely forgot it, as far as the fight was concerned or holding any grudge, or feeling that he had done any great damage to any body's feelings or character. He simply is not made up like any other man on earth, and when he made the statement in the Fundamentalist in reference to any man's character or any one's reputation harmed by any thing that he is calculated to have said, he meant that exactly as he stated it.[69]

To Ketcham, Ingle's reply was almost as exasperating as the *Fundamentalist* article had been. In the first place, Peak and Ingle should not have drafted

---

66. Cited in Ketcham to Ingle, June 3, 1952.
67. Ibid.
68. Ibid.
69. Robert D. Ingle to Robert T. Ketcham, June 23, 1952.

Norris's apology. Norris himself "knew exactly what wording it would take to rub out the wounding words which he had hurled at good and godly men and movements over the past 20 years and more. He did not need a 'lawyer' to write his copy for him, and then for him to add his signature."[70]

As for the question of whether Ketcham knew Norris well enough to judge him, Ketcham replied, "I doubt, Brother Ingle, if there is another man in the United States who has better reason to know him than I do." Then Ketcham responded to the subject of Norris being a ruthless fighter who completely laid down the conflicts and even forgot about them when they were over:

> [Y]ou inadvertently and unconsciously laid bare the characteristic of Dr. J. Frank Norris. . . . You picture him as a man who ruthlessly stalks across the battlefield with his sword drawn, plunging it into lives and characters, assassinating men's characters and reputations right and left, and then leaves the battlefield strewn with their wounded and bleeding bodies, hearts, souls, and minds. When the battle is over, he straightway "forgets" the whole thing, and never thinks of the damage that he has done to lives and characters and careers. You certainly drew a full-length pen picture of Dr. Norris when you said that. That's exactly what he does, and it is exactly what he is trying to do now. With a ruthlessness that amounted almost to godlessness, he walked over the names and characters of outstanding men of God here in the North, and now he wants to forget it, and he wants everyone else to forget it, and go on as though it had never occurred.[71]

Ketcham went on to warn Ingle against the disease of "Norrisism." He expressed concern that the disease was far advanced in both Ingle and Peak. There the matter stood. Norris died on August 20, 1952, just over a month after Ketcham's last letter to Ingle. Four years later, Luther Peak led his church back into the Southern Baptist Convention, publishing an article explaining why he was leaving fundamentalism. At the time of his death, Norris had seven judgments standing against him in Tarrant County for slander and libel.[72]

Years earlier, in her letter of accusation against Norris, Dorothy Jackson had told how Norris responded when she confronted him personally with her charges.

> Dr. Norris's reply to my charges at the time was "If any man dared make any reflection on my wife's husband I would resign from the ministry for fifteen minutes, call him a S__ of a B____ (which he pronounced in full) and beat H___ out of him, and then go down and pay my fine.[73]

70. Robert T. Ketcham to Robert D. Ingle, July 11, 1952.
71. Ibid.
72. Luther Peak, "Why We Left Fundamentalism to Work with Southern Baptists," *Baptist Standard*, April 1956, 6–7; Vick, interview.
73. Dorothy Jackson, mass letter, June 14, 1940.

One of the people who replied to the letter was W. B. Riley, pastor of First Baptist Church in Minneapolis, Minnesota. Riley said,

> I had to smile when I read what he said he would do to any man who would dare to make a reflection on his wife's husband's character. There isn't a man living, or any tongue in existence, that could reflect upon his character! It's incapable of defamation. The half of his infamy will never be told. This is my conviction after years of observation and audience.[74]

In these words, Riley may have written Norris's most fitting epitaph.

Does It Matter?

Both the World Baptist Fellowship and the Baptist Bible Fellowship trace their origins to J. Frank Norris, but not all of Norris's heirs ended up in these two groups. For example, John R. Rice began his ministry as a Norris protégé, but broke with Norris while still pastoring in Dallas. As an evangelist he relocated to Wheaton, Illinois, and then to Murfreesboro, Tennessee. Rice was one of the founders of the Southwide Baptist Fellowship in 1956. Because of the prominence of Rice within this movement, it is sometimes called "the Sword crowd," reflecting the influence of Rice's popular paper, *The Sword of the Lord*.

The Southwide Baptist Fellowship is a preachers' fellowship. It has considerably less structure than the World Baptist Fellowship and the Baptist Bible Fellowship. While the WBF and the BBF operate their own schools and missions, the Southwide exists basically for the annual fellowship meeting. Its pastors have typically supported Tennessee Temple College and Baptist International Missions, Inc. (BIMI). The WBF, the BBF, and the SWBF have never been entirely sealed off from each other, and a good bit of crossing over between groups has occurred. Together, they constitute virtually a single movement, sometimes known as Independent Baptist Fundamentalism.

One of the most prominent pastors to represent Independent Baptist Fundamentalism was Jack Hyles. While he never attended Norris's school, Hyles was strongly influenced by Norris's philosophy of ministry. He carried this philosophy into the pastorates of Miller Road Baptist Church in Garland, Texas, and First Baptist Church in Hammond, Indiana. Identified loosely with the Sword crowd, Hyles really developed a sub-movement of his own. For decades he was probably the most prominent representative of Independent Baptist Fundamentalism.

74. W. B. Riley to Ralph Jackson, June 27, 1940.

In one of his books, *The Church*, Hyles devoted a chapter to reflecting upon "Where We Are in Fundamentalism." He posited that American fundamentalists fit into three categories or types. The first type he called "American Baptist Fundamentalists," consisting of those who withdrew from the Northern (later, American) Baptist Convention. The second type was "Protestant Fundamentalism," comprising the interdenominational fundamentalists. Hyles's label for the third type was "Southern Baptist Fundamentalism," that is, those fundamentalists whose roots were in the Southern Baptist Convention. Examples of this type included J. Frank Norris, Lee Roberson, and G. Beauchamp Vick. Hyles listed both the Baptist Bible Fellowship and the Southwide Baptist Fellowship as examples of Southern Baptist fundamentalism. Educational institutions included Baptist Bible College, Tennessee Temple College, and his own Hyles-Anderson College, as well as local church schools such as those operated by Bob Gray in Longview, Texas, and by Jim Vineyard in Oklahoma City.[75]

Southern Baptist fundamentalism (as Hyles labeled it) is not strictly a Southern phenomenon. Norris and Vick pastored in Detroit. John R. Rice spent two decades in Illinois. Both the BBF and the Southwide have developed significant networks in the geographical North. In a few cases Northern fundamentalists have exported their version of fundamentalism to the South. The labels *Northern* and *Southern* distinguish types of fundamentalists more than geographical locations.

Hyles suggested that Southern Baptist fundamentalism is "where the action has been." He also noted that Northern and Southern fundamentalists do not always see eye to eye.

> These people are part of the big circle of *fundamentalism*, but we have some basic disagreements. There have been some invisible fences between us that are now rising up and becoming more visible. We do not build those fences. They started saying that we are shallow and too evangelistic. They started accusing us of promoting easybelievism. We have no choice but to say that they are wrong. They criticize us because of our excitement and our informality. The action in *fundamentalism* in this generation has come from Southern Baptist *fundamentalists*, that is, those who left the Southern Baptist Convention and those they have influenced.[76]

75. Jack Hyles, *The Church* (Hammond, IN: Prepare Now Resources, n.d. but 1992), chapter 4. Hyles's books seem to have gone out of print after his death, but this volume is now available in a Kindle edition through Amazon. The Kindle edition has not preserved the pagination. What Hyles called "Southern Baptist fundamentalism" is not the same thing as the conservative resurgence in the Southern Baptist Convention. Hyles was referring to a version of fundamentalism that existed as a distinguishable movement from the 1920s onward and consisted of Baptist fundamentalists who left the Southern Baptist Convention.

76. Ibid., chapter 4.

Hyles also saw separation as a marker that distinguished Northern Baptist from Southern Baptist fundamentalism. Both groups were separatistic, but what they meant by separation was not the same thing.

> The GARB and the American Baptists divided basically over doctrine. When Dr. J. Frank Norris pulled out of the Southern Baptist Convention, most Southern Baptist preachers believed that the Bible was the Word of God. The Bible was not issue in those days. It was an ecclesiastical issue, a type of worship issue, and a separation issue. They pulled out over mixed bathing being wrong. They pulled out over social drinking being wrong. They pulled out over teaching evolution. They pulled out over matters of separation, and matters of type [of] worship.[77]

As Hyles saw it, one of the weaknesses of Southern Baptist fundamentalism was that this group had to rely upon Protestant fundamentalism for most of its literature. This situation, however, could be easily explained. The Southern Baptist fundamentalists "are the ones that have been red-hot . . . the guy that is red-hot does not want to take time to write a commentary." Nevertheless, Hyles concluded, "I happen to think that we are as smart as they are."

According to Hyles, an unseen wall existed between Southern Baptist fundamentalism and the other two types. For the most part, the Southern fundamentalist leaders had not said much about it, but the other two groups were now beginning to attack the Southern fundamentalist position. Consequently, Southern Baptist fundamentalists would have to defend the things they thought were important.

> We must defend altar calls. We must defend the old-time religion, because groups one and two are basically going back to their origin of formal worship services. In order to preserve what we have had through these years those of us in group three are going to have to stand for what we have had. They are shooting at us, and we have no recourse but to defend our position.[78]

Specifically, Southern Baptist fundamentalists should guard their pulpits, because "when a church in [Southern Baptist fundamentalism] calls a pastor from [Northern Baptist fundamentalism], there is a catastrophe ahead." Most church members would not be able to recognize the difference, but pastors from the first two types of fundamentalism would want to teach the existence of an invisible church. They would also want to go back to "formal worship

77. Ibid.
78. Ibid.

services." They might be good men, but let them be good within their own groups.

Such was Jack Hyles's typology of American fundamentalism. While few would consider Hyles to be an authoritative student of fundamentalist history, and while his evaluation does exhibit a fair amount of distortion, its general outlines contain an important truth. Fundamentalists—even Baptist fundamentalists—come in different varieties. Evaluating all fundamentalists by the characteristics of a single type will inevitably lead to a skewed judgment of fundamentalism as a whole.

Hyles captured several of the marks that distinguish varieties of Baptist fundamentalism, though he gave them his own twist. It is worth taking a few paragraphs to sort out these characteristics and to examine their role in distinguishing versions of Baptist fundamentalism. Of course, these distinctions must be expressed as general characteristics, and not all fundamentalists of either type will reflect all of these characteristics to the same degree.

First, Hyles noted that the Northerners accused the Southerners of "shallowness" and "easybelievism." What Hyles was noting was that the two versions of fundamentalism differ in their presentation of the gospel. Southern Baptist fundamentalists tend to stress the gospel invitation and the profession of faith, while Northern Baptist fundamentalists prioritize repentance and conversion. Typically, Southern Baptist fundamentalists have assumed that their listeners knew and understood a good bit of the gospel. The challenge was to move hearers to make a decision to profess Christ. Northern Baptist fundamentalists have generally focused upon the content of the gospel, trusting in the persuasive power of the message itself. In other words, among Northern Baptist fundamentalists, evangelism is primarily a matter of declaration and presentation, while among Southern Baptist fundamentalists it is primarily a matter of invitation and persuasion.

Another contrast plays into Hyles's remark about "easybelievism." The two versions of fundamentalism hold different visions of the Christian life. In the Southern fundamentalist view, the Christian life is primarily propelled by crisis decisions which are often made in response to what is called "hard preaching." While Northern fundamentalists do not discount the importance of some crisis decisions, they see the Christian life as a matter of progressive sanctification, a series of comparatively small spiritual adjustments that, over time, add up to significant growth and change.

The contrast between these two visions of the Christian life plays directly into a contrast between pulpit ministries. The "hard preaching" of Southern fundamentalism aims to motivate listeners by contrasting their Christian obligations (the "standards") with their spiritual lethargy and failure; in other words, it aims to shame listeners. Its goal is primarily to motivate the listener to engage in "soul winning" and to abandon practices that are considered worldly. On the other hand, Northern fundamentalists, aiming for incremental growth, tend to emphasize biblical content and teaching as an important aspect of their preaching. Southern preaching tends to aim more for exhortation, while Northern preaching tends to aim more for exposition.

What Hyles had to say about the excitement and informality of Southern Baptist fundamentalism also ties in at this point. The two versions of Baptist fundamentalism are driven by significantly different priorities in their church gatherings. Both believe that the gospel should be preached at most or all public services of the church. For Northern Baptist fundamentalists, however, evangelism is only one, and not necessarily the most important, function of the gathered church. Their services are heavily weighted toward worship and instruction. Southern Baptist fundamentalists, however, downplay the importance of public worship or even reject it altogether.

Hyles also mentioned that Southern and Northern Baptist fundamentalists differed in their understanding of separation. As he implied, the difference operates at two levels. First, Northern fundamentalists tend to be more concerned than Southern fundamentalists with ecclesiastical separation. This means that the Northerners are more alert to religious activities that involve institutional cooperation and platform identification with apostates and erring believers. Both groups also emphasize personal separation, or non-participation in activities that are considered worldly. Southern fundamentalists, however, tend to have a longer list of worldly activities in which Christians are not allowed to participate.

As Hyles observed, the two groups have different doctrinal emphases. He mentioned that Northern Baptist fundamentalists believe in an invisible (universal) church, while Southern Baptist fundamentalists do not. To put it in other words, the Northern version of fundamentalism tends to be more influenced by historic Baptist ecclesiology while the Southern version tends to be more influenced by the theories of Landmark Baptists. The Southerners are more likely to believe in Baptist successionism, to deny the existence of a universal church, and to require that baptism be performed by a Baptist in order to be valid.

Another doctrinal difference, one that Hyles knew about but did not mention, is in the area of soteriology. Historically, Northern Baptist fundamentalism has been led mainly by men who were at least moderately influenced by Calvinism. With some exceptions, however, Southern Baptist fundamentalism has been vocally anti-Calvinistic.

One of the greatest differences between Northern Baptist and Southern

Baptist fundamentalism involves disparate understandings of pastoral leadership. Concerning the Northerners, Hyles wrote, "They think we should have committees to run everything in the church."[79] While this is not quite an accurate description, it does point to a contrast. Southern Baptist fundamentalists emphasize a form of pastoral leadership that is paternalistic and authoritarian. For them, the pastor leads by making most of the important decisions for the congregation. The pastor may seek counsel from the church or from other church leaders, but he is able to make his decisions unilaterally. The people are expected to accept his decisions, and any serious recalcitrance may become grounds for church discipline (which is often carried out by the pastor unilaterally). If the pastor has assistants, they are viewed as extensions of his ministry and not as pastors in their own right. Congregational polity means that the church votes to receive new members and that it votes to call the pastor. Beyond that point, the congregation makes few real decisions.

By way of contrast, Northern Baptist fundamentalists emphasize congregational polity. The church is expected to determine its own policies and direction. Pastors do lead, but their leadership consists mainly in their teaching of the Word of God and their example of holy living. They certainly have a voice in establishing policy and direction, but they are not free to impose their will upon the church. In Northern Baptist fundamentalism, a church may have multiple pastors, each of whom is called by and ultimately responsible to the congregation. Each is recognized as a pastor in his own right. Finally, since the important decisions are made by the congregation, much of pastoral leadership involves bringing individual members to a point at which they can make informed, mature, biblical decisions.

In short, Southern Baptist fundamentalists get their vision of church polity from J. Frank Norris's style of Great Man leadership. Within the church, every pastor tries to fill the role of a Great Man. Many Northern Baptist fundamentalists (particularly Regular Baptists) tend to follow Ketcham (and, before him, Van Osdel) in his rejection of Great Man leadership. They want the decision-making process to be spread broadly among the brethren, whether internally within an individual church's membership, or externally within a church's broader fellowship.

Given their strong emphasis upon Great Man leadership, it is not surprising that the Southern Baptist fundamentalists also reject associationalism. Baptist church associations derive their power from the churches, and the will of the churches is expressed through the consensus (usually expressed by vote) of their fellowship. Instead of associations, Southern Baptist fundamentalists

79. Ibid.

prefer to organize preachers' fellowships in which the pastors of the supporting churches make the decisions.

Hyles noted the existence of at least two versions of Baptist fundamentalism. Ketcham and Norris exemplified these two versions—in fact, each of them helped to define a version. As Hyles also noted, when these two versions are brought into too-close contact with each other, conflict almost inevitably ensues. The reason is simple. A church or fellowship cannot work in both ways. The two philosophies of ministry are ultimately irreconcilable. Leaders of these two fundamentalisms can maintain a cordial relationship from a distance. They can even become allies in some kinds of conflicts. When they are brought too close together, however, each philosophy of ministry works directly to erode the other.

Northern Baptist fundamentalism has made few advances in the Southern states, but Southern Baptist fundamentalism has proliferated in the Northern. It was well entrenched at Temple Baptist in Detroit from the 1930s onward. It received further impetus when John R. Rice, an erstwhile Norris protégé, moved his ministry from Dallas, Texas, to Wheaton, Illinois. When Jack Hyles came to Hammond, Indiana, from Garland, Texas, in 1959, he built another capital for Southern Baptist fundamentalism. In time, every Northern state came to have at least one organization that represented the heirs of J. Frank Norris.

Consequently, from about 1940 onward, the history of Baptist fundamentalism in the North involves at least three parties. The first consists of those Northern Baptist fundamentalists who left the convention on their own initiative. These pioneer separatists are represented primarily by the Regular Baptist movement. The second party comprises those Northern Baptist fundamentalists who attempted to remain in the convention, but who were ultimately forced out. This group is represented primarily by the Conservative Baptist movement and those organizations that survived its breakup. The third party includes the heirs of J. Frank Norris who brought their philosophy and methodology into Northern churches. This group is represented in the North primarily by the Baptist Bible Fellowship and the churches connected with the Sword crowd.

Indeed, the Sword crowd may even represent a fourth party within Baptist fundamentalism. While it is certainly a version of Southern fundamentalism, it developed along a unique trajectory. Since its influences were different, its values and practices are also somewhat different. In order to understand the Sword crowd, one must first understand something about John R. Rice, from whose ministry it developed. That is the next story that needs to be told.

J. Frank Norris and G. Beauchamp Vick.

J. Frank Norris in his office at First Baptist Church, Fort Worth, Texas. The motto above his desk reads, "Life ain't in holding a good hand, But in playing a poor hand well."

John R. Rice, evangelist and *Sword of the Lord* editor.

9 The Sword Movement

THE GENERAL ASSOCIATION OF REGULAR BAPTIST CHURCHES adopted Ketcham's proposed constitution in 1938 at Waterloo, Iowa. With minor adjustments, the new form of organization would remain virtually unchanged for more than half a century. Agreement on the new constitution meant that Regular Baptists were among the first important fundamentalist groups to achieve organizational equilibrium and to erect a stable platform for growth.

Other branches of fundamentalism were soon to develop, but they were still in flux. During the period from 1938 to 1948 various strands of fundamentalism coalesced into identifiable movements. As these new groups emerged, the differences between them became clearer. By the end of the decade, deep fault lines had appeared. Baptist fundamentalism would eventually fracture along these lines, never to be repaired.

One noteworthy development was the growth of the "Sword crowd," which was named for John R. Rice's paper, the *Sword of the Lord*. Rice began publishing the paper while he was an ally of J. Frank Norris. His reputation spread as he began to gain more contacts among Northern fundamentalists. Rice moved to Wheaton, Illinois, in 1940, after which the Sword movement grew into a nationwide phenomenon.

While Rice certainly represents a branch of Southern Baptist fundamentalism, his influence developed separately from the World Baptist Fellowship and the Bible Baptist Fellowship. The Sword crowd and the Norris groups overlapped to some extent, but Rice's ideas and influence were distinctive in some of their key features. This distinctiveness accounts for some of his initial appeal to Northern fundamentalists and explains how Rice's popularity grew in the North. It also explains how many Northern fundamentalists became uneasy with Rice, leading to a decline of his influence among Regular Baptists and others.

John R. Rice

Rather than setting out to become a minister, John R. Rice meant to be a college professor and perhaps eventually a politician.[1] A graduate of Baylor University, he taught English at Wayland Baptist College in Plainview, Texas, before commencing graduate studies at the University of Chicago. During his studies at Chicago, Rice found his interest strongly directed toward preaching and leading souls to Christ. He subsequently completed about two-thirds of a seminary program at Southwestern Baptist Seminary in Fort Worth, Texas, leaving seminary because he urgently wanted to preach the gospel.

Rice planted and pastored churches on multiple occasions. He also became the editor of probably the most widely circulated fundamentalist weekly in the world. Through all of this activity, however, he identified himself as an evangelist and felt that his primary call was to preach the gospel and to lead souls to Jesus Christ.

Rice's ministry began in Southern Baptist circles. During the 1920s the teaching of evolution became an issue within the Baptist General Convention of Texas. Rice stood against it. His unwillingness to toe the line eroded his support among Southern Baptists. Rice heard about J. Frank Norris, who was battling the convention, and Rice found camaraderie in Norris's orbit.

As an evangelist, Rice would even go where no church would support him. During his early ministry he often preached in communities where the churches opposed evangelistic campaigns. Rice would just set up a big tent and begin to preach the gospel. Sometimes he even had to hold his meetings in the open air. Many people professed Christ, and when they did, Rice was left with a problem. He did not want to send converts into a church that had opposed the preaching of the gospel. Consequently, he would often organize his converts into a new church and then find a pastor for the fledgling congregation. This was the pattern that he followed in 1932 with a series of revivals in the

---

1. Three important biographies of Rice have been published. The oldest is Robert L. Sumner, *Man Sent from God* (Grand Rapids: Eerdmans, 1959; repr. Murfreesboro, TN: Sword of the Lord Publishers), which was written before Rice moved his ministry to Tennessee. Viola Walden, *John R. Rice: The Captain of Our Team* (Murfreesboro, TN: Sword of the Lord Publishers, 1990) was written by one of Rice's oldest coworkers. The newest is Andrew Himes, *The Sword of the Lord: The Roots of Fundamentalism in an American Family* (Seattle: Chiara Press, 2011). Himes is Rice's grandson and presents himself as the black sheep of the Rice family. He has written a biography that is a mixture of whimsy, criticism, and self-evaluation. A shorter biographical work is Fred M. Barlow, *Dr. John R. Rice: Giant of Evangelism* (Murfreesboro, TN: Sword of the Lord Publishers, 1983). Three unpublished dissertations deal with Rice: Howard Edgar Moore, "The Emergence of Moderate Fundamentalism: John R. Rice and the Sword of the Lord" (PhD diss., George Washington University, 1990); David Keith Bates Jr., "Moving Fundamentalism Toward the Mainstream: John R. Rice and the Reengagement of America's Religious and Political Cultures" (PhD diss., Kansas State University, 2006); Nathan A. Finn, "The Development of Baptist Fundamentalism in the South" (PhD diss., Southeastern Baptist Theological Seminary, 2007).

Oak Cliff neighborhood of Dallas. He set up his tent, preached his sermons, saw numbers of conversions, and organized the converts into the Fundamentalist Baptist Tabernacle. In this case, however, Rice himself became the pastor. By 1934 this church had grown until it registered nearly a thousand members on its rolls. Most of them had been converted directly under Rice's preaching. The church erected a building, which subsequently burnt to the ground. With a new building, the church also adopted a new name: Galilean Baptist Church.

Besides evangelistic campaigns and pastoral work, Rice's ministry was developing in other ways. He got his first taste of radio ministry, preaching daily over Norris's station in Fort Worth, then over other stations. He won a reputation as an able debater for his public disputations with W. L. Oliphant, minister of the Oak Cliff Church of Christ. Most importantly, in September 1934 he began publishing the weekly paper that would become his principal legacy— the *Sword of the Lord*. Originating as a little neighborhood paper in Dallas, the *Sword* soon expanded into a major periodical with national circulation.

Rice's preaching style during those years ran somewhere between confrontational and pugilistic. A sermon from the period, *What's Wrong with the Dance?*, illustrates the pulpit demeanor that Rice could adopt.

> I am telling you now, if God Almighty lets me live, later on you will not like me one-half as well as you do now! If God gives me grace, I am going to drive the dance out of the schools, and if God gives me power, in two or three or four years or five. I give you fair warning, you bunch of hens. . . . If anybody doesn't like that, you can swell up and burst as far as I am concerned. If anybody in this church doesn't like that kind of preaching, we will give you a check out any time you say. You can check out now. If I hear any complaint about it, I think I will preach again on it next Sunday night. I will say right now; under God, I don't have to have your help. Nobody pays you to come to hear me preach. As God is my witness, no man is my boss. This Bible and the Lord Jesus Christ decides what I am going to preach, and I am going to preach it![2]

This sermon was delivered at Galilean Baptist about 1935. By the 1940s Rice seems to have moderated his preaching style, at least in his published sermons. He used less posturing and hectoring, more pleading. As he grew older, Rice rarely preached without tears. To be fair, Rice probably borrowed his earlier style. It is one that some fundamentalists prefer. Some branches of fundamentalism have imitated this bullying pulpit manner, as have some nonfundamentalists. In certain circles it is viewed as a sine qua non of robust fundamentalism.

2. John R. Rice, *What's Wrong with the Dance?* (Grand Rapids: Zondervan, n.d. but c. 1935), 21–22.

Controversy with Norris

In 1936 John R. Rice and J. Frank Norris parted ways—and not amicably. According to Robert Sumner, trouble had been brewing for some time. Norris was using the *Fundamentalist* to attack other fundamentalist leaders. The breaking point came when Norris wrote an article against Sam Morris, a Southern Baptist pastor who was a close friend of Rice. Norris sent a copy of the article for Rice to proofread. Rice responded by telling Norris's secretary: "You tell Dr. Norris he must not publish that in THE FUNDAMENTALIST.... It is not true. It will do Sam great harm, and it would be wrong to print it."[3]

The article had already been typeset, but Norris withdrew it at Rice's insistence. He was far from pleased, however. He wrote to Rice, "No one can get anywhere in the North, East, or outside of Texas in this fundamentalist movement without the love and confidence of the First Baptist Church." Of course, the reference to First Baptist Church might as well have been a direct reference to Norris himself.[4]

Rather than cowing Rice, Norris's threat stiffened his attitude. Rice pointed out that he had stood with Norris because of their shared convictions. The two men had labored together in the cause of Christ and the Bible. Rice had never asked for compensation or promotion, and he never would. Rice then quoted Psalm 75:6 and 7, "For promotion cometh neither from the east, nor from the west, nor from the south. But God is the judge: he putteth down one, and setteth up another."[5]

If Rice thought that Norris was going to let the matter drop, he was about to learn better. Although he was a pastor, Rice was heavily involved in preaching evangelistic campaigns. He had scheduled one for January 1936 at Grace Baptist Church in Binghamton, New York. It was to be his first major campaign in a Northern city. Rice planned to take several days driving to Binghamton with his family and a stenographer. He was actually loading the car to leave when he received a telegram from Fred R. Hawley, the pastor at Binghamton. Hawley told Rice that the meeting was canceled.

In a flurry of telegrams, Rice learned that several men who claimed to be his friends had contacted Hawley, accusing him of straying into Pentecostalism. Dumbfounded, Rice took time to prepare a long letter denying the charges. He enclosed copies of pamphlets and articles in which he had dealt with speaking in tongues, divine healing, and related issues. He closed the letter by stating that he was starting out for Binghamton, that he would be

---

3. Sumner, *Man Sent from God*, 102; Walden, *Captain of Our Team*, 42–43.
4. Walden, *Captain of Our Team* 43.
5. Ibid.

unable to communicate until he arrived, but that he intended to conduct an evangelistic campaign in the city whether Hawley would have him or not.[6]

During the week that Rice was on the road, Hawley did his own investigation, partly by asking neighboring pastors what they knew about Rice. He found the charges against Rice to be completely false, and he greeted the evangelist quite literally with open arms. Not only that: the controversy had drawn interest from a number of other pastors from Binghamton. Once Rice was vindicated, they grew incensed at the slanders against him, and they threw their influence behind the campaign. The attendance quickly outgrew the church's auditorium, so the meetings were moved into a downtown theater. With a nightly attendance of around 1,600, the monthlong campaign eventually saw more than three hundred professions of faith.

Norris, however, refused to relent. While the Binghamton campaign was still going on, he published a telegram over his own signature in the *Fundamentalist*.

> It is with deepest personal sorrow that a sense of loyalty to the truth compels me to publish the platform of Holy Rollerism as advocated by Rice. For many years orthodox brethren have protested to me concerning his unscriptural teaching but I trusted him implicitly and further because of overwhelming duties I never read his writing or heard him except very little. But now have made a thorough review and found he advocated the platform of Pentecostalism or Holy Rollerism. Next week's *Fundamentalist* will give review of his unsound teaching on so-called Holy Spirit baptism. He takes hundred percent platform of Holy Rollerism.[7]

In this case, Norris was true to his word. The next week's *Fundamentalist* carried an article by Louis Entzminger purporting to describe the "Rice heresy." Other attacks followed. Rice, however, was able to show that Norris had previously known his real views and actually endorsed them in print. He also claimed that Norris was fabricating quotations to use against him. As events developed, Norris was unable to produce any documentation to back up his charges against Rice.[8]

Of course, lack of proof never stopped Norris. As the attacks continued, Rice used the pages of the *Sword* to respond in print. The contrast between his attitude and Norris's was marked: "I have personally, earnestly prayed that no harm would come to Dr. Norris or these other men who have followed his leadership in attacking me. They are good men." Rice excused Norris on the

---

6. Sumner, *Man Sent from God*, 103–04; Walden *Captain of Our Team*, 42–44.

7. J. Frank Norris to the *Fundamentalist*, January 23, 1936. Reproduced in Sumner, *Man Sent from God*, 105.

8. Sumner, *Man Sent from God*, 105–06.

grounds that his greater temptations grew out of his greater blessings. Furthermore, Rice encouraged his readers to continue to listen to what Norris said and to read what Norris wrote. He continued, "I pray that no friend he has loved and been true to will forsake him, falsely accuse him, try to block his revivals and assassinate his ministry. And may the dear Lord deal with him in just such tender mercy as all of us so sorely need."[9]

On the one hand, Rice's attitude toward Norris seems like a sterling example of Christian grace and charity. On the other hand, one wonders whether such apparent charity was actually the very thing that enabled Norris to continue his predatory behavior. Rice's grandson, Andrew Himes, offers this observation:

> Norris helped to launch John R. Rice's career as a prominent and influential fundamentalist leader, but their friendship could only last so long. In the end, Norris appeared to be much more concerned about his own ego and reputation than about "saving souls" or building the fundamentalist movement, and he felt threatened by Rice's growing influence and popularity among grassroots fundamentalists. It is striking to me that my granddad did not attack and expose Norris for his . . . many provocative and public lies. Instead, Rice made good use of Norris' endorsement and resources, and then split from him only when conflict with Norris became unavoidable.[10]

What if Norris had been held accountable in 1936? Might the attacks upon Ketcham, Fuller, Strathearn, and others have been avoided? Might the split of 1950 never have occurred? Remarkably, those whom Norris slandered did not often hold him accountable in public. Furthermore, some leaders within Norris's own crowd must have known of the slanders, yet they did little to oppose them. These men must be held responsible to some degree. Men like Vick, Dowell, Smith, and Zimmerman could grieve for their wounds at Norris's hands in 1950, but where was their protest when Norris was savaging others? By their own testimony they had seen what he was capable of doing, and they feared it. Did not their lack of action make them at least partly complicit in the evil that he did?

Northern Influence

Norris intended to hurt Rice, but his attacks turned out to be the very thing that opened doors for the evangelist in the North. For example, Norris's defamation was what solidified citywide support for Rice's Binghamton campaign.

9. Sumner, *Man Sent from God*, 112; Walden, *Captain of Our Team*, 44–45.
10. Himes, *The Sword of the Lord*, 211 (note).

The evident success of that campaign spread Rice's reputation throughout the North. It also gave Rice a taste of citywide evangelism and fired his longing for more.

The next years brought Rice an increasing number of Northern campaigns, and he began to develop friendships with a growing crowd of Northern pastors. In 1937 he received an honorary doctorate from Los Angeles Baptist Theological Seminary, an approved school of the GARBC. In September 1938 a GARBC church brought him to Waterloo, Iowa, to conduct a campaign. There he formed a close friendship with P. B. Chenault, the aggressive young pastor of Walnut Street Baptist Church.

Rice was still pastoring the Fundamentalist Baptist Tabernacle in Dallas. In October 1938, the church's building burned to the ground. The congregation moved into an unused church building about two miles away and then began construction of a new facility. Rice determined that he would not allow the church to languish during the time of transition. He invited Chenault to come down from Iowa to conduct revival meetings early in 1939. After a successful campaign, Chenault, his wife, and his infant daughter left for home following an evening service. Near McKinney, Texas, a drunk driver crossed into Chenault's lane, crowding Chenault off the road. Chenault was killed in the ensuing crash.

News of the death electrified Baptist fundamentalists throughout the nation. At thirty-five years of age, Chenault had been one of the rising stars of the Regular Baptist movement. His dramatic leadership in pulling the Walnut Street church out of the convention had captured the attention of fundamentalists everywhere.

John R. Rice accompanied Chenault's body to Waterloo, where he preached the funeral sermon. Both Robert T. Ketcham and Will H. Houghton (president of Moody Bible Institute, of which Chenault was an alumnus) also spoke. Nearly three thousand mourners jammed into the Walnut Street building. Mrs. Chenault was carried into the service on a hospital cot, which was placed in a screened-off area near the pulpit steps. As a duet sang, "God's Way Is the Best Way," her voice was heard joining the song.

When Rice concluded the funeral sermon, he offered a public invitation. About twenty-five people stood to profess faith in Christ. The church was so impressed with his ministry that he was asked to stay in Waterloo for revival meetings. He preached for the next thirteen nights, and the campaign yielded more than 150 decisions.[11]

These events had a profound effect upon Rice. He went home to finish

---

11. Walden, *The Captain of Our Team*, 48–50; Robert T. Ketcham, "P. B. Chenault—At Home with the Lord," *Baptist Bulletin*, May 1939, 2.

erecting the new building for the Fundamentalist Baptist Church, which now renamed itself Galilean Baptist Church. Rice's heart, however, was no longer in Dallas. He was an evangelist, and he saw the great cities of the North as a field ripe for evangelism. In January 1940 he resigned the pastorate of Galilean Baptist Church and relocated his ministry—including the *Sword of the Lord*—to Wheaton, Illinois.

Growing Influence

Wheaton was one of the capitals of fundamentalism in the United States. It was the location of Wheaton College, the most influential evangelical school of its day. It was home to many Christian workers, including professors from Moody Bible Institute. It was also a popular location for missionaries to retire. Wheaton would give Rice a base for expanding his influence throughout the North. He would stay there for the next twenty-three years.

Rice's influence grew rapidly. During 1940 he preached twenty-two meetings, all in Illinois, Indiana, and Michigan. In 1941 he formed an alliance with Theodore Epp that involved him in the ministry of the *Back to the Bible* radio broadcast. In 1942 he participated in a conference on evangelism at Bethany Reformed Church in Chicago. There he shared the platform with Oswald J. Smith, Harry A. Ironside, and other luminaries of interdenominational fundamentalism.

As the result of this conference, Rice deliberately committed himself to rejuvenating the practice of citywide revivals in the United States—a practice that had fallen into disfavor during Billy Sunday's later years. One of his first efforts was a union campaign in north Minneapolis during June and July 1943. The monthlong meeting was considered a success, and it is probably where Rice became acquainted with Richard V. Clearwaters, the new pastor of Fourth Baptist Church.

Also in 1943 Rice led in forming a Partnership of Evangelists to Promote Union Campaigns. The affiliating evangelists adopted a code of ethics and agreed to hold one another accountable for adherence to the code. The idea behind the organization was to bring churches of various denominations together for citywide evangelism and revival. During the next couple of years, Rice participated in successful campaigns in Everett, Washington; Buffalo, New York; and Cleveland, Ohio.

Not satisfied with these successes, Rice launched another new endeavor in 1945. Under the auspices of the *Sword of the Lord*, he sponsored a weeklong conference on evangelism, meeting in Winona Lake, Indiana. The conference met annually in Winona Lake for the next two years, then in Toronto, Los Angeles, and Chicago. Later these "Sword conferences" became a significant focal point for an entire branch of Baptist fundamentalism that paradoxically maintained an interdenominational flavor.

The *Sword of the Lord* reached five thousand paid subscriptions shortly after Rice moved to Wheaton. The list continued to grow year by year until it eventually numbered in six digits. The main articles were usually transcriptions of sermons. Rice also used the *Sword* to promote Bob Jones College (later University). Jones was a regular contributor to the *Sword*, while other institutions received scant attention. For example, Los Angeles Baptist Theological Seminary had given Rice an honorary doctorate, but received virtually no ongoing exposure in the *Sword*.

By the mid-1940s Rice was becoming at least a minor celebrity among Northern Baptist fundamentalists. He had shown that he would work with both Regular Baptists and convention fundamentalists. He had preached or participated in several important evangelistic campaigns. He was sponsoring a popular annual conference and publishing a growing paper, the *Sword of the Lord*. His influence was damaged, however, when he issued a series of public attacks against Lewis Sperry Chafer during the mid-to-late 1940s. Those attacks centered upon a book that Chafer had written years earlier.

Lewis Sperry Chafer and *True Evangelism*

Lewis Sperry Chafer was a prominent Bible teacher who became the founder of Dallas Theological Seminary, but he spent his early ministry in evangelism. He first worked with great evangelists such as J. Wilbur Chapman, then eventually conducted his own evangelistic campaigns. After about 1907 he left evangelism and came under the influence of prominent Bible teachers such as F. B. Meyer and especially C. I. Scofield. His perspective on his previous work began to change. Published in 1911 *True Evangelism* represented Chafer's rejection of many ideas he had once held and methods he had once practiced.[12]

By his own testimony, Chafer wrote *True Evangelism* to express his shift "away from emotional and superficial methods, which are too often thought to be the only possible expression of earnestness and enthusiasm in soul-winning, and toward an entire dependence upon the Spirit to do every phase of the work." He had come to the conclusion that not only the work of saving the lost, but also the work of seeking them, was a divine undertaking. He

---

12. Lewis Sperry Chafer, *True Evangelism* (New York: Gospel Publishing House, 1911); biographical information about Chafer can be found in John D. Hannah, *An Uncommon Union: Dallas Theological Seminary and American Evangelicalism* (Grand Rapids: Zondervan, 2009), 47–72.

believed that a failure to recognize the subordinate role of human effort in soul winning had led to a series of "false forces" in evangelism.[13]

Among these false forces was a wrong understanding of evangelists and their work. On Chafer's view, a biblical evangelist was not primarily an itinerant preacher who went about reviving established churches, but a "pioneer missionary to the hitherto unevangelized" who would "prepare the way for the pastor and teacher in his more constant ministry in the church." The modern itinerant evangelist or revivalist was "unexpected in Scripture," a merely human invention. The modern notion of revival operated on the assumption that Christians needed to recover spiritual ground that they had lost, like an awakening out of sleep. According to Chafer, however, Scripture assumed that the normal condition of believers would be "alertness and erectness."[14]

Consequently, what moderns called a "revival" was "abnormal rather than normal." While such an event could occasionally become necessary, Chafer thought that it had to be viewed as an emergency measure to return believers to their normal alertness. Once alerted, churches should not require ongoing revivals as a habit of life or a "sanctioned method of work." Normally, if a church seemed powerless and needed to be brought to a position of fruit-bearing, this restoration could be "accomplished only through a ministry of teaching and pastoral care." In other words, a spiritually lethargic congregation would be aroused through regular biblical exposition and ongoing shepherding.

Chafer granted that some individuals might be so gifted in this particular work that they could travel from church to church, working as temporary assistants alongside the resident pastor. If an awakening occurred, they could then "do the work of an evangelist" in leading souls to Christ, even though they did not hold the calling of an evangelist. While Chafer admitted that such a ministry was possible, however, he insisted that it constituted a confession of decadence on the part of the church. Such a congregation was so far gone that the Holy Spirit could not perform His normal work. Furthermore, seeking this kind of revival betrayed that the church's confidence was in the itinerant preacher rather than in the Holy Spirit.[15]

To accomplish a scriptural work, even this sort of itinerant preacher or evangelist (Chafer slipped back into the use of the term) would need to build a scriptural foundation for producing fruit that would abide. Building such a foundation required an extended time of pastoral instruction to the congregation. Modern evangelists, however, were motivated by a different set of concerns. The modern evangelist found that his "reputation, and often his

---

13. Chafer, *True Evangelism*, 3, 13–15.
14. Ibid., 15–18.
15. Ibid., 18–19.

remuneration, are dependent upon apparent results." The reason was because most churches were more interested in the number of decisions rather than their genuineness. The pressure to produce numbers of decisions created "a great temptation for the evangelist to be superficial in his aim and undertakings." Consequently, modern evangelists tended to place an undue emphasis upon methods that would secure the kind of results they wanted.[16]

While Chafer affirmed the usefulness of protracted meetings, he thought that they could be disastrous if relied upon as a major evangelistic method. The way that modern evangelists conducted their invitations was also problematic: to require a public demonstration (such as going forward or raising a hand) would confuse people about the biblical conditions of salvation. Chafer insisted that public confession ought to follow genuine conversion. It should never be permitted to look like a means of attaining salvation. The way that modern evangelists conducted their invitations left a false impression upon people who wanted to be saved. It also opened the possibility of false assurance for people who could end up trusting their public confession rather than trusting the gospel. Chafer was convinced that by appealing for public actions at the moment of conversion, such invitations had resulted in an appalling rate of backsliding among those who made professions.[17]

According to Chafer, these evangelistic appeals for public decisions also overlooked the Holy Spirit's work in preparing hearts to trust Christ. One practice to which Chafer particularly objected was sending workers into the audience during the invitation, expecting these workers to urge people to make public decisions. This and other attempts to embarrass people into public professions of faith were worse than useless. They were intrusive and they dishonored the Holy Spirit. "By adopting such a programme the evangelist or pastor is positively hindering the very work of God he is attempting to do."[18]

If they were so destructive, then why were such methods employed? Chafer believed he could pinpoint the reason. "Where the spectacular element in public soul-winning is eliminated there is little opportunity to count supposed results." In other words, the evangelist had to have something to show for his efforts, and the easiest way to achieve that goal was to count professions of faith. From Chafer's perspective, however, conversion should never by tested merely by profession of faith, but by the "reality of a changed life afterwards."[19]

Chafer also believed that modern evangelists had altered their message in order to achieve greater visible results. Rather than simply proclaiming the

16. Ibid., 19–21.
17. Ibid., 21–30.
18. Ibid., 30–32.
19. Ibid., 32.

gospel, they had become preachers of moral conduct and civic righteousness. Consequently, they ended up making an appeal that was not so much for re-generation as for reformation. Chafer objected that the unsaved did not need to hear exhortations concerning Christian living, forms of amusement, or church membership, as if these matters were somehow conditions of salvation. By inserting them into the presentation, modern evangelists almost unavoid-ably created confusion for lost people as to the real issue in salvation.[20]

Evangelists did further damage by relying upon the persuasive power of their own preaching rather than upon the persuasive power of the Holy Spirit. The Spirit's work was to take the message of the gospel and "to make the mean-ing of the Cross sufficiently clear to [the unsaved] person to enable him to abandon all hope of self-works, and to turn to the finished work of Christ alone in intelligent saving faith." For Chafer, this convicting ministry of the Holy Spirit was the only ground upon which the evangelist should make an appeal to the unsaved person. The skill of the evangelist consisted simply in "the ability to present the limited body of redemptive truth repeatedly, yet with freshness and variety." The evangelist was properly limited to the evangel itself as his message.[21]

Evangelists who departed from the simple gospel message faced the danger of trying to secure decisions through their own persuasive power. Chafer ad-mitted that superficial decisions could be produced easily and that apparently great results could be accomplished. The reason was simple, "for some minds are so dependent upon the opinions of others that the earnest dominating ap-peal of the evangelist, with the obvious value of a religious life, are sufficient to move them to follow almost any plan that is made to appear to be expedient." The problem was that people who responded to this sort of appeal would be acting only from the evangelist's conviction, for "they have received no suf-ficient vision for themselves." Such decisions did not meet the condition of "believing with the heart," and they accounted for the multitude of supposed converts who simply slipped back into their sins.[22]

Chafer admitted that some genuine conversions did occur along with the multitude of false professions, but these did not justify the use of the evange-lists' methods. The harm that was done far outweighed the good. Some few were saved, but many were left unapproachable and hopeless after their false conversions had dissolved. He granted that urging sinners to believe was not always wrong, but it ought to be done only when the Holy Spirit had clearly moved in the hearts of the unsaved.[23]

20. Ibid., 32–33.
21. Ibid., 33–34, 87–90.
22. Ibid., 93–94.
23. Ibid., 94–96.

John R. Rice and Moody Press

Although Chafer published *True Evangelism* in 1911, Rice did not read the work until the mid-1940s. He might never have read it except that Chafer wrote an editorial in October 1944 on "Salient Facts Regarding Evangelism" for Dallas Seminary's journal, *Bibliotheca Sacra*. At about the same time, Rice was opining that evangelists *as evangelists* "have a definite ministry to the saints of God." Rice wrote, "The way to have a revival, the way to get many lost sinners saved, is to reprove and rebuke and exhort God's people, according to the Scripture, until their sins are felt and abhorred, confessed and forsaken." This was the very approach to evangelism that Chafer had rejected.[24]

Chafer's editorial in *Bibliotheca Sacra* reiterated several points from *True Evangelism*. Chafer still insisted that the biblical evangelist of Ephesians 4:11 is a pioneer missionary who works in unevangelized fields. He stated that the "efforts of a high-powered specialist to revive a dead church have no Biblical recognition, especially when the church has the habit of sinking back at once into its former dead estate as soon as the revivalist's effort has ceased." He thought that modern evangelism had too often "given opportunity for self-promoting men to turn this work of God into a *racket* and a *graft*." The high-pressure tactics of modern evangelism had been born in Arminianism, he said, and were to be rejected by those who, like Chafer and Dallas Seminary, held a more Calvinistic soteriology. Faithful evangelists should rely upon the Holy Spirit and limit themselves to the gospel message, "with such clarifying declarations as to its acceptance as may be needed." Furthermore, the evangelist should "avoid giving the evil heart of man—ever prone to turn to useless works—something to *do* in order to be saved; he will rather give him Someone to *believe*."[25]

In light of this editorial, Rice began to read *True Evangelism*. He understood the book as an attack upon the entire earlier generation of evangelists. As it happened, these earlier evangelists—figures like R. A. Torrey, J. Wilbur Chapman, and Billy Sunday—were the very individuals upon whom Rice was trying to pattern his own ministry. They were his heroes. Viewing Chafer's work as an assault upon them, he could hardly take it kindly. He also became alarmed that Moody Press was now republishing the book.

Rice wanted to put the book out of circulation. He wrote a long letter to Don Norman, director of Moody Press, in which he urged Norman to

24. John R. Rice, *The Ruin of a Christian* (Wheaton, IL: Sword of the Lord Publishers, 1944), 3.
25. Lewis Sperry Chafer, "Salient Facts Regarding Evangelism, *Bibliotheca Sacra* 101 (October 1944), 384–388.

withdraw *True Evangelism* from publication. In the process, he responded to several of Chafer's arguments.

First, Rice noted that Chafer objected to modern evangelists on the grounds of the large numbers of superficial decisions that were supposed to result from their work. He replied that this objection was "primarily the argument of unbelievers, wicked people who have fought revivals down through the years." He charged that Chafer had joined "the wicked unbelievers and Christ-rejectors in accusing mass evangelism of superficial results and doing more harm than good." Rice added, "I think it is very sad that a preacher should help spread the attacks of the infidels and modernists, and that Moody Press should print it and circulate it."[26]

Rice also objected to Chafer's insistence that a revival is abnormal rather than normal. He indignantly noted that Chafer "does not sanction revivals as a method of work in churches." Rather than arguing against Chafer's view, Rice simply noted that it was unpopular. Chafer might not want revivals, but "D. L. Moody and R. A. Torrey did. Dr. J. Wilbur Chapman did. So did all the men who founded the Moody Bible Institute. So did B. H. Carroll, who founded Southwestern Baptist Seminary, and Dr. L. R. Scarborough, who was used of God to triumphantly carry on that work. So do Bible believers generally think that evangelistic campaigns in churches are normal."[27]

Since he envisioned himself as an evangelist, Rice was particularly stung by Chafer's suggestion that biblical evangelists were primarily pioneer missionaries. At this point, Rice did not even attempt to reply to Chafer. He simply repeated Chafer's position as if the expression of Chafer's ideas constituted an indictment against him. "[Chafer] is in favor of diminishing the influence of evangelists, of not having evangelistic campaigns in churches save in the time of direst needs, and never to have big, co-operative revival campaigns like those so familiar in the day when the book was written."[28]

Rice further dismissed Chafer's opinion that the evangelist should limit himself to preaching the message of the gospel. Rice responded that the great evangelists such as Moody, Torrey, and Sunday had never restricted their message in this way. Neither had the "evangelist Paul," who preached to Felix of righteousness, temperance, and judgment to come. Paul and other "Bible evangelists" did far more than simply to preach the gospel. Indeed, arguing from the order of gifts in Ephesians 4:11 and 12, Rice insisted that Scripture assigns the evangelist an office next to that of apostle and prophet, and higher than the position of pastor and teacher. Furthermore, the ministry of the

---

26. John R. Rice to Don Norman, December 16, 1944; reprinted in John R. Rice, "A Hurtful, Unscriptural Attack on Evangelism and Evangelists," *Sword of the Lord*, June 21, 1946, 5.
27. Ibid.
28. Ibid., 6.

evangelist could not be restricted to the unsaved, for evangelists were given for "the perfecting of the saints, for the work of the ministry, for the edifying of the body of Christ." Consequently, Rice argued, Chafer's view was "dangerously unscriptural and does tremendous harm."[29]

Also scandalous was Chafer's rejection of the public invitation. Rice dismissed Chafer's concern that the invitation confused the lost. He noted, "Very rarely in dealing with thousands of lost sinners have I ever found one who thought that going forward had anything to do with salvation except to claim it after he had already decided for Christ in his heart." Rice noted that the custom of giving a public invitation was widespread within American evangelicalism. He stated that he used it himself, for the benefit of both the convert and others. "Often, the Holy Spirit will not make His presence much felt until public confession has been made. Public confession greatly honors God. It rejoices the hearts of believers. It has a great effect on unbelievers. It strengthens and safeguards the new convert."[30]

Rice closed his letter with a direct appeal for Norman and Moody Press to pull Chafer's book from publication.

> I think the book ought to be taken off the market completely. I think it does tremendous harm. I know it irritates and alienates evangelists who ought to be friends of Moody Bible Institute and Moody Press. I know it is a constant thorn in the flesh of great evangelistic groups. . . . Unfortunately, among the large group of independent fundamental churches and preachers, Dr. Chafer's influence on this matter has been large, and hundreds of pastors in little unsuccessful churches that rarely ever win a soul struggle along trying to win souls but suspicious of mass evangelism and evangelists. I hope you and other good men at Moody in whom I have great confidence will move to stop this hurtful influence and take the book off the market.[31]

Norman did not remove the book from publication, but (with Rice's permission) he did send a copy of Rice's letter to Chafer. According to Robert L. Sumner, an attempt was made to get Chafer to rewrite the book. By now, however, Chafer was well up into his seventies, and his views were set. According to Sumner, he sent a letter to Rice in which he stated that, if he were to rewrite the book, it would be even more strongly worded than the original.[32]

Rice would not let the matter drop. He used his influence to recruit others to apply pressure to Moody Press. John Brown, founder of John Brown University, joined him in protesting Chafer's Calvinism. W. B. Riley walked out

---

29. Ibid.
30. Ibid.
31. Ibid., 7.
32. Sumner, *Man Sent from God*, 196.

of a meeting in which Chafer was speaking. When the Sword conference met at Winona Lake in 1945, more than forty leaders—mostly evangelists—put their names to a resolution moved by Bob Jones Sr., pressuring Moody Press to withdraw the book.[33]

Don Norman and Moody Press stood fast and refused to censor Chafer's work. Rice's next move was to write directly to Will H. Houghton, president of Moody Bible Institute. In his letter he reiterated the same complaints that he had already made to Norman about *True Evangelism*. The letter makes it clear that Rice was far from resigned—if anything, his language was even less temperate than when he had written to Norman. He accused Chafer of "unholy slander against D. L. Moody and R. A. Torrey and every good evangelist in the world widely known as a soul winner." He noted that the book sold only a few hundred copies each year, and commented, "I can understand that. It is so amateurish, so naïve, so obviously impractical, that very few people could hope to be helped in soul-winning by it." Rice suggested that the unpopularity of the book was enough reason to withdraw it from publication.[34]

Rice attempted to emphasize the damage that Chafer's book was doing: "The few thousand copies that have been distributed have done enormous harm. . . . The results have been disastrous in hundreds of cases." Yet Rice also argued, "I cannot find a single prominent fundamental Christian leader in America outside of Dr. Chafer himself who believes the doctrines and principles laid down in this book. Not one man rises to defend it." Rice did not explain how such severe damage could occur in hundreds of cases when not one man was willing to defend Chafer's ideas.[35]

Also contained within Rice's letter was a clear threat. The evangelist repeatedly emphasized how reasonable he had been with Moody Press. That, however, was about to change.

> Now I feel that unless you and Moody Institute can be prevailed upon to stop the promotion and sale and distribution of this misleading and hurtful book of false doctrine and attack on evangelists and evangelism, I will have no recourse but to take the matter to the public and warn people everywhere about this book, and, as far as I am able to do so, stop its circulation among and support by Bible believers.[36]

Rice emphasized that the best solution would be if the book were quietly

---

33. Ibid., 191–95. Sumner reproduces the text of the resolution along with the names of the forty-one evangelists who signed it. He omits the names of the six non-evangelists whose signatures appeared.

34. John R. Rice to Will H. Houghton, February 6, 1946; reprinted in John R. Rice, "Moody Institute Reprints Book Attacking Evangelists," *Sword of the Lord*, October 25, 1946, 4.

35. Ibid.

36. Ibid.

withdrawn and all stocks destroyed. If Houghton refused to burn the books, however, "then I believe the leading Christians in America can be led to repudiate it."[37]

When Houghton kept the book on the market, Rice was true to his word. In June 1946 he used the *Sword of the Lord* to print his original letter to Norman, along with a number of editorial comments. He told the public that *True Evangelism* was a "direct attack," not upon the excesses of some evangelists, but upon "evangelism itself, as known and practiced in America by the greatest soul-winners." He hinted at the possibility that he might later publish the Winona Lake petition, as well as his correspondence with Houghton. He expressed hope that when the publishers knew "the feeling of soul-winning Christians all over America, . . . they will withdraw the book from circulation." In case anyone doubted Rice's perspective, he closed his editorial by stating, "We cannot expect anything else but that modernists, atheists, communists and false cults will be against Bible evangelism, but we feel that no evangelical Christian should join those enemies of Christianity in opposing the office and work of God-called and anointed and proven evangelists."[38]

This editorial was a bald appeal for the readers of the *Sword* to pressure Moody Press and to silence Chafer. Rice wanted Chafer's book out of the hands of the public, and he was perfectly willing to engineer public pressure to get Moody Press to withdraw it. He repeated this public appeal more explicitly a couple of months later. While asking for Christian charity, he said, "Write to officials of Moody Institute, or Moody Press, if you feel you should, and ask them to withdraw Dr. Chafer's book, "True Evangelism," from publication, for Jesus' sake. . . . I hope you feel like helping to encourage the withdrawal of the book, which certainly hinders evangelism, discourages personal work, teaches there should be no public invitation to accept and confess Christ openly."[39]

The alternative of simple, charitable disagreement seems never to have occurred to Rice. From the very beginning of the conflict, he positioned himself as the aggressor. His primary wish was not to respond to Chafer's book, but to suppress it. He did not want the Christian public to be able to encounter Chafer's views, let alone to consider them as a possible alternative to his own. He wanted Chafer silenced.

So far the Moody administration had not responded to pressure. Rice wondered whether they might respond to money. He wrote to R. L. Constable of Moody Press, offering to purchase the entire inventory of *True Evangelism*

37. Ibid.

38. Rice, "A Hurtful Attack," 5.

39. John R. Rice, "Christian Leaders Join Sword In Defending Evangelism," *Sword of the Lord*, September 6, 1946, 8.

at cost, together with the printing plates, if Moody Press would agree in writing not to publish the work again. Ironically, however, Rice's opposition to the book had become its best advertisement, and sales had risen sharply. Constable informed Rice that he could purchase as many copies as he liked at wholesale prices, but that the book was not going to be withdrawn. Perhaps adding insult to injury, Constable suggested that if Rice were to create less controversy, perhaps demand for the book would decline to the point that "economic consideration would mitigate against its publication."[40]

Rice replied in a sharp letter accusing Constable of adopting a policy that was "arrogant and arbitrary." He was irked that money was the deciding factor (though Rice himself had offered money to purchase the remaining stock). He jibed, "Moody could also make money out of publishing other kinds of heresy." As far as Rice was concerned, the result was going to be a "definite division" between those who believed in evangelism and those who did not. "Of course I find it my duty to defend evangelists and evangelism. If you continue to sell the book, we evangelists will have to continue to warn against it." For Rice, the "attack on evangelists" was now the "official position of Moody Bible Institute."[41]

The Ongoing Controversy

Throughout most of the controversy, Chafer offered no public reply to Rice's attacks. In October 1946 he did publish a short editorial about "Modern Evangelism." He never referred to Rice or the controversy, but the editorial was clearly motivated by Rice's insistence that public invitatiıons were necessary. Chafer believed that the preacher should simply give the Word of God and then depend upon the Holy Spirit to apply it "apart from all public requirements or actions."[42]

Also in October, Rice raised the stakes in the controversy. He devoted nearly half an issue of the *Sword* to presenting his side of the story. He published the resolution that had been adopted in 1945 at the Sword conference in Winona Lake. He printed his correspondence with Will H. Houghton. He included his letters to and from R. L. Constable. While Rice's supporters saw

---

40. John R. Rice to R. L. Constable, August 17, 1946; R. L. Constable to John R. Rice, October 15, 1946; both reprinted in John R. Rice, "Moody Institute Reprints Book Attacking Evangelists," 5.

41. John R. Rice to R. L. Constable October 15, 1946; reprinted in John R. Rice, "Moody Institute Reprints Book Attacking Evangelists," 5.

42. Lewis Sperry Chafer, "Modern Evangelism," *Bibliotheca Sacra* 103 (October 1946), 385-386.

him as a charitable man who had been pushed to extremes, the publication of these letters came across as a declaration of war.[43]

Rice struck again in December 1946. He printed a three-part defense of evangelists that singled out Chafer for special criticism. As his defense of evangelists turned into an attack upon Chafer, he made statements that many fundamentalists must have found extreme or even alarming.

In the first editorial Rice discussed the office of evangelist in relationship to other church offices. During that discussion he focused briefly on the office of prophet. He defined prophets as those who received special divine revelation, adding, "There is no statement in the Bible that God has withdrawn the gift of prophecy. A backslidden church has few evidences of the ministry of prophecy." Rice also argued that evangelists were more important than pastors and teachers. Furthermore, Rice began to refer to Chafer's position as "ultra-dispensationalism," a label that had previously been reserved for those who distinguished a dispensation that began with Paul from the dispensation of the earlier apostles.[44]

In his second attack article, Rice attempted to vindicate the contributions evangelists had made. Against Chafer, he asserted that evangelists had been leaders in the pursuit of civic righteousness and moral reform. He retold the history of the evangelists' social involvement from Whitefield and the Wesleys through Billy Sunday. Rice also emphasized the role of evangelists in education, Christian literature, and Christian hymnody. Rice further argued that the vast majority of conversions occurred in evangelistic meetings. Consequently, "The churches in America will die when they kill evangelism. And they ought to die for when they kill evangelism they have forsaken New Testament Christianity and become apostate and unchristian."[45] Rice was not talking about personal soul-winning, but about the public activity directed by professional evangelists.

In the third article, Rice tried to deliver evangelists from the accusation of extremism. He admitted that some evangelists really were extremists, just as some pastors were. He insisted, however, that evangelists were attacked far more often for being right than for being wrong. Then Rice again turned his attention toward Chafer, charging that *True Evangelism* was "bitter and unreasoning." He accused Chafer of rejecting evangelists because evangelism required a special enduement from the Holy Spirit that Rice identified as the baptism in the Holy Spirit. He stated that ultra-dispensationalists (such as

---

43. John R. Rice, "Moody Institute Reprints Book Attacking Evangelists," 1-5.

44. John R. Rice, "Evangelists—Their God-Given Position and Influence in the Church," *Sword of the Lord*, December 6, 1946, 1, 3-5.

45. John R. Rice, "The Contribution of Evangelists to Christianity," *Sword of the Lord*, December 13, 1946, 1, 4-5.

Chafer) balked at this theory of Holy Spirit baptism. Therefore, ultra-dispensationalism was at the root of Chafer's error, as was hyper-Calvinism (Rice's label for four-point Calvinism). Perhaps most pernicious of all, however, was the fact that "men who are themselves unsuccessful as soul winners are often jealous of evangelism."[46]

As Rice hammered Chafer, he also attempted to rebuild his fractured relationship with Moody Bible Institute. The school sent copy for an advertisement to be run in the *Sword of the Lord*. One line in the ad mentioned Chafer's *True Evangelism*. Rice rejected the ad, instead running an article about Moody Bible Institute. He said, "We could not run the ad with an endorsement of this book which, we believe, is unscriptural and harmful, and could not have that line taken out." Then Rice added, "One wrong book published does not make the school bad and we trust that Moody Institute will yet get rid of the bad book." Throughout the article, Rice tried to make it clear that he supported Moody except for the dispute over *True Evangelism*. His article actually reproduced most of the text that would have appeared in Moody's ad.[47]

Though he was trying to befriend Moody again, Rice followed his three-article series with another attack upon Chafer. He was particularly irritated by Chafer's comment that high pressure evangelism gave self-promoting men the opportunity "to turn this work of God into a *racket* and a *graft*." Rice, whose attitude toward money was genuinely sacrificial, took these words personally. He spent nearly three pages in the *Sword of the Lord* in "A Defense of Reputable Evangelists Against a Heartbreaking Slander." Rice read Chafer in the most extreme possible terms, as if the Dallas theologian were accusing all evangelists of what Rice called "money grubbing." In response to Chafer, Rice intoned, "To break down the influence of evangelists, to accuse them, to allow suspicion against them is a wicked sin that God Himself must surely punish."[48]

By this point Rice's assault upon Chafer had become quite personal. As far as Rice was concerned, Chafer was jealous. He was guilty of a wicked sin. God would surely punish him. Rice's long-time associate and biographer, Viola Walden, quotes Rice as saying that Chafer was "so largely influenced by John Nelson Darby that he was a hyper-Calvinist and an ultra-dispensationalist, and this viewpoint made it impossible to have much success as a soul winner. Under his leadership, the [Scofield Memorial] church dried up, few souls were saved, and pressure compelled him to surrender the pastorate." She also

---

46. John R. Rice, "Evangelists and the Reproach of Christ," *Sword of the Lord*, December 27, 1946, 1-4.

47. John R. Rice, "Moody Bible Institute and Evangelism," *Sword of the Lord*, December 13, 1936, 6.

48. Chafer, "Salient Facts Regarding Evangelism," 385; John R. Rice, "Money-Grubbing Evangelists," *Sword of the Lord*, January 3, 1947, 2-4.

quotes Rice as feeling strongly that "the curse of God is on this book [*True Evangelism*]." [49]

Rice had badly overestimated his own strength. He was probably right that few fundamentalists agreed completely with Chafer. By early 1947, however, he had begun pounding Chafer almost weekly, and readers were getting tired of it. While he continued to speak cordially of Moody Bible Institute, the language that he used toward Chafer was far from reasonable. He was also beginning to express views of his own that, by mainstream fundamentalist standards, were pretty extreme. His allowance for present-day prophecy and for a post-conversion baptism in the Spirit would startle most dispensationalists, as would his references to Chafer as an ultra- or hyper-dispensationalist (he used both terms). Furthermore, though Chafer was certainly a moderate Calvinist, the label *hyper-Calvinist* was entirely unwarranted. Simple fair-mindedness alienated some of Rice's readers.

Among them was Harry A. Ironside, pastor of Moody Church in Chicago. Ironside knew Rice well. The two men had worked together and Ironside had Rice's respect. Rice had published Ironside's sermons in the *Sword*. Throughout his conflict with Chafer, Rice had named Ironside as an example of the kind of evangelist that he thought Chafer was rejecting. What Rice had not reckoned upon, however, was that Ironside was a strong dispensationalist. He was pointedly anti-Pentecostal and had written a book that was critical of Holiness theology. Rice's concessions about ongoing prophecy and about a post-conversion baptism in the Spirit alarmed him. Speaking of Holy Spirit baptism, Ironside had written that "individual believers no longer wait for the promise of the Father, expecting a new descent of the Spirit."[50] Rice directly contradicted this position. Furthermore, Ironside was a personal friend of Lewis Sperry Chafer.

Sometime in early 1947 Ironside finally concluded that the controversy was damaging the cause of fundamentalism. He wrote an opinion piece for the May edition of the *Moody Church News*. While the article did not name any names, it was a sustained rebuke against those who were attacking Chafer, and against Rice in particular.

Ironside insisted that *True Evangelism* was not a critique of evangelists like Moody, Torrey, and Chapman. In fact, he claimed that Torrey, Chapman, and the British evangelist Henry Varley had all read the manuscript and approved the work. Ironside noted that many had accused *True Evangelism* of being a bad book. He asked, "In what does its badness consist?" Then he answered his own question:

49. Walden, *The Captain of Our Team*, 86 (footnotes).
50. Harry A. Ironside, *Holiness the False and the True* (New York: Bible Truth Press, 1912), 96–97.

Simply this: it shows the folly of pressing men to make professions of salvation who give no evidence of a work of the Spirit of God in their souls. It points out the evil of trying to count up large numbers of converts rather than of looking to God to work in the power of the Holy Ghost in bringing people to see their need of Christ and trusting Him as their own Savior. The present writer read this 'bad book' over thirty years ago and has been working in accordance with the principles it lays down ever since. We recommend it unqualifiedly as one of the best books on clear-cut, sane, Scriptural evangelism ever published.[51]

Encouraged by Ironside's support, Chafer offered his own brief defense in *Bibliotheca Sacra*. Besides reprinting Ironside's remarks, he reviewed the history of the book's publication, then addressed the controversy directly: "Whatever evangelists of the present day are contending for in attacking this volume, just by reason of the attack *True Evangelism* is injuring their cause more than they can possibly realize. If their methods are clean and their motives pure, let them demonstrate this by the work they do." Probably thinking of Charles Fuller's *Old Fashioned Revival Hour*, he noted that the momentum for evangelism had shifted away from crusading evangelists and toward radio evangelism. He was not sure whether evangelistic campaigns could be restored, but noted that "evangelists can easily become the main hindrance to restoring such a work." This statement was most likely an oblique reference to Rice.[52]

Ironside's unqualified endorsement of *True Evangelism* seems to have solidified resistance against Rice. Hannah reports that Ironside actually broke fellowship with Rice over the issue. After the 1947 Sword Conference (held shortly after Ironside's editorial was published), the Winona Lake conference ground refused to permit Rice to use its facilities again. Rice and his evangelists were forced to go elsewhere.[53]

John R. Rice and *The Power of Pentecost*

By late 1947 the current of fundamentalist opinion was running decidedly in favor of Chafer. Rice, however, was unwilling to concede defeat. He wrote a book-length defense of his views, published in 1949 as *The Power of Pentecost*. This volume was meant to be a sustained argument against the position of Scofield and Chafer, whom Rice still insisted upon labeling ultra-dispensationalists. At its heart, the book attempted to prove just two ideas.

The first was that Pentecost was neither the beginning of the church nor an unrepeatable event. Instead, Rice took Pentecost as a model for revival. As

51. Quoted by Lewis Sperry Chafer in "An Attack Upon a Book," *Bibliotheca Sacra* 104 (April 1947), 132–134.

52. Lewis Sperry Chafer, "An Attack Upon a Book," 130–132.

53. Hannah, *An Uncommon Union*, 128; Sumner, *Man Sent from God*, 177.

Rice understood it, the church began, not with Pentecost, but with the first believer. Consequently, Pentecost must have a different significance. Rice believed that Pentecost was a clear instance of God pouring out His power upon those who wished to do His will in soul winning. God had promised such an outpouring in Joel 2, and that promise was fulfilled in Acts 2. Consequently, "Pentecost was the first time Christianity got a strong foothold on this earth." Rice insisted that this outpouring of divine power, with its subsequent evangelistic success, could and should be reproduced in the church of his day.[54]

The other point that Rice tried to prove was that the baptism in the Holy Spirit was an anointing or filling of the Holy Spirit, an enduement with power from on high for the purpose of power in evangelism. It was not equivalent to the baptism *by* the Spirit into the Body of Christ in 1 Corinthians 12:13, but it was what the apostles experienced on the Day of Pentecost. To be truly effective in evangelism, this baptism in, or anointing with, the Spirit was absolutely essential. Furthermore, it was not a ministry of the Spirit that every believer received. Normally, God granted it only to those who yearned for it, pleaded for it, waited for it, and patiently obeyed God by soul-winning while waiting.[55]

Rice also emphasized that the baptism in the Spirit—the special anointing or enduement for evangelism—was distinct from other operations of the Holy Spirit in the believer's life. It was not the same thing as the indwelling of the Spirit. It was not the same thing as growth in Christian grace. It was not the same thing as sanctification.[56]

While Rice objected strongly to the idea that speaking in tongues was a necessary evidence of baptism in the Holy Spirit, he did not rule it out entirely. Addressing the miraculous gifts, he said that "God may see fit to give any of these gifts to his people today." More than tongues, "it would be perfectly proper, therefore, for every Christian to seek to prophesy." Indeed, Rice insisted that miraculous events had occurred in connection with the ministries of such Christian notables as R. A. Torrey, Jonathan Goforth, and J. Hudson Taylor. He even claimed that miracles had been wrought in connection with his own ministry.[57]

For Rice, anyone who rejected these views was guilty, not simply of an error, but of infidelity. This kind of infidelity would fail to reproduce the "life and power and fruitfulness of New Testament Christianity." He compared people like Chafer to those infidels who rejected New Testament doctrines

54. John R. Rice, *The Power of Pentecost or the Fullness of the Spirit* (Wheaton, IL: Sword of the Lord Publications, 1949), 77–82.

55. Ibid., 123–72, 293–390, 413–31.

56. Ibid., 113–17, 286, 372–74.

57. Ibid., 248–50; 182–83, 188.

such as "the authority of the Bible, the deity of Christ, and salvation by the blood." These two forms of infidelity were "not far apart in wickedness."[58]

Thinking of dispensationalists such as Chafer—those who affirmed the uniqueness of Pentecost and denied that the baptism in the Spirit was a post-conversion experience—Rice wrote,

> A revulsion of feeling took place among leaders of Christian thought and it became popular to explain away Pentecost. Pentecost was the technical beginning of a new dispensation, people said. Pentecost could never be repeated. It was simply the origin of the Christian church. All of us were already baptized in the Holy Spirit, at least potentially, and therefore we did not need to have more. . . . Since Pentecost, said these worldly-wise Bible teachers, that was never in order. The teachings of Darby were substituted for the great doctrinal position of D. L. Moody and R. A. Torrey. . . . Oh, the dearth, the famine, the spiritual wilderness, the powerlessness resulting from this retreat from the clear Bible teaching of the power of the Holy Spirit![59]

According to Rice, neglect of Holy Spirit enduement was responsible for the decline in revival, the growth of modernism and formalism, and the worldliness of church members. Where Holy Spirit enduement was insufficiently emphasized, Christians would drift toward worldliness and away from soul winning. They would magnify abstract Bible teaching at the expense of evangelism. They would seek to please people rather than to arouse and convict them. These negative effects were the responsibility of the ultra-dispensationalism represented by *True Evangelism*.[60]

The difference between Chafer and Rice was not simply over the office of evangelist, much less the aberrant use of that office. They disagreed about the origin of the church, the function of Pentecost, the appropriate way to appeal to the lost, and the continuation of miraculous gifts. Most of all, they fundamentally disagreed about the nature of the Christian life. For Chafer, the normal (as opposed to the average) Christian life was ideally a matter of steady growth, facilitated by the careful teaching of Scripture. For Rice, the normal Christian life was one in which inevitable worldliness and spiritual decline had to be interrupted periodically by a revivalistic shock.

Different understandings of the Christian life led to dramatically different visions of Christian leadership. For Chafer, Christian leadership primarily involved the exposition of the Scriptures. For Rice, Christian leadership required a special, post-conversion work of the Spirit that enabled the leader to administer the right kind of revivalistic shock. For Chafer, a revival was

58. Ibid., 24.
59. Ibid., 88–89.
60. Ibid., 152.

an abnormal event, needed only under unusual circumstances. For Rice, a revival was the standard way of doing business.

Throughout the controversy, Chafer remained largely silent. Just as the controversy was beginning, he lost his wife to a protracted illness. He himself passed through a crisis of health in 1945, resulting in John Walvoord taking the presidency of Dallas Theological Seminary. Throughout the crisis, Walvoord attempted to shelter Chafer from even knowing about Rice's attacks. He also encouraged Chafer not to respond. To Chafer, Walvoord wrote, "It is utterly useless to attempt to reason with a man like John R. Rice and I consider it a waste of time." Walvoord had already said privately that "I do not believe it is possible to instruct [Rice] on the points of the issue and it would only arouse him to further steps." Chafer employed his remaining strength to work on his *Systematic Theology*, which he completed in 1947. Thereafter he was incrementally incapacitated by a series of small strokes. He died within two days of J. Frank Norris in 1952.[61]

Aftermath

John R. Rice had moved his ministry from Dallas to Wheaton in order to gain a larger following in the North. His hearing among fundamentalists did grow, but primarily in the South and among Southern transplants (of which Northern industrial centers had many). He developed some allies in the North, but few of them had actually started out as Northern Baptists.

In particular, Rice never exactly overwhelmed the GARBC. Probably his controversy with Chafer helps to explain why. During those years, the most important Regular Baptist training institution was the Baptist Bible Seminary of Johnson City, New York. The views of the Johnson City faculty—and of the mainstream of the GARBC—are fairly represented by the school's cofounder and dean, Emery H. Bancroft.

Bancroft taught that God had elected certain individuals to salvation. Their election was not conditioned by divine foresight of any human merit or moral action, either before or after regeneration. In other words, Bancroft affirmed that election was the cause of faith rather than vice versa. Bancroft's articulation of these teachings matched the definition of the Calvinistic doctrine of unconditional election.[62]

Furthermore, Bancroft taught that, in addition to God's general call for all

61. John F. Walvoord to Lewis Sperry Chafer, July 2, 1946; reprinted in Hannah, *An Uncommon Union*, 132; John F. Walvoord to Ernest L. Hoover, December 5, 1945, 336n183. Norris died on August 20, Chafer on August 22.

62. Emery H. Bancroft, *Elemental Theology*, 3rd ed. (Grand Rapids: Zondervan, 1960), 72–73; Emery H. Bancroft, *Christian Theology: Systematic and Biblical* 2nd rev. ed. (Grand Rapids: Zondervan, 1976), 237–41.

humans to repent and be saved, the Holy Spirit also issued a special call to the elect. This special calling was efficacious because it communicated a new spiritual life and nature, making a "new mode of spiritual activity possible and desirable." This special calling effectually brought the elect to repentance and faith in Christ. Bancroft's articulation of these teachings matched the definition of the Calvinistic doctrine of irresistible grace.[63]

In other words, Bancroft was a moderate Calvinist. His sympathies in this area were fully in keeping with those of Lewis Sperry Chafer. This moderately Calvinistic soteriology was just what John R. Rice dismissed as hyper-Calvinism.

Bancroft was not only a moderate Calvinist, he was also a dispensationalist. He believed that the church consists of regenerate believers during the present age, that is, between the two advents of Christ. Specifically, the church began on the Day of Pentecost and would end with the Rapture. Bancroft wrote, "On the Day of Pentecost, the Spirit was made manifest on the earth as the witness of the risen, ascended Christ; then and there the Lord baptized the disciples in the Spirit, into the body in which and through which He was henceforth to manifest Himself on the earth (1 Cor. 12:13)." In the debate over the meaning of Pentecost, Bancroft clearly disagreed with Rice.[64]

Furthermore, Bancroft affirmed that Holy Spirit baptism occurred for all believers at their conversion. This baptism made each believer a member of the Body of Christ. Bancroft insisted that this ministry of the Spirit began at Pentecost, though it was also an ongoing work that the Spirit performs for each believer. Since the baptizing work of the Spirit takes place for each believer at regeneration, it must not be sought as an experience after regeneration. In other words, Bancroft directly rejected Rice's teaching about a post-conversion baptism in the Holy Spirit that communicated a special endurement for evangelism.[65]

While the two men articulated their ideas a bit differently, Bancroft's dispensationalism was hardly distinguishable from Chafer's. Both men saw Pentecost as the birthday of the church and as an unrepeatable event. Both taught that the Holy Spirit's baptism was simply His work in joining individual believers to the Body of Christ. Neither admitted the possibility of a post-conversion baptism of the Spirit. In short, both held the position that Rice insisted upon calling ultra-dispensationalism.

Bancroft's views reflected the education that he had received at Moody Bible Institute. Many other Regular Baptists had also been trained in these views, and Bancroft himself trained a whole generation more. Bancroft's theology represents the center and mainstream of Regular Baptist thought.

---

63. Bancroft, *Elemental Theology*, 73–76; Bancroft, *Christian Theology*, 241–42.
64. Bancroft, *Elemental Theology*, 238; Bancroft, *Christian Theology*, 289, 291.
65. Bancroft, *Elemental Theology*, 165–66; Bancroft, *Christian Theology*, 169–70, 261.

Consequently, Rice's attack on Chafer had to be taken as an implicit (if un-intentional) attack upon most Regular Baptist pastors. The longer Rice pro-longed the attack and the more strident his tone became, the less comfortable many Regular Baptists would feel with him.

While Ironside responded directly to Rice's attacks, most Northern fun-damentalists—including Regular Baptists—simply ignored them. Perhaps because the feud with Norris was a very recent memory, no one seemed eager to argue with Rice. Yet his influence among Northern fundamentalists, and especially among Regular Baptists, plummeted after this point. Exceptions did exist, such as Robert Sumner, who was Rice's biographer and a member of the GARBC Council of Fourteen. Not many Regular Baptists, however, tried to maintain substantial links with Rice.

Rice's views would lead to yet further division. After fifteen years as a mem-ber of Wheaton Bible Church, Rice left in 1955 to establish Calvary Baptist Church in Wheaton. Ostensibly, the reason was the older church's decision to stop conducting public baptisms. Yet Rice chose not to affiliate with any of the existing churches in the area—including any Regular Baptist church. This choice amounted to a tacit admission that the differences were too great for happy fellowship at close quarters.[66]

Rice continued to dwell on the issues that had led to his attack upon Chafer. Two examples of his writing, chosen almost randomly, will serve to illustrate Rice's commitment to these ideas. The first comes from a 1961 book on personal soul winning. In a chapter titled "Power from On High," Rice reiterated his objection to the dispensational understanding of Pentecost. He still denied that the church began on the Day of Pentecost, and he insisted that Pentecost had to be a repeatable event. For Rice, Pentecost still represented the special indue-ment, or empowerment, of the Holy Spirit that all Christians need in order to be effective soul winners. Christians who wanted to receive this empowerment needed to come repeatedly to God in "penitent waiting and pleading."[67]

The second illustration comes from a book on false doctrines that Rice published in 1970. In this book, he responded to Roman Catholicism, bap-tismal regeneration, Christian Science, Seventh-day Adventism, British Is-raelism, and the Jehovah's Witnesses. He also included a chapter against what he called hyper-Calvinism.

By *hyper-Calvinism* Rice meant simply ordinary Calvinism as it was de-fined at the Synod of Dort. He considered this form of Calvinism to be "a perversion by proud intellectuals who thus may try to excuse themselves from any spiritual accountability for soul winning." In this attack upon Calvinism,

---

66. Walden, *The Captain of Our Team*, 151–53.
67. John R. Rice, *The Golden Path to Successful Personal Soul Winning* (Murfreesboro, TN: Sword of the Lord Publishers, 1961), 141–59.

Rice stated several specific objections: unconditional election was not a biblical doctrine, limited atonement was an unscriptural slander against God, and irresistible grace implied irresistible damnation. By critiquing unconditional election and irresistible grace, Rice extended his attack beyond traditional Calvinism and brought it to bear against the moderate Calvinism that had been represented by Chafer and Bancroft. Even very moderate Calvinists were still, in his opinion, hyper-Calvinists.[68]

Interestingly, the same volume included a brief chapter in response to ultra-dispensationalism. The remarkable thing about this chapter is that it was aimed at an entirely different doctrinal theory than the dispensationalism of Scofield and Chafer. In this chapter, Rice correctly understood ultra-dispensationalism as a teaching that posits a break in biblical history between the ministry of the Jerusalem apostles and the ministry of Paul. Evidently Rice did eventually figure out what ultra-dispensationalism actually is. Still, he never apologized for hanging this label on Scofield, Chafer, and others. Indeed, Rice's most sympathetic biographer continued to employ these labels years after his death.[69]

Fundamentalists in the North never saw John R. Rice as an enemy, but many were uneasy with his ideas. His largest base of support grew up in and around the Southwide Baptist Fellowship, while his influence waned among Baptist fundamentalists in the North. Perhaps this factor contributed to the decision to move his ministry from Wheaton to Murfreesboro, Tennessee, in 1963. From Murfreesboro, Rice continued to exert influence. The Sword was probably the most widely read fundamentalist periodical of the 1960s and '70s. Indeed, many nonfundamentalists have assumed that Rice exemplified the movement. He did actually exemplify one version of fundamentalism, but there were other versions that felt less than wholly comfortable with him.

After 1963 Rice's influence in Northern Baptist fundamentalism diminished, though it did not vanish. His influence over other versions of fundamentalism actually increased. When Jerry Falwell wanted to found the Moral Majority in the late 1970s, Rice supplied him with the Sword mailing list. Falwell's success was due in no small part to Rice's backing. That, however, is another story.

To Rice's credit, no whiff of scandal ever touched his ministry. No one ever questioned his personal integrity, his devotion to the Lord, or his passion for evangelism. Even those who disagreed with his ideas could respect him as a man of God.

---

68. John R. Rice, *False Doctrines* (Murfreesboro, TN: Sword of the Lord Publishers, 1970), 273–89.

69. Rice, *False Doctrines* 319–325; Walden, *The Captain of Our Team*, 88. Different versions of hyper- or ultra-dispensationalism have been articulated. Rice was responding specifically to the Acts 28 theory.

One part of the story of Rice's involvement with Northern Baptist fundamentalism remains to be told, namely, his role in the development of opposition to the new evangelicalism. Rice was one of the founders of the National Association of Evangelicals, later viewed as a prominent neoevangelical institution. He was also a close friend of evangelist Billy Graham, and it was his break with Graham that signaled the beginning of a formal division between neoevangelicals and fundamentalists. That story, however, awaits telling at a later time.

Lee Roberson, founder of the Southwide Baptist Fellowship, with John R. Rice.

Conservative Baptist Leaders: Richard Clearwaters, Monroe Parker, Myron Cedarholm.

10 Conservative Baptists and Regular Baptists

By the late 1930s the Regular Baptists had begun to put their association into its final form. In the South, J. Frank Norris was building his own fellowship of Baptist fundamentalists while the Regular Baptists tried to keep out of his way. In 1940 John R. Rice moved from Dallas to Wheaton, and this move marked the beginning of a distinct segment of Baptist fundamentalism built around the *Sword of the Lord*. While the participants sometimes overlapped, each of these movements developed its own brand of Baptist fundamentalism.

One other principal movement within Baptist fundamentalism was yet to emerge. During the 1940s a substantial proportion of the Fundamentalist Fellowship began to break away from the Northern Baptist Convention to organize the Conservative Baptist movement. By the end of the decade the Conservative Baptists had created five major organizations and had established an ethos that, while different from that of the conservatives who remained at peace within the convention, was also distinct from the clear separatism of the Regular Baptists.

Tensions within the Convention

After 1922 the controversy within the Northern Baptist Convention focused primarily upon foreign missions. The missions controversy began in 1923, when Bertha Henshaw's allegations led John R. Straton and the Fundamentalist League of New York to investigate the American Baptist Foreign Mission Society. The society not only blocked outsiders from access to documentation, but announced what it called the "Inclusive Policy," which was widely understood to mean that ABFMS intended to keep sending out liberal missionaries.

The board took so much criticism over the announcement that it was forced to issue a clarification, the so-called "Evangelical Policy." First articulated at the 1924 convention, the Evangelical Policy stated that the mission would send out only those missionaries who were "loyal to the gospel." These words reassured some, but others noted the vagueness of the statement.

The situation was exacerbated by controversy when the foreign board approved W. R. Hartley, who had explicitly denied the deity of Christ. The Hartley controversy seemed like just the issue that the fundamentalists needed if they were going to hold the mission accountable. At the last moment, however, liberals induced the fundamentalist leadership to abandon its prosecution of Hartley by agreeing to an investigation of the foreign board. While fundamentalists thought they had won a victory, the liberals simply traded an immediate and heated issue for a committee that could be packed with their own sympathizers.

The investigating committee contained only a minority of identifiable fundamentalists, none of whom had a reputation for rocking the denominational boat. Nevertheless, at the 1925 convention it delivered a report that actually admitted the presence of some liberals on the mission field. The Hinson Resolution, if adopted, would have stipulated doctrinal boundaries for missionaries, but it was amended out of existence. The convention contented itself with encouraging the foreign board to be more careful in its appointments.

Conservative missionaries on some fields found the modernism intolerable. One of those fields was the Philippines. A conservative physician, Dr. Raphael Thomas, believed that his ministry included gospel preaching, but the board told him to stick to medicine. Thomas resigned from ABFMS in 1927 and, following the leadership of Lucy Peabody, organized the Association of Baptists for the Evangelism of the Orient. This mission later aligned with the General Association of Regular Baptist Churches.

The Fundamentalist Fellowship disapproved of that kind of separatism. Its leaders protested liberalism, but over the next fifteen years they threw their support behind the convention program, though liberalism continued to flourish. A controversy erupted in 1933 over the book *Re-Thinking Missions*, edited by William Ernest Hocking. The book was radically liberal. The Fundamentalist Fellowship wanted to see it denounced. The ABFMS, however, expressed only mild disagreement with some of the book's conclusions.[1]

In spite of their unhappiness, convention fundamentalists yearned to believe the best. In 1934 Earle V. Pierce—at that time the president of the Fundamentalist Fellowship—wrote to Robert Ketcham that, "when it is stated that our Foreign Mission Society is sending out modernistic missionaries, the

---

1. Hocking, William Ernest, ed., *Re-Thinking Missions: A Laymen's Inquiry after One Hundred Years* (New York: Harper and Brothers, 1932).

person who makes that statement is either ignorant or mendacious."[2] Pierce's pronouncement amounted to little more than whistling past the graveyard.

The next year (1935) found the convention fundamentalists reacting against a report from the convention's Commission on Social Action. Not only was the report strongly tilted toward a social gospel, but it was also overtly pacifistic and implicitly socialistic. W. B. Riley of Minneapolis denounced this report in a sermon titled "Bloodless but Red." In spite of the fundamentalist outcry, the convention adopted the report. The only concession that the fundamentalists could secure was a promise that the report would only be circulated to those who requested it. The Fundamentalist Fellowship claimed this concession as a victory—a claim that seemed ludicrous to those who had already left the convention.

By the time the "Bloodless but Red" controversy had died down, H. H. Savage was already working quietly with ABFMS to keep the Tondo station open in the Belgian Congo. He gathered considerable support for this mission outpost on the promises that only orthodox missionaries would be appointed to the station and that his group would be given veto power over appointees. In January 1937 the foreign board reneged on these commitments, leading Savage and others to a complete break with ABFMS. For the first time, a prominent member of the convention's Fundamentalist Fellowship called publicly for the rejection of the convention's mission society.

The fundamentalist leadership continued to voice public support for the convention program, but the numbers indicate that support was dwindling. In 1921, the Northern Baptist Convention had received almost $10 million in giving. By 1938 the convention reported receipts of only $2.5 million. Between 1928 and 1938 missions giving declined from nearly $2 million per year to less than $1 million per year. In 1939 the foreign mission society was forced to reduce its budget by $60 thousand. Faced with these grim figures, the foreign board had to begin calling missionaries home from the field. The number of supported missionaries plummeted. In 1923 the Northern Baptist Convention supported 844 foreign missionaries. By 1943 this number had fallen to 459.[3]

Of course, much of this decline can be attributed to the Depression. Those were bleak years, full of despair for most people. Nevertheless, the independent boards such as Baptist Mid-Missions and ABWE were growing during

2. Quoted in Robert T. Ketcham, "The Northern Baptist Situation," *Baptist Bulletin*, November 1943, 2.

3. C. H. Heaton, *The Baptist Fundamentalist Fellowship* (Chicago: Fundamentalist Fellowship of the Northern Baptist Convention, n.d.), 8; cited by Herbert Earl Rogers, "A Study of the Doctrinal Principles which Brought About the Conservative Baptist Movement" (BD thesis, Central Baptist Theological Seminary of Minneapolis, 1960), 24; "Northern Convention Receipts," *Watchman Examiner*, May 26, 1938, 570; "The Tragedy of Northern Baptist Foreign Missions," *Watchman Examiner*, March 16, 1939, 265.

the same period. Even after the Depression ended, Northern Baptist giving increased only incrementally. By 1943, it had returned to only about a third of the 1921 high point.

The Northern Baptist Convention met in Los Angeles in 1939, electing Elmer A. Fridell as its president for the ensuing year. Fridell was an alumnus of Des Moines College (one of the predecessors of Des Moines University), who had pastored churches in Seattle, Washington, and Fresno, California. He was also a teacher at the liberal Berkeley Divinity School. He held several denominational posts and had been particularly active in foreign missions. The rise of his star within the NBC clearly signaled the dominance of the liberal party. In time, Fridell's influence would precipitate the departure of the Fundamentalist Fellowship and transform it into a separatist organization.

What was the attitude of the convention's rank and file? By some estimates, at least 80 to 90 percent of the NBC constituency was still conservative, though they remained loyal to the convention for the moment. Several considerations kept them in. Many simply could not or would not see a problem. Of those who did, some hoped for a revival and restoration. Others were held in place by their friendships within the convention. Still others felt that the convention was their home, so the liberals could be the ones to leave.

No one could overlook the fact that convention executives and state secretaries had a virtual monopoly on pulpit placement. Every pastor knew that he was likely to need another pulpit some day, and these convention functionaries were the gatekeepers. They could provide job security for the compliant. They could also close doors against the recalcitrant. For many pastors, independence seemed like a lonesome path. Granted, the GARBC was growing, but would it hold together?

Many seemed to fear the rebuke or contempt of their fellow pastors. Northern Baptists had a long and prestigious history. To belong to the convention was to be somebody. The separatists (especially the Regular Baptists) were widely perceived as cranks and yokels. The sophistication and prestige of the convention was enough to hold some pastors in place.

Legal pressures also kept pastors from leading churches out of the convention. Many churches had received gift mortgages from convention agencies—mortgages that did not have to be repaid as long as the churches remained loyal. Sometimes convention officials encouraged churches to store their title deeds in the state offices for safekeeping. Not infrequently, if a church tried to separate, the convention would claim legal title to the property. If the convention could find a disgruntled minority in a separating church, the officials would go to work to assist the minority in filing suit against the majority for the building and grounds.

Ordinations were another tool that convention officials could use to keep pastors in line. If a candidate wanted to be ordained, he would first appear before a committee of his local association, then before a state committee, then before an ordination council in his local church. Often, the main business of the local and state committees was to ensure loyalty to the convention.[4]

Perhaps the key problem was the pension fund. The Ministers' and Missionaries' Benefit Board provided generous terms of retirement. If a pastor broke his ties with the convention, however, he was almost certain to lose everything except his personal contributions. For many pastors, the loss would be devastating.

Any separatist organization had to wrestle with the problems created by the M&M Board. The GARBC simply required a clean break with the convention. Many fundamentalist pastors—especially older ones—found that break too difficult. They remained in the convention. Perhaps that is one reason that the Regular Baptist Movement was built primarily by young men.

Regular Baptist Developments

When the GARBC met at Waterloo in 1938, Robert T. Ketcham proposed a complete overhaul of the organization's constitution. His proposal was adopted and, though minor alterations have been made, its core provisions still govern the Regular Baptist fellowship. What remained was to test the plan in actual use.

An opportunity did not take long to present itself. Los Angeles Baptist Theological Seminary had been approved by the executive committee of the GARBC in 1935. During the late 1930s, however, the Council of Fourteen began to hear rumblings about "local conditions which seemed to bring a question as to its trustworthiness as a thoroughly Baptist institution." According to the recollections of some Regular Baptists, Pentecostal teachings were surfacing on the campus. This situation confronted the GARBC with a decision: Would the Council of Fourteen defend the seminary because of its links to the association, or would it withdraw approval?[5]

In April 1939 the council asked two of its members, David Gillespie and Ralph W. Neighbour, to prepare a questionnaire for all trustees and teachers of the Los Angeles Seminary. The answers were compiled prior to the September meeting of the council, and the results were less than satisfactory.

---

4. One of the authors (Delnay) stood before such a committee in the state of Illinois. One of his questioners warned him that "anyone trained at Northern [Baptist Theological Seminary] under [President Charles W.] Koller was hardly to be trusted." And Koller was by all accounts a convention loyalist.

5. Joseph Stowell, *Background and History of the General Association of Regular Baptist Churches* (Hayward, CA: Gospel Tracts Unlimited, 1949), 52; Minutes of the Council of Fourteen, General Association of Regular Baptist Churches, April 1, 1939.

On Ketcham's motion, the council voted that the association's approval be withdrawn from the seminary.[6]

During the same session Ketcham also offered a motion concerning Wheaton College: "That the Council of the G.A.R.B.C. in recognition of the peculiar service that Wheaton College is rendering to our fundamentalist Baptist youth, commend Wheaton College to the favorable consideration of our churches."[7] This motion also passed, effectively making the interdenominational Wheaton an approved agency of the General Association of Regular Baptist Churches. The council had removed its approval from a Baptist institution while granting approval to an interdenominational school.

The irony was not lost on William Matthews, president of Los Angeles Baptist Theological Seminary. Though a member of the Council of Fourteen, Matthews had been absent from the September meeting. The council's decision left him incredulous. When the council met again in February 1940, Matthews boycotted the meeting and sent an airmail letter to J. Irving Reese, the chairman of the council. Matthews thought it was bad enough that Los Angeles Seminary had been denied approval, but he was incensed that the council had approved Wheaton. Besides dissenting from the council's action, he threatened to bring a minority report to the GARBC annual meeting in Erie, Pennsylvania.

Matthews's letter only strengthened the council's resolve. The members authorized Reese to respond with a letter that expressed surprise at Matthews's dissent, defended the council's action in approving Wheaton, and warned Matthews that a protest would be unlikely to move the messengers at Erie. Instead, Reese advised Matthews to "meet with the Council at Erie as we stand ready to discuss any of these issues fully with you at that time." The only member of the council who did not participate in the discussion or vote was Earle G. Griffith, president of Baptist Bible College of Johnson City, New York. Griffith deliberately recused himself from the discussion of a sister school.[8]

This response was the final blow for Matthews. He resigned his seat on the council and published an article attacking the GARBC. In its September meeting the council discussed putting a response in the *Baptist Bulletin*, but concluded that a public statement would only provoke further attacks from Matthews. After deliberation the council adopted an official policy of silence about the Los Angeles Seminary. The decision proved to be the right one, and Matthews set about correcting the problems in his own institution. In 1945

6. Minutes of the Council of Fourteen, General Association of Regular Baptist Churches, September 5–7, 1939.

7. Ibid.

8. Minutes of the Council of Fourteen, General Association of Regular Baptist Churches, February 20–22, 1940.

the Council of Fourteen returned Los Angeles Baptist Theological Seminary to the list of approved institutions.[9]

Incidentally, the Council of Fourteen approved Wheaton College only for a single year. In February 1940 Wheaton College announced that J. Oliver Buswell was leaving the presidency. As it turned out, Buswell was being forced out. He claimed that the reasons were related to his strict ecclesiastical separation and to his stand against alcohol, "extreme dispensationalism," perfectionism, amillennialism, and a "Spinozistic tendency in the theology." Some of these were exactly the factors that made Wheaton appealing to Regular Baptists, and with Buswell's departure their ardor for Wheaton began to cool.[10]

At any rate, the Los Angeles incident shows something about how the approval system worked in the early GARBC. It allowed the fellowship to distance itself quickly from an institution that was beginning to deviate from Regular Baptist norms. It provided a way to hold the institution accountable while limiting the influence that the institution or its leadership could exert upon the association as a whole.

During this period, Regular Baptists were also engaged in an ongoing battle to defend separatist churches from the predatory tactics of convention officials. One of the most notorious cases involved the First Baptist Church of Princeton, Indiana. Pastored by Ford Porter since 1926, the church had shown significant growth even during the Depression. By 1938, First Baptist could claim about 450 members. Porter had become active in the Regular Baptist movement and was elected to the first Council of Fourteen. On January 31, 1938, First Baptist voted out of the Northern Baptist Convention, the Indiana state convention, and the Evansville Baptist Association.

The vote, however, was not quite unanimous. Eighteen members wanted the church to retain its old connections, and by canvassing the absentee membership they increased their number to twenty-seven. This minority group called an ex parte council of churches from the Evansville association. In calling the council, the church was assisted by Allie Stith, moderator of the Evansville Baptist Association. To the association churches, Stith wrote,

> I think it is time that we stood out against these preachers and factions that are causing so much trouble in our churches. . . . The minority members (of the First Baptist Church of Princeton) are cooperating with the Convention, and unquestionably constitute the true church as originally organized. I hope you will see to it, if possible, to have

9. Minutes of the Council of Fourteen, General Association of Regular Baptist Churches, September 3–5, 1940; Stowell, *Background and History*, 52.

10. J. Oliver Buswell, statement for Wheaton College, February 2, 1940; reprinted in "Dr. Buswell Leaves Wheaton," *Baptist Bulletin*, March 1940, 3–4.

your representatives at this council, of the type who are in sympathy with our organized work.[11]

Not surprisingly, the council voted 17–3 that the minority constituted the First Baptist Church of Princeton. Furthermore, it advised the group to take whatever steps were necessary to gain control of the church's property, building, and parsonage. The minority then gave public notice that it would meet to elect new trustees for the First Baptist Church. At this point, Pastor Porter led the majority to seek a court injunction that restrained the minority from representing itself as the First Baptist Church. After hearing representatives from both groups, the judge granted the injunction.

The minority quickly filed for a plea in abatement, effectively asking the judge to set aside the injunction. The judge granted a hearing in January 1939, and the minority appeared with several expert witnesses. These included both Allie Stith and T. J. Parsons, the executive secretary of the Indiana Baptist Association. For two and one half days, attorneys for the minority argued that their clients should be recognized as the true church and allowed to elect trustees. Each of the expert witnesses testified that a church that left the convention was no longer in fellowship with the Baptist denomination and ceased to be a Baptist church.

The church's attorney pressed these witnesses repeatedly for authority to back up their claims, but they produced none. Finally, the church's attorney asked Parsons, the convention secretary, whether it was not true that Baptists accepted the Bible as their sole authority. When Parsons replied in the affirmative, the attorney asked for the chapter and verse that declared a church to be outside the Baptist denomination when it withdrew from the convention. Parsons admitted that no such verse existed.

Finally, the minority rested its case. Immediately, and without calling a witness, the church's attorney asked the judge to rule in favor of the church, since the expert witnesses had presented no authority as warrant for their claims. The minority attorneys responded with a two-hour barrage of quotations from law books and citations from other cases, but the judge's decision declared in favor of the church.[12]

Not satisfied, the minority changed venue to the next county and filed suit against the church. The case was tried on March 11 and 12, 1940, in Booneville, Indiana. Once again the minority presented expert witnesses, and once again the witnesses withered under cross-examination. Once again the judge ruled in favor of the church without ever having to listen to the church's witnesses. By now, both the church and the minority were bearing stiff legal

11. Allie Sith to the churches of the Evansville Baptist Association, n.d.; cited by Robert T. Ketcham, "The Princeton Case," *Baptist Bulletin*, February 1939, 3.

12. Ketcham, "The Princeton Case," 2–4.

costs. Regular Baptist churches and individuals began to contribute toward the church's costs, but they suspected that the minority was being bankrolled by the state convention.[13]

The Princeton case was only one in a long series of similar court actions. If a church voted unanimously to separate from the convention, it might get away without a challenge. If any dissenting votes were cast, however, convention officials would try to rally the minority into a faction that would claim to be the church. In some cases like Princeton, the church won. In other cases (most notoriously, the much later case of the First Baptist Church of Wichita, Kansas) the church lost. For pastors of smaller churches, this kind of intimidation was often enough to head off any overtly separatist moves. Over time, however, the GARBC leadership—especially Ketcham—developed a fair amount of legal finesse and helped many separatist churches to retain their buildings and properties.[14]

While Regular Baptists certainly faced challenges and conflicts, their focus remained on positive ministry. Every issue of the *Baptist Bulletin* carried reports of ordinations and local church work, and large sections were devoted to missionary letters and news. During the early 1940s Ketcham noted that if the convention kept losing missionaries and the independent Baptists kept appointing them at the current rate, then independent Baptist missionaries would outnumber convention missionaries within about three years. Even after the beginning of World War II, Regular Baptist missionaries remained active in most fields.

The Regular Baptists' interest in missions was not confined to the foreign fields. They shared a growing sense that many areas of North America needed Bible-preaching churches. The Interstate Evangelistic Association was the only approved domestic mission agency, but most of its work was directed toward pastoral placement and pulpit supply. In July 1941 pastors and Christian workers met in Elyria, Ohio, to discuss the problem of home missions. Their solution was to organize a new agency, the Fellowship of Baptists for Home Missions. J. Irving Reese, who had left the Interstate Evangelistic Association to become pastor of First Baptist Church in Elyria, was appointed head of the new mission.[15]

13. "The Princeton Case—Another Victory," *Baptist Bulletin*, April 1940, 6; Herbert Lockyer, *The Berean Miracle: The Story of the Life and Labors of Ford Porter* (Indianapolis: Berean Gospel Distributors, 1963), 43.

14. The Wichita case was conducted in 1970. The state court ruled that a Baptist church cannot change its denominational affiliation, even by majority vote. For a brief summary of the Wichita case, see H. Leon McBeth, *The Baptist Heritage: Four Centuries of Baptist Witness* (Nashville: Broadman, 1987), 696. After about 1950, Conservative Baptist leaders like B. Myron Cedarholm and Richard V. Clearwaters also developed legal expertise to help churches escape the convention unscathed.

15. "Fellowship of Baptists for Home Missions," *Baptist Bulletin*, September 1941, 20;

Other home mission agencies were being organized at about the same time. The Columbia Basin Baptist Mission was organized in 1940 to work in central and eastern Washington, Idaho, and western Montana. The Hiawathaland Baptist Mission was incorporated in 1942 under the leadership of H. H. Savage and Arthur Glenn. It worked in the lumber camps of upper Michigan, Wisconsin, and Minnesota. Together with FBHM, these missions were approved by the GARBC. The addition of these three agencies provided the Regular Baptist movement with a platform for vigorous church planting that would produce significant growth over the next half century.[16]

World War II began in Europe in 1939. Though the United States did not enter the war until near the end of 1941, most Americans had a growing sense that their country could not remain neutral. The prospect of American involvement in the war brought new concerns to Baptist fundamentalists. One of the most important was to find a way to get fundamentalist chaplains into the military. To be appointed as a chaplain, a candidate had to receive endorsement from a recognized denomination. Protestant churches typically secured this recognition by participating in the Federal Council of Churches. Since the Federal Council was dominated by liberals, fundamentalist bodies like the GARBC refused to get involved with it. Consequently, these separatist organizations had no recognition or standing to endorse chaplains for the military.

In October 1941 the Bible Presbyterian Church and the Bible Protestant Church organized a fundamentalist alternative to the Federal Council of Churches. Led by Carl McIntire, the new body was called the American Council of Christian Churches. It aimed to challenge the monopoly that the Federal Council held over military chaplaincy and in other areas. In January 1942, just weeks after Pearl Harbor, the GARBC's Council of Fourteen met with officials from the American Council of Christian Churches, then voted to recommend that the GARBC declare itself in fellowship with the ACCC. That motion was approved by the entire association at its annual meeting in May. Because of the nature of Baptist organization, Regular Baptist churches then had to vote individually to identify with the ACCC.

The cooperation of the ACCC helped the GARBC get chaplains into the armed forces. By the end of 1942 the GARBC had about six men who had applied for appointment to military chaplaincy. The government's General Commission on Army and Navy Chaplains was dominated by the Federal

---

Minutes, Fellowship of Baptists for Home Missions, July 15–16, 1941.

16. William J. Hopewell, *The Missionary Emphasis of the General Association of Regular Baptist Churches* (Chicago: Regular Baptist Press, 1963), 43.

Council of Churches. Since the GARBC was not a constituent of that commission, Regular Baptists were given no quota for military chaplains.[17]

The ACCC, however, went to work in Washington and won a hearing for its constituents. The result was that in April 1943 Vernon Bliss received notice of temporary appointment as a chaplain and First Lieutenant in the United States Army. So sudden was this announcement that it caught the Regular Baptist leadership by surprise. Ketcham wondered whether Bliss had been "actually certified and only so by the G.A.R.B. and the American Council," or whether he had been inadvertently placed under the Federal Council's commission. Bliss's appointment, however, was legitimate—the first of many to follow.[18]

As the GARBC continued to grow, it eventually became the largest and perhaps the most active constituent of the American Council of Christian Churches. This relationship played a significant role in the controversy over neoevangelicalism that developed during the 1950s. The American Council and the GARBC would continue their collaboration into the 1990s.

The 1943 meeting of the General Association of Regular Baptist Churches was held in Johnson City, New York. At this meeting T. T. Shields spoke for the last time from the association's national platform. The GARBC now counted 256 churches within its fellowship. Its leaders knew of yet more churches leaving the Northern Baptist Convention. They saw the need for a permanent field representative who could present the work of the association to unaffiliated churches. On the council's recommendation, the messengers at the 1944 conference voted to employ a field representative.[19]

The position, called simply the national representative, was offered to Heber O. Van Gilder. A graduate of Philadelphia Bible Institute, Van Gilder had spent more than two decades in pastoral ministry in Pennsylvania and Ohio. With Ketcham and Griffith, he had been one of the organizers of the Ohio Association of Independent Baptist Churches. Now in his mid-forties, he was pastor of Temple Baptist Church in Portsmouth, Ohio, and serving as a member of the Council of Fourteen. In 1948 he would accept the presidency of Western Baptist College (now Corban University) in Salem, Oregon. Van Gilder opened an office for the GARBC on North Clark Street in Chicago, hiring Ruth Ryburn to staff the office while he was traveling. In early 1945 Ketcham resigned as editor of the *Baptist Bulletin* and Van Gilder added that responsibility to his job description.

17. General Commission on Army and Navy Chaplains to Vernon Bliss, February 17, 1943.
18. Robert T. Ketcham to Vernon Bliss, March 2, 1943; Ketcham to Bliss, April 26, 1943.
19. Minutes of the Council of Fourteen, General Association of Regular Baptist Churches, January 26–28, 1944; May 15–18, 1944. The association minutes are interspersed with the Council of Fourteen minutes for May 1944.

Van Gilder served as the national representative until 1948. Upon his resignation, Robert T. Ketcham was chosen as his successor. Ketcham would hold the office of national representative until his retirement twelve years later. At that time the association created the office of national consultant to allow Ketcham to retain a formal title and office.

Also at the 1948 conference, the GARBC reversed an earlier decision. Years before, while J. Frank Norris was still on friendly terms with the GARBC leadership, an informal agreement had stipulated that Norris's group would minister in the South and the GARBC would minister in the North. In fact, the word *north* was even added to the name. A decade later, the GARBC had seen plenty of Norris's tactics. He was now an old man, and the GARBC was receiving interested inquiries from churches in the Southern states. The association was beginning to grasp its potential as a nationwide organization, and the messengers voted to drop *north* from the name.

In 1948 the GARBC was sixteen years old. During those years, the Regular Baptist movement had faced a number of theological, practical, and institutional issues. It had grown and matured, adapting its form of organization to fit a developing understanding of church fellowship, associationalism, and separatism. While these developments were taking place, fundamentalism within the Northern Baptist Convention was also changing.

The Conservative Baptist Foreign Mission Society

The Northern Baptist Convention had long since rejected any attempt to make fundamental doctrines a test for convention office or missionary appointment. The convention could talk in vague terms about Christ and the Bible, but it would not require belief in verbal inspiration, the deity of Christ, His virgin birth or miracles, the plan of salvation, the creation, or the culmination. Organizationally, it had become a self-perpetuating body with an agenda very different from that of the churches whose money it was taking. An attitude of institutional arrogance had developed, and that attitude eventually led the Fundamentalist Fellowship to break completely with the convention. The trouble began in the foreign mission society.

The foreign mission board did include some fundamentalists. Typically, four out of the eighteen board members who interviewed new missionaries were known to be committed conservatives. Only rarely would they vote against a candidate. More often, they abstained from voting, which left the record showing a unanimous vote. Sometimes they simply accepted the reassurances of other board members concerning questionable candidates.

There were reports—some of them substantiated—of candidates who would spend the morning of their interview giving modernistic answers to the board's questions. Then someone would take them out to lunch. What was said over the table remained a mystery, but for the afternoon session the candidates would make a complete turnaround. Their answers now gave all the ideas and values that a conservative could wish. It was a matter of some wonder that an hour and a half of instruction could turn modernists into believers.[20]

Why would a modernist even want to endure the hardships of the mission field? One reason was that the foreign field was a relatively safe place to be a liberal. Another was the liberal commitment to the social gospel: undeveloped countries provided the perfect laboratory for demonstrating the efficacy of medicine, agriculture, and education to advance the kingdom. Developed countries such as Japan offered a good venue for the exchange of cultures, which facilitated brotherhood and again advanced the kingdom.

After the 1926 convention, the missions controversy simmered with only periodic flareups. As long as the controversy was in the background, the conservatives felt like they held the steering wheel—and the liberals were happy to let them. When the time came for important decisions, however, the liberals would either pressure the fundamentalists for concessions or simply outvote the conservative minority. That is what happened in February 1943 when the board appointed Elmer Fridell as the foreign secretary of the mission.

Fridell had served as president of the NBC in 1940 and was identified with the modernist party. He tried to present himself as a moderate, but his pronouncements on social issues were at odds with that claim. The Fundamentalist Fellowship thought that Fridell's appointment to such a sensitive position was more than disturbing. The situation was complicated, however. Because of wartime restrictions, the Northern Baptist Convention did not meet in 1943. All elective offices were held over from the year before. Conservatives who might have challenged Fridell's appointment on the floor of the convention were left with few ways to voice their concerns.

On May 20–22 the Fundamentalist Fellowship sent two representatives to meet with the ABFMS board at Springfield, Illinois. They pleaded for almost anybody but Fridell to be appointed as foreign secretary. They implied that the appointment had the potential to split the convention. Predictably,

20. One particular case involved the Rev. and Mrs. Gordon Gilbert. Gilbert was a graduate of Colgate Rochester. The candidate committee of the ABFMS examined the Gilberts in May 1943, and the conservative members were not satisfied with their views. Then Dr. Nathan R. Wood, former president of Gordon College, took an interest and tried to instruct the Gilberts. At their interview in the fall of 1944, their answers were again unsatisfactory. Thereupon Wood took them to lunch for more instruction. That afternoon they reversed their position and were converted to orthodox doctrine. The committee voted unanimously to appoint them for missions work in China. The story was told in a mimeographed report from Chester E. Tulga, 1945.

the board refused to budge—this time, without even the façade of sweet reasonableness.[21]

Two days later the Fundamentalist Fellowship met at the Lawson YMCA in Chicago, not far from Moody Bible Institute. Wartime travel was difficult, but forty members from eleven states managed to attend the meeting. Earle V. Pierce was in the chair. One of the speakers was Peder Stiansen, noted professor of church history at Northern Baptist Seminary. Over the years Stiansen had served as one of the conservatives on the ABFMS board. He now articulated three alternatives for the group to consider—none of which, however, involved separation from the Northern Baptist Convention. First, the fundamentalists could let the matter stand, but according to Stiansen, that would accomplish nothing. Second, they could continue to protest, and that, too, would accomplish nothing. Stiansen's third alternative was to organize a new mission society.

The group seemed to realize that Stiansen was right, that in good conscience they were duty bound to found a new mission agency. They resolved to organize a new board that would operate within the NBC but would not be controlled by it. They hoped to be able to direct their support toward strictly orthodox missionaries and a conservative mission agency without having to surrender any of their standing within the convention. As subsequent events would reveal, however, the NBC had no tolerance for any agency that it could not control.

For the moment, the Fundamentalist Fellowship appointed a committee of nine, with E. Myers Harrison as secretary. The committee worked through the summer to develop a plan. To encourage national participation, they decided to hold three regional meetings, one each in the West, the East, and the Central United States. They also hoped to change the image of their movement by changing its name. According to Chester Tulga, the label *fundamentalist* had been debased by radicals such as J. Frank Norris and Gerald Winrod. In Utah, some extreme Mormons were even calling themselves fundamentalists. Consequently, the committee chose to go with the name *conservative* rather than *fundamentalist*. Their new mission would be named the Conservative Baptist Foreign Mission Society, and as they created other new agencies, they would keep the label *conservative* for all of them.[22]

While the committee labored that summer, spats broke out between convention representatives and fundamentalist leaders. Earle V. Pierce published

---

21. Most of this history is detailed in Chester E. Tulga, *The Foreign Missions Controversy in the Northern Baptist Convention* (Chicago: Conservative Baptist Fellowship, 1950). Tulga's work tends not to follow the timeline, often anticipating later events or reminiscing about earlier ones.

22. Chester E. Tulga, recorded interview with Robert Delnay, April 6, 1962.

a two-part series on Northern Baptist Foreign Missions in the *Watchman Examiner*. He argued that the Evangelical Policy had been applied only loosely, insisted that the virgin birth of Christ was essential to the gospel, and noted that "during the past twenty years, by actual record, 65% of the missionary appointments have been made from liberal theological seminaries." Pierce admitted that some of these missionaries turned out to be orthodox, but questioned whether their preparation left them fully committed to focusing upon the gospel.[23] Attempting to put content to the word *evangelical*, Pierce stated,

> In the minds of our people the dictionary definition is what they think of, which is: "(1) Of or pertaining to the gospel or the four Gospels. (2) Holding or conformed to what the majority of Protestants regard as the fundamental doctrines of the gospel, such as personal union with Christ, the Trinity, the fallen condition of man, Christ's atonement for sin, salvation by faith, not by works, and regeneration by the Holy Spirit. . . ." *Let our Foreign Board hold strictly to that definition and there will be no need of another society.*[24]

Orrin Judd replied to Pierce on behalf of the ABFMS. Judd, who had served on the foreign missions board for eight years, stated, "I have not known one to be appointed in that period who did not meet the definition which Dr. Pierce quotes." He further insisted that if such a person had been appointed, then Pierce should have named him. For example, no candidates had denied the virgin birth of Christ, though, as Judd saw it, a virgin birth was not really essential to the Christian message or to the uniqueness of Jesus. Judd flatly denied Pierce's assertion that 65 percent of missionary candidates came from liberal schools (or, as Judd put it, from "schools which deny the historic Biblical faith and substitute man's philosophy"). Furthermore, he challenged Pierce's right to question whether any missionary was truly committed to preaching the gospel. He suggested that the new society actually arose from rivalries between the old and new seminaries—a clear swipe at Northern Baptist Theological Seminary. Judd insisted that Fridell could not be charged with liberal theology. The real complaint was about his strongly stated position on social issues.[25]

At about that time, the foreign mission board began promoting the book *Burma Surgeon* by Gordon Seagrave. The author had been appointed to the

---

23. Earle V. Pierce, "Northern Baptist Foreign Missions—Part II," *Watchman Examiner*, August 26, 1943, 818–20.

24. Earle V. Pierce, "Northern Baptist Foreign Missions—Part I," *Watchman Examiner*, August 19, 1943, 796.

25. Orrin G. Judd, "Northern Baptist Foreign Missions," *Watchman Examiner* October 28, 1943, 1033, 1037. Judd's reply did not appear until the end of October, and it also referenced some of the intervening events. Pierce subsequently rejoined in "Northern Baptist Foreign Missions," *Watchman Examiner*, December 9, 1943, 1178–79.

ABFMS as a medical missionary in 1922. His book was an edited version of his personal journal. It contained some surprising admissions. For example, Seagrave revealed that "Tiny is quite annoyed at the way I operate. She says that all through my operations I am either praying out loud, singing, or swearing. She is wrong. They are all three just my peculiar way of praying." He later commented, "Had to swear at those nurses today." Seagrave expressed frustration at another episode: "I was a minute late getting started and took the wrong turn in town and then had a hell of a time catching up with the others."[26]

Near the end of the book, Seagrave told of trying to pole a boat downriver with several companions:

> Grindlay was cussing me from the stern. "Damn it, Doc, why don't you push us off those snags?"
>
> "Damn it yourself! If I had a flashlight that would work I would keep us off them." I had the advantage of him, for I could cuss roundly in Burmese and Shan, and make a good effort of it in Chinese, without his even knowing I was cussing! I could have done a better job of it also if there had been anything for me to stand on. . . .
>
> After three hours of cussing I turned my pole over to Paul with a sigh of relief. I found my bed was partly under water, so I moved over to a six-inch-wide stretch between a couple of nurses on the other side. But I hadn't had more than a beauty nap when I was wakened.
>
> "God damn. God damn. God damn!" Breathless, fervent, a real prayer! Was that Paul? It certainly was none other! Something must have happened if that most discreet, self-contained, he-man saint, Paul Geren, was cussing![27]

Orrin Judd had objected that no one had the right to question the commitment of foreign missionaries to preaching the gospel. Yet here was clear evidence that the surgeon Seagrave, while doubtless a committed humanitarian, was not only personally profane, but was also the kind of man who found amusement in the profanity of others. What was worse, the foreign mission board was selling his book. In view of the Evangelical Policy of the ABFMS, conservatives found themselves asking, "Was Dr. Seagraves an evangelical?"[28]

On September 9 the executive committee of the Fundamentalist Fellowship met with a committee from the board of the ABFMS at the La Salle Hotel in Chicago. The board claimed to want peace, and the fundamentalists wanted tangible assurance that the board would honor its policy of appointing only evangelical missionaries. One of the board representatives observed, "It seems that your position is that while the language of the evangelical policy is thoroughly satisfactory, you feel that the Board has not honestly lived up to

26. Gordon Seagrave, *Burma Surgeon* (New York: W. W. Norton, 1943), 30–31, 193, 239.
27. Ibid., 252–53.
28. Tulga, *Foreign Missions Controversy*, 98.

it." The reply was, "That is exactly it! The 'evangelical policy' is excellent. All any of us ask is that it be strictly followed." [29]

In other words, the fundamentalists believed that the board had used the Evangelical Policy as an evasion so that they could continue the Inclusive Policy. To correct that deficiency, the conservatives proposed a resolution that was meant as an interpretation of the Evangelical Policy. Specifically, they wanted assurances that the board would not appoint missionaries or secretaries who denied certain core doctrines, namely,

> the inspiration of the Bible as the authoritative Word of God; the preexistence, virgin birth, sinless life, miraculous works, and other revelations that Jesus is God the Father's only begotten Son; the atonement for our sins wrought by the death of our Lord; His bodily resurrection from the dead; His priesthood on behalf of believers and His Kingly glory; the necessity of regeneration for all human beings and the requirement of this faith as a basis of salvation for sinners.[30]

On September 21 the entire board of the ABFMS met for four hours to consider the resolution. One key member of the board stated flatly, "I am not ready to disenfranchise the liberals," to which he received the reply, "You are evidently ready to disenfranchise the fundamentalists." By a vote of thirteen to four, the board rejected the fundamentalists' proposed resolution. Instead, the board reiterated its commitment to the Evangelical Policy, adding, "Within the Northern Baptist Convention there has always been latitude of interpretation of the New Testament teachings that support this policy." The majority report then reaffirmed the old NBC statement first proposed by Cornelius Woelfkin, "The New Testament is the all-sufficient ground of our faith and practice."[31]

A key consideration for the majority report was that no charges were being brought against any particular missionary. For that matter, the "official minutes for the last 20 years show no dissenting or divided votes on the appointment of any candidate." Whatever reservations the conservatives may have had, the board's votes were unanimous.[32]

The four-member minority issued its own report on the same day as the majority. The minority report insisted that the fundamentalists were not proposing a creed, but merely trying to clarify the Evangelical Policy. Clarification was necessary because the Inclusive Policy (as it was now being interpreted) and the Evangelical Policy could not be followed simultaneously. The

---

29. Earle V. Pierce, "The Foreign Board Has Spoken," *Watchman Examiner* February 24, 1944, 180.
30. "Foreign Board and Fundamentalists," *Watchman Examiner*, September 30, 1943, 929.
31. Ibid.; Pierce, "Call to Conservatives," 986–987; Pierce, "The Foreign Board Has Spoken," 180; "Statement of Board of A.B.F.M.S.," *Watchman Examiner*, 2 December 2, 1943, 1159–60.
32. "Statement of the A.B.F.M.S.," 1159.

report also alleged that the seemingly unanimous approval of all candidates was deceiving. When the fundamentalists expressed reservations, they had been pressured to abstain from voting so that the board would seem united. The votes appeared to be unanimous only because the fundamentalists had bowed to the pressure and abstained. As for bringing charges against specific missionaries, the report stated, "None knows better than do the members of the Majority that such a procedure is impossible and all the more so by virtue of the refusal to define the 'Evangelical Policy' except in general terms. No charges against specific missionaries will be made, for to do so would be useless and employed only to discredit those who made them."[33]

The majority report constituted an evasion, and Pierce wrote that the fundamentalists intended to move ahead with the three regional meetings. These would be held in New York, Chicago, and San Francisco. The intent was to organize a Conservative Baptist Foreign Mission Society.[34]

The Western Regional met as announced, in San Francisco, with R. S. Beal in charge. Albert Johnson of Portland, Oregon, delivered the main address, affirming that the base problem before them was the denial of the supernatural. He called for a new mission that would work within the convention, operating much as the Women's ABFMS was already functioning.[35]

The Central Regional met a week later at Tabernacle Baptist Church in Chicago. The meeting was under the direction of R. V. Clearwaters of Minneapolis, who would become a leader on the board and in the Central Regional. The speaker on the second night was W. B. Riley, who delivered an address on "Divinely Ordained Divisions."

The Eastern Regional met November 4 and 5 at the historic Calvary Baptist Church of New York City, with W. T. Taylor in charge. The three regional meetings had fulfilled their purpose in facilitating national participation. So well did they work that the regional plan became a foundation principle of the Conservative Baptist movement. It was retained to 1985, long after the fundamentalists had left.

The three regional meetings led to an organizational meeting, December 16, at Tabernacle Baptist of Chicago. George J. Carlson was the church's pastor. At this meeting, the nascent Conservative Baptist movement officially adopted the proposed constitution. As if to ratify this action, two missionary couples came down the aisle to offer themselves as the first missionaries of the

33. Quoted by Tulga, *Foreign Missions Controversy*, 112. The conservative members of the ABFMS board were H. A. Davidson, F. Arvid Hagstrom, Earle V. Pierce, and Peder Stiansen. See Bruce L. Shelley, *Conservative Baptists: A Story of Twentieth-Century Dissent*, 42.

34. Pamphlet by Earle V. Pierce, "The Call to Conservatives," *Watchman Examiner*, October 14, 1943, 986–87.

35. Pamphlet by Albert Johnson, "Northern Baptist Missions," published after the Western Regional of October 1943.

new board. For its first president, the new society chose E. Myers Harrison, a former missionary to Burma who was now pastoring Woodlawn Baptist Church in Chicago.[36]

The new constitution allowed for individual membership. To protect the society, it also included a doctrinal statement that drew a clear line against modernism. To join the new Conservative Baptist Foreign Mission Society (CBFMS), one had to declare, "I state without reservation that the Doctrinal Statement of the Conservative Baptist Foreign Mission Society as given above represents my own personal beliefs. Furthermore, I have contributed financially (either directly or through my church) during the past year to the work of the Conservative Baptist Foreign Mission Society."

The Conservative Baptist movement now had a mission agency around which to rally. They seem to have thought that the NBC would welcome the new society. It did not. In December 1943 the convention appointed a Committee on Conference and Cooperative Unity, ostensibly to settle the differences between the two missions. The committee did meet over lunch with a few fundamentalists, but that was as close as it ever came to a conference about the issues. After these ad hoc meetings, committee chairman W. C. Coleman produced a document known as the "Coleman Report." Issued early in 1944, it was highly critical of the new mission.[37]

The Coleman Report alleged that a group of individuals had attempted to impose a doctrinal statement as a limitation upon the foreign board's policy, and that this attempt had been "refused with some show of resentment." Against the Fundamentalist Fellowship, the report insisted that "we cannot hide behind 'conscience' as a bar to cooperation since conscience is applicable only to individual action and not corporate action." It argued that the fundamentalists were dishonest in trying to co-opt the word *conservative*, as though there were no other conservatives in the convention or the ABFMS. It defended the Inclusive Policy as a legitimate course of action for Northern Baptist missions. It noted the conservatives' provision for individual membership, then attacked this provision as unbaptistic. Most importantly, the report rejected the fundamentalist attempt to impose a "code of belief" upon the larger body. The report insisted that any effort to require missionaries or board members to sign a confession of faith was coercive and would lead to intellectual dishonesty.[38]

The CBFMS appointed a committee to prepare a reply to the Coleman

36. Carl F. H. Henry, "Conservative Baptist Foreign Mission Society," *Watchman Examiner*, January 6, 1944, 17.

37. Eventually Coleman produced two reports. This one is sometimes designated the "first Coleman Report."

38. "Report of the Coleman Committee," *Watchman Examiner*, March 30, 1944, 301–03; "Report of the Coleman Commission (Continued)," *Watchman Examiner*, April 6, 1944, 325–27.

Report. Written primarily by Clarence S. Roddy, the reply originally appeared in the *Watchman Examiner*. Later reprinted by CBFMS, it was usually referred to simply as the *Answer*.[39]

The *Answer* noted that the Coleman committee had been appointed to compose the differences between ABFMS and CBFMS, but charged that the committee had never conferred with representatives of CBFMS. Instead, it had conferred at length with representatives of the ABFMS, who had resorted to ad hominem accusations against the CBFMS organizers. The *Answer* further maintained that, given the liberal bias of the foreign board, the CBFMS had a perfect right to call itself *conservative*. The *Answer* rejected the claim that a confessional requirement was coercive or that it would lead to dishonesty, replying that a confession was both appropriate and necessary under the present circumstances. Contrary to the statements of the foreign board, the *Answer* asserted that the controversy was deeply theological. Arguing that the New Testament clearly taught the virgin birth of Christ, the *Answer* inquired, "*May we ask the why of this apparent reluctance of certain Board members and officials to speak clearly about the birth of our Lord?*" In short, the *Answer* took the position that the controversy could be laid at the feet of the Inclusive Policy, which was why the CBFMS had been organized.[40]

The formal answer from the CBFMS was only one document in a storm of protests over the Coleman Report. The vigor of the disagreement seems to have caught the Coleman commission by surprise. By the time the Northern Baptist Convention met in Atlantic City, the commission had begun to backpedal, producing a second and much more moderately worded report.

The second Coleman Report actually disavowed the Inclusive Policy "in any sense that would imply the inclusion of appointees under the board who are not in wholehearted agreement with our established 'evangelical policy.'" The report also reaffirmed the Evangelical Policy, though that policy was again stated in terms that were designed to accommodate most liberals. Included as part of the report was a response from the foreign board that took back some of what the actual report appeared to concede, but that also encouraged the recognition of the new society "as a missionary agency through which conservatives can channel their missionary interests and gifts." In its appended response, the foreign board also encouraged CBFMS to pursue comity agreements with ABFMS.[41]

One effect of the second Coleman Report was to divide the ranks of the

39. E. Myers Harrison, Clarence S. Roddy, W. Theodore Taylor, and Carey S. Thomas, "The Coleman Report—The Reply of the C.B.F.M.S.," *Watchman Examiner*, April 20, 1944, 372–75.
40. Ibid.
41. *Yearbook of the Northern Baptist Convention 1944* (n.p.: American Baptist Publication Society, 1944), 45, 240–45.

conservatives. Some believed that the concessions of the second Coleman Report were adequate, or at least a step in the right direction. Others noted that the report really said nothing new. The Evangelical Policy was still too foggy, and it was the merest veil against liberalism on the mission field.

The second Coleman Report led to the appointment of the Committee on Conference and Cooperative Unity, again intended to resolve the matter and provide a basis for working together. This committee consisted of nine members. Three were from CBFMS, three from ABFMS, and three from the General Council of the Northern Baptist Convention, which was acting as something of an executive board for the entire convention. This committee was commonly known as the Committee of Nine. It would not report until the 1945 convention, which was scheduled to meet in Grand Rapids, Michigan.

In the meanwhile, the second Coleman Report had encouraged CBFMS to pursue comity agreements with ABFMS. A comity agreement was an arrangement between two mission societies in which they consented to work in different territories, with each agreeing not to encroach upon the territory of the other. Often, comity agreements were negotiated between the missions of different denominations. They might not approve of all the doctrines being taught by the other mission on a neighboring field, but the agreement kept the two boards from tripping over each other. If nothing else, they could assure themselves that they were not confusing the nationals with intramural debates. After all, no individual mission was able to reach the entire world. From a pragmatic point of view, comity agreements seemed justifiable.

The ABFMS held vast territories under such agreements. The problem for the foreign board was that both its funding and its workers had been declining for decades. Even if all of its missionaries had been faithful to the Scriptures and devoted to evangelism, the ABFMS had no hope of reaching all the territories it held—and was blocking other boards from entering.

When the Coleman Report, with the approval of the foreign board, encouraged the CBFMS to negotiate comity agreements with ABFMS, the conservatives assumed that ABFMS would be willing to release some of these territories to the new mission. That was the attitude with which they approached the ABFMS. What they received, however, was a clear rebuff. What ABFMS wanted was to ensure that CBFMS would stay out of all of its territories. The CBFMS could find its own fields. The convention board was conceding nothing, not an acre in the desert.

Only in May 1945 did the CBFMS work out an agreement with the Unevangelized Africa Mission to take over its Congo field under the existing comity agreements. That territory was in eastern Congo, and the CBFMS board scheduled thirteen missionaries to enter it. About that time, Dr. and Mrs. Eric Frykenberg arrived safely in Ellichpur, India, and five single women were sent to help them. CBFMS had twenty missionaries under appointment to India, thirteen to Africa, six to South America, three to China, and two whose fields were yet undetermined. These developments took place just as the war was ending in Europe, with transportation suddenly becoming easier and safer. The war in the Pacific theater still had some months to run.[42]

Meanwhile, the government had imposed new travel restrictions, with the result that the Northern Baptist Convention canceled its Grand Rapids meeting in 1945. Instead, convention officials gathered in the LaSalle Hotel in Chicago to hear reports and act on convention business. Among their business was the latest report from the Committee on Cooperative Unity (the so-called Committee of Nine).

The work of the committee had not gone well. The majority comprised representatives of the ABFMS and of the convention hierarchy; the minority included the representatives of CBFMS. Predictably, the majority wanted concessions that the minority was not willing to grant. The committee fractured, presenting two reports to the convention officials in Chicago.

The majority report was straightforward. CBFMS had to drop the word "conservative" from its name, since that word implied that other Northern Baptists were not conservative. It had to cease operating as a foreign mission and become a fellowship for encouraging churches to contribute to acceptable convention missionaries. It had to be careful not to undermine confidence in the missionaries and projects that it did not support. In short, if the majority prevailed, the CBFMS had no future. It might as well go out of existence.[43]

Of course, the majority knew that the conservatives were not about to abandon their new board. Consequently, the second part of their report expressed confidence in the ABFMS, its policies, officers, missionaries, and its loyalty to the "revealed will of God as seen in the Bible." The report further expressed regret that the CBFMS leadership had used the interim period to entrench itself as a "divisive and competing organization." Since reconciliation seemed impossible, the CBFMS should stop calling itself *conservative* and start calling itself *fundamental*. Finally, the majority report stated that this "fundamentalist foreign mission society is not another society within the framework of the NBC." Therefore, the convention structure must not be used to channel gifts to the new society.[44]

If adopted, the majority report would make the CBFMS a strictly independent mission agency. It would have no standing whatever in the Northern

---

42. Conservative Baptist Foreign Mission Society, *News and Views*, July 1945.
43. John W. Bradbury, "Report of the Northern Baptist Convention Meetings," *Watchman Examiner*, June 14, 1945, 579.
44. Ibid.

Baptist Convention. Participation in the CBFMS would not be recognized by the convention as participation in the work of the denomination.

The conservative minority of the Committee of Nine saw no reason that the CBFMS should not be recognized as another foreign mission agency within the Northern Baptist Convention. They argued that their work was not competitive but supplemental to that of the ABFMS. Far from dividing the convention, they insisted that they had kept many churches in the convention that might otherwise have departed. Consequently, they urged the convention to recognize CBFMS, stipulating that the supporters of the new board would abstain from voting on officers for the ABFMS. They agreed to avoid fields occupied by ABFMS unless comity agreements could be worked out. They also wanted officers and missionaries of the CBFMS to remain eligible for pensions from the M&M Board. In the case of future differences, the Committee on Conference and Cooperative Unity would continue to act as mediator.[45]

Both reports were presented to the General Council, which was operating with full authority to make decisions for the convention between meetings. Someone moved that a decision be delayed until the next full meeting of the convention. The motion was voted down eleven to seven. Then the General Council adopted the Majority Report by a vote of twelve to six. To the dismay of the minority, twelve individuals were able to rule that the Conservative Baptist Foreign Mission Society would not be recognized as an agency of the Northern Baptist Convention.[46]

The Conservative Baptist Movement

Early in 1944 the CBFMS opened an office in Chicago. Shortly thereafter, the Fundamentalist Fellowship opened its office virtually next door. Vincent Brushwyler was appointed as General Director of the CBFMS sometime in early 1945. In May, Raymond Buker was appointed as foreign secretary.[47]

In February 1945 the Fundamentalist Fellowship engaged Chester Tulga to become its Field and Research Secretary. Twenty years earlier, when Tulga was pastoring in Ohio, he had participated in the Baptist Bible Union. After moving to North Platte, Nebraska, he threw in his lot briefly with the Fundamentalist Fellowship. Near the end of that pastorate he quietly attempted to shift into the position of convention loyalist, a posture that he maintained through the years that he was ministering in Brookings, South Dakota. In

45. Ibid., 579–80. The minority members were F. Russell Purdy, I. Cedric Peterson, and W. Theodore Taylor.

46. Ibid., 580.

47. Vincent Brushwyler, "C.B.F.M.S. Annual Board Meeting," *Watchman Examiner*, June 21, 1945, 609.

December 1943 he was called to Norwood Park Baptist Church in Chicago, where he again shifted his loyalty back toward the Fundamentalist Fellowship. Since he was in Chicago, he probably attended the founding of the CBFMS. At any rate, he quickly became visible as an ally of the new mission. His new job with the Fundamentalist Fellowship placed him in national leadership for the first time. It also effectively removed Earle V. Pierce from leadership in the Fundamentalist Fellowship.

Tulga's periodical, called the *News Letter*, first appeared in February 1945. It was a relatively small affair, a single sheet folded in half. Tulga soon began to supplement the little *News Letter* by preparing longer, mimeographed white papers that he called the *Bulletins*. The first appeared on September 11. Soon, the Fundamentalist Fellowship was cranking out a stream of pamphlets, bulletins, newsletters, and booklets, most of which came from Tulga's pen. These publications, mailed directly to pastors and church members, could be relied upon to articulate the Conservative Baptist view on convention issues. This stream of literature fed much of the growth during the early years of the Conservative Baptist movement.[48]

In July 1945, the Swedish Baptist conference (which had maintained loose ties to the ABFMS) passed a resolution asking the board whether missionary candidates were required to affirm the virgin birth of Christ. The foreign board gave a vague answer that the Swedish Baptists found entirely unacceptable. In a move that angered other board members, Earle V. Pierce (still a member of the foreign board, though no longer the leader of the Fundamentalist Fellowship) offered a resolution that would have given an affirmative reply to the Swedish Baptists. His resolution was outvoted by the usual margin, twelve to four. Pierce responded by issuing a public appeal for conservatives throughout the convention to apply pressure to the foreign board. It was clear that he intended to make this episode an issue at the upcoming convention.[49]

In January 1946, the *News Letter* ran an article in which R. S. Beal of Tucson listed grievances against the Northern Baptist Convention. The first was that somebody was using the M&M Board to keep pastors and churches under control. Another was that the Council on Finance and Promotion, which had been formed in 1934, was now assuming dictatorial powers over state conventions by controlling nominations, appointments, and pastoral placements.

---

48. Kenneth W. Rhodes, "Ambivalent Fundamentalist: The Life and Ministry of Chester Tulga," (PhD diss.: University of Akron, 2001), 198–200. The second bulletin, undated but numbered #2, was also mimeographed. It devoted ten pages mainly to the Federal Council of Churches, and was probably edited by Tulga. The next issue was dated August 1946, and numbered Vol. 1, No. 1, edited by Tulga and from the Chicago address. After that a number of extended, mimeographed articles came out that year, but without numbering. The *News Letter* ran until about 1956, when Tulga left the CBF.

49. Earle V. Pierce, "What Will Conservatives Do?" *Watchman Examiner*, March 21, 1946, 280–82.

A third complaint was that the General Council, by operating as if it were the convention between meetings, gave a handful of individuals authority over the whole convention. Beal also protested the amount of money that the convention spent on overhead, the convention's lack of transparency, and its commitment to the Inclusive Policy.[50]

Other conservatives were also going into print. One of their most frequently voiced concerns was that the salaried servants of the convention were permitted to vote on convention business, creating a clear conflict of interest. Articulating the fundamentalist position, Charles H. Heaton published an article in which he stated that disenfranchising the salaried servants would be an important question at the Northern Baptist Convention for 1946.[51]

The convention was scheduled to meet in Grand Rapids, May 21–26. With the end of the war, travel was easier, and as the date drew near, feelings were running high. Then, somebody started a rumor that the conservatives were out to capture the convention. The convention's Law Committee responded by preparing a constitutional amendment that would effectively disenfranchise the supporters of CBFMS. The Council on Finance and Promotion intimated that the conservatives were lying. D. R. Sharpe, executive secretary of the Cleveland Baptist Association, threatened to fight the fundamentalists. As events would prove, he had plenty of ammunition.[52]

The conservatives had high hopes for the 1946 convention. Michigan was fundamentalist territory. The Fundamentalist Fellowship held its preconvention conference at Mel Trotter's mission, May 18–20. One matter of business was to change the name from Fundamentalist Fellowship to Conservative Baptist Fellowship. That name stuck for the next twenty years. On May 19 (Sunday afternoon), I. Cedric Peterson—the same I. Cedric Peterson who had incited the Des Moines University riot—preached on the subject, "The M&M as the Power Structure of the Liberals." The title said it all. Driven by a sense of frustration and desperation, and with victory plausibly within their grasp, the Conservative Baptists began planning their strategy for the convention.

The liberals already had their strategy in place. While the conservatives were still meeting, D. R. Sharpe drew first blood. In his files he had correspondence with Chester Tulga from years before. Tulga, presenting himself as a convention loyalist and distancing himself from fundamentalism, had asked Sharpe for help finding a pastorate. Now Sharpe printed an open letter to Tulga in pamphlet form, reviewing their correspondence and questioning

---

50. R. S. Beal, "Executive Committee of the Fundamentalist Fellowship Faces Convention Issues," *News Letter*, January 1946.

51. C. H. Heaton, "Shall Secretaries Vote?" *Watchman Examiner*, March 21, 1946, 282–83.

52. "Human Temper at the Convention," *Watchman Examiner*, May 9, 1946, 471; "The Proposed Amendment to the By-Laws of the Northern Baptist Convention," *Watchman Examiner*, May 9, 1946, 472–73.

Tulga's integrity: "In the light of your chameleon-like changes, from one position to another, are you competent to judge and especially are you qualified to lead a movement which you so recently repudiated as being factional, un-Christian, narrow, and intellectually bankrupt?" When delegates arrived at the convention, Sharpe had people stationed at the doors distributing the pamphlet. The contents shocked even the conservatives, and Tulga's credibility dropped to nothing. The damage was incalculable.[53]

The Regular Baptists had been watching the conservatives closely. Ketcham, still pastoring in Waterloo, read Sharpe's publication with dismay. He wrote to Tulga, "Frankly, Chester, in all of the twenty-five years of conflict I have had nothing which has left me with such a grieved spirit as this disclosure from the pen of Dr. Sharpe. . . . I am amazed and shocked when I read many of these quotations." Ketcham continued, "But Chester, the thing I can't understand is why, knowing as you did, that these statements were in the files of the enemy, you ever permitted yourself to be elevated to the place of prominent leadership which you occupied among Convention Fundamentalists."[54]

Upon receiving Ketcham's letter, Tulga crumpled it angrily, then smoothed it out to work on a reply. The core of his defense, repeated not only to Ketcham but to the board of the Fundamentalist Fellowship, was that Sharpe had misrepresented the quotations from their correspondence. Since Sharpe had been proven less than truthful on other matters, the board accepted his explanation (more or less), and decided that removing him would do more damage than leaving him as Research Secretary. Ketcham, however, was not so easily pacified. He insisted that "many of Dr. Sharpe's quotations seem to be thoroughly genuine." Ketcham then rehearsed a long list of these quotations, beginning each by asking, "Did you say. . . ." Then he wrote, "I repeat, Chester, even granting that you had repented of such statements and forsaken them fully, the fact that you knew they were in the files of the enemy should have been sufficient reason for you to have stayed out of range of their gun fire."[55]

The 1946 convention became a watershed for the Conservative Baptist movement. It represented one last, all-out effort by the fundamentalists to purge the convention and remove control from the liberals. The fundamentalists attended the convention in force. There they proposed four initiatives that, if adopted, would give them a major victory.[56]

First, Earle V. Pierce presented a constitutional amendment that would

53. D. R. Sharpe, "An Open Letter," May 7, 1946.

54. Robert T. Ketcham to Chester E. Tulga, July 18, 1946.

55. Chester E. Tulga to Robert T. Ketcham, July 20, 1946; Robert T. Ketcham to Chester E. Tulga, July 24, 1946.

56. Charles H. Heaton, *The Baptist Fundamentalist Fellowship* (Chicago: Fundamentalist Fellowship of the Northern Baptist Convention, 1946), 5.

have disenfranchised the paid executives of the convention. This motion was voted down.[57]

Second, in view of the oft-stated Inclusive Policy, the conservatives proposed a motion that would have required all convention personnel to affirm the virgin birth, bodily resurrection, and miracles of Christ, as well as the inspiration of all the contents of Scripture.[58] The convention, however, passed a substitute resolution that "we reaffirm our faith in the New Testament as a divinely inspired record and therefore a trustworthy, authoritative and all-sufficient rule of our faith and practice. We rededicate ourselves to Jesus Christ as Lord and Saviour and call our entire denomination to the common task of sharing the whole Gospel with the whole world."[59]

Third, the conservatives attempted to remove the Federal Council of Churches and the World Council of Churches from the convention's unified budget. This attempt was also defeated.[60]

Fourth, the conservatives offered a substitute ballot of convention officers. The Baptist Bible Union had tried something like this in 1927 and it was defeated then. The strategy fared no better now. The substitute ballot was defeated by 2,483 to 605.[61]

In short, the conservatives were outmaneuvered in every initiative. They had pinned their hopes on this convention. They were present in force. If they could not win in Grand Rapids, they knew they could not win anywhere. That by itself would have been a crushing defeat. Worse, however, was to come.

Under the convention rules, every member church was permitted to send two delegates to the convention meetings. For every one hundred members over the first one hundred, the church was allowed an additional delegate. So a church of 200 members would be allowed three delegates, a church of five hundred would be allowed six delegates, and so forth.[62]

H. C. Hassrick, speaking for the General Council, presented a motion that revised the number of delegates who would be recognized. A church would be allowed to send only that ratio of its delegates that matched the percentage of its benevolent funds that it directed into convention agencies. For example, a church of nine hundred members would normally be permitted ten delegates.

57. *Year Book of the Northern Baptist Convention, 1946* (Philadelphia: Judson Press, 1946), 48.

58. "Report of the Northern Baptist Convention," *Watchman Examiner*, June 13, 1946, 611–12.

59. *Year Book of the Northern Baptist Convention*, 97; Ibid., 96–97; "Report of the Northern Baptist Convention," 613.

60. *Year Book of the Northern Baptist Convention*, 138–39; "Report of the Northern Baptist Convention," 613–14.

61. *Year Book of the Northern Baptist Convention*, 166. The original motion had been made by Earle V. Pierce at Atlantic City in 1944. It was only being debated now.

62. *Year Book of the Northern Baptist Convention*, 145.

If the church gave half its benevolent money to convention agencies and half to CBFMS, then it would be allowed to seat only five delegates. A church that gave no financial support to the convention would be given no representation at all. If the Hassrick amendment passed, it would effectively disenfranchise the conservatives and de facto place them outside the convention.

Extended debate on the Hassrick amendment took place that evening, when G. E. Dawkins of Pennsylvania moved that it be adopted. Conservatives tried and failed to get it tabled. Then they pleaded for more time. Finally, when the conservatives had run out of maneuvers, the convention voted to accept the amendment, 2,298 to 585.[63]

At this point, a break was imminent. Indeed, the Hassrick amendment had effectively made the break already. Before the convention adjourned, the Fundamentalist Fellowship assembled and appointed a committee, popularly known as the Committee of Fifteen, to investigate the possibility of forming a new Conservative Baptist association of churches. Richard V. Clearwaters would later recall that many fundamentalists fled that meeting, never to return.

Other organizations were also in view. As early as February 1946, E. Myers Harrison had written to several fundamentalist leaders, including Chester Tulga, about the possibility of a Conservative Baptist Home Mission Society. Though a home mission society would not become a reality for another two years, Harrison's letter clearly indicates that conservative leaders were looking beyond the convention structures for the ministries and outreaches of their churches.[64]

Now the Committee of Fifteen was feeling its way toward an association of churches. Tulga, who was on the committee, wrote to several other members near the end of July. He opined that the time was not ripe to separate from the convention. To pull out now would mean leaving some brethren behind. They would have trouble leading their churches out, and there would surely be legal battles. As yet, Conservative Baptists had no seminary that they could take out with them. Besides, numbers of churches were in sound state conventions that might yet be captured by conservatives. Those included Arizona and Minnesota, and perhaps Colorado and Oregon.[65]

Some were asking whether they might not want to look for some sort of union with the GARBC. Perhaps still smarting from Ketcham's rebukes, Tulga responded to this suggestion in a letter addressed to the Conservative Baptist leadership. He observed that the GARBC would only be interested

63. Ibid., 147; "Report of the Northern Baptist Convention," 615–16.
64. E. Myers Harrison to Chester E. Tulga, February 26, 1946.
65. Chester E. Tulga to R. S. Beal, July 23, 1946; Chester E. Tulga to John Bradbury, July 27, 1946; Chester E. Tulga to Gabriel Guedj, July 27, 1946.

in churches that would leave the convention. Then he concluded, "As I see it, there is no immediate future for us in trying to amalgamate with any group."[66]

That winter, the Committee of Fifteen sent out a report on its progress. The members had met on September 17–20 at the Westminster Hotel in Winona Lake, Indiana. They claimed to have polled about twelve hundred convention pastors and to have met with several Baptist bodies that were looking toward closer cooperation. They then added these recommendations:

1. That we purpose to continue fellowship with those of like faith and practice both within and without the Northern Baptist Convention.

2. That for the present the Conservative Baptist Fellowship reaffirm its policy of recommending that our churches remain within the Northern Baptist Convention.

3. That the Conservative Baptist Fellowship continue as an organization within the Northern Baptist Convention.

4. That we support any group within the Convention (N.B.C.) whose efforts will be made toward the accomplishment of the objectives which the Conservative Baptist Fellowship has advocated.

5. That the three proposed regional conferences give consideration to the formation of a united conservative Baptist association of America, to which any sovereign Baptist church may belong regardless of other affiliations, providing that each church subscribes to our (C.B.F.) doctrinal statement. (It is understood that the number of affiliations is not an ethical problem for an autonomous Baptist church.) And that this Committee shall supply each conference with a tentative and specific outline of the scope and activity of such a group.[67]

As the committee drafted a constitution, it followed the pattern of the CBFMS in calling three regional fellowships. Following the above recommendations, Article Four of the constitution allowed for dual affiliation with the Northern Baptist Convention. That provision would later become a matter of contention. To some of the founders, dual affiliation was a means of helping candidate churches get out of the convention. From their perspective, the new association was asking churches to join, after which the association would help those churches in their struggle to get free. To others of the founders, Article Four was a sort of Bill of Rights, affirming their entitlement to identify with the Conservative Baptist movement while permanently maintaining their links with the convention.

To this point, the Conservative Baptist movement consisted of the CBFMS and the Conservative Baptist Fellowship. At Atlantic City, 1947, the Conservative Baptist Association of America was born, becoming the third

---

66. Chester E. Tulga to the Conservative Baptist Leadership, July 29, 1946.
67. Conservative Baptist Fellowship, Committee of Fifteen Report, n.d. but winter 1946–47.

Conservative Baptist organization. The new association elected I. Cedric Peterson as its general director.

The following year, 1948, the CBF organized the Conservative Baptist Home Mission Society, probably upon the urging of B. Myron Cedarholm. CBHMS was authorized at the annual Conservative Baptist conference in Milwaukee and held its first meeting June 24. It operated with a board of ten. L. M. Clark of Chicago was chosen as president, Walter Fricke as secretary, Mitch Seidler as treasurer, and F. D. McFadden as assistant treasurer. From the beginning the new home mission aimed to avoid needless competition with other sound Baptist works, but it refused to be bound by comity agreements. It would accept only candidates who expressed unqualified agreement with the doctrinal statement. Candidates would also have to give evidence of adequate training, experience, and spirituality for the task and field to which they were called. Office work would be done in the central division (Chicago) office.

In 1948 the CBF elected Richard V. Clearwaters as its president. He served until 1951, and was then replaced by J. Palmer Muntz. In 1949 B. Myron Cedarholm replaced I. Cedric Peterson as general director of Conservative Baptist Association of America. This was a pivotal move. Cedarholm was a capable promoter, and in sixteen years he brought the membership of CBA from about ninety to around eighteen hundred churches, many of which he had helped to plant. He remained general director until 1965.

With the close of the decade, several men (among them, William Whittemore, Hale Davis, Sam Bradford, and R. V. Clearwaters) saw a need for a Conservative Baptist seminary. By this time Riley had started a seminary as part of the Northwestern organization. Those who wanted a Baptist school were sending their young men and women primarily to Northern Baptist Theological Seminary. At the time, Northern had over three hundred students, a blue-ribbon faculty, adequate buildings (though in an increasingly hazardous neighborhood), a tradition of loyalty to the Scriptures, and regional accreditation for its undergraduate programs. On the negative side, the seminary was still connected to the Northern Baptist Convention.

During those years Northern's president, Charles Koller, seemed to go through some agony of soul over the school's position, but his loyalty to the NBC hardly wavered. A few events drove him into deeper loyalty to the convention, one of them being a telephone interview with Tulga, during which Tulga secretly had a stenographer transcribe the conversation.[68] The convention had its own way of applying pressure, and in 1949 Koller came to a final decision. In November he invited several convention executives for a week

68. A copy of the transcript was in the Tulga files in 1962.

of chapels to sell the M&M Board, Judson Press, and the mission societies to the students. He then took the position in class that Northern was in the convention, not in spite of the liberals, but because of them. He claimed that Northern could lose all the battles and still win the war, flooding the convention pulpits with good men. His optimism had some basis in fact: Northern was graduating about as many preachers as the liberal convention seminaries together. Nevertheless, those good men never came close to purifying the convention.

Conservative Baptists saw Koller's declaration as the beginning of the end. For Northern there could be no return. One fundamentalist board member resigned in a public letter, predicting to Koller that his successor would be a man very different from himself and that his successor would be an outright modernist. The prophecy was not far wrong.

Early in 1951, R. V. Clearwaters wrote to Koller, answering Koller's optimism about flooding the convention's pulpits with good men, thereby losing the battles but winning the war.

> Since the Minnesota Baptist Convention has been committed to the Conservative Baptist program and objectives, the graduates of Northern Baptist Theological Seminary one by one have come into Minnesota, accepted pastorates, and consistently stood with the modernist minority in opposing the Minnesota Baptist Convention. Why? Because true to their training, they are schooled to an ecclesiastical loyalty to the Northern Baptist Convention (now the American Baptist Convention) "inclusive policy" which they put ahead of their theological loyalty to the Word of God.[69]

Koller would not remain president at Northern much longer. With the worsening neighborhood and after several muggings (including Stiansen), the board gave Koller an extended leave, appointing Ben Browne, a home office establishment man, as interim president. As it turned out, Koller's leave was so extended that he never returned.

By the time that Conservative Baptists felt that they could no longer look to Northern, they had already begun organizing their own school. The spring of 1950 brought the announcement of a new seminary to be opened in Denver. A mansion near downtown had been purchased, and the organizers chose William Kerr, the theologian from Northern, as dean.

Kerr was given the responsibility of putting the school together. He brought four young men from Northern: William Burdick to teach New Testament, Joseph Edwards to teach Old Testament, William McLaughlin for homiletics, and Douglas Birk, who had run the bookstore, to be business manager. It

---

69. Richard V. Clearwaters to Charles W. Koller, January 17, 1951.

seemed like an ideal team, with a faculty young enough to provide stability for many years to come. The seminary opened that fall with about thirty students.

At that point the picture seemed complete. The new Conservative Baptist movement had, in seven years, established five essential organizations. It boasted a constituency of churches whose membership numbered in the thousands. Under Brushwyler's leadership, CBFMS had nearly three hundred missionaries under appointment. The Conservative Baptist Association of America was growing rapidly; the growth rate under Cedarholm surpassed that of any other Baptist fellowship during that century. Yet the weaknesses in the organizational scheme would ultimately prove to be critical in the face of the differences among the Conservative Baptists themselves.

Regular Baptists and Conservative Baptists

Regular Baptists had left the convention in 1932, and they required separation from 1938 onward. Still, they followed the doings of the convention fundamentalists with keen interest, particularly as events transformed the Fundamentalist Fellowship into the Conservative Baptist movement. To explain the relationship of Regular Baptists to Conservative Baptists, it is necessary to return the narrative to the late 1930s.

As early as 1939 W. B. Riley published a challenge to convention fundamentalists in his *Pilot*. The *Baptist Bulletin* immediately reprinted the article. Riley argued that the Fundamentalist Fellowship "ought to put up a worthy fight or cease from it altogether." He observed that "as politicians we have been signal failures; not once since the anniversaries at Buffalo, N.Y., and at Des Moines, Iowa, have we had formulated any definite and adequate plan, or courageously attempted to carry anything through!" This failure was particularly distressing in view of the liberals' inability to maintain the institutions that they had captured. Riley optimistically posited that, with a determined effort, the fundamentalists could take control of the convention within a year, or within two or three at the most.[70]

Editorializing on Riley's essay, Ketcham endorsed the dictum that the convention fundamentalists ought to fight or quit. Ketcham also noticed that Riley had said, "*The Regular Baptists* will take in more churches the coming year than they have any year in the past, and their increase will grow in proportion as the present modernist control continues." To this, Ketcham simply responded, "Thank you, Doctor."[71]

With Ketcham as editor, the *Baptist Bulletin* continued to reprint articles

70. "Dr. W. B. Riley on the Northern Baptist Convention," *Baptist Bulletin*, September 1939, 1, 5–6.
71. Ibid.

from Riley every few months. Ketcham was also following reports on the Northern Baptist Convention in the *Watchman Examiner*, and he would occasionally comment on these in the *Baptist Bulletin*. In 1941 the GARBC met at First Baptist Church of Pontiac, pastored by H. H. Savage. The meeting was notable because Savage was still identified with the Fundamentalist Fellowship rather than the Regular Baptist movement.

The meeting in Pontiac illustrates that the GARBC did not perceive the convention fundamentalists as opponents. Indeed, in February 1943 the Fundamentalist Fellowship of eastern Michigan played host to the GARBC Council of Fourteen. The council reciprocated by presenting a major conference under the sponsorship of the Alpha Baptist Church of Detroit. The meeting featured nine of the fourteen council members and was promoted among both convention and non-convention Baptist churches. Both groups were delighted with the result, and the *Baptist Bulletin* opined, "We trust that in the future like gatherings may be held in strategic metropolitan areas [of] the country."[72]

When the Fridell controversy erupted between convention fundamentalists and the ABFMS, Regular Baptists seem hardly to have noticed. It finally came to their attention through an editorial that W. B. Riley published in the *Pilot*. The next month, Ketcham noted that Fridell's modernism was so obnoxious that it got the attention even of fundamentalists who were convention loyalists.[73]

When in 1943 the fundamentalists appointed a committee to form a conservative mission board, Ketcham could barely restrain himself. For years the conservatives had been boasting that they had displaced the liberals on the convention boards and were in de facto control of the convention. They had complained that the Regular Baptist exposure of modernism was dated, perhaps true at one time, but no longer the case. Now Ketcham gave voice to his exasperation.

> The Convention Fundamentalists have been especially emphatic in their statements that the condition within the Foreign Board in particular has improved. They have claimed that one by one they have been putting fundamentalists on the Foreign Board, and that they are there in such numbers as to practically control the fundamental interests of that Board. They have said over and over again that now Baptists everywhere could send their missionary money through the Foreign Board with safety and assurance and that it would be properly used for the propagation of old-fashioned Baptist faith. And now comes the crash! And the crash reveals exactly what we have all along

72. "Eastern Michigan Baptist Fundamental Fellowship Plays Host to G.A.R.B. Council Members," *Baptist Bulletin*, March 1943, 2.

73. Robert T. Ketcham, "Facts for Baptists to Face," *Baptist Bulletin*, May 1943, 10.

contended, that the situation is not one whit better than it has ever been. The crash reveals that slow-going, compromising fundamentalists within the Convention have come up against something that even they cannot countenance.[74]

Ketcham expressed particular disdain for Earle V. Pierce. For years Pierce had been the main voice denouncing the Regular Baptist criticisms of the convention. He had even gone so far as to question the Regular Baptists' truthfulness. Now Ketcham reprinted an entire editorial in which Pierce claimed that conditions in the ABFMS had been getting worse for years. Ketcham observed, "Here over his own signature he admits the fact that the situation within the Foreign Board has never been settled and that it has been increasingly difficult to deal with it, and that now in order to hold the 'loyalties' of a large number of Baptist churches, the old Board must be completely deserted and a new one set up."[75]

As far as Ketcham was concerned, the plan for a new board within the convention was doomed from the start. He pointed back to the Tondo Station controversy, when H. H. Savage tried to work alongside the foreign board. Ketcham remembered that Savage was told "in no uncertain terms that he could not publicize, propagate, or develop the particular mission station or field which he and his churches took over. . . . How could missionaries from the two boards ever work side-by-side on the same field? "The inevitable result of such a set up will be discord and conflict with resultant discouragement to the missionaries and to the churches."[76]

From Ketcham's perspective, the only real solution for the convention fundamentalists was separation. Trying to set up a new, conservative mission society within the convention would never work. Not just the foreign board, but the whole convention was filled with liberalism. Ketcham tried to appeal directly to the disgruntled conservatives:

> Brethren of the new mission society, why not do the job right while you are at it and make the separation complete, and join the forces of those who saw this situation years ahead of you, and have put into operation a great Baptist fellowship based upon the old historic Baptist principles as found in the sure Word of God? . . . May God give a great host of pastors and churches within the Northern Baptist Convention courage even yet to take the step and the stand that alone will honor God.[77]

---

74. Robert T. Ketcham, "Northern Baptist Convention Splits over Foreign Board," *Baptist Bulletin*, July 1943, 1.
75. Ibid., 3.
76. Ibid., 4.
77. Ibid., 4.

Two months later Ketcham was again editorializing about "the competence of the leaders of the convention fundamentalist movement." He reproduced a statement from 1935 in which Earle V. Pierce had stated that "anyone who contends that the Foreign Board is sending modernist missionaries to the field is either ignorant or mendacious." He also reproduced a statement in which John W. Bradbury had claimed that convention conservatives "have gained control of the Foreign Mission Board; have an approximate control of the Home Mission Boards; have reformed the publication society; have built up three of our largest seminaries and training schools"; and accomplished other great advances within the convention.[78]

Then Ketcham told how, in a recent address, Bradbury admitted that modernist missionaries were being sent to the field and that three-quarters of recent missionaries had graduated from liberal schools. When asked how long he had known about this state of affairs, Bradbury replied, "For fifteen years." He was then asked why he had not warned Northern Baptists of what he knew, and he had no reply. Bradbury did state later that he was admitting these facts "to his shame."[79]

Turning his attention to Pierce, Ketcham noted that when Elmer Fridell was elected secretary of the foreign board, four votes opposed his selection. It was Pierce who rose and moved that the vote be made unanimous—the same Pierce who said that no modernist missionaries had gone to the field during the previous twelve years. Ketcham objected to the trustworthiness of the kind of leadership that Pierce and Bradbury had provided. He urged convention fundamentalists to think twice before following such mistaken leaders any further. Then he added,

> We repeat with renewed insistence that the only solution for the rank and file of Baptist churches and pastors who still want to be true to the historic Baptist faith is to completely separate from the apostate convention itself and to repudiate the leadership of men who mistakenly or otherwise have deliberately tried to make them believe that things were under control while at the same time they themselves knew that the situation was as wretched and deplorable as ever.[80]

Ketcham raised the subject again in the November *Baptist Bulletin*. He printed a six-page article that pushed many regular features out of the magazine. In the article, he summarized the situation in the convention, including the appointment of Fridell, the conservative reaction, the joint meeting between the fundamentalists and ABFMS on September 9, the foreign board's

---

78. Robert T. Ketcham, "The Tragedy of a Mistaken Leadership," *Baptist Bulletin*, September 1943, 1.
79. Ibid., 1–2.
80. Ibid. 2.

decision on September 21, and the conservatives' call for regional meetings leading up to a new mission society. Ketcham then briefly reviewed his reasons for believing that the new society would not work. The bulk of the article, however, was devoted to a comparison of what the fundamentalist leadership (especially Pierce and Bradbury) had been saying for years versus what they were saying now. The contrasts were stark, which led Ketcham to wonder how anybody could follow their leadership.

> Certainly if a man has proven himself untrustworthy in leadership in past experiences, there would seem to be no particular call for trusting him for leadership in some new venture. . . . We know it is not nice to say, "We told you so." But we did! And we do not hesitate a moment to tell you again that this same leadership is proposing to take this same unsuspecting crowd of Baptists out upon another venture which is already doomed to failure because it violates the fundamental principle of God's Word, to come out from among them and be separate.[81]

Contrary to Ketcham's advice, many of the convention fundamentalists did trust the conservative leadership and followed Earle V. Pierce in organizing the new Conservative Baptist Foreign Mission Society. Ketcham did not address the topic again until after the Coleman Commission had delivered its first report and the replies had begun to appear. Then Ketcham fastened particularly to a response that Pierce published in the *Watchman Examiner*. Pierce had tried to explain how votes to send liberals to the mission field could appear to be unanimous. Pierce admitted that the conservatives had bowed to pressure and abstained from some votes, then explained, "But when one knows that his vote will amount to nothing except to mark him as an obstructor, there often arises a serious question as to what he should do." Ketcham's response to this explanation was pointed: "The shame and shallowness of this admission must be apparent to all and certainly needs no editorial comment to emphasize it."[82]

If Ketcham's words seem brittle, it is worth remembering that Pierce had spent ten years accusing him of misrepresenting the situation in the convention. Now Pierce was admitting the truth of the very things that Ketcham had been saying all along. Worse, Pierce was leading a separation from the ABFMS because of its liberalism, but at the same moment he and his fellow leaders were trying to keep churches and pastors in an equally liberal convention. Ketcham insisted that convention fundamentalists could not have it both ways.

---

81. Robert T. Ketcham, "The Northern Baptist Situation," *Baptist Bulletin*, November 1943, 1–6.
82. Robert T. Ketcham, "The New Conservative Baptist Foreign Mission Society," *Baptist Bulletin*, April 1944, 1.

Why penalize the Foreign Board by separating from it and at the same time stay within the framework of everything else that is equally modernistic. If these conservative brethren feel called upon now to create a Conservative Baptist Mission Board, then why not obey God fully and create a Conservative Baptist Convention. We would gladly welcome these fundamental Baptists into the fold of the G.A.R.B., which saw this issue fifteen years ago and pioneered the way and set up just such a Baptist body.[83]

From this point the *Baptist Bulletin* maintained more or less of a silence about the convention fundamentalists. Ketcham was enduring a series of unsuccessful procedures to restore his failing eyesight, so the editorship of the *Bulletin* went to the new national representative, H. O. Van Gilder. At least in their official publication, the Regular Baptists ignored the Fundamentalist Fellowship for upwards of a year. They broke their silence, however, after the conservatives were badly beaten at the 1946 Grand Rapids convention.

In a front page article the *Baptist Bulletin* reported every disastrous blow to the conservatives: the failure to disenfranchise the convention officials, the failure to defund the National Council and World Council of Churches, the failure to pass even a barely minimal doctrinal standard, the proportioning of voting rights to financial contributions, and the failure to elect a conservative ballot of officers. The *Baptist Bulletin* noted that the convention fundamentalists were beginning to divide into two camps: those who were "openly advocating separation," and those who were "clamoring for more moderation." The *Bulletin* observed,

> Whether the compromising attitude of a few will temper the policies of the Fundamentalist group remains to be seen. We know the temper and spirit of many of their leaders, and are convinced that they will not compromise. However, it will certainly prove extremely difficult for them to rally their forces in any campaign now for reforms in the Convention, and we predict that many churches this year will be coming out. We trust that many of them will find their fellowship with us and devote their strength in constructive efforts, while they enjoy the happy fellowship and freedom from conflict to be found within the G.A.R.B.C.[84]

Two months later national representative H. O. Van Gilder devoted an article to the problems that convention fundamentalists were about to face. On the one hand, many had moved rather quickly into a separatist stance. They were likely to discover, however, that separation would not be easy—especially for churches that were financially indebted to state conventions. On the

---

83. Ibid., 2.
84. "Convention Fundamentalists Defeated at Grand Rapids," *Baptist Bulletin*, July 1946, 1, 14–15.

other hand, in Minnesota the fundamentalists had actually captured the state convention. Van Gilder observed, "For the Fundamentalists of that state officially to sever with the Convention, would be not only to lose the advantage which these resources give them, but to surrender these funds into the hands of those who would use them for the destruction of our historic Baptist faith." Furthermore, in many cases conservative pastors had only recently been informed about the issues, and they would need time to give their churches the necessary information to be prepared for separation. In spite of these considerations, the Fundamentalist Fellowship had to develop a working program almost immediately, and that program would probably not satisfy everyone.[85]

As the situation now stood, Van Gilder expressed one great hope: "that those who are like-minded in the things of the Lord may find some way to establish a more united testimony, or at least to avoid further division with its consequent weakening of the cause of evangelical Christianity." These were more than mere words on Van Gilder's part. The Council of Fourteen had already sent a communication to prominent Conservative Baptist leaders, pleading that "they would not set up another organization of Bible-believing Baptists without first considering with us the possibility of some sort of united testimony." The hope was genuine, and the terms in which it was expressed were deliberately vague. Exactly what Van Gilder and the council had in mind would soon become apparent.[86]

The fact is that the Regular Baptist leadership had been quietly courting the Conservative Baptist leadership for over a year. The first overture took the form of a letter from Ketcham to R. S. Beal and Albert Johnson in early March 1945. Ketcham probably chose these two because they were more sympathetic than some to Regular Baptists. The letter was both an irenicum and an appeal. He began by noting that he was not speaking in any official capacity, but that he judged his associates to be sympathetic with what he was about to say. Then he mentioned his recent editorials—a necessary move, since these publications could hardly have failed to offend some Conservative Baptists.

> [N]o doubt you have felt that in many respects I was over critical and somewhat skeptical. May I say to you that many of the points of criticism which appeared in my editorials have been greatly modified and in some instances completely eliminated, by the fact that the Conservative movement has changed its leadership. I think you made a tremendous step in the right direction when the leadership of this movement was taken out of the hands of Dr. Pierce, and I, of course, would include with him Dr. Bradbury, for I think he was equally at fault with Dr. Pierce in his "coverup" of the true situation.[87]

85. H. O. Van Gilder, "Editorial Comment," *Baptist Bulletin*, September 1946, 3, 30–31.
86. Ibid., 31.
87. Robert T. Ketcham to H. H. Savage and Albert Johnson, March 10, 1945, copied in,

The letter went on to predict that the conservatives would not be able to cleanse the convention. Eventually, the supporters of the new mission board would either be thrown out of the convention or they would be forced to walk out, taking their new board with them. Some would balk, but many would separate. When that happened, Ketcham said, he wanted to avoid the "tragic spectacle" of a second Baptist fellowship outside the convention. He pleaded with Beal and Johnson at least to sit down and explore the possibility of a union between Regular Baptists and Conservative Baptists. [88]

Two months later, on May 15, Ketcham presented this letter to the Council of Fourteen. He had judged his colleagues rightly—they were delighted with the sentiments that he had expressed. Consequently, the council endorsed the letter and sent copies to other convention fundamentalist leaders. [89]

The convention conservatives, however, were not yet ready to turn their attention to separation. Into 1946, the Fundamentalist Fellowship remained adamant that separation was not one of its objectives. Not until the Grand Rapids convention did the minds of the Conservative Baptist leadership begin to change. Even after the debacle at Grand Rapids, however, Conservative Baptist leaders remained cool toward the GARBC.[90]

In October 1946 the Conservative Baptists' Committee of Fifteen arranged for a meeting with representatives of other groups at Winona Lake, Indiana. Among those invited was H. O. Van Gilder. The result was a cordial conversation between the GARBC national representative and the Committee of Fifteen. The next month, Gabriel Guedj contacted Van Gilder and asked for specific suggestions for ways that Conservative Baptists and Regular Baptists could try to work toward union. To prepare an answer, the Council of Fourteen met in Los Angeles during the first week of December and drafted a four-point plan that projected a merger between Regular Baptists and Conservative Baptists in May 1950. A copy of this plan was sent to each member of the Committee of Fifteen.

To achieve the merger, the first step would be for the Conservative Baptists to form an organization of churches. The process of organization would permit the Conservative Baptists to discover for themselves who would be included in rather an amorphous movement. It would also give them a platform to negotiate as a group with the Regular Baptists.

"Convention Conservatives—Can We Get Together?" *Baptist Bulletin*, April 1947, 4–5.

88. Ibid.

89. Resolution of the Council of Fourteen, General Association of Regular Baptist Churches, May 15, 1945, copied in "Convention Conservatives—Can We Get Together?" *Baptist Bulletin*, April 1947, 5.

90. Charles H. Heaton, *The Baptist Fundamentalist Fellowship* (Chicago: Fundamentalist Fellowship of the Northern Baptist Convention, 1946), 5; Chester E. Tulga to the Conservative Baptist leadership, July 29, 1946.

The second step, to be taken at the same time as the first, would be to announce publicly that the two groups intended to merge. In fact, Conservative Baptists and Regular Baptists would immediately begin to cooperate in every way except organizational structure. This cooperation would silence critics who saw one or the other of the groups as troublemakers who could not get along with anyone.

The third step would be to work through the remaining prejudices and differences between the Regular Baptists and the Conservative Baptists. The cooperation specified in the second step would provide a natural venue for airing and negotiating these differences. A three-year courtship would provide ample opportunity to discover any insurmountable differences before the merger would be finalized.

The fourth step would be for the GARBC to authorize the Council of Fourteen to negotiate the actual merger. Presumably the Conservative Baptists' Committee of Fifteen would have the same authorization. The council was optimistic about the possibility of bringing the two groups together by 1950, but was also quite willing for either group to speed up the proceedings or to slow them down. In any case, a final plan would have to be submitted to all churches as a referendum for final ratification before it could be adopted.[91]

In January 1947 the Committee of Fifteen met with the Council of Fourteen at the Stevens Hotel in Chicago. Thirteen Conservative Baptists and nine Regular Baptists (including the national representative) attended the meeting. The chief topic of discussion was the relationship of the Conservative Baptist movement to the Northern Baptist Convention. Most members of the Committee of Fifteen thought that the convention fundamentalists were headed toward separation, but they considered it unwise to state their intentions publicly. The opposite sentiment had also been expressed, however—most recently in a letter sent out by Carl Truax, a prominent Conservative Baptist leader from California. Truax had written to Conservative Baptists on the West Coast,

> There has been a persistent rumor out for some time that the Conservative Baptist Foreign Mission Society, the Conservative Baptist Fellowship and I have been advising churches to leave the Northern Baptist Convention. . . . Please be fully advised that neither the CBFMS, nor the CBF, nor I are advising any church to withdraw from the Northern Baptist Convention. The contrary is true."[92]

91. Resolution of the Council of Fourteen, General Association of Regular Baptist Churches, early December, 1946; reprinted in "Convention Conservatives—Can We Get Together?" *Baptist Bulletin*, April 1947, 4–5.

92. Carl Truax to Conservative Baptist pastors on the West Coast, January 7, 1947; cited in "The Difference Between the CBA of A and the GARBC," mimeographed paper from the GARBC home office, n.d. but 1960.

Clearly the Conservative Baptists did not agree among themselves about whether or when they might be headed for separation. Some wondered aloud whether they would end up creating an association that would be half in and half out of the convention.

In view of these differences, H. O. Van Gilder suggested that the Committee of Fifteen might at least pass a declaration recognizing the principle of separation. He received support from committee member H. H. Savage. Eventually the Committee of Fifteen passed the following declaration:

> Since the Northern Baptist Convention has resolved "That we reaffirm our faith in the New Testament as the divinely inspired record and therefore the trustworthy, authoritative and all sufficient rule of our faith and practice" and since we believe the New Testament teaches the virgin birth, the atoning death, the bodily resurrection, and other great truths historically held by Baptists, and since we believe the New Testament teaches refusal to cooperate with those who do not hold such like precious truths, therefore: we are opposed to the inclusive policy (which condones unbelief while recognizing truth and violates conscience) and refuse to support it financially or promotionally directly or indirectly.[93]

While this Chicago Resolution did express separation of a sort, it was miles away from the GARBC brand of separatism. As late as September 1946 the Committee of Fifteen was directing the Conservative Baptist Fellowship to encourage conservative churches to remain in the convention. The Chicago Resolution did nothing to repudiate that direction. Nevertheless, it appeared to give some credence to separatism, if only indirectly, and it was passed unanimously by those Committee of Fifteen members who were present.

Some within the GARBC felt that "real progress had been made" at the Chicago meeting. R. S. Beal thought that the Council of Fourteen's proposal for full fellowship (except for organizational union) should be implemented immediately. As the proposal indicated, the Committee of Fifteen moved ahead with its plan for organizing a fellowship of churches. The feeling was that the three regional meetings had worked well when establishing the CBFMS and that the process ought to be repeated.[94]

The three regional meetings were held in Brooklyn, Chicago, and San Francisco, all during February 1947. These meetings culminated in a plan to launch the new Conservative Baptist Association in Atlantic City that summer. Even

---

93. Minutes of the Combined Meeting of the Council of Fourteen of the General Association of Regular Baptist Churches and the Committee of Fifteen of the Conservative Baptist Fellowship, held at the Stevens Hotel in Chicago, Illinois, January 28, 1947; see also "Convention Conservatives—Can We Get Together?" *Baptist Bulletin*, April 1947, 5–6.

94. "Convention Conservatives—Can We Get Together?" *Baptist Bulletin*, April 1947, 6.

during the regional meetings, however, many expressed the sentiment that the new CBA should permit its churches to continue in fellowship with the Northern Baptist Convention.[95]

Regular Baptists were both surprised and disappointed by developments at these meetings. The Chicago Resolution, passed unanimously by the Committee of Fifteen, was supposed to be read at all three regionals. At the Central Regional, however, it had been heavily amended to remove much of its already-mild separatism. At the Eastern Regional, no mention was made of the Chicago Resolution until a question was raised from the floor by a visiting GARBC pastor—and then chairman Gabriel Guedj simply summarized the resolution from memory. At the Western Regional, the Chicago Resolution was not brought up at all.[96]

The recommendation of the Committee of Fifteen to the regional meetings reiterated the commitment to permit dual affiliation with the Northern Baptist Convention. Both the Central and Eastern regionals declared themselves in favor of this plan. Before the Western Regional met, Gabriel Guedj wrote to H. O. Van Gilder, again emphasizing that the CBA would be a fellowship of autonomous churches, "regardless of other affiliations." Then he suggested that the Council of Fourteen try to persuade GARBC churches to join the new Conservative Baptist association.[97]

Van Gilder immediately wired Guedj. The telegram expresses some of the disappointment and even alarm that the GARBC leadership must have felt at this point: "Believe invitation to our churches to participate in constitution convention of CBA will be widely regarded as unfriendly effort to disrupt GARB." Van Gilder went on, "Course approved by our Council outlined in proposal already submitted. This proposal will be published in April Bulletin with full history of negotiations."[98]

In fact, Van Gilder's terse cable could hardly have conveyed the dismay of the Regular Baptist leadership. They had left the Chicago meeting in January full of optimism. Now things appeared to have gone badly awry. The Committee of Fifteen was clearly rethinking its already-limited commitment to separation. Two of the three regionals had adopted a plan that explicitly disavowed separatism. Further, it appeared that the Committee of Fifteen had every intention of trying to co-opt the merger by involving GARBC churches

95. Bruce Shelley, *A History of Conservative Baptists*, 57.

96. "Convention Conservatives—Can We Get Together?" *Baptist Bulletin*, April 1947, 6; "Is the GARBC Unfriendly to the CBA?" mimeographed paper from the GARBC Home Office, n.d. but early 1950s, 9.

97. "Convention Conservatives—Can We Get Together?" *Baptist Bulletin*, April 1947, 6; Gabriel Guedj to H. O. Van Gilder, February 14, 1947; reprinted in "Convention Conservatives—Can We Get Together?" *Baptist Bulletin*, April 1947, 7.

98. H. O. Van Gilder to Gabriel Guedj, n.d. but mid-February 1947; reproduced in "Convention Conservatives—Can We Get Together?" *Baptist Bulletin*, April 1947, 6–7.

as part of the Conservative Baptist Association of America from the very beginning. Clearly Van Gilder took this move as an attempt to divide the Regular Baptist forces so as to weaken the Council of Fourteen's bargaining position.

Van Gilder's telegram did not catch up with Guedj until after the Western Regional had already met. Guedj bristled at it. He told Van Gilder that the conservatives were not approaching GARBC churches "at this time," but rather asking the Council of Fourteen to make the approach. Second, Guedj insisted that the Chicago Resolution had been "presented in substance and adopted unanimously" at the three regional conferences. Furthermore, Guedj disclaimed "any vestige of desire to disrupt and that also applies to our entire leadership." As far as he was concerned, the Committee of Fifteen was simply calling for a convention of churches. While he did not deny that some of them might already be fellowshipping with the GARBC, he asked, "How can that be regarded as disruptive?"[99]

Guedj's claim that the Chicago Declaration had been presented and adopted unanimously at the three regionals was hardly credible. An edited version had been presented at the Central Regional. It had been summarized from memory at the Eastern Regional. It had never been introduced at the Western Regional. Regular Baptists knew the facts because many had attended each meeting and were witnesses to the proceedings. Van Gilder himself had been present at the Central Regional. For the Regular Baptist leadership, Guedj's reply constituted clear evidence that he was willing to play loosely with the truth.

Van Gilder's response betrayed little of the irritation that he must have felt. He welcomed Guedj's disavowal of any intention to disrupt the GARBC. Nevertheless, he pointed out that the conservatives were supposed to be organizing the churches *"which now comprise your constituency,"* not seeking a larger and partly Regular Baptist constituency. Van Gilder emphasized, *"Frankly, I hold that anything else would be unethical."* He continued,

> Let me remind you again that our proposal was that you brethren organize *your own group*, and that our two associations, after maintaining cordial relations, and conducting cooperative enterprises, undertake a merger. This I believe to be the course of courtesy, brotherhood, and Christian statesmanship, and I sincerely hope you will use your influence in this direction.[100]

Van Gilder tried to make it clear that his only objection was to the fact that

99. Gabriel Guedj to H. O. Van Gilder (n.d. but late February 1947); reproduced in "Convention Conservatives—Can We Get Together?" *Baptist Bulletin*, April 1947, 7.

100. H. O. Van Gilder to Gabriel Guedj, March 5, 1947; reproduced in "Convention Conservatives—Can We Get Together?" *Baptist Bulletin*, April 1947, 7.

the Conservative Baptists had not yet thought through all of their organizational convictions, especially in the matter of separation. If the Conservative Baptists could get clear on that, then he would be more than prepared to abandon the GARBC. For the moment, however, the Conservative Baptists were still in transition. Van Gilder continued, "If our brethren get the idea that you Conservatives are attempting to 'raid' our group, any real union may be delayed by years."[101]

The discussion now stood at an impasse. Van Gilder ran an article in the April 1947 edition of the *Baptist Bulletin* that documented the history of the conversation to that point. The Council of Fourteen had already accepted an invitation from the Committee of Fifteen to hold the GARBC annual conference in Atlantic City that May. The plan was for both groups to schedule the same meeting hall, with the Conservative Baptists commencing their meeting the day after the Regular Baptists ended theirs. That way, Conservative Baptists could come a day early for the last day of the GARBC meetings, while the Regular Baptists could stay over an extra day and catch the opening of the Conservative Baptist Association of America meetings.

After Van Gilder published his article, however, the Committee of Fifteen changed the plan. With everyone's travel plans already set, they rescheduled the CBA convention to open a day early. Since the meeting hall had already been programmed for Regular Baptist use, the committee rented a local Presbyterian church building in which to convene. This move had the effect of keeping Conservative Baptists out of the Regular Baptist meeting. Whatever factors may have influenced this decision, it threw a wrench into the exchange between the two groups. Rightly or wrongly, the Council of Fourteen had the sense that they were being snubbed.

Even so, the council agreed to a second meeting with the Committee of Fifteen while both groups were in Atlantic City. Ketcham later described that meeting as uneasy from the start. Gabriel Guedj was in the chair. The Committee of Fifteen led off by having H. H. Savage read their draft constitution for the Conservative Baptist Association of America. After Savage had finished reading it, he tapped the draft and said, "This is separation. This is separation." Whereupon Lester Thompson, a committee member from Colorado, rejoined, "Well, this is the first time I've heard that this is a separatist organization, and what's more, if that's separation, I don't want to have any part of it." For the next hour and a half the Conservative Baptists argued among themselves about the sort of association they were putting together. Finally someone looked at Ketcham, whose men had sat silently through the whole encounter, and asked what he thought. He replied to the effect that the Regular Baptists were not

101. Ibid.

ready to join a group that could not decide what it was. At that point Guedj abruptly stalked out of the meeting.[102]

Upon the motion of David Otis Fuller, a committee of six was elected to continue discussions about a merger. The Council of Fourteen selected three members from the Committee of Fifteen, and vice versa. As events unfolded, however, this committee of six would never even meet.

Over the next few days, the Conservative Baptist Association of America was born. From the beginning it followed the Committee of Fifteen's recommendation in allowing for dual affiliation. Evidently, all of the Conservative Baptist leaders favored this policy, but they had different reasons for preferring it. Some wanted time to lead their churches out of the convention with minimal risk of litigation and minimal damage to their retirement fund. Others seem to have hoped to keep one foot in the convention and the other in the CBA indefinitely. Before a decade passed, this difference would tear the Conservative Baptist movement to pieces.

In retrospect, the desire for a merger was almost all on the Regular Baptist side. According to Ketcham, the Council of Fourteen actually offered to dissolve the GARBC and to encourage all of its churches to join the new Conservative Baptist Association of America. The only condition was that the CBA had to require separation from the convention and from other organizations that tolerated liberal theology. This was a concession that the Conservative Baptist movement was never willing to make.[103]

The Conservative Baptists never seem to have shared the yearning for a united testimony within Baptist fundamentalism. Not one leader went on record strongly favoring a merger with the Regular Baptists. At best, the Conservative Baptist leadership hoped to lure churches from the GARBC into its fold. Understandably, the Regular Baptist leadership considered this ploy obnoxious.

Were the two groups really so far apart? They were indeed. Some Conservative Baptists thought that the GARBC had an aura of contentiousness that they wanted to avoid. Furthermore, some Conservative Baptists wanted a movement with more prestige than the Regular Baptists would be able to provide. Moreover, Conservative Baptists were led by Great Men, and such leaders were not viewed with favor among Regular Baptists. The most substantial issue, however, was separation, and on this question the two groups remained far apart. The Regular Baptists had taken a firm position in 1938, and they were showing no sign of modifying that stand. The Conservatives, on the

102. Robert T. Ketcham, recorded interview with Robert Delnay, April 7, 1962.
103. Ibid.

other hand, were clearly a mixed multitude, and after another decade many could accurately be described by Harold Ockenga's new label, *neoevangelical*.

That, however, is another story, and one that needs to be told separately. Through the end of the 1940s, Baptist fundamentalism was defined primarily by its struggle against liberal theology (including the various forms into which old modernism morphed during and after the Depression). After about 1950, Baptist fundamentalism was increasingly defined by its struggle with neoevangelicalism. The emergence of a new evangelical movement and its rejection by fundamentalists constitutes the next great chapter in the history of Baptist fundamentalism.

The attempts to merge with the Conservative Baptists did have one other effect upon the GARBC. Faced with the possibility of rapid growth, the Regular Baptist leadership was forced to think through the approval system and the relationship between the association and the agencies. The conclusion was that the agencies needed to be made more accountable in ways that did not infringe upon their autonomy. Consequently, the Council of Fourteen recommended, and the messengers approved, a more specific application process and an annual review of all agencies. These procedures continued in place until the approval system was dropped during the late 1990s.[104]

Thus ends this first part of the story of Baptist fundamentalism. After 1947 the Conservative Baptist movement and the Regular Baptist movement never again came close to a merger. Indeed, when the Conservative Baptist movement broke to pieces two decades later, the more separatistic faction would still reject union with the GARBC. Its leaders preferred to erect entirely new organizations, much as they had during the 1940s. For its part, the GARBC continued to flourish, enjoying relative harmony and steady growth into the 1980s. Decades later, it still retains its commitment to what is sometimes called "secondary separation," in that it refuses to admit churches into its fellowship unless they separate from organizations that tolerate nonevangelical theology. All of that is the part of the story that still remains to be told.

104. Hopewell, *Missionary Emphasis*, 45–51.

Belden Avenue Baptist Church youth group, 1945.

Epilogue

THE PERIOD AROUND 1950 was definitive for Baptist fundamentalism. Mass evangelism was still working. There were between 150 and 200 Bible conferences in the USA, most of them strong on prophecy, evangelism, and missions. Radio evangelism was widespread, from local stations to Charles Fuller's *Old Fashioned Revival Hour,* which was heard coast to coast through about six hundred stations. M. R. DeHaan's *Radio Bible Class* was also widely heard. A cultural morality existed, frowning on divorce and cohabitation, closing up downtown on Sunday except for the drugstores, and banning profanity on the radio. Baptist churches attempted to maintain a testimony of godly conduct, sometimes drawing the charge of legalism. Men running for public office felt it helpful to mention their church membership.

The postwar awareness made itself felt in the GI Bill, enabling veterans in large numbers to get a college education. Bible institutes turned into Bible colleges as enrollments soared. Gasoline still sold for around twenty cents a gallon, but the interstate highway system was yet to be built, so two-lane highways took people right through the center of the next town. Train travel was still attractive. Travel by air cost more, but you could fly in one of the newer DC-6s or Constellations. Television was just beginning to enter the living room; two more years and almost everyone had it, in blurry black and white, of course.

Of the issues for the churches, probably the most pressing was modernism, beginning to enter about 1870 from Germany, and dominant in the Protestant denominations by about 1910. By that time it had slipped into most seminaries and denominational colleges, and from there to downtown pulpits. It seemed warm and friendly, but believers with any discernment realized that the modernists doubted or denied the supernatural. Modernist pastors tended to be educated and suave, and they were clever enough not to be too bold in preaching their beliefs and denials.

For Baptists in the North, the most pressing concern was the way that modernists organized the Northern Baptist Convention in 1907. Churches did not vote into it; they found themselves in it, mainly by being in a local association and then in a state convention. Modernists controlled the NBC. When in 1911 the godly head of the home mission society led in beginning a retirement program, the M&M Board, the modernists found its generous terms to be ideal for promoting loyalty among the pastors. Disharmony with the convention could mean the loss of one's pension, and that was long before Social Security.

The first to treat the problem seriously were the men of the Baptist Bible Union, who organized in 1922–23, mainly under the leadership of Oliver W. Van Osdel, then of Grand Rapids, Michigan. Under Riley, Norris, and Shields, they kept their separatism in check and were in no hurry to leave the convention. They knew that the NBC was doctrinally and morally corrupt, but only after 1926 did they resolve to separate. In 1932 their successors began the GARBC, and in 1938 they took the hard position that to join them meant breaking ties with all liberal connections, meaning the convention. That can be labeled "come out" separatism, and it proved durable.

By 1950 the GARBC was a working form of Baptist separatism. It had an accepted method of operating, with a Council of Fourteen and an office staff headed by a national representative, Robert T. Ketcham. It had found a way to forge relationships with already-existing missions and schools by approving but not controlling them.

The second notable effort among Northern Baptists was the Conservative Baptist movement, first called the Fundamentalist Fellowship. Tracing to 1920 under the Brooklyn committee, J. C. Massee and then Earle V. Pierce, they seemed to look for an eventual separation, perhaps by easing the modernists out. They were more urbane than the Bible Union men, but they could find ways to cooperate with them. They found no way to expel the modernists, however, and it is hard to pinpoint one achievement from their efforts. When during the 1930s the GARBC men were slowly gathering churches and pastors, Pierce was persuading pastors to stay in.

Finally the provocations, or perhaps the modernist arrogance, proved to be too much, and in 1943 the Fundamentalist Fellowship organized the Conservative Baptist Foreign Mission Society. In 1946 the Fundamentalist Fellowship became the Conservative Baptist Fellowship. In 1947 it organized an association of churches, the CBA. Then in 1948 the CBF organized the home mission society, the CBHMS, followed by the Conservative Baptist Theological Seminary of Denver in 1950. In seven years the movement with its five agencies became a denomination. No Conservative Baptist agency required its members to leave the convention yet, or for years to come.

There were reasons to move slowly. Otherwise, the convention could seize church property, whose mortgages or deeds they often held. Why should churches be abandoned to the convention when the judicious use of printed materials could help them get out? Most importantly, pastors could lose their pensions. Hence, the attitude was, "Go slowly; we will get out eventually."

What, then, was it that these and other Baptists held in common? Certainly the fundamentals, but what does that convey? First, the plenary, verbal inspiration of the Bible, together with its inerrancy. Then the Virgin Birth, the full deity of Christ, and His miracles. The substitutionary death on the cross, His bodily resurrection, and His ascension to Heaven. Eventually His bodily return. As to the order of end-time events, there was as yet no standard view.

What did it mean to be a fundamentalist? Clearly more than just orthodoxy. A first mark was devotion to the Scripture. Among many (though certainly not all), a second mark was the hope of an any-moment return of Christ (Scofield was often their text—in many churches the pastor would announce a biblical passage both by its reference and by its page in the Scofield Bible). A third mark was separation, both from apostasy and from the world. A fourth mark was an attitude of conviction, even militancy. Since a person could hold all these four and still be a scoundrel, one might add a fifth mark of those they would identify as fundamentalists: a genuine devotion to Christ, a walk in the Spirit. Many showed that last mark; some did not.

As of 1950 notable events were happening among Baptist fundamentalists. That year the Conservative Baptist movement founded its final agency. Almost before the year was out, however, some leaders began to realize that they were a divided movement. For the moment, they could all assent to separatism, as they did with the Portland Manifesto in 1953, but the missions and the seminary moved toward new evangelicalism, while the Fellowship and the Association stayed fundamentalist. Under Myron Cedarholm's promotion, the CBA was growing faster than any comparable fellowship.

Another notable event among Baptists was the disruption in the Norris empire and its division into the World Baptist Fellowship and the Baptist Bible Fellowship. Norris himself would die two years later. Both groups, together with the Sword crowd, represented a uniquely Southern version of Baptist fundamentalism. In common with Northern fundamentalism, this Southern variety held the fundamentals listed above. They did not, however, face as much obvious liberalism as the Northern versions. They reacted against the teaching of evolution in the schools, against the relaxing of cultural mores, and against the heavy-handedness of denominational officials. The two Norris groups had churches in the North, but their influence there was uneven.

To some extent, the outworking of separatism distinguished the different branches of Baptist fundamentalism from each other—particularly in the

case of Regular Baptists and Conservative Baptists. Otherwise, fundamentalists reflected all the dissimilarities of the larger Baptist denomination from
which they had emerged. Most of the GARBC held the Moody and Dallas
version of dispensationalism, but Shields opposed the Scofield Bible and Rice
rejected Chafer as an ultra-dispensationalist. Rice was unsparing in his invective against "hyper" (i.e., four-point) Calvinism, while Shields and some of
the Johnson City faculty were five-pointers. Baptist fundamentalists differed
over the nature of preaching, the necessity of revival, the role of evangelists,
the shape of the normal Christian life, the requirement of a second blessing or
anointing from the Spirit for effective ministry, and whether or not they ought
to be led by Great Men. They also perpetuated the old Baptist debate over the
desirability of service organizations versus associations. To this debate they
added two other forms of organization that were less commonly seen in older
Baptist life: the preachers' fellowship and the ecclesiastical empire.

In their peculiarities, none of the four branches of Baptist fundamentalism
was really unique. They reflected concerns that characterized various groups
of nonfundamentalists. Their diverse philosophies of preaching, understandings of the Christian life, models of church life, and visions of leadership identified them as subsets of larger movements among North American Baptists.

In other words, all Baptist fundamentalists held certain commonalities
with other Baptist fundamentalists, while each branch of Baptist fundamentalism held its unique features in common with branches of non-fundamen-
talist Baptists. The common factor among fundamentalists was militancy or
separatism. Other considerations were not uniquely fundamentalist and do
not enter into the definition of fundamentalism.

The idea of fundamentalism, then, is the idea that the gospel forms the
boundary of Christian fellowship. The gospel is defined by the fundamentals:
to deny a fundamental is to deny the gospel itself. Consequently, no Christian
fellowship can be entertained with those who (like theological liberals) deny
one or more fundamental doctrines.

Up to about 1950 the debate between Baptist fundamentalists was over
"purge out" versus "come out" separation. One or the other was considered
necessary to maintain the integrity of Christian fellowship. After 1950, however, the debate turned increasingly to the question of what to do about those
who affirmed the fundamentals but showed little interest in truncating fellowship with deniers of fundamental doctrines. Fundamentalists were forced to
confront this attitude with the emergence of the neoevangelical movement.

Both external and internal pressures have continued to mold the various
branches of Baptist fundamentalism. The 1950s and 1960s brought the conflict
with neoevangelicalism. Then concerns over communism, the Civil Rights
movement, and eroding morality drove some Baptist fundamentalists into

highly political ministries. Others reacted against such politicization. The 1960s and 1970s saw the beginnings of a King James Only movement that has affected every branch of fundamentalism. Disagreement over how to appropriate an increasingly secularized popular culture has further divided fundamentalists, as has debate over the proper boundaries in the application of ecclesiastical separation.

All of that is part of the story that still needs to be told. It will be, God willing. In the meanwhile, this part of the story is finished.

Index